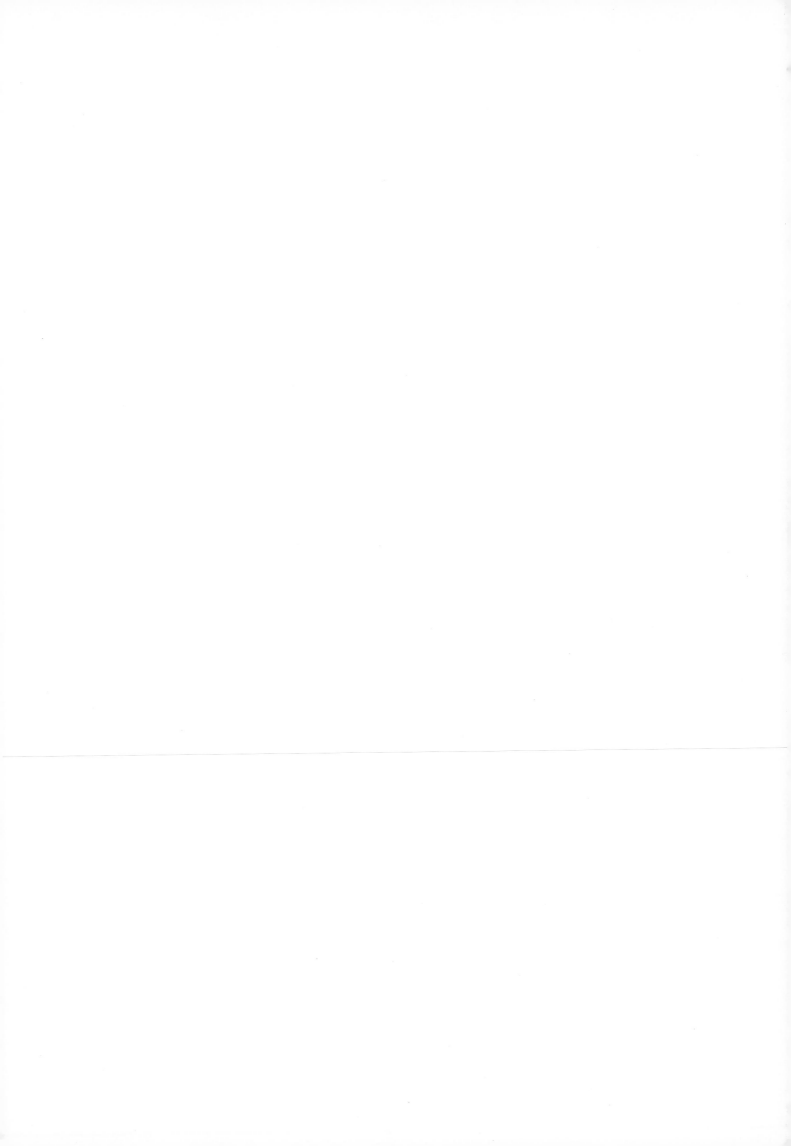

BOLLINGEN SERIES LX

SAMOTHRACE

EXCAVATIONS

CONDUCTED BY THE INSTITUTE OF FINE ARTS

OF NEW YORK UNIVERSITY

KARL LEHMANN

PHYLLIS WILLIAMS LEHMANN

Editors

Volume 3

View of the Hieron from the northwest

SAMOTHRACE

THE HIERON

BY

PHYLLIS WILLIAMS LEHMANN

WITH CONTRIBUTIONS BY

MARTIN R. JONES   KARL LEHMANN

GILBERT CASS, ALEC DAYKIN, MARTHA LEEB HADZI, ELAINE P. LOEFFLER,
IRIS C. LOVE, AND PHILIP OLIVER-SMITH

Text I

BOLLINGEN SERIES LX·3

PRINCETON UNIVERSITY PRESS

THIS IS PART ONE OF THE THIRD VOLUME
IN A PUBLICATION ON SAMOTHRACE
CONSTITUTING NUMBER LX IN BOLLINGEN SERIES,
SPONSORED BY AND PUBLISHED FOR BOLLINGEN FOUNDATION

Library of Congress Catalogue Card No. 58–8985

Manufactured in the U.S.A.
Plates printed by The Meriden Gravure Company,
Meriden, Conn.
Composed in Monotype Bulmer, printed, and bound
by Kingsport Press, Inc., Kingsport, Tenn.
Designed by Andor Braun

To

MABEL McAFEE GABRIEL

PREFACE

Many an excavator has not survived to explore the evidence gained through his own work in the field, as many a building has been published decades after excavation by archaeologists entirely dependent on the records of earlier excavators. I have had the good fortune both to excavate the Hieron and to participate in piecing together the evidence yielded by its fragments—to remember it as an overgrown ruin as I submit for publication the plates that show it fully restored. They form part of a volume more extensive than its predecessors in this series as a result of the special importance of the Hieron in its Samothracian context and the degree of its preservation, factors which have imposed on us the obligation to wring from the physical remains of this building all that could be deduced from them regarding the mysterious rites that culminated in it.

Many have collaborated in this task, chief among them Martin R. Jones, with whom I have worked out the reconstruction of the architectural features of the building. His plates (III–CIX) provide the basis for my presentation in Chapters I and II. The description and interpretation of the evidence recorded in these plates, presented in Chapter I, reflect our common view of every problem and every detail, although Mr. Jones is not responsible for its literary form. The reconstruction of the Hellenistic and Roman floral akroteria of the Hieron is the product of similar joint activity on the part of Philip Oliver-Smith and myself, and their description and justification in Chapters III and V again reflect our common observations and conclusions, although the responsibility for their formulation in these chapters is wholly mine, as the credit for Plates CXI–CXVI is entirely his. I am also indebted to Mr. Oliver-Smith for providing diagrams to illustrate my reconstruction of the sculptures of the northern pediment. I am grateful to both Mr. Jones and Mr. Oliver-Smith for the sharpness of their visual observation and for their patience in considering and reconsidering over a number of years the complicated evidence before us. A third team, of which Alec Daykin, aided by Denys Spittle, was the chief member, recorded the plan and sections of the building, incorporating in them features of the northern and southern extremities originally drawn by Stuart M. Shaw and Roy Fraser. Ultimately emended and partially redrawn by Mr. Jones, their collective work appears as Plates I–II.

As in our previously published volumes, the Catalogue of Finds is the work of Martha Leeb Hadzi, Elaine P. Loeffler, and Iris C. Love, each of whom is individually responsible for her section. Miss Love and I are greatly indebted to Elsbeth B. Dusenbery and Andreas Vavritsas for their courtesy in allowing us to draw on unpublished material from their joint excavation in the Southern Nekropolis of particular relevance in determining the date of the first major repairs made to the building—those involving replacement of its original southern akroteria.

All those interested in the cult of the Great Gods in Samothrace will be thankful that in the summer of 1959 Karl Lehmann was willing to interrupt his work on other projected volumes of our publication and, at my request, to write Chapter IV: "The *Epopteia* and the Function of the Hieron." It must stand as his longest printed statement on the religion of the Sanctuary—the topic that led him to undertake excavations in Samothrace, that preoccupied him increasingly in the last years of his life, and to which he anticipated devoting a large part of the final volume of the publication.

It is a pleasure to record our indebtedness to Gilbert Cass for his perspective view of the Hieron, Plate CX; to Stuart M. Shaw for providing a partial restoration of the interior of the Arsinoeion; to François Salviat for having put at our disposal drawings and photographs recording the investigation of the cella in 1925 by his teacher, the late Fernand Chapouthier (figs. 11–14); to Jiří Frel for having brought to our attention waterspouts and antefixes from the building in the Archaeological Museum of the Charles University in Prague and for providing us with photographs of them; and to a series of generous volunteers who have helped Miss Love draw and reproduce the ceramic profiles published in the Catalogue: Susi Bloch, Philip Oliver-Smith, Joannah Clapton Wilmerding, and, in particular, Madelaine De Huszar and Fredrica Wachsberger. Again, it is a pleasure to acknowledge the generous collaboration of Alison Frantz and Anna Wachsmann, many of whose fine photographs appear in this volume. The remainder of the photographs of Samothracian monuments published here were taken by members of the staff. Among them, I should like to single out for special thanks James R. Mc-Credie, who has supplemented our earlier negatives in many instances with photographs taken during his own strenuous days as field director of our current campaigns.

We are especially indebted to successive directors of the Antikenabteilung of the Kunsthistorisches Museum in Vienna—in particular, to Fritz Eichler, Rudolf Noll, and his assistant, Wolfgang Oberleitner—for providing us with every facility and courtesy during repeated stays in Vienna in order to examine the architectural and sculptural fragments from the Hieron in the Museum's possession. Without their co-operation, reconstruction of the pedimental and akroterial sculptures and of the sculptured coffers of the pronaos ceiling would have been impossible. Above all, we are grateful to Dr. Noll for his generosity in allowing us to publish our reconstruction of the Roman floral akroterion, almost all the fragments of which are in Vienna. In this, as in all volumes of our publication in which buildings explored by our Austrian predecessors are reconsidered, we are partially dependent on evidence in the possession of the Kunsthistorisches Museum. That it is always at our disposal is an incalculable asset. The Museum's special role in helping us to effect a partial reconstruction of the porch of the Hieron in 1956—like that of all the other institutions and individuals who assisted us in this enterprise—is acknowledged in the Appendix to this volume.

I should like to extend my personal thanks to the directors and staffs of a number of libraries whose hospitality and facilities have been indispensable to my investigation of the Hieron: those of the American School of Classical Studies in Athens, the German Archaeological Institutes in Athens and Rome, and the William Allen Neilson Library of Smith College. Thanks to Karl Schefold's kindness, I was able to use the Archaeological Seminar of the University of Basel as my study in the bleak autumn of 1960.

Again, I am personally indebted to a host of friends and colleagues for sharing opinions and information with me and for providing photographs for this volume. Their individual contributions are for the most part indicated in relevant footnotes, but I would like gratefully to acknowledge their assistance here: Peter H. von Blanckenhagen, Herbert Bloch, Axel Boëthius, Jean Charbonneaux,

Ahmet Dönmez, Elsbeth B. Dusenbery, the late Erwin Goodenough, Virginia Grace, George Hanfmann, Robert M. Harris, Evelyn Harrison, Dorothy K. Hill, Louise A. Holland, D. E. L. Haynes, Kenneth Jenkins, V. G. Kallipolitis, Christos Karousos, Semni Karousou, Naphtali Lewis, Eleanor T. Lincoln, Reinhard Lullies, Benjamin Meritt, Mary Moore, Nicholas D. Ohly, Bonnie Orr, Louis Robert, Georges Roux, Helen Stobbe, D. E. Strong, Dorothy Burr Thompson, Patricia Tobacco, Franz Willemsen, Charles K. Williams, and Rodney Young. Mrs. Hadzi is similarly indebted to Frances Follin Jones, Simone Mollard-Becques, Francesco Roncalli, and Hermione Speier.

Special thanks go to Jean Kyle and the editorial and production departments of Bollingen Series for their patience and skill in coping with this bulky volume, and to Erna G. Huber for typing the manuscript. It has profited repeatedly from Mrs. Kyle's care and editorial suggestions, as I have continuously from Mrs. Huber's unfailing readiness to help me in numberless ways throughout the long years of our association.

Finally, it is appropriate to acknowledge here a longstanding personal indebtedness to the American Association of University Women and the John Simon Guggenheim Memorial Foundation for grants that have enabled me to study Hellenistic religious architecture in the library and in the field. Circumstances have forced me to interrupt and possibly never complete the specific investigation that they sponsored. It has, nevertheless, formed the basis of my work on the Hieron and provided the comparative material that I have used in Chapter II.

These grants reflect an interest in Hellenistic art stimulated in me nearly thirty years ago by Karl Lehmann, an interest which led him to assign to me, in 1948, the task of excavating and investigating the Hieron. When Mr. Jones and I began to reconstruct the building and Miss Love commenced her study of the pottery associated with it, we had the constant advantage of his rigorous criticism, as I later had of discussing with him the problems posed by its so fragmentary sculptures. He did not live to see any portion of our manuscript or any of our restoration drawings; whatever their shortcomings, they are ours. Yet it is to him and his guiding presence that we owe our greatest debt.

We dedicate this volume to Mabel McAfee Gabriel, faithful friend and sponsor, in grateful tribute.

Samothrace
July, 1965

PHYLLIS WILLIAMS LEHMANN

A year after *The Hieron* was submitted for publication, too late to be incorporated in its references, a third edition, revised and enlarged, of Karl Lehmann's *Samothrace, A Guide to the Excavations and the Museum* was published. Readers of Bollingen Series LX should consult this edition for the most recent information on our work in the Sanctuary.

In this interval, too, Elsbeth B. Dusenbery and Lucy Talcott have read page proof of the ceramic portion of the Catalogue of Finds of the present volume, and James R. McCredie has read the remainder of Texts I and II. It is a pleasure to record my indebtedness to them for this generous contribution to the volume, which has benefited greatly from their knowledge, care, and criticism.

P. W. L.

Samothrace
July, 1967

CONTENTS

TEXT I

page

PREFACE vii

ABBREVIATIONS xiii

LIST OF TEXT FIGURES xvii

Introduction 3

I. Description and Reconstruction 34

II. The Hellenistic Hieron: Structure and Style 154

III. The Hellenistic Sculptures of the Hieron 237

TEXT II

IV. The *Epopteia* and the Function of the Hieron, *by Karl Lehmann* 3

V. The History of the Hieron 51

Appendix: The Partial Reconstruction of the Porch 132

CATALOGUE OF FINDS

1. Ceramics 143
   By Iris C. Love

   I. The Fill of the Foundation Ditches (1–42) 145

   II. Fill from the Cella and the Porch (43–60) 165

   III. The Fill of the Pronaos (61–90) 173

   IV. Fill from the Area between the Cella and the Terrace Wall (91–117) 191

   V. Inscribed Ceramics (118–153) 211

2. Minor Objects 237
   By Elaine P. Loeffler

   I. Lamp (154) 239

II. Coins (155–159)   241

III. Door and Ceiling Attachments (160–171)   244

3. Varia (172–177)   251

By Elaine P. Loeffler and Martha Leeb Hadzi

INDEXES

1. Topographical Index of Architectural Monuments   261

2. Ancient Authors   278

3. Inscriptions and Papyri   282

4. Principal Greek and Latin Words   284

5. Ceramic Inscriptions and Graffiti   289

6. General Index   290

The Plates are bound separately.

ABBREVIATIONS

AA	*Archäologischer Anzeiger.*
Abh. preuss. Ak.	*Abhandlungen der (königlichen) preussischen Akademie der Wissenschaften.* Berlin.
Abh. sächs. Ak.	*Abhandlungen der sächsischen Akademie der Wissenschaften.* Leipzig.
ActaA	*Acta Archaeologica.*
Aegina	Adolf Furtwängler. *Aegina, Das Heiligtum der Aphaia.* Munich, 1906.
AJA	*American Journal of Archaeology.*
AM	*Mitteilungen des deutschen archäologischen Instituts, Athenische Abteilung.*
Annuario	*Annuario della (Regia) Scuola Archeologica di Atene.*
Anrich	Gustav Anrich. *Das antike Mysterienwesen in seinem Einfluss auf das Christentum.* Göttingen, 1894.
AnzWien	*Anzeiger der Akademie der Wissenschaften.* Vienna.
ArchDelt	Δελτίον ἀρχαιολογικόν.
ArchEph	᾽Εφημερὶς ἀρχαιολογική.
ArchP	*Archiv für Papyrusforschung.*
ArchRW	*Archiv für Religionswissenschaft.*
BCH	*Bulletin de correspondance hellénique.*
Berl. Ber.	Preussischen Akademie der Wissenschaften, Berlin. *Monatsberichte.*
BIBulg	*Bulletin de l'Institut archéologique bulgare.*
Bousquet	Jean Bousquet. *Le Trésor de Cyrène.* (École française d'Athènes, *Fouilles de Delphes,* II.) Paris, 1952.
BSA	*Annual of the British School at Athens.*
Bulard	Marcel Bulard. *Peintures murales et mosaiques de Délos.* (Fondation Eugène Piot, *Monuments et mémoires,* XIV.) Paris, 1908.
Chapouthier	Fernand Chapouthier. *Les Dioscures au service d'une déesse.* (Bibliothèque des Écoles françaises d'Athènes et de Rome, 137.) Paris, 1935.
CIG	*Corpus Inscriptionum Graecarum.*
CIL	*Corpus Inscriptionum Latinarum.*
Clara Rhodos	*Clara Rhodos.* Studi e materiali pubblicati a cura dell'Istituto Storico-Archeologico di Rodi. Rhodes, 1928– .
Corinth	Results of Excavations Conducted by the American School of Classical Studies at Athens. *Corinth.* Princeton, 1929– .
Courby-Picard	Fernand Courby and Charles Picard. *Recherches archéologiques à Stratos.* Paris, 1924.
CVA	*Corpus Vasorum Antiquorum.*
Délos	École française d'Athènes. *Exploration archéologique de Délos.* Paris, 1909– .

Didyma	Theodor Wiegand, ed. *Didyma*. Berlin, 1941– .
Dinsmoor	William Bell Dinsmoor. *The Architecture of Ancient Greece*. London and New York, 1950.
Dugas	Charles Dugas et al. *Le Sanctuaire d'Aléa Athéna à Tégée au IVᵉ siècle*. Paris, 1924.
Études thasiennes	École française d'Athènes. *Études thasiennes*. Paris, 1944– .
Farnell	L. R. Farnell. *The Cults of the Greek City States*. Oxford, 1907.
FdDelphes	École française d'Athènes. *Fouilles de Delphes*. Paris, 1909– .
FGrHist	F. Jacoby. *Die Fragmente der griechischen Historiker*. Berlin and Leiden, 1923– .
GöttNachr	*Nachrichten von der Gesellschaft der Wissenschaften zu Göttingen*.
Guide	Karl Lehmann. *Samothrace. A Guide to the Excavations and the Museum*. New York, 1955.
*Guide*²	Idem. 2d edn., revised, Locust Valley, New York, 1960.
Hemberg	Bengt Hemberg. *Die Kabiren*. Uppsala, 1950.
Hepding	Hugo Hepding. *Attis, seine Mythen und sein Kult*. Giessen, 1903.
IG	*Inscriptiones Graecae*.
Inscr. Délos	*Inscriptions de Délos*. Paris, 1926– .
JDAI	*Jahrbuch des deutschen archäologischen Instituts*.
JHS	*Journal of Hellenic Studies*.
JIAN	*Journal international d'archéologie numismatique*.
JÖAI	*Jahreshefte des österreichischen archäologischen Institutes in Wien*.
JRS	*Journal of Roman Studies*.
Kabirenheiligtum	P. Wolters et al. *Das Kabirenheiligtum bei Theben*. Berlin, 1939– .
Kos	Rudolf Herzog. *Kos. Ergebnisse der deutschen Ausgrabungen und Forschungen*, Vol. I (P. Schazmann, *Asklepieion*). Berlin, 1932.
K.P.	R. Koldewey and O. Puchstein. *Die griechischen Tempel in Unteritalien und Sicilien*. Berlin, 1899.
Lagina	Arnold Schober. *Der Fries des Hekateions von Lagina*. (*Istanbuler Forschungen*, II.) Baden bei Wien, 1933.
Larisa	J. Boehlau et al. *Larisa am Hermos*. Berlin, 1940– .
Lindos	C. Blinkenberg et al. *Lindos. Fouilles et recherches, 1902–1914*. Berlin, 1931– .
Linforth	Ivan M. Linforth. *The Arts of Orpheus*. Berkeley and Los Angeles, 1941.
Magnesia	Carl Humann, Julius Kohte, and Carl Watzinger. *Magnesia am Maeander*. Berlin, 1904.
MélRome	École française de Rome. *Mélanges d'archéologie et d'histoire*.
MemAccLinc	*Memorie dell'Accademia Nazionale dei Lincei*.
MemPontAcc	*Atti della Pontificia Accademia Romana di Archeologia, Memorie*.
Migne	J. P. Migne. *Patrologiae cursus completus. Series graeca*. Paris, 1857–1912.
Milet	Theodor Wiegand, ed. *Milet*. Berlin, 1906– .
MonAnt	*Monumenti Antichi pubblicati per cura dell'Accademia dei Lincei*.
MusHelv	*Museum Helveticum*.
Neandria	Robert Koldewey. *Neandria*. (*51. Programm zum Winckelmannsfeste*.) Berlin, 1891.

Nilsson	Martin P. Nilsson. *Geschichte der griechischen Religion*. Munich, 1941, 1950.
Noack	Ferdinand Noack. *Eleusis*. Berlin, 1927.
OGIS	Wilhelm Dittenberger. *Orientis Graeci Inscriptiones Selectae*. Leipzig, 1903–5.
Olympia	E. Curtius and F. Adler. *Olympia*. Berlin, 1890–97.
Olynthus	D. M. Robinson et al. *Excavations at Olynthus*. Baltimore, 1929–52.
Pedimental Sculptures	Phyllis Williams Lehmann. *The Pedimental Sculptures of the Hieron in Samothrace*. Locust Valley, New York, 1962.
Pergamon	Königliche (Staatliche) Museen zu Berlin. *Altertümer von Pergamon*. Berlin, 1885– .
Praktika	Πρακτικὰ τῆς ἐν ᾿Αθήναις ᾿Αρχαιολογικῆς ῾Εταιρίας.
Priene	T. Wiegand and H. Schrader. *Priene. Ergebnisse der Ausgrabungen und Untersuchungen in den Jahren 1895–1898*. Berlin, 1904.
RA	*Revue archéologique*.
RE	G. Wissowa et al. *Paulys Real-Encyclopädie der classischen Altertumswissenschaft*. Stuttgart, 1894– .
RhM	*Rheinisches Museum für Philologie*.
Roscher	W. H. Roscher. *Ausführliches Lexikon der griechischen und römischen Mythologie*. Leipzig, 1884–1937.
Roux	Georges Roux. *L'architecture de l'Argolide aux IVe et IIIe siècles avant J.-C.* Paris, 1961.
RM	*Mitteilungen des deutschen archäologischen Instituts, Römische Abteilung*.
RVV	*Religionsgeschichtliche Versuche und Vorarbeiten*.
S,I	A. Conze, A. Hauser, and G. Niemann. *Archäologische Untersuchungen auf Samothrake*. Vienna, 1875.
S,II	A. Conze, A. Hauser, and O. Benndorf. *Neue archäologische Untersuchungen auf Samothrake*. Vienna, 1880.
SB bayer. Ak.	*Sitzungsberichte der königlichen bayerischen Akademie der Wissenschaften*. Munich.
Schober	Arnold Schober. "Der Neue Tempel von Samothrake," *JÖAI*, 29 (1935), 1 ff.
Shoe	Lucy T. Shoe. *Profiles of Greek Mouldings*. Cambridge, 1936.
Sokolowski	F. Sokolowski. *Lois sacrées de l'Asie Mineure*. (École française d'Athènes, *Travaux et mémoires*, IX.) Paris, 1955.
Syll²	Wilhelm Dittenberger. *Sylloge Inscriptionum Graecarum*. 2d edn., Leipzig, 1898–1901.
Syll⁴	Idem. 4th edn., revised, Hildesheim, 1960.
Thiersch	Hermann Thiersch. *Pro Samothrake*. (Akademie der Wissenschaften in Wien. Philosophisch-historische Klasse. *Sitzungsberichte*, Vol. 212, I.) Vienna, 1930.
Ziehen	L. Ziehen. *Leges Graeciae et Insularum*. (J. de Prott and L. Ziehen. *Leges Graecorum Sacrae e Titulis Collectae*, Pt. II, fasc. 1.) Leipzig, 1906.

LIST OF TEXT FIGURES

TEXT I

Frontispiece. View of the Hieron from the northwest. (P: P. W. L.)

1. View of the Hieron, 1964. (P: Nicholas D. Ohly.) — 3

2. Coquart's plan of the Sanctuary after the French excavation of 1866. *Archives des missions scientifiques et littéraires*, 2d ser., 4 (1867), pl. 1. — 5

3. View of the main threshold and adjacent pavement after excavation in 1873. *S,I*, pl. 15. — 6

4. View of the abaton after excavation in 1873. *S,I*, pl. 20. — 7

5. Hauser's plan of the Hieron after the Austrian excavation of 1873. *S,I*, pl. 11. — 8

6. View of the Hieron from the northeast after the Austrian excavations of 1873–75. (P: Deutsches Archäologisches Institut, Athens.) — 9

7. Hauser's reconstruction of the façade of the Hieron. *S,I*, pl. 42. — 10

8. Hauser's restored lateral elevation of the Hieron. *S,II*, p. 29, fig. 7. — 10

9. Hauser's restored plan of the Hieron. *S,II*, p. 29, fig. 6. — 11

10. Restored plan of the Hieron. Anton Springer, *Handbuch der Kunstgeschichte*, I: *Das Altertum*, 5th edn., rev. by Adolf Michaelis (Leipzig, 1898), p. 93, fig. 155. — 12

11. Diagram by Chapouthier, showing his trench across the cella. — 14

12. Schematic plan by Chapouthier of the area investigated in the cella. — 14

13. View of Chapouthier's trench across the cella, seen from the west. (P: Fernand Chapouthier.) — 15

14. View of underpavement exposed by Chapouthier in the cella. (P: Fernand Chapouthier.) — 15

15. Chapouthier's restored plan of the Hieron. (*Les Dioscures*, p. 163.) — 16

16. View of the Hieron after the Austrian excavations of 1873–75. (P: Deutsches Archäologisches Institut, Athens.) — 18

17. View of the porch from the east before excavation, 1948. — 18

18. View of the porch from the northeast before excavation, 1948. — 18

19. View of the northeastern corner of the pronaos after excavation, 1948. — 19

20. View of the cella at the end of the campaign of 1948, looking toward the abaton. — 20

21. Detail of the apse, showing the apses of the two predecessors of the Hieron. (P: Anna Wachsmann.)   21

22. View of the cella, seen from the south, 1949.   22

23. View of the terrace wall, 1949.   23

24. Lower part of the southwestern akroterion, after discovery in 1949.   23

25. View of the Hieron, seen from the northwest, after the campaign of 1952; in foreground, the Hall of Votive Gifts; at right, the Altar Court.   25

26. View of the Hieron, seen from the northwest, at the end of the campaign of 1953; in foreground, the Hall of Votive Gifts; at right, the Altar Court.   26

27. View of the Hieron, seen from the Nike Fountain, 1954; in foreground, the Altar Court and the Hall of Votive Gifts; in left background, the Arsinoeion. (P: Anna Wachsmann.)   27

28. View of the anastelosis, 1956. (P: Panagiotou.)   28

29. View of the Hieron, seen from the southeast after the anastelosis. (P: Alison Frantz.)   29

30. View of the Sanctuary, seen from the north, 1956. (P: P. W. L.)   30

31. Plaster reconstruction of the central floral akroterion. (P: J. R. McCredie)   32

32. Air view of the Sanctuary, 1957. (P: Royal Hellenic Air Force, by courtesy.)   34

33. Detail of the abaton, showing the apse of the Hieron and the foundations for the apses of its predecessors.   35

34. View of the Hellenistic apse, showing the foundations for the apses of its predecessors.   35

35. View of the northwestern corner of the foundation.   38

36. View of the southwestern corner, showing the foundation and euthynteria.   40

37. Partial view of the southern foundation, euthynteria, and apse wall.   40

38. Detail of the southwestern corner, showing the euthynteria, blocks of the stereobate, and the apse wall.   40

39. Southeastern corner block 284; view of bottom. (P: Anna Wachsmann.)   46

40. A. 52.525, bronze Π-clamp in lead pouring (Scale 1:2). B. 53.584, bronze dowel (Scale 1:1). Samothrace Museum. (Drawn by Martin R. Jones.)   47

41. Southeastern pilaster capital and adjacent southern binder, after Hauser. *S,II,* pl. 11, fig. II.   49

42. Plan of the abaton, after Hauser. *S,I,* pl. 17.   51

43. Partial view of the abaton after the excavation of 1873. *S,I,* pl. 18.   52

44. View of the cella from the south. (P: Anna Wachsmann.)   53

45. Detail of the southwestern corner, showing packing between the cella and apse walls. 54

46. Remodeled Roman doorway. A. Diagrammatic elevation. B. Diagrammatic plan. (Drawn by Martin R. Jones.) 59

47. Fragmentary eastern end of the main threshold, 36. 60

48. Fragmentary western end of the main threshold, 62 A. 60

49. Main lintel fragment 346 E. Kunsthistorisches Museum, Vienna. (P: By courtesy of the Museum.) 62

50. Fragmentary inscription prohibiting the uninitiated entrance to the Hieron. Samothrace Museum. (P: Anna Wachsmann.) 64

51. Southeastern corner architrave block 234. (P: Anna Wachsmann.) 70

52. Setting marks. (Drawn by Martin R. Jones.) 73

53. Fragmentary lateral sima block, including waterspout 49.544. (P: Anna Wachsmann.) 74

54. Fragmentary southeastern corner geison block 348 A. (P: Anna Wachsmann.) 76

55. Lost southwestern corner sima block. *S,II,* pl. 14. 77

56. Lateral elevation and section of marble kalypter 49.514. (Drawn by Martin R. Jones.) 81

57. Projected plan of the early Hellenistic Hieron. (Drawn by Martin R. Jones.) 85

58. View of the pronaos from the west, showing the juncture of the earlier and later foundations. 86

59. View of the northwestern corner of the pronaos foundation. 87

60. View of the northern foundation of the pronaos, seen from the south. 87

61. View of the pronaos, showing the western foundation. 87

62. Detail of the pronaos, showing the eastern foundation. 87

63. Detail of the eastern foundation of the pronaos. 88

64. View of the northern foundation of the pronaos and the inner stylobate, seen from the south. (P: Anna Wachsmann.) 89

65. Detail of the porch foundation, showing the southwestern corner block of the euthynteria. 93

66. Detail of the pronaos after refilling in 1951, showing part of the northern foundation and inner stylobate, seen from the south. 95

67. Capital 43. (P: Anna Wachsmann.) 96

68. Detail of the inner stylobate. (P: Anna Wachsmann.) 97

69. Fragmentary northwestern corner entablature blocks, after Hauser. A. Architrave. B. Frieze. *S,I,* pls. 23, fig. I; 25, fig. I. 103

70. Ridge block of raking geison, after Hauser. *S,I,* pl. 26, fig. III.   107

71. Fragmentary beam 40 from the pronaos ceiling.   111

72. Fragmentary porch coffer 442. (P: Anna Wachsmann.)   112

73. Fragmentary pronaos coffer 30-33. (P: Anna Wachsmann.)   113

74. Detail of the cella, showing pavement and underpavement north of the abaton.   119

75. Plan of the northern end of the cella, showing main threshold and adjacent pavement, after Hauser. *S,I,* pl. 14, fig. II.   119

76. View of the cella looking south. (P: Anna Wachsmann.)   120

77. Detail of the western aisle of the cella.   121

78. Detail of the eastern aisle of the cella.   121

79. Detail of the packing in the eastern aisle.   123

80. Fragmentary Hellenistic bench support 56.18. A. Front. B. Side. (P: Panagiotou.)   125

81. Plan and elevation of the drain below the northwestern corner of the cella, after Hauser. *S,II,* pl. 15.   127

82. View of the western euthynteria in 1875, showing outlet; above, drain block. *S,II,* pl. 16.   127

83. A. Fragmentary Hellenistic outlet 54.29. B. Roman replacement 54.28. Samothrace Museum. (P: Alison Frantz.)   127

84. Recut drain block.   127

85. View of the eschara in the central aisle.   128

86. View of the abaton from the east.   129

87. View of the abaton and the bema-pouring stone. (P: Anna Wachsmann.)   132

88. Detail of the western side of the abaton.   133

89. Fragment of marble torch 49.28. Samothrace Museum. A. Elevation. (P: Anna Wachsmann.) B. Elevation. C. Plan. (Drawn by Martin R. Jones.)   136

90. Lost fragment of a marble torch drawn by Hauser. *S,I,* p. 14, fig. 6.   136

91. Delos, Maison de Kerdon. Detail of wall in Room 3. Bulard, fig. 30.   141

92. Delos, Maison du Trident. Detail of Room *a*. Bulard, fig. 39.   141

93. Detail of coffering from the Mausoleum at Halikarnassos. A. S. Murray in *Transactions of the Glasgow Archaeological Society,* n.s., 2 (1894), 10, pl. 3.   143

94. Restored coffer from the cella ceiling (Scale 1:3). (Drawn by Martin R. Jones.)   144

95. Roman bench support. (P: Anna Wachsmann.)   146

96. Fragmentary foot of Roman bench support 49.536 B. (P: Panagiotou.) — 148

97. Fragmentary foot of Roman bench support 49.536 B. — 148

98. Fragmentary foot of Roman bench support 50.124. — 148

99. Fragment of Roman bench support 51.200. — 148

100. Fragment of Roman bench support 49.537 A. — 148

101. Late Hellenistic bench support. Samothrace Museum. (P: Anna Wachsmann.) — 149

102. Detail of late Hellenistic bench support. Samothrace Museum. (P: Anna Wachsmann.) — 149

103. View of the Hieron and the Altar Court from the Theater, 1960. (P: Alison Frantz.) — 154

104. Delphi, Temple of Ge. Plan of the extant ruin. *FdDelphes*, II, pt. 1², fig. 142. — 156

105. Dreros, Geometric Temple. Detail of eschara. (P: P. W. L.) — 157

106. Prinias, Temple A. View showing eschara. (P: P. W. L.) — 158

107. Megalopolis, Sanctuary of Zeus. Restored plan. *Excavations at Megalopolis 1890–1891* (London, 1892), p. 58, fig. 55. — 160

108. Selinus, Temple C. Restored plan. A. W. Lawrence, *Greek Architecture* (The Pelican History of Art, Baltimore, 1957), p. 122. — 161

109. Priene, Temple of Athena. Restored elevation. Martin Schede, *Die Ruinen von Priene* (Berlin and Leipzig, 1934), fig. 32. — 163

110. Sardis, Temple of Artemis. Detail of the wall. (P: John Sloan.) — 164

111. Samothrace, the Altar Court. Profiles of moldings. 5, 6: the epikranitis. *Samothrace*, Vol. 4, pt. II, pl. XXXVIII. — 165

112. Partial reconstruction of the wall entablature of the Hieron. Samothrace Museum. (P: Alison Frantz.) — 167

113. Partial reconstruction of the wall entablature of the Altar Court. Samothrace Museum. (P: Alison Frantz.) — 167

114. Samothrace, the Altar Court. Corner frieze block 586. *Samothrace*, Vol. 4, pt. II, pl. XXIX. — 169

115. Samothrace, the Altar Court. Profile of geison (Scale 1:3). *Samothrace*, Vol. 4, pt. II, pl. XXXIX. — 170

116. Detail of lateral sima. (P: Anna Wachsmann.) — 171

117. Detail of lateral sima. (P: Anna Wachsmann.) — 171

118. Fragment of the lateral sima of the Propylon of the Temenos. Kunsthistorisches Museum, Vienna. (P: By courtesy of the Museum.) — 171

119. Epidauros, Tholos. Detail of the sima. (P: Deutsches Archäologisches Institut, Athens.) — 173

120. Corinth, South Stoa. Sima and antefix. (P: American School of Classical Studies, Athens [No. 5504], by courtesy.) 173

121. Fragment of the sima of the Arsinoeion. Kunsthistorisches Museum, Vienna. (P: By courtesy of the Museum.) 173

122. Detail of sima block 49.453. Samothrace Museum. (P: Alison Frantz.) 175

123. Detail of sima block 49.544. Samothrace Museum. (P: Alison Frantz.) 175

124. Detail of sima block 49.545. Samothrace Museum. (P: Alison Frantz.) 175

125. Detail of sima block 49.452. Samothrace Museum. (P: Alison Frantz.) 175

126. Detail of sima block 52.493. Samothrace Museum. (P: Alison Frantz.) 175

127. Lion's-head waterspout from the Arsinoeion. Kunsthistorisches Museum, Vienna. (P: By courtesy of the Museum.) 177

128. Detail of the sima of the Tholos at Epidauros. National Archaeological Museum, Athens. (P: Deutsches Archäologisches Institut, Athens.) 177

129. Fragment of the sima of the Tholos at Epidauros. National Archaeological Museum, Athens. (P: Deutsches Archäologisches Institut, Athens.) 177

130. Olympia, Leonidaion. Waterspout. (P: F. Willemsen, by courtesy.) 177

131. Fragment of the southern raking sima. Samothrace Museum. (P: Anna Wachsmann.) 178

132. Priene, Temple of Zeus. Fragment of the raking sima. Archaeological Museums of Istanbul. (P: By courtesy of the Museums.) 179

133. Priene, Temple of Athena. Anta capital. Schede, *Die Ruinen von Priene*, fig. 36. 179

134. Antefix 48.578. Samothrace Museum. (P: Anna Wachsmann.) 180

135. Antefix from the Altar Court. Samothrace Museum. (P: Anna Wachsmann.) 180

136. Antefix from the Propylon of the Temenos. Kunsthistorisches Museum, Vienna. (P: By courtesy of the Museum.) 181

137. Terracotta antefix from the Anaktoron, 39.657. Samothrace Museum. (P: Anna Wachsmann.) 182

138. Phigaleia, Temple of Apollo. Antefix. (P: Deutsches Archäologisches Institut, Athens, by courtesy.) 183

139. Didyma, Temple of Apollo. Sima and antefix. (P: Deutsches Archäologisches Institut, Rome, by courtesy.) 183

140. Terracotta antefix 61.186. Samothrace Museum. (P: J. R. McCredie.) 184

141. Fragmentary terracotta ridge antefix 53.210. Samothrace Museum. (P: Anna Wachsmann.) 185

142. Fragmentary terracotta ridge antefix 53.152. Samothrace Museum. (P: Anna Wachsmann.) 185

143. Delphi, Temple of Apollo. Sima and antefixes. (P: Bildarchiv, Marburg.) 187

144. Didyma, Temple of Apollo. Antefixes. *Didyma*, I, pl. 203. 187

145. Terracotta antefix from the Stoa. Samothrace Museum. (P: J. R. McCredie.) 187

146. Terracotta kalypter from the Anaktoron. Samothrace Museum. (P: Anna Wachsmann.) 187

147. Magnesia, Temple of Artemis. Restored elevation. *Magnesia*, fig. 32. 189

148. Didyma, Temple of Apollo. Die-wall door. *Didyma*, I, pl. 87. 190

149. Outer wooden door from the Tomb at Langaza. T. Macridy, "Un tumulus macédonien à Langaza," *JDAI*, 26 (1911), fig. 8. 190

150. Marble door from the Tomb at Vergina. K. A. Rhomaios, Ὁ Μακεδονικὸς τάφος τῆς Βεργίνας (Μακεδονικὴ Βιβλιοθήκη, 14 [Athens, 1951]), pl. A. 191

151. Marble door from the Tomb at Palatitza. Léon Heuzey and H. Daumet, *Mission archéologique de Macédoine* (Paris, 1876), pl. 21. 192

152. Prinias, Temple A. Restored entrance. Charles Picard, *Manuel d'archéologie grecque: La sculpture*, I (Paris, 1935), fig. 127. 193

153. Kylix by Aison. Museo Arqueológico Nacional, Madrid. *CVA, Espagne,* fasc. 2, Museo Arqueológico Nacional, fasc. 2, III, I D, no. 1, pl. II. 194

154. Detail of a lekythos from Vari. National Archaeological Museum, Athens. A. B. Cook, *Zeus*, I (Cambridge, 1914), fig. 330. 194

155. Didyma, Temple of Apollo. View of ceiling in southern stairwell. *Didyma*, I, pl. 85, F327. 195

156. Ephyra, Sanctuary of Hades. Plan. *BCH*, 86 (1962), 767. 197

157. Delos, Thesmophorion. Outlet in the western foundation. (P: P. W. L.) 201

158. Delos, Serapeion A. Bench support. *Délos*, XVIII, p. 13, fig. 11. 203

159. Fragmentary Hellenistic bench support 52.154-53.568. Samothrace Museum. (P: Panagiotou.) 204

160. Fragmentary Hellenistic bench support A. Samothrace Museum. (P: Panagiotou.) 205

161. Roman bench support from the Gymnasium at Pergamon. P. Schazmann, *AM*, 36 (1911), 111. 205

162. Pydna. Entrance to tomb chamber. Heuzey and Daumet, *Mission archéologique de Macédoine*, pl. 18. 207

163. Delos, Maison de la Colline. Restored section. *Délos*, VIII, pt. 2, pl. 18. 208

164. Delos, Maison de Dionysos. Partial restoration of a wall. Bulard, pl. 6 A, fig. a. 209

165. Partial restoration of a wall in Delos. Bulard, pl. 6 A, fig. c. 209

166. Delos, Maison du Trident. Partial restoration of a wall. Bulard, pl. 6 A, fig. b. 209

167. Partial restoration of a wall in Delos. Bulard, fig. 41. 209

168. Partial restoration of the interior of the Arsinoeion by Stuart M. Shaw. 211

169. View of the Hieron after the anastelosis of 1956. (p: Panagiotou.) — 219

170. Lykosoura, Temple of Despoina. Restored façade. B. Leonardos, *Praktika,* 1896, pl. 4. — 222

171. Kos, Temple A. Restored façade. P. Schazmann, *Kos,* I, pl. 6. — 222

172. Fragment of the northern raking sima. (p: Anna Wachsmann.) — 224

173. Detail from the wall of the Arsinoeion. (p: J. R. McCredie.) — 224

174. Pergamon, Precinct of Athena. Entablature of an Ionic niche in the Stoa. (p: Deutsches Archäologisches Institut, Athens.) — 224

175. Lion's-head waterspout 346 K 2. Kunsthistorisches Museum, Vienna. (p: By courtesy of the Museum.) — 225

176. Lion's-head waterspout 346 K 1. Kunsthistorisches Museum, Vienna. (p: By courtesy of the Museum.) — 225

177. Lion's-head waterspout. Archaeological Collection of the Charles University, Prague. (p: By courtesy of the Collection.) — 225

178. Antefixes 346 L 1, 2. Kunsthistorisches Museum, Vienna. (p: By courtesy of the Museum.) — 227

179. Antefixes from the Hieron in the Archaeological Collection of the Charles University, Prague. (p: By courtesy of the Collection.) — 227

180. Antefixes 346 L 4, 6. Kunsthistorisches Museum, Vienna. (p: By courtesy of the Museum.) — 227

181. Inner architrave block 53. (p: Anna Wachsmann.) — 230

182. Detail of inner architrave block 260 from the Ptolemaion. (p: J. R. McCredie.) — 230

183. Magnesia, Temple of Artemis. Detail of column capital. *Magnesia,* p. 50, fig. 34. — 231

184. Magnesia, Temple of Artemis. Detail of anta capital. *Magnesia,* p. 74, fig. 64. — 231

185. Coffer lid from the Propylon of the Temenos, 55.149. Samothrace Museum. (p: J. R. McCredie.) — 232

186. Fragmentary coffer lid from the Temple of Athena at Priene, No. 1171. The British Museum, London. (p: By courtesy of the Museum.) — 233

187. *C(V)1.* Kunsthistorisches Museum, Vienna. (p: By courtesy of the Museum.) — 238

188. *C(V)2.* Kunsthistorisches Museum, Vienna. (p: By courtesy of the Museum.) — 239

189. *C(V)3.* Kunsthistorisches Museum, Vienna. (p: By courtesy of the Museum.) — 239

190. *C(V)4.* Kunsthistorisches Museum, Vienna. (p: By courtesy of the Museum.) — 239

191. *C(V)5.* Kunsthistorisches Museum, Vienna. (p: By courtesy of the Museum.) — 239

192. *C(V)6.* Kunsthistorisches Museum, Vienna. (p: By courtesy of the Museum.) — 240

193. *C(S)1.* Samothrace Museum. (p: J. R. McCredie.) — 241

194. *C*(*S*)*2.* Samothrace Museum. (P: J. R. McCredie.)   241

195. *C*(*S*)*4.* Samothrace Museum. (P: Anna Wachsmann.)   241

196. *C*(*S*)*5.* Samothrace Museum. (P: J. R. McCredie.)   242

197. *C*(*S*)*7.* Samothrace Museum. (P: J. R. McCredie.)   242

198. *C*(*S*)*8.* Samothrace Museum. (P: J. R. McCredie.)   242

199. *C*(*S*)*9,* seen from the side. Samothrace Museum. (P: Alison Frantz.)   243

200. *C*(*S*)*9,* seen from above. Samothrace Museum. (P: Alison Frantz.)   243

201. *C*(*S*)*9,* seen from below. Samothrace Museum. (P: Alison Frantz.)   243

202. *C*(*S*)*10.* Samothrace Museum. (P: Anna Wachsmann.)   244

203. Fragmentary coffer lid from the Temple of Athena at Priene, No. 1165. The British Museum, London. (P: By courtesy of the Museum.)   246

204. Detail of centaur relief. Kunsthistorisches Museum, Vienna. (P: By courtesy of the Museum.)   248

205. Detail of giant opposing Moira from the Great Altar. The Pergamon Museum, Berlin. Heinz Kähler, *Der grosse Fries von Pergamon* (Berlin, 1948), pl. 53, right.   248

206. Head of a centaur or satyr. Palazzo dei Conservatori, Rome. (P: J. Felbermeyer.)   249

207. Detail of Poseidon Jameson. Musée du Louvre, Paris. (P: By courtesy of the Museum.)   249

208. Detail from the frieze of the Temple of Dionysos at Teos. Depot Museum, Izmir. (P: Halit Gökberk.)   250

209. Terracotta statuette of a centaur from Priene. Staatliche Museen, Berlin. (P: By courtesy of the Museums.)   251

210. Misthia. Rock-cut relief. H. Swoboda, J. Keil, F. Knoll, *Denkmäler aus Lykaonien, Pamphylien und Isaurien* (Brünn, 1935), pp. 17 f., no. 16.   252

211. Diagram showing the positions of the extant fragments of the northern pedimental sculptures. Roman numerals indicate the positions of the thirteen original figures; arabic numbers show the location of the preserved fragments or figures. (Drawn by Philip Oliver-Smith.)   *facing* 253

212. Reconstruction of the northern pedimental sculptures by Phyllis Williams Lehmann. (Drawn by Philip Oliver-Smith.)   *facing* 253

213. *NP*(*V*)*1.* Kunsthistorisches Museum, Vienna. (P: By courtesy of the Museum.)   255

214. *NP*(*V*)*1.* Kunsthistorisches Museum, Vienna. (P: By courtesy of the Museum.)   255

215. *NP*(*V*)*2.* Kunsthistorisches Museum, Vienna. (P: By courtesy of the Museum.)   256

216. *NP*(*V*)*3,* seen from the side. Kunsthistorisches Museum, Vienna. (P: By courtesy of the Museum.)   257

217. *NP*(*V*)*3,* seen from beneath. Kunsthistorisches Museum, Vienna. (P: By courtesy of the Museum.)   257

218. *NP(V)4.* Kunsthistorisches Museum, Vienna. (P: By courtesy of the Museum.) 257

219. *NP(V)5,* seen from the outside. Kunsthistorisches Museum, Vienna. (P: By courtesy of the Museum.) 258

220. *NP(V)5,* seen from the inside. Kunsthistorisches Museum, Vienna. (P: By courtesy of the Museum.) 258

221. *NP(V)6.* Kunsthistorisches Museum, Vienna. (P: By courtesy of the Museum.) 259

222. *NP(V)7.* Kunsthistorisches Museum, Vienna. (P: By courtesy of the Museum.) 260

223. *NP(V)8.* Kunsthistorisches Museum, Vienna. (P: By courtesy of the Museum.) 262

224. *NP(S)9,* seen from above. Samothrace Museum. (P: Anna Wachsmann.) 262

225. *NP(S)9,* seen from the outside. Samothrace Museum. (P: Alison Frantz.) 262

226. *NP(S)9,* seen from the inside. Samothrace Museum. (P: Alison Frantz.) 262

227. *NP(S)10.* Samothrace Museum. (P: Panagiotou.) 263

228. *NP(V)11.* Kunsthistorisches Museum, Vienna. (P: By courtesy of the Museum.) 265

229. *NP(V)12.* Kunsthistorisches Museum, Vienna. (P: By courtesy of the Museum.) 266

230. *NP(V)13.* Kunsthistorisches Museum, Vienna. (P: By courtesy of the Museum.) 267

231. *NP(V)14.* Kunsthistorisches Museum, Vienna. (P: By courtesy of the Museum.) 269

232. *NP(S)15.* Samothrace Museum. (P: J. R. McCredie.) 270

233. *NP(V)16.* Kunsthistorisches Museum, Vienna. (P: By courtesy of the Museum.) 271

234. *NP(S)17,* seen from above. Samothrace Museum. (P: Alison Frantz.) 272

235. *NP(S)17,* seen from the side. Samothrace Museum. (P: Alison Frantz.) 272

236. *NP(S)17,* seen from below. Samothrace Museum. (P: Alison Frantz.) 272

237. *NP(V)18,* seen from the inside. Kunsthistorisches Museum, Vienna. (P: By courtesy of the Museum.) 273

238. *NP(V)19,* seen from the outside. Kunsthistorisches Museum, Vienna. (P: By courtesy of the Museum.) 274

239. *NP(V)19,* seen from the inside. Kunsthistorisches Museum, Vienna. (P: By courtesy of the Museum.) 274

240. *NP(S)20.* Samothrace Museum. (P: Anna Wachsmann.) 275

241. *NP(S)20,* seen from the side. Samothrace Museum. 275

242. *NP(S)21.* Samothrace Museum. (P: Alison Frantz.) 275

243. *NP(S)22.* Samothrace Museum. (P: Panagiotou.) 277

244. *NP(S)23*, seen from below. Samothrace Museum. (P: Alison Frantz.)   277

245. *NP(S)23*, seen from above. Samothrace Museum. (P: Alison Frantz.)   277

246. *NP(S)24*, seen from above. Samothrace Museum. (P: J. R. McCredie.)   277

247. *NP(S)25*, seen from above. Samothrace Museum. (P: Alison Frantz.)   277

248. *NP(S)25*, seen from below. Samothrace Museum. (P: Alison Frantz.)   277

249. *NP(S)26*. Samothrace Museum. (P: Panagiotou.)   278

250. *NP(V)27*. Kunsthistorisches Museum, Vienna. (P: By courtesy of the Museum.)   279

251. Reconstruction of the northern pediment by A. Schober. *JÖAI*, 29 (1935), 16.   287

252. Detail of a red-figured Apulian amphora from Ruvo. The Hermitage, Leningrad. (P: By courtesy of the Museum.)   291

253. Fragmentary striding female figure (VII.1). Kunsthistorisches Museum, Vienna. *S,I*, pl. 40.   295

254. Fragmentary striding female figure (VII.1). Kunsthistorisches Museum, Vienna. (P: By courtesy of the Museum.)   304

255. Reclining male figure (XI.11). Kunsthistorisches Museum, Vienna. (P: By courtesy of the Museum.)   305

256. Fragmentary seated draped figure (V.16). Kunsthistorisches Museum, Vienna. *S,I*, pl. 38.   306

257. Reclining female figure (XII.12). Kunsthistorisches Museum, Vienna. (P: By courtesy of the Museum.)   308

258. Detail from the Telephos frieze. The Pergamon Museum, Berlin. *Pergamon*, III, pt. 2, pl. 36, fig. 8.   309

259. Fragmentary marble group. The Walters Art Gallery, Baltimore. (P: By courtesy of the Gallery.)   309

260. Detail of the frieze of the Hekateion at Lagina. Archaeological Museums of Istanbul. *Lagina*, pl. 4.   311

261. Detail of the frieze of the Hekateion at Lagina. Archaeological Museums of Istanbul. *Lagina*, pl. 15.   312

262. Pedimental statue from the Temple of Dionysos at Teos. Depot Museum, Izmir. (P: Halit Gökberk.)   314

263. Pedimental statue from the Temple of Dionysos at Teos. Depot Museum, Izmir. (P: Halit Gökberk.)   314

264. Detail of the frieze of the Temple of Dionysos at Teos. Depot Museum, Izmir. (P: Halit Gökberk.)   315

265. Seated figure from Athens. National Archaeological Museum, Athens. (P: By courtesy of the Museum.)   316

266. *SP(V)1*. Kunsthistorisches Museum, Vienna. (P: By courtesy of the Museum.)   318

267. *SP(V)2*. Kunsthistorisches Museum, Vienna. (P: By courtesy of the Museum.)   320

268. *SP(V)3.* Kunsthistorisches Museum, Vienna. (P: By courtesy of the Museum.) — 320

269. *SP(V)4.* Kunsthistorisches Museum, Vienna. (P: By courtesy of the Museum.) — 320

270. *SP(S)1.* Samothrace Museum. (P: Panagiotou.) — 321

271. *SP(S)2.* Samothrace Museum. (P: J. R. McCredie.) — 321

272. *SP(S)3.* Samothrace Museum. (P: J. R. McCredie.) — 321

273. *SP(S)4.* Samothrace Museum. (P: Panagiotou.) — 322

274. *SP(S)5.* Samothrace Museum. (P: Panagiotou.) — 322

275. *SP(S)6.* Samothrace Museum. (P: Panagiotou.) — 322

276. Delos, Serapeion A. View of the Temple of Isis. — 324

277. Delos, Samothrakion. Restored façade of the Monument of Mithradates Eupator. *Délos,* XVI, fig. 56. — 325

278. Grave stele from Kertsch. G. von Kieseritzky and Carl Watzinger, *Griechische Grabreliefs aus Südrussland* (Berlin, 1909), pl. 28. — 326

279. Relief from the Monument of the Haterii. The Lateran Museum, Rome. (P: Anderson.) — 327

280. Detail of Aphrodite from Melos. Musée du Louvre, Paris. (P: Maurice Chuzeville.) — 328

281. Diagram of the restored Hellenistic central akroterion, showing the location of the preserved fragments. (Drawn by Philip Oliver-Smith.) — *facing* 329

282. *SCA 1.* Samothrace Museum. (P: J. R. McCredie.) — 330

283. *SCA 5.* Samothrace Museum. — 331

284. *SCA 8.* Samothrace Museum. (P: Anna Wachsmann.) — 332

285. *SCA 11.* Samothrace Museum. (P: Anna Wachsmann.) — 333

286. *SCA 19.* Samothrace Museum. — 334

287. *SCA 21.* Samothrace Museum. — 335

288. *SCA 22.* Samothrace Museum. (P: Anna Wachsmann.) — 335

289. *SCA 27.* Samothrace Museum. (P: Anna Wachsmann.) — 337

290. *SCA 28.* Samothrace Museum. (P: Anna Wachsmann.) — 337

291. *SCA 33.* Samothrace Museum. (P: Anna Wachsmann.) — 337

292. *SCA 36.* Samothrace Museum. — 337

293. *SCA 45.* Samothrace Museum. (P: Anna Wachsmann.) — 339

294. *SCA 60.* Samothrace Museum. — 341

295. *NCA(S)6*. Samothrace Museum. (P: Anna Wachsmann.) — 343

296. *NCA(V)1*. Kunsthistorisches Museum, Vienna. (P: By courtesy of the Museum.) — 345

297. *NCA(V)3*. Kunsthistorisches Museum, Vienna. (P: By courtesy of the Museum.) — 345

298. *NCA(V)4*. Kunsthistorisches Museum, Vienna. (P: By courtesy of the Museum.) — 345

299. *NCA(V)6*. Kunsthistorisches Museum, Vienna. (P: By courtesy of the Museum.) — 345

300. Base of the Roman central akroterion. Kunsthistorisches Museum, Vienna. (P: By courtesy of the Museum.) — 349

301. Fragmentary stalk from the Hellenistic central akroterion, seen from the side. Samothrace Museum. (P: J. R. McCredie.) — 350

302. Plaster reconstruction of the Hellenistic floral akroterion. Samothrace Museum. (P: J. R. McCredie.) — 352

303. Restored central akroterion from the Temple of Aphaia at Aegina. *Aegina*, II, pl. 107. — 354

304. Fragmentary central akroterion from the Temple of Poseidon at Sounion. National Archaeological Museum, Athens. (P: By courtesy of the Museum.) — 355

305. Restored akroterion from Kaulonia. Paolo Orsi, *MonAnt*, 29, pt. 2 (1924), pl. 10. — 356

306. Reconstruction of Akroterion A from the Parthenon. Hildegund Gropengiesser, *Die pflanzlichen Akrotere klassischer Tempel* (Mainz, 1961), pl. 6. — 356

307. Reconstruction of the akroterion of the Tholos at Epidauros. (After Roux, fig. 40.) — 357

308. Terracotta antefix from the Leonidaion at Olympia. (P: F. Willemsen, by courtesy.) — 359

309. Pilaster capital from the Temple of Apollo at Didyma. *Didyma*, I, pl. 118, F272. — 359

310. Fragment from the floral akroterion of the Propylon to the Temenos. (P: Anna Wachsmann.) — 360

311. Pilaster capital from the Hekateion at Lagina. *Lagina*, fig. 9. — 360

312. Akroterion on the Sarcophagus of Mourning Women. Archaeological Museums of Istanbul. (After O. Hamdy, *Une nékropole royale à Sidon* [Paris, 1892], pl. 5.) — 361

313. Fragmentary tendrils from the Hellenistic central akroterion. Samothrace Museum. — 361

314. Akroteria from the Temple of Despoina at Lykosoura. Lykosoura Museum. (P: Bildarchiv, Marburg.) — 362

315. Fragmentary central akroterion from the Temple of Hera Basileia at Pergamon. *Pergamon*, VI, pl. 34, fig. 25. — 362

316. Fragmentary floral akroterion from the Temple of Dionysos at Teos, after Pullan, Notebook II, in the Department of Greek and Roman Antiquities of the British Museum, London. (P: By courtesy of the Museum.) — 363

317. *SLA 1*. Samothrace Museum. (P: Anna Wachsmann.) — 365

318.   *SLA 1.* Samothrace Museum. (P: Anna Wachsmann.) — 366

319.   *SLA 1,* right side. Samothrace Museum. — 367

320.   *SLA 1,* seen from the rear. Samothrace Museum. (P: Anna Wachsmann.) — 367

321.   *SLA 1,* detail. Samothrace Museum. — 369

322.   *SLA 1,* left side, detail. Samothrace Museum. — 369

323.   *SLA 1,* detail. Samothrace Museum. — 369

324.   *SLA 1,* left side, detail. Samothrace Museum. (P: Anna Wachsmann.) — 369

325.   *SLA 4.* Samothrace Museum. (P: J. R. McCredie.) — 371

326.   *SLA 4,* seen from the rear. Samothrace Museum. (P: J. R. McCredie.) — 371

327.   *NLA 1.* Samothrace Museum. (P: J. R. McCredie.) — 373

328.   *NLA 2.* Samothrace Museum. (P: J. R. McCredie.) — 373

329.   *NLA 3.* Samothrace Museum. (P: J. R. McCredie.) — 373

330.   *NLA 5.* Samothrace Museum. — 373

331.   *NLA 7.* Samothrace Museum. (P: Alison Frantz.) — 375

332.   *NLA 7,* seen from the side. Samothrace Museum. (P: Panagiotou.) — 375

333.   *NLA 8,* seen from above. Samothrace Museum. (P: Panagiotou.) — 375

334.   Southwestern Hellenistic akroterion of the Hieron. Samothrace Museum. — 378

335.   Southwestern Hellenistic akroterion of the Hieron, seen from the left side. Samothrace Museum. (P: Anna Wachsmann.) — 379

336.   Southwestern Hellenistic akroterion of the Hieron. Samothrace Museum. — 380

337.   Southwestern Hellenistic akroterion of the Hieron. Samothrace Museum. — 380

338.   Detail of the frieze of the Hekateion at Lagina. Archaeological Museums of Istanbul. *Lagina,* fig. 18. — 381

339.   Detail of the frieze of the Hekateion at Lagina. Archaeological Museums of Istanbul. *Lagina,* pl. 5. — 381

340.   Bronze statuette of Athena from Caesarea in Cappadocia. Staatliche Museen, Berlin. (P: By courtesy of the Museums.) — 382

341.   Reverse of silver tetradrachm of Alexander I Balas. The British Museum, London. (P: Beryl Sokoloff, after a cast, by courtesy of the Museum.) — 382

342.   Detail of the frieze of the Hekateion at Lagina. Archaeological Museums of Istanbul. *Lagina,* pl. 21. — 382

343. Bronze statuette of Athena from Caesarea in Cappadocia, seen from the rear. Staatliche Museen, Berlin. (P: By courtesy of the Museums.)   383

344. Southwestern Hellenistic akroterion of the Hieron. Samothrace Museum.   383

TEXT II

Frontispiece. View of the Hieron from the north. (P: Alison Frantz.)

345. View of the Hieron and the Altar Court, seen from the Theater. (P: Nicholas D. Ohly.)   3

346. Bilingual inscription from the Anaktoron. Samothrace Museum. (P: Anna Wachsmann.)   5

347. Inscription recording the initiation of C. Marius Schinas and household. Samothrace Museum. (P: Anna Wachsmann.)   12

348. View of the *bathra* and torch-stone east of the cella.   18

349. Detail of the Anaktoron, showing supports for grandstand. (P: Anna Wachsmann.)   22

350. Antioch-ad-Pisidiam, Sanctuary of Men. Restored plan. *BSA*, 18 (1911/12), fig. 1, opp. p. 40.   24

351. Votive relief from Eleusis. Eleusis Museum.   25

352. Restored drawing of an inscription recording initiations. *Hesperia*, 12 (1943), pl. 5 c.   27

353. Detail from a Roman sarcophagus. Museo dei Conservatori, Braccio Nuovo, Rome. (P: J. Felbermeyer.)   28

354. View of the eschara in the central aisle.   31

355. Detail of a cinerary urn from the cemetery of the Gens Statilia. *JIAN*, 1901, pl. 17.   32

356. Fragment of an Arretine bowl. Munich. H. Dragendorff and C. Watzinger, *Arretinische Reliefkeramik* (Reutlingen, 1948), Beilage 6, fig. 49.   33

357. Bothros in the southeastern corner of the Anaktoron.   34

358. Bema-pouring stone in the abaton.   35

359. Delos. View of the Kabeirion on Mount Kynthos. H. Berve and G. Gruben, *Greek Temples, Theaters, and Shrines* (New York, 1962), pl. 102.   37

360. View of the Hieron, showing the parapets in the remodeled cella. (P: P. W. L.)   43

361. Plan of the Sanctuary of Magna Mater at Ostia. *MemPontAcc*, 3d ser., 6, pt. 2 (1947), pl. III.   44

362. Altars from the Sanctuary of Ge at Phlya. National Archaeological Museum, Athens. (P: By courtesy of the Museum.)   46

363. Air view of the Sanctuary. (P: Royal Hellenic Air Force, by courtesy.)   51

364. Fragmentary Doric geison block. Kunsthistorisches Museum, Vienna. (P: By courtesy of the Museum.)   52

365. Plan and section of the *bathra* and torch-stone east of the cella. (Drawn by Martin R. Jones.)   54

366. View of the *bathra* and torch-stone east of the cella, seen from the south.   55

367. View of the northern stone from the northwest.   55

368. View of the northern stone from the southeast.   55

369. Sketch plan of the Hieron and the structures in its vicinity (excluding monuments) in the late second century B.C. A: the Hieron; B: the Altar Court; C: the Hall of Votive Gifts; D: the Temenos; E: the Theater; F: the Nike Fountain; G: the Stoa; X: archaic altar; Y: drain. (Drawn by Martin R. Jones.)   57

370. Detail of altar foundation.   58

371. Marble bust from the Sanctuary. Samothrace Museum. (P: Anna Wachsmann.)   60

372. Rear view of marble bust from the Sanctuary. Samothrace Museum. (P: Anna Wachsmann.)   60

373. Marble bust from the Sanctuary, seen from the right side. Samothrace Museum. (P: Anna Wachsmann.)   60

374. Marble bust from the Sanctuary, seen from the left side. Samothrace Museum. (P: Anna Wachsmann.)   60

375. Bust of Homer. Glyptothek, Munich. (P: F. Kaufmann.)   61

376. Bust of Homer. Museo del Vaticano, Rome. (P: By courtesy of the Museum.)   61

377. Drawing of Samothracian bust by Cyriacus of Ancona. Ms. Lat. misc. d. 85, fol. 141 r. Bodleian Library, Oxford. (P: By courtesy of the Library.)   63

378. Detail from an Apulian krater. Bibliothèque Nationale, Paris. A. Furtwängler and K. Reichhold, *Griechische Vasenmalerei*, I (Munich, 1904), pl. 60.   64

379. Marble statue from the Sanctuary. Samothrace Museum. (P: Alison Frantz.)   66

380. View of the Hieron and its vicinity from the west. (P: J. R. McCredie.)   68

381. View of the terrace wall in 1949, seen from the east.   71

382. Stairway to the south of the Altar Court.   72

383. Detail of the terrace wall. (P: J. R. McCredie.)   72

384. Torch-stone. A. View. B. Plan and sections. (Drawn by Martin R. Jones.)   73

385. View of the Hieron from the northeast, with the site of the Theater in the background. (P: P. W. L.)   75

386. View of the Stoa from the south. (P: J. R. McCredie.)   77

387. Fragmentary sima block 49.453. Samothrace Museum. (P: Anna Wachsmann.)   80

388. Lion's-head waterspout 38.366 A. Samothrace Museum. (P: Anna Wachsmann.)   80

389. Antefix 49.515. Samothrace Museum. (P: Panagiotou.)   82

390. Antefix 52.494. Samothrace Museum. (P: Panagiotou.) 82

391. Antefix 49.514 A-B. Samothrace Museum. (P: Anna Wachsmann.) 82

392. Diagram of the restored Roman central akroterion, showing the location of the preserved fragments. (Drawn by Philip Oliver-Smith.) *facing* 83

393. *RCA(V)1.* Kunsthistorisches Museum, Vienna. (P: By courtesy of the Museum.) 85

394. *RCA(V)3.* A. Front. B. Rear. Kunsthistorisches Museum, Vienna. (P: By courtesy of the Museum.) 87

395. *RCA(V)4.* Kunsthistorisches Museum, Vienna. (P: By courtesy of the Museum.) 87

396. *RCA(V)8.* Kunsthistorisches Museum, Vienna. (P: By courtesy of the Museum.) 87

397. *RCA(V)13.* Kunsthistorisches Museum, Vienna. (P: By courtesy of the Museum.) 89

398. *RCA(V)15,* seen from the front. Kunsthistorisches Museum, Vienna. (P: By courtesy of the Museum.) 89

399. *RCA(V)15,* seen from the outer side. Kunsthistorisches Museum, Vienna. (P: By courtesy of the Museum.) 89

400. *RCA(V)15,* seen from the inner side. Kunsthistorisches Museum, Vienna. (P: By courtesy of the Museum.) 89

401. *RCA(V)17.* Kunsthistorisches Museum, Vienna. (P: By courtesy of the Museum.) 91

402. *RCA(V)17,* seen from the side. Kunsthistorisches Museum, Vienna. (P: By courtesy of the Museum.) 91

403. *RCA(V)21.* Kunsthistorisches Museum, Vienna. (P: By courtesy of the Museum.) 92

404. *RCA(V)21,* seen from the left side. Kunsthistorisches Museum, Vienna. (P: By courtesy of the Museum.) 92

405. *RCA(V)22.* Kunsthistorisches Museum, Vienna. (P: By courtesy of the Museum.) 92

406. *RCA(V)22,* seen from the top. Kunsthistorisches Museum, Vienna. (P: By courtesy of the Museum.) 92

407. *RCA(V)23.* Kunsthistorisches Museum, Vienna. (P: By courtesy of the Museum.) 93

408. *RCA(V)23,* seen from the left side. Kunsthistorisches Museum, Vienna. (P: By courtesy of the Museum.) 94

409. *RCA(V)23,* seen from the rear. Kunsthistorisches Museum, Vienna. (P: By courtesy of the Museum.) 94

410. *RCA(S)5.* Samothrace Museum. 95

411. *RCA(V)24.* Kunsthistorisches Museum, Vienna. (P: By courtesy of the Museum.) 95

412. *RCA(V)25.* Kunsthistorisches Museum, Vienna. (P: By courtesy of the Museum.) 95

413.   *RCA(V)26.* Kunsthistorisches Museum, Vienna. (P: By courtesy of the Museum.)   95

414.   *RCA(V)27.* Kunsthistorisches Museum, Vienna. (P: By courtesy of the Museum.)   95

415.   *RCA(V)26,* seen from the side. Kunsthistorisches Museum, Vienna. (P: By courtesy of the Museum.)   95

416.   *RCA(V)33.* Kunsthistorisches Museum, Vienna. (P: By courtesy of the Museum.)   97

417.   *RCA(V)33,* seen from the left side. Kunsthistorisches Museum, Vienna. (P: By courtesy of the Museum.)   97

418.   *RCA(V)39.* A. Front. B. Rear. Kunsthistorisches Museum, Vienna. (P: By courtesy of the Museum.)   98

419.   *RCA(V)45.* Kunsthistorisches Museum, Vienna. (P: By courtesy of the Museum.)   99

420.   *RCA(V)46.* Kunsthistorisches Museum, Vienna. (P: By courtesy of the Museum.)   99

421.   *RCA(V)47.* Kunsthistorisches Museum, Vienna. (P: By courtesy of the Museum.)   99

422.   *RCA(V)48.* Kunsthistorisches Museum, Vienna. (P: By courtesy of the Museum.)   100

423.   *RCA(V)49.* Kunsthistorisches Museum, Vienna. (P: By courtesy of the Museum.)   100

424.   Petal tips from the Roman central akroterion. Kunsthistorisches Museum, Vienna. (P: By courtesy of the Museum.)   103

425.   Didyma, Temple of Apollo. Rear corner pilaster capital. (P: Alinari.)   104

426.   Fragmentary tendrils from the Roman central akroterion. Kunsthistorisches Museum, Vienna. (P: By courtesy of the Museum.)   106

427.   Restored rear central akroterion, after Hauser. *S,I,* pl. 46.   108

428.   *SCA 22.* Fragment of a fluted stalk from the Hellenistic central akroterion, seen from the left side. Samothrace Museum. (P: J. R. McCredie.)   111

429.   *RCA(V)12.* Fragment of a fluted stalk from the Roman central akroterion, seen from the left side. Kunsthistorisches Museum, Vienna. (P: By courtesy of the Museum.)   111

430.   *SCA 1.* Fragment of the base of the Hellenistic central akroterion. Samothrace Museum. (P: J. R. McCredie.)   112

431.   *RLA(V)1,* seen from the rear. Kunsthistorisches Museum, Vienna. (P: By courtesy of the Museum.)   114

432.   *RLA(V)1.* Kunsthistorisches Museum, Vienna. (P: By courtesy of the Museum.)   114

433.   *RLA(V)1.* A. Seen from the right side. B. Seen from the left side. Kunsthistorisches Museum, Vienna. (P: By courtesy of the Museum.)   115

434.   *RLA(V)2.* Kunsthistorisches Museum, Vienna. (P: By courtesy of the Museum.)   117

435.   *RLA(S)1.* A. Seen from the rear. B. Seen from the front. Samothrace Museum.   118

436.   Southwestern Hellenistic akroterion of the Hieron. Samothrace Museum. (P: Anna Wachsmann.)   121

437. Southeastern Roman akroterion of the Hieron. Kunsthistorisches Museum, Vienna. (P: By courtesy of the Museum.)   121

438. View of the Hieron from the west in 1953; in foreground, the Hall of Votive Gifts and the Altar Court.   125

439. Detail of the lintel of the main door.   126

440. Detail of the western parapet, showing repair.   127

441. Detail of the covered drain north of the Hieron.   128

442. Trough found in the cella.   129

443. Top of capital 346 A 1. (Drawn by Martin R. Jones.)   *following* 136

444. Schematic detail of the plan of the extant antique porch, showing the re-erected columns on their modern crepidoma or stylobate. (Drawn by Martin R. Jones.)   *following* 136

445. Front elevation of the anastelosis: diagram showing the number, position, and dimensions of the reconstructed ancient blocks. Modern marble blocks are marked with a cross. (Drawn by Martin R. Jones.)   *following* 136

446. Lateral elevation of the anastelosis: diagram showing the number, position, and dimensions of the reconstructed ancient blocks. Modern marble blocks are marked with a cross. (Drawn by Martin R. Jones.)   *following* 136

447. Detail of the anastelosis, seen from the west. (P: Nicholas D. Ohly.)   139

SAMOTHRACE:

THE HIERON

Text I

1. View of the Hieron, 1964

Introduction

W HEN Cyriacus of Ancona visited the Sanctuary of the Great Gods in October, 1444, the building in which pious initiates had entered the higher degree of the Samothracian mysteries throughout antiquity had lain in ruins for nine hundred years. Yet it had never wholly disappeared beneath the creeping vegetation of the centuries after its destruction by earthquake. Deprived of its identity but vaguely definable, its scattered marbles had remained a recognizable feature of the deserted landscape. Here, on this island which he thought of in Homeric fashion as the "ancient seat of Neptune," Cyriacus did not hesitate to interpret the blocks of the Hieron as the immense ruins of a marble temple of Neptune.[1]

1. For Cyriacus' visit to Samothrace, see especially: Erich Ziebarth, "Cyriacus von Ancona in Samothrake," *AM,* 31 (1906), 405 ff.; Karl Lehmann-Hartleben, "Cyriacus of Ancona, Aristotle, and Teiresias in

First and most influential of all the learned travelers who were ultimately to investigate the antiquities of Samothrace, Cyriacus was followed, nearly four centuries later, by another breed of explorers. Abandoning his characteristic effort to interpret unknown monuments in the light of literary documents, they were content to record their observations in less speculative terms. But they, too, continued to draw attention to the ruins of the building and to call it a temple. Blau and Schlottmann, reporting on a visit to Samothrace in the summer of 1854,[2] singled out the ruins of the Doric Temple as seemingly among the greatest on the island and, citing the existence of some of the very blocks mentioned by Cyriacus, were impressed with the degree to which it could be reconstructed. A few years later, early in June, 1857, Alexander Conze made his first visit to Samothrace. Like his predecessors, he included the Doric marble building among the conspicuous ruins in the Sanctuary and considered that it might have been a temple.[3] Realizing that the marble used for Samothracian buildings was probably imported from Thasos, he linked the Doric marble building with two other marble ruins, the Round Building and the φυλακή, and concluded that all three dated from the period following Alexander the Great. This statement, correct in itself, contained within it the germ of an assumption that for more than a century was to take on the proportions of a dogma: that the "New Temple," as the Hieron came to be called, like the rotunda dedicated by Arsinoe and the monumental propylon given by Ptolemy II, was a Ptolemaic dedication of the first half of the third century B.C. Conze concluded his report on the antiquities of Samothrace with an eloquent statement on the desirability of conducting large-scale excavation in the Sanctuary.[4]

Before he could himself undertake this task, two members of the École française d'Athènes, Gustave Deville and E. Coquart, inaugurated excavation in the Sanctuary. Among the areas they explored and charted in the summer of 1866 was the region of the "Temple dorique" (fig. 2).[5] Like all their successors, they were shocked by abundant evidence that this ruin, in particular, served as a quarry for the islanders, whether its marbles were broken up for re-use or reduced to lime. They confined their excavation of the building to *sondages* made at the northwest corner of the porch, where one step block was uncovered *in situ,* to two other strips along the northern and eastern sides of the porch (the areas in-

Samothrace," *Hesperia,* 12 (1943), 115 ff.; the references cited in both these articles; and text ii, pp. 63 ff. The allusion to the Hieron mentioned above occurs in Cod. Vat. lat. 5250, fol. 14 r: *Vidimus et ingentia neptuni marmorei templi vestigia, immanium columnarum fragmenta, epistyliaque et bases. . . .* The passage recurs in Ms. I, 138, fol. 192 v, in the Biblioteca Capitolare in Treviso, and is reprinted in *S,I,* p. 1, n. 1, and Ziebarth, op. cit., p. 407.

2. "Altertümer von Samothrake und Imbros," *Berl. Ber.,* 1855, p. 608. For the reports of earlier nineteenth-century visitors, see *S,I,* p. 3, nn. 1–3.

3. *Reise auf den Inseln des thrakischen Meeres* (Hannover, 1860), pp. 59, 61.

4. Ibid., pp. 73 f.

5. "Rapport sur une mission dans l'île de Samothrace," *Archives des missions scientifiques et littéraires,* 2d ser., 4 (1867), 259 f., 262 f., 268, 275 f.

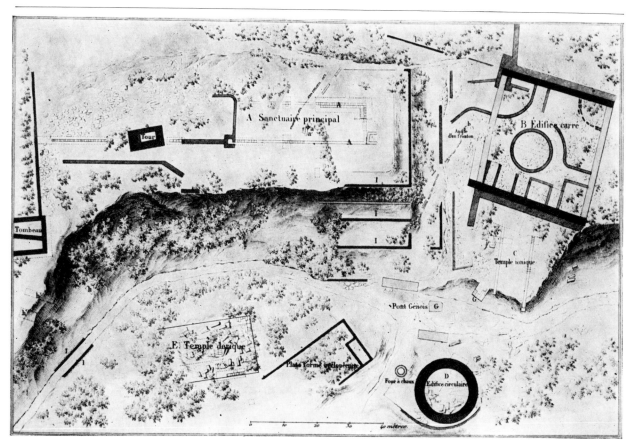

2. Coquart's plan of the Sanctuary after the French excavation of 1866

dicated by dotted lines in fig. 2), and a trench placed in the center of the cella.[6] Then, discouraged by the degree to which the southern part of the building lay buried beneath vegetation and encumbered by blocks, they abandoned hope of determining its full extent and concluded, in obvious disappointment, that the excavation of this area had yielded no results of any interest.[7] Coquart recorded what he thought sufficient blocks to enable the excavators to reconstruct the order of this Hellenistic building and its external appearance,[8] but they were never published, partially as a result of Deville's death.[9]

6. The areas indicated as excavated in the general plan illustrated above should not be taken too literally. Had the excavators actually uncovered the specific rectangular field shown on the eastern side of the building, for example, they could not have avoided discovering the point at which the cella abuts the wider porch —a significant feature of the plan that is not mentioned or recorded in this report, hence, was presumably not visible.

7. Deville, ibid., p. 263: "Les fouilles faites sur ce point n'ont eu aucun résultat intéressant."

8. Ibid., pp. 275 f. "Les détails que nous avons mesurés et dessinés peuvent servir à reconstituer l'ordre et l'aspect extérieur du temple, qui à d'autres égards ne mérite pas grand intérêt."

9. After the first Austrian campaign, Coquart published a list of the drawings he had made in Samothrace which evidently included two sheets devoted to the Doric marble temple—one, a plan; the other, elements of the order and coffers. See "A Monsieur le Président de l'Académie des Inscriptions et Belles-Lettres, Institut de France," *RA*, n.s. XV, 27 (1874), 24 f.

3. View of the main threshold and adjacent pavement after excavation in 1873

Seven years later, when Conze had organized an expedition remarkable for its day, he returned to Samothrace with the express intention of excavating at least one building in the Sanctuary thoroughly.[10] Although he would have liked to attack the enormous limestone ruin on the western hill of the Sanctuary which at the time he, as well as Deville and Coquart, assumed to have been the principal and earliest temple,[11] restrictions of time and money forced him to postpone this task and to concentrate on the two marble ruins that had attracted Cyriacus—the Doric temple and the rotunda.[12]

When Conze and Alois Hauser, to whom investigation of the Doric temple had been assigned, began excavation of the building early in May, 1873, the trenches of their predecessors were still discernible.[13] Taking advantage of the French plan, they again began to work at the northwest corner of the building. Continuing across the northern foundation and its vicinity, where they found blocks from the façade and fragments of the pedimental sculptures in fallen position, they then moved southward along the outer eastern and western edges of the building in an attempt to discover its perimeter. Especially along the eastern side, where excavation was easier and the debris less high, they recovered blocks from the

10. *S,I*, p. 6.
11. Ibid.; *Reise*, p. 58.
12. *S,I*, p. 6.
13. The following brief summary of the Aus-

trians' procedure is based on Conze's description, supplemented by Hauser's statements in *S,I*, pp. 6, 9–15, 47–49.

4. View of the abaton after excavation in 1873

wall entablature, where they, too, lay in fallen position. Eager to find the southern end of the long cella and to ascertain its plan, they dug trenches across the building and were rewarded by discovery of the main threshold and the marble pavement adjacent to it, as well as the wholly unexpected apse and its singular installation (figs. 3–5). Outside it, to the south of the building, there appeared the scattered fragments of the floral and figural akroteria now in Vienna. Figure 5 illustrates the extent to which the building was explored in that first six-week campaign. More than two years later, in another brief campaign in the summer of 1875, excavation was continued to the south of the building and along its western side.[14]

The results of this second exploration of the Doric marble temple were published in two monumental volumes printed in 1875 and 1880.[15] They have proved indispensable to our own investigation, because they record evidence that had vanished long before the mid-twentieth century. Upon his return to Samothrace in 1875, Conze was aghast to discover that the ruin had suffered grievous damage in the short interlude after the expedition's departure and before its return, in spite of his efforts to arrange for its protection.[16] Especially

14. Reported in *S,II,* pp. 9 f., 27–32.

15. *S,I,* 1875; *S,II,* 1880.

16. See *S,II,* pp. 9 f. This experience doubtless seemed to justify Conze's earlier decision to transport

to Vienna representative blocks of the building, as well as its fragmentary sculptures, even when this action involved dismembering blocks to obtain a portion of their ornamental carving.

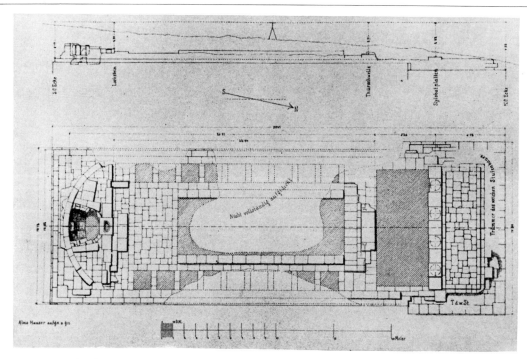

5. Hauser's plan of the Hieron after the Austrian excavation of 1873

painful was the brutal destruction of the great marble threshold of the main door and the adjacent pavement, with its revealing traces of the grille door through which initiates were admitted to the cella,[17] and of the installation of the apse, a unique feature of the building.[18] Under the circumstances, Hauser's drawings of detailed areas within the cella or of blocks later destroyed (for example, figs. 41, 42, 70, 75) are a priceless record. We have invariably used his plates to supplement our own observations in describing and reconstructing the original appearance of the building. It is the more necessary, therefore, to make a few comments on the character of this early excavation and its records.

Comparison of figs. 5 and 6, a view of the ruin some years after "excavation," with Pl. I will indicate that it was explored rather than excavated. The plan reproduced in fig. 5 is especially misleading, since by scrupulously marking certain areas of the building as incompletely uncovered, Hauser implied, and in fact stated,[19] that the remaining areas were fully excavated. But this was not the case. Nor do individual blocks shown in the plan represent elements actually seen and recorded.[20] The underpavement of the porch and

17. For discussion of this grille and its implications, see below, pp. 118 ff.

18. Discussed below, pp. 129 ff.

19. *S,I*, p. 58.

20. Hauser reported, ibid., that there was insufficient time to move blocks and investigate thoroughly in the areas enclosed by dotted contours on pl. 11 (= our fig. 5), and that along the eastern foundation individual stones could not be examined. This statement is so explicit that it does not prepare one for the fact that elsewhere on the plan precisely drawn elements are incorrect (for example, the number of blocks in the southern euthynteria), or for the omission of the majority but not all of the clamp, dowel, and pry holes in this same file of blocks (pl. 17).

6. View of the Hieron from the northeast after the Austrian excavations of 1873–75

cella, for example, which looks so specific and convincing, is wholly different in character, as we discovered to our surprise. This single instance will suffice to suggest that the plan as a whole cannot be taken literally, that it is a curious mixture of the precise and the schematic in which recorded observations were combined with unverified assumptions.

In two other respects, Hauser's procedure reflects the period at which he worked. The restored elevations (figs. 7, 8) were based on investigation of a very limited amount of the available evidence: only eight of the several hundred extant wall blocks appear to have been measured; less than a quarter of the well-preserved column drums.[21] Here, too, investigation was schematic and restricted to a sampling of the available material. It was further complicated by the fact that a foundation adjacent to the Hieron, of which Conze, in particular, was aware, had also supported a Doric superstructure (the Altar Court) and that the blocks of the two structures had become intermingled on the western side of the Hieron when the buildings were thrown to the ground.[22] Confronted with two sets of dimen-

21. Cf. the charts in *S,I*, pp. 62; *S,II*, p. 27.
22. See text II, p. 130, and *Samothrace*, Vol. 4, pt. II, pp. 4, n. 5, and 9. For the frieze of the Altar Court, ibid., Pls. XXVI–XXIX, and below, pp. 168 f.

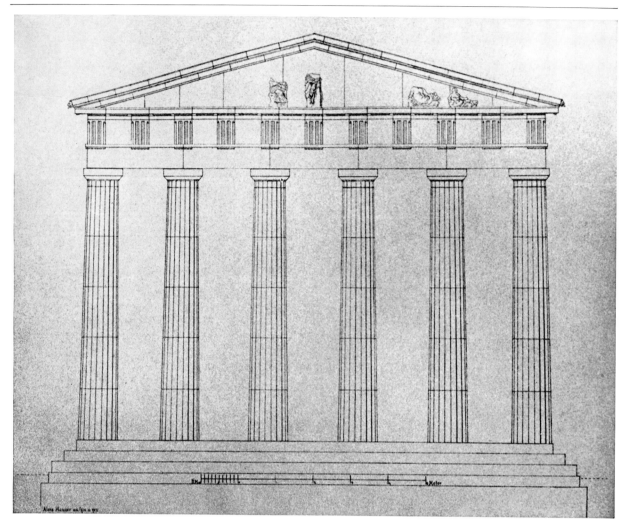

7. Hauser's reconstruction of the façade of the Hieron

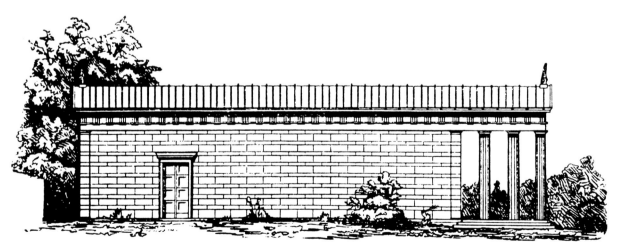

8. Hauser's restored lateral elevation of the Hieron

sions for his frieze and unaware of the existence of a second Doric structure, Hauser resolved what must have seemed a discrepancy in his measurements by ascribing to the frieze blocks of the Hieron a nonexistent height midway between their actual height and the height of the frieze of the Altar Court—thereby introducing another incorrect factor into the delicate problem of the proportions of his Doric entablature and its relationship to the colonnade. Finally, as these nineteenth-century excavators did not, in general, dig into the depths,[23] so they did not think in terms of successive building periods or observe evidence of later additions or repairs to this building, but accepted it as the homogeneous product of one period.

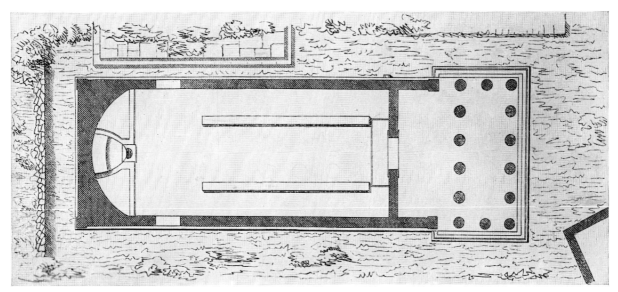

9. Hauser's restored plan of the Hieron

Hence, the ill-built late parapets dividing the interior into nave and aisles were automatically introduced into the restored plan of the Hellenistic building (fig. 9), thus preparing the way for future misinterpretation of it.[24]

Whatever its shortcomings by present standards, this investigation constituted a prodigious advance in Samothracian studies—indeed, in contemporary archaeological publication. Coupled with the exceptional nature of the Doric marble temple, or, as Conze finally called it, the "New Temple," [25] it ensured widespread interest in that building. Soon its unorthodox plan, its anticipation of elements associated with Early Christian architecture, and its seemingly fixed date in the first half of the third century B.C. made it become part

23. Excavation into the depths of the apse was a notable exception. For the most part, as Conze stated in *S,I*, p. 14, the Austrians did not excavate below the level at which they expected finds—i.e., the late antique ground level.

24. For refutation of the many features of Hau-

ser's restored plan and elevations which, being based on a combination of incomplete evidence, incorrect observation, and insufficiently supported hypothesis, are at fault, see below, chap. I, passim.

25. To distinguish it from the so-called "Old Temple," for which see *Hesperia*, 20 (1951), 12 ff., and, ultimately, *Samothrace*, Vol. 5.

of the repertory of monuments included in handbooks on Greek architecture.[26] For Conze, partly as a result of his conviction that the third century was of paramount importance in the history of the Sanctuary, partly because of his continuing assumption that the "New Temple" should be grouped with the Rotunda of Arsinoe and the Propylon of Ptolemy II, if only because of material and scale, inclined to date the building in the first half of the third century B.C.[27]

In the interval between the Austrian excavation of the building and renewed exploration of it by a French-Czech expedition half a century later, two variations on Conze's

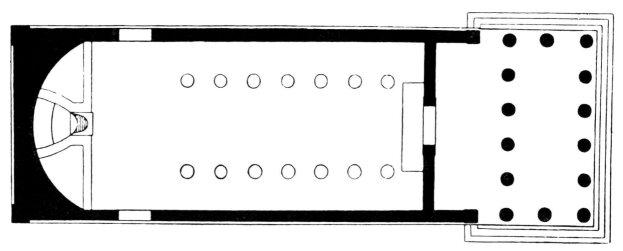

10. Restored plan of the Hieron, after Springer-Michaelis

and Hauser's conclusions regarding its date and plan gained considerable acceptance. Both were stated or implicit in Otto Rubensohn's discussion of the Sanctuary in 1892, in which he assumed that the "New Temple" was a Ptolemaic dedication and, unaware of the true nature or date of the rectangular subdivisions between nave and aisles in Hauser's plan, suggested that the interior of the cella must have been divided into three aisles by either columns or piers.[28] Some years later, the former alternative was given graphic expression in two widely-used volumes (cf. fig. 10),[29] thereby stimulating acceptance and retention

26. It is needless to cite the innumerable publications in which the "New Temple" has been quoted or Hauser's restored plan reproduced, from the appearance of S,I in 1875 until the mid-twentieth century. The review of this first volume by G. Matz and F. von Duhn in Bullettino dell'Instituto di correspondenza archeologica, 1876, pp. 106 ff., will suffice to illustrate the character of its reception.

27. Cf. S,I, p. 24, and, more explicitly, S,II, pp. 112 f., where the extreme limits for the date of the "New Temple" are defined as the second half of the fourth century, on the one hand, and the mid-third

century, on the other. The former date, quoted from Rayet's review of S,I in Gazette des beaux-arts, 2d ser., 13 (1876), 591, and based on presumed analogies with the Temple of Athena at Priene, is of particular interest. See below, pp. 179 f.

28. Die Mysterienheiligtümer in Eleusis und Samothrake (Berlin, 1892), pp. 183 ff., and especially p. 184.

29. Anton Springer, Handbuch der Kunstgeschichte, I: Das Altertum, 5th edn., rev. by Adolf Michaelis (Leipzig, 1898), p. 93, fig. 155; and Gabriel Leroux, Les origines de l'édifice hypostyle (Bibliothèque des

12

until the mid-twentieth century[30] of an erroneous plan conducive to emphasis on the presumed archetypal relationship between the Hieron and the Christian basilica.[31]

Assumption that the building was a dedication of Ptolemy Philadelphos was promoted in 1925, when Antoine Salač reported his discovery of a fragmentary inscribed architrave block two years earlier in the course of work carried on in the Sanctuary in collaboration with Fernand Chapouthier, a fellow member of the École française d'Athènes.[32] Although this block bearing the letters ΩΝΘΕΟ was found at a considerable distance from the façade of the Hieron, near the northwestern corner of the Altar Court, Salač did not recognize that the foundation he had excavated to the west of the "New Temple" had once supported a marble structure. Hence he attributed the fragment to the porch of the "New Temple" and, drawing on the analogy of the inscribed architraves of Ptolemy's Propylon, proposed that the "New Temple," too, had been a donation of Ptolemy II and that its architrave had been inscribed with an identical text. Actually, the solitary fragment of this otherwise hypothetical inscription comes from the dedicatory inscription of the building beside which it was found,[33] but its attribution to the Hieron was accepted as further evidence in support of a traditional theory.[34]

In the meantime, Chapouthier had reinvestigated the interior of the building, presumably with the intention of clarifying the nature of its plan. Digging an irregular trench across the cella (cf. figs. 11, 12, 14),[35] he discovered that it had been paved and that, con-

---

Écoles françaises d'Athènes et de Rome, 108 [Paris, 1913]), p. 191, fig. 59. In both these volumes, the building was provided with the increasingly popular date ca. 260 B.C. Two still more inaccurate and misleading simplifications of this restored plan appear in Valentin Müller, "The Roman Basilica," *AJA*, 41 (1937), fig. 1, III, and Emerson H. Swift, *Roman Sources of Christian Art* (New York, 1951), p. 25, fig. 16, no. 6.

30. For example, by Roberto Paribeni, *I grandi santuari dell'antica Grecia* (Milan, 1947), p. 72, and Dinsmoor, p. 269.

31. Most recently by Émile Mâle, *The Early Churches of Rome*, tr. David Buxton (Chicago, 1960), pp. 47, 51.

32. "Inscriptions inédites de Samothrace, I," *BCH*, 49 (1925), 245–53.

33. See Vol. 2, pt. I, **9**, and especially Vol. 4, pt. II, pp. 4 ff., 117 ff., for discussion of this inscription. Although its text may be debatable, the fact that it comes from the dedicatory inscription of the Altar Court and not from the Hieron is indisputable.

34. For example, by Thiersch, pp. 8 f.

35. We are greatly indebted to François Salviat for the unpublished drawings and photographs illustrated in figs. 11–14 which he inherited from Professor Chapouthier. They provide valuable evidence of his procedure and the purpose of his excavation in the "New Temple" and supplement the brief lines published in *BCH*, 49 (1925), 466, which he evidently intended to elaborate at a later date (cf. his statement in *Les Dioscures*, p. 162, n. 6).

Figure 11 is clearly a tracing made from *S,I*, pl. 11, to which has been added a general indication of the area uncovered. Unavoidably, therefore, it retains the errors of its source, including the too great length of the parapet walls which do not extend as far south as they appear to. Comparison of figs. 11–14 with our Pl. I makes it clear that Chapouthier dug immediately to the south of the eschara, on the eastern side of the cella, and that he actually uncovered the southernmost extension of the parapets, although this point may not have been apparent without excavation farther to the south. It is also evident that a large part of the area now lacking underpavement or packing in the central and lateral aisles immediately to the south of the parapets was included in Chapouthier's trench— i.e., that it was reduced to its present state, whether through destruction or disintegration, in the years following his excavation and preceding our own.

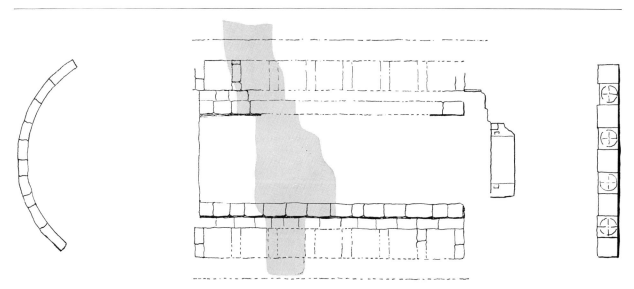

11. Diagram by Chapouthier, showing his trench across the cella

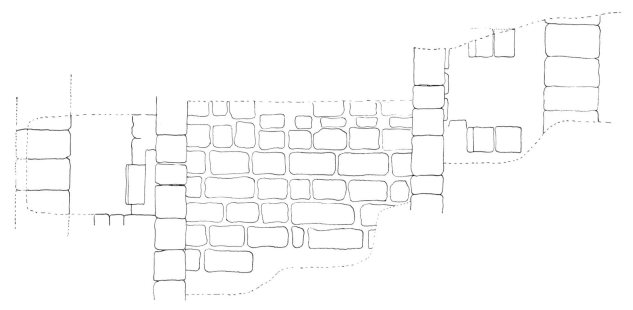

12. Schematic plan by Chapouthier of the area investigated in the cella

trary to the accepted view, it had never been subdivided by colonnades.[36] Evidently, he concluded that the low walls long misinterpreted in Hauser's plan as the foundations for such colonnades were to be associated with the short, transverse foundations that he un-covered on both sides of the cella (figs. 12, 13). For some years later, in publishing a

36. *BCH*, 49 (1925), 466. He also announced that there were no remains earlier than the fourth century B.C. beneath the building. Presumably, he drew this incorrect conclusion from the lack of any evidence of an earlier structure in his transverse trench in the cella —the only point at which he re-examined the building. (For discussion of the predecessors of the Hieron, see text II, pp. 51 ff.) He did not state (nor, given contemporary views about the chronology of the building, can I suggest) his reason for referring to traces antedating the fourth century, a phrase that certainly implies an earlier date for it than had been advanced since Rayet.

13. View of Chapouthier's trench across the cella, seen from
the west

14. View of underpavement exposed by Chapouthier in the cella

15

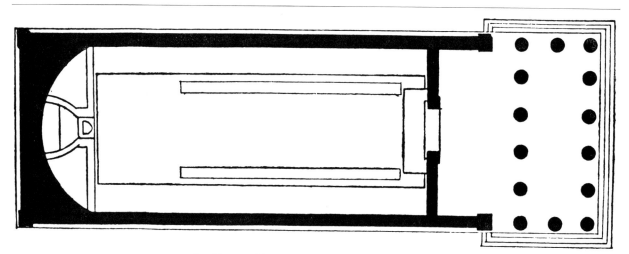

15. Chapouthier's restored plan of the Hieron

modified version of Hauser's restored plan (fig. 15), he assumed that the interior of the building had been flanked by two rows of niches or banquettes.[37]

At about the same time, Arnold Schober published the results of his re-examination of the architecture and sculpture of the "New Temple," an investigation concerned, in particular, with the pedimental and akroterial sculptures in Vienna.[38] Pointing out that portions of the columnar architrave of the porch had long been known and that they provided proof that it had never been inscribed, he rejected Salač' thesis and attributed the fragmentary inscribed block which had provoked that theory to the building beside which it was found[39]—a logical assumption borne out by subsequent excavation.[40] Having disposed of the latest "evidence" in support of the established theory that the "New Temple" was a dedication of Ptolemy II, he attempted to prove that the building and its sculptures should be dated a hundred years later, in the mid-second century B.C.[41] This radical proposal, based solely on stylistic analysis, was both correct and incorrect: correct in its general evaluation of the date of the pedimental sculptures,[42] but faulty in its analysis of

37. *Les Dioscures*, p. 163. A few years earlier, Thiersch, pp. 5 f., n. 6, evidently unaware of Chapouthier's original statement about the floor of the cella but anticipating one of his suggestions about the function of the side aisles, proposed that the unpaved floor of the cella had been used for ritual dances or dramas performed before spectators seated in the side aisles, and that the well-known frieze of dancing maidens had been mounted on or fastened to the long low walls dividing the cella into nave and aisles, thereby providing an appropriately decorated parapet behind which the spectators sat. (For this frieze, which we now know comes from the small Ionic propylon giving access to the Temenos northeast of the Hieron, see

Hesperia, 20 [1951], 16 ff., pls. 8 ff.; *Guide*, pp. 57 ff., 80 f.; *Guide²*, pp. 57 ff., 83 f.; and Vol. 5 of this series, forthcoming.) Chapouthier's suggestions in regard to the side aisles were further developed by René Vallois, *L'architecture hellénique et hellénistique à Délos* (Paris, 1943), p. 154, who interpreted the combined evidence of Hauser's and Chapouthier's plans and comments as indication that they were occupied by steps.

38. "Der Neue Temple von Samothrake," *JÖAI*, 29 (1935), 1–22.

39. Ibid., pp. 1 f.

40. See the references cited above, n. 33.

41. See *JÖAI*, 29 (1935), 4–6, 21 f.

42. For detailed consideration of Schober's dis-

architectural detail,[43] as renewed and, for the first time, stratigraphic excavation of the building was later to establish.[44] Accepted by some,[45] rejected by others,[46] Schober's article gave rise to a new theory or, rather, a new variation on the old. For Salač, reiterating that the structure uncovered to the west of the "New Temple" had been fully excavated and denying that it could ever have supported a superstructure, but unable, a second time, to disregard the uninscribed columnar architrave blocks discovered in the nineteenth century, announced that the "New Temple" had had two building periods: that it had been built at the beginning of the third century by Ptolemy Philadelphos and provided with a dedicatory inscription attesting that donation, but reconstructed in the second century without such an inscription.[47] Ironically enough, this pronouncement, born of the refusal to relinquish a mistaken theory, was to prove partially correct, for the Hieron is the product of two building campaigns, if neither a Ptolemaic dedication nor third century in date.

Repeatedly explored but never fully excavated, the "New Temple" demanded reinvestigation. On July 14, 1948, we were able to turn to that task. In the nearly three-quarters of

---

cussion of the sculptures of the Hieron, see below, chap. III, passim, and text II, pp. 113 ff. It is only necessary to remark here that, like all his predecessors, Schober assumed that the Vienna Nike was contemporary with the pedimental sculptures—an assumption perhaps natural before the discovery of the original akroteria of the southern pediment, but one that mars or invalidates certain of his statements.

43. Again, in analyzing certain details that occur only on the second-century porch, Schober naturally assumed that it was contemporary with the cella. But, working as he did in the Kunsthistorisches Museum, he should have measured the frieze blocks before his eyes instead of using Hauser's incorrect figure for their height as a basis for proportional comparisons. These two examples will suffice to suggest and explain the origin of certain of his mistakes.

44. For description of the two major building periods of the Hieron and their dates, see below, especially chaps. I, pp. 84 ff.; II, passim; III, pp. 246 ff., 301 ff., 327 f., 381 ff.; and the Catalogue, text II, pp. 145 f., 165 f., 173 ff.

45. For example, by two authors who had previously accepted the traditional date: Schede in Daniel Krencker and Martin Schede, *Der Tempel in Ankara* (*Denkmäler antiker Architektur*, III [Berlin and Leipzig, 1936]), p. 46, n. 10; and Otto Kern, *Die Religion der Griechen*, III (Berlin, 1938), 118.

46. For example, Gerhard Kleiner, *Tanagrafiguren* (*JDAI*, Suppl. 15 [Berlin, 1942]), pp. 153 ff.,

288 f.; and Heinz Kähler, *Der grosse Fries von Pergamon* (Berlin, 1948), pp. 74, 103, 178, n. 58. Chapouthier himself, in an addendum to *Les Dioscures*, pp. 347 f., reported Schober's conclusions without taking a decisive stand for or against them.

47. "La dédicace du nouveau temple des grands dieux à Samothrace," *BCH*, 70 (1946), 537–39. This article, as the author emphasized in his first footnote, is the unchanged text of a paper delivered in Amsterdam in the summer of 1938 relatively soon after the publication of Schober's article. It is a stubborn restatement of his original position modified only by grudging acceptance of sufficient of Schober's argument to motivate the conclusion that the "New Temple" was reconstructed at a later date. No additional evidence is offered in support of this "reconstruction," which is simply announced.

Before our excavation of the building to which Salač's inscribed block actually belonged and its subsequent publication (see the references cited above, n. 33), this modified version of his original theory was accepted by Jiří Frel, "Deux étapes de la construction du nouveau Cabirion de Samothrace," *Listy Filologické*, 74 (1950), 65–69 (reported in *Fasti Archaeologici*, 5 [1950], 232 f.), and Hemberg, p. 71. Salač' original conclusion still circulates as fact in 1965—witness Charles Picard, "Sur les dédicaces monumentales apposées en Grèce aux entablements de façades d'édifices sacrés ou civils," Χαριστήριον εἰς ᾽Αναστάσιον Κ. ᾽Ορλάνδον (Athens, 1965), I, 103!

16. View of the Hieron after the Austrian excavations of 1873–75

17. View of the porch from the east before excavation, 1948

18. View of the porch from the northeast before excavation, 1948

a century since Conze and Hauser had partially exposed it, the ruin had again become overgrown with trees and shrubs. But the marble blocks littering the porch and its periphery in the late nineteenth century were, for the most part, undisturbed—drums still teetered on the edge of the foundation or lay embedded before it, as they had lain for centuries (cf. figs. 16–18). It soon became apparent that a great proportion of the extant blocks of the superstructure lay in fallen position [48] and that they had either crashed down directly over the interior of the building and its immediate vicinity or been flung to the

48. Others had been only slightly dislodged from their original positions. Those that had never been

19. View of the northeastern corner of the pronaos after excavation, 1948

north and northwest.[49] As these fallen blocks were removed from the surface of the building, they were numbered and their original positions recorded before they were provisionally placed on its northern, eastern, and western sides in order to free it for excavation (fig. 22). In the brief remaining weeks of this first postwar campaign, the porch, the pronaos, and the greater part of the cella up to the abaton were uncovered (fig. 20). The exploratory character of earlier investigation of the building, the hypothetical nature of many features of Hauser's plan of the extant remains, was immediately apparent.[50]

Once the foundation had been cleared of blocks from the superstructure, it was possible, at certain points, to excavate within the building.[51] The largest and, as it proved, the most significant field for such activity was the pronaos, where excavation into the depths revealed that the porch had, indeed, been attached to an earlier building (fig. 19).[52] The date of that earlier building remained uncertain until the rich ceramic material recovered in the fill and, subsequently, in the foundation ditches of the porch and cella [53] could be studied and the building itself fully investigated. But that the cella of the "New Temple" antedated the porch was clear.

It was equally clear that the short transverse foundations indicated along the sides of

touched in the course of repeated "excavation" of the building often retained a creamy freshness of color on their long-buried undersurfaces. Unfortunately, they have grown increasingly dark with exposure to the air.

49. The specific provenance of individual blocks or fragments is cited below in chap. I wherever it is significant. In general, they were found over or near the portions of the building to which they had belonged: the column drums over, around, and north of the porch; the great pronaos beams over the pronaos;

the wall blocks over and in the periphery of the cella, and so forth. There were, of course, exceptions—notably where previous excavators had moved blocks to one or another side of the cella in order to dig a trench.

50. Cf. fig. 5 and Pl. I.

51. These areas are specified, and representative examples of the finds from their fills are published in the Catalogue. See text II, pp. 165 ff., 173 ff.

52. See below, pp. 85 ff.

53. For these fills, see text II, pp. 145 ff.

20. View of the cella at the end of the campaign of 1948, looking toward the abaton

the cella in the Austrian plan had once supported marble benches, fragments of which were found throughout the length of the building, and that spectators seated in these lateral aisles had witnessed some liturgical action. For embedded in the limestone underpavement of the central aisle there appeared a wholly unexpected feature, a sacrificial hearth or eschara (fig. 85) —evidence, once again, of the incompleteness of previous excavation of the building. Throughout the entire area, a jumble of wall blocks, both marble and limestone, had covered the cella, and, as cleaning of it progressed, increasing quantities of fragments of the red, white, and black stucco that had once adhered to its walls were recovered. As we neared the apsidal termination of the cella (fig. 20), we gained a foretaste of the continuing vandalism to which the building had been subjected in the decades following the Austrian excavation; crumbs of marble and missing blocks of the tufa and porphyry underpavement previously preserved in this part of the cella testified to the destructive activity of stone-robbers (cf. fig. 5 and Pl. I).

The following summer, when we resumed excavation of the building by uncovering the southern end of the cella, a scene of indescribable chaos met our eyes. The eastern frame of the central area within the apse had been stripped of its marbles,[54] and the deep pit in

54. Like other dislodged blocks edging the opening in the apse, they were subsequently recovered and replaced in their original positions. The supporting blocks directly beneath them are not part of the original construction, which had been torn away. (For further details, see below, pp. 130 ff.)

21. Detail of the apse, showing the apses of the two
predecessors of the Hieron

this area excavated by the Austrians lay choked with blocks, especially blocks from the
adjacent corners of the cella. Among them was a fragment of a snake-entwined marble
torch, part of the installation of the abaton,[55] and a fragment of the relief sculptures of the
rear pediment.[56] And there, in the depths, below the jumble of extraneous blocks and fragments of sculpture, there appeared the arcs of the salient apses of the two predecessors of
the Hellenistic building (Pl. I; fig. 21).[57]

By early July, 1949, the ruin had been cleared of fallen blocks and fully exposed (fig.
22). South of the pronaos, the underpavement of the cella or the field-stone packing on
which it rests was either wholly or partially intact, except at one point: the irregular strip
south of the parapet walls, where earlier Chapouthier had dug a trench across the then
preserved underpavement, as we were later to learn.[58] There, where the underpavement was
entirely lacking and there was hope of obtaining evidence regarding the date of these predecessors of the Hellenistic building without inflicting further damage on it, we excavated.[59]

55. See below, pp. 135 ff.

56. See below, p. 321, *SP(S)3*.

57. For description of the Hellenistic apse and its
forebears and discussion of the predecessors of the
present building, see below, pp. 35 ff., and text II,
pp. 51 ff.

58. The anticipated report on this excavation was
never published. It was not until after Professor

Chapouthier's death, when the diagrams and photographs reproduced in figs. 11–14 were forwarded to us
through M. Salviat, that the precise location of his
trench was confirmed. See above, pp. 13 ff.

59. In a trench 4.70 m. east-west by 2.30 m.
north-south. After digging to a depth of 1 m. below the
level of the adjacent underpavement, we abandoned
this unproductive attempt to obtain evidence of earlier

22. View of the cella, seen from the south, 1949

Unfortunately, the little earth present in the dense packing of boulders that proved to support the underpavement did not contain a single potsherd.

Once the building itself had been uncovered and the long task of recording its plan and sections begun,[60] we attacked its periphery, turning first to the interval between the cella and the field-stone terrace wall to its south (fig. 23). Scattered over this area, down to the level of the euthynteria, lay blocks of the superstructure, including the great corner blocks of the wall, broken pieces of the raking sima, and occasional fragments of the akroterial sculptures. Soon it became apparent that these fragments, as well as the akroterial sculptures discovered by our Austrian predecessors to which they belonged, were Roman replacements of the original southern akroteria. For on July 7, 1949, in the course of excavating the narrow passage between the cella and the as yet unexcavated structure immediately to its west, we discovered the greater part of the original southwestern akroterion lying, face down, at the level of the euthynteria and the top foundation course (fig. 24). Near it and, like it, neatly buried ca. 9 m. north of the corner lay the fragments of the winged torso.[61]

This splendid statue buried beneath the late antique ground level, hence not uncovered

---

fills beneath the Hellenistic building and refilled the trench. The fact that our Austrian predecessors had already dug to the bottom of the open area in the apse precluded the recovery of stratigraphic evidence at that crucial point.

60. See below, n. 85.

61. For the Hellenistic akroteria, see below, pp. 329 ff.; for their Roman counterparts, text II, pp. 83 ff.

23. View of the terrace wall, 1949

24. Lower part of the southwestern akroterion, after discovery in 1949

by our predecessors, lay below a dense accumulation of marbles, in particular, sima blocks, lion's-head waterspouts, and kalypters—all clearly in fallen position. By mid-July, we realized that the welter of blocks along the western side of the cella included the elements of still another Doric entablature—an entablature greater in height and in some respects bolder in detail than that of the "New Temple"—which must belong to a marble structure adjacent to it on this side.[62] Full excavation of the "New Temple" had also made us aware that the cella had been repaired more than once in later antiquity,[63] that the main threshold, the parapet walls, and the installation of the abaton all gave evidence of having been re-modeled. But we, too, continued to labor under the mistaken theory that the cella had been built in the mid-third century B.C.[64]—a theory dispelled only by subsequent investigation of the fabric of the building and its fills.

In 1950, we concentrated on the area north of the porch. As far as 15 m. to the north and 7.50 m. to the west of the northwest corner of the building and some 7 m. north of the archaic altar discovered before the war in the course of our first exploratory work in the Sanctuary,[65] the sloping terrain was strewn with blocks from the porch: architrave, frieze, geison, and sima blocks; blocks from the tympanum and fragments of the raking sima; double-faced blocks from the anta walls; coffers and column drums. Northeast of the porch, on the eastern side of the nearby Temenos, lay a chain of drums assembled for transport by Byzantine builders but later abandoned. Immediately to the north of the porch we recovered additional fragments of the pedimental sculptures, as well as precious remnants of the northern akroteria—few in number and small in size, but sufficient to establish the fact that the northern akroteria were identical in type and workmanship with the original southern akroteria, and that, unlike these Hellenistic counterparts, they had never been replaced but remained in position until the building collapsed.[66]

Excavation and removal of an Austrian dump to the west of the porch yielded other fragmentary sculptures, including pieces that proved to come from the carved lids of the pronaos coffers, parts of which had already appeared in the northern part of the cella in 1948. The triangular area north of the porch framed by the Temenos on the east and a Roman drain uncovered that summer on the west was excavated to the level of the fifth course of the northern foundation of the porch. The revealing variations in the coursing of this foundation and the character of its fill, later supplemented by investigation of the lateral foundations of the porch and their fills, began to emerge.[67]

62. See Vol. 4, pt. ii, for this structure, to which the inscribed block found by Salač belonged and which we subsequently excavated and called the Altar Court.

63. For the Roman repairs and revisions of the building, see text ii, pp. 79 ff., 124 ff.

64. See *Hesperia*, 20 (1951), 21 ff., and subsequent preliminary reports. The traditional date was inadvertently retained by Mrs. Hadzi in *The Arts*, 37 (1963), 36.

65. See text ii, pp. 58 f.

66. See below, pp. 372 ff.

67. The builders of the porch worked in soil containing an outcropping of rock (as in the pronaos), which they filled in with a loose packing of stone. On

25. View of the Hieron, seen from the northwest, after the campaign of 1952; in foreground, the Hall of Votive Gifts; at right, the Altar Court

The next summer, after having ascertained that no additional structures or foundations for monuments existed in the area to the north of the porch or on the sloping terrain above the river bed to its northwest, we excavated to the west of the porch and the northern part of the cella. There, beneath the previously removed Austrian dump, the ground was strewn with marble blocks from the "New Temple" and the as yet unexcavated Doric structure adjacent to the southern half of the cella, intermingled with blocks of fine marine limestone from a hitherto unknown building immediately to its north—the archaic Hall of Votive Gifts (fig. 25).[68] In the interval between the two northerly buildings we found the same purplish fill that had occurred on the northern side of the porch and, in the western foundation ditch of the "New Temple," sufficient potsherds ultimately to corroborate the testimony of the northern and eastern foundation ditches and the foundations themselves and to indi-

the northern side of the building only the foundation ditch for the porch (ca. 0.30 m. wide) contained potsherds.

At the end of the season, this area was partially refilled and its level raised to facilitate future access to the building.

68. For this building, see Vol. 4, pt. 1.

26. View of the Hieron, seen from the northwest, at the end of the campaign of 1953; in foreground, the Hall of Votive Gifts; at right, the Altar Court

cate that the lower courses of the porch-pronaos foundations were contemporary with the cella and that the plan of the early Hellenistic building had called for a porch, although that porch was not completed for nearly two centuries.[69]

Here, to the west of the porch, in the vicinity of the Austrian dump, we found further fragments of the sculptured lids of the pronaos coffers in addition to recovering the dislodged carved outlet of a drain that our Austrian predecessors had discovered *in situ* in the euthynteria outside the northwestern corner of the cella (figs. 82, 83 B).[70] More important, it was here, to the west of the pronaos, that we found the fragmentary inscription originally mounted on the threshold of the main door, as well as a portion of the base in which it was later inserted—that late Hellenistic *lex sacra* prohibiting the uninitiated from entering the building which both confirmed its function as the *epopteion* and revealed its name: the Hieron (fig. 50).[71]

The following June, 1952, we completed excavation on the western side of the cella and began to explore its eastern, more particularly, its southeastern, periphery. Moving southward

69. See below, pp. 84 ff. The interval between the buildings was later leveled to serve as a small block field (see figs. 25–27).

70. Below, pp. 126 ff.

71. For this inscription, see below, pp. 63 ff.; text II, pp. 4 ff. It was first published in *Hesperia,* 22 (1953), 14 f.

27. View of the Hieron, seen from the Nike Fountain, 1954; in foreground, the Altar Court and the
Hall of Votive Gifts; in left background, the Arsinoeion

in the narrow lane between the Hieron and the Altar Court toward the point reached in this
area in 1949, we continued to find blocks from the two Doric structures lying side by side
over the eastern part of the Altar Court. Still farther to the west, in the orchestra of the nearby
Theater, we uncovered a group of blocks from the Hieron that had fallen over the neighboring enclosure and been transported to the Theater by former excavators of the Altar Court.
Others, including the fragmentary eastern threshold and blocks from the stereobate, lay above
the terrace wall to the south of the cella, obviously having been carried there by our Austrian
predecessors.[72] In the course of tracing this wall somewhat to the east of the Hieron where it
disappears beneath the unexcavated surface of the rising terrain (fig. 25),[73] we encountered
and excavated a limekiln strategically placed above the southeastern corner of the cella—
melancholy reminder of the continuing depredation to which this extensively preserved marble ruin had been subjected for more than three-quarters of a century after its wanton destruction was first reported by earlier excavators.[74]

During the summer of 1953, we continued to explore the southeastern periphery of the

72. Excavation of a small area 5.75 north-south
by 5.25 east-west immediately behind this wall and
south of the southeastern corner of the cella yielded

no finds or foundations.

73. Text II, pp. 71 f.

74. See above, pp. 4 ff.; text II, p. 130. The bottom

28. View of the anastelosis, 1956

building and to excavate a strip some 5 m. wide along its entire eastern flank (fig. 26). East of the southeastern corner of the cella, we found evidence of an early Imperial road ascending to the east along the terrace wall. Its earth fill rested on a stone packing laid on the purple fill from the building period of the cella which was itself covered with marble chips from the construction of the Hieron. The compact fill of this road contained a dense accumulation of pottery, especially bowls and dishes of local manufacture, as well as fragments of terracotta figurines, and a sparse number of bronze studs and fragmentary cymatia from the lateral doors and coffered ceiling of the cella.[75] Buried in this fill, near the corner of the building, were the fragments of the late Hellenistic floral akroterion[76]—evidence, once again, of damage to the rear façade in the early Imperial period.

---

of this kiln, which contained an immense accumulation of lime, was 1.70 m. above the euthynteria.

The single act of vandalism from which the Hieron has suffered since 1948 occurred between the campaigns of 1949 and 1950, when the well preserved blocks of the euthynteria at the southern end of the cella were defaced by a local resident bent on extract-

ing lead from their dowel and clamp holes (below, p. 40, n. 16).

75. For the material contained in this fill, see text II, pp. 191 ff. and **91–117, 161, 163–165, 169, 170, 175–177.**

76. See below, pp. 329 ff. The biggest fragment, *SCA 1*, was found 1 m. east and 0.75 m. north of the

29. View of the Hieron, seen from the southeast after the anastelosis

Along the eastern side of the building, we continued to find marble blocks lying in fallen position, but no trace of another building or monument.[77] One significant discovery remained for the final phase of this last excavation campaign in and around the Hieron: exposure of the triad of stones outside the northern part of the cella, where the confession of sins required of all candidates for admission to the *epopteia* took place (figs. 348, 365–368).[78]

During these last years, we had arranged the blocks of the superstructure on or near the building in such a fashion as to suggest their original location, wherever that proved feasible, and to make them accessible for future study. Blocks once discovered *in situ* but later dislodged, like the fragments of the main threshold, the marbles of the abaton, or the southeast corner stereobate block, were replaced in their original positions;[79] others found near their original positions—dislodged limestone foundations for benches or marble bench supports—were put back in place. In so far as possible, groups of blocks were restored to the quarter of the building to which they had belonged: column drums, capitals, and columnar architrave

southeastern corner at the level of the euthynteria; the majority of the other fragments lay in its immediate vicinity or slightly to the south, near the terrace wall.

77. On this side, as on the west, we encountered the deep pits made by Chapouthier at the outer edges of his trench across the cella (figs. 12, 13) and a stack of blocks removed from the building in the course of this work. We also cut through our own initial trial trench east of the northeast corner of the porch, reported in *AJA*, 43 (1939), 140.

78. Text II, pp. 17 ff., 54 ff.

79. Below, p. 60, n. 55; p. 50, n. 35; p. 41, n. 19.

30. View of the Sanctuary, seen from the north, 1956

blocks were placed on the porch; coffers and beams in the pronaos; [80] jamb and lintel fragments from the main door near the threshold; blocks from the eastern wall on the eastern foundation, from the western wall on the western foundation; and stereobate blocks were restored to provisional positions on the euthynteria.[81] The remainder of the extant blocks were grouped in fields on all four sides of the building (figs. 26, 27).[82]

In 1954, a typical section of the wall entablature was erected in Hall A of the Museum (Pl. LVI; fig. 112). At the same time, the four best preserved lion's-head waterspouts from the lateral simas were mounted on the outer wall of Hall C facing the courtyard (figs. 122–125, 387). The following year, other fragments from the building were placed on exhibition in Halls A, B, and C: a portion of the raking sima; the best preserved fragments of the Hellenistic floral akroteria; the fragmentary *lex sacra;* fragments of the coffer reliefs, pedimental, and akroterial sculptures; the southwestern figural akroterion.[83] Finally, in the summer of 1956, the generosity of the Bollingen Foundation enabled us to fulfill a long cherished dream and to reconstruct part of the porch. On the basis of drawings provided by Mr. Jones and with the co-operation of the Greek Anastelosis Service, five columns together with the architrave blocks of the central intercolumniation were re-erected on a modern crepidoma (frontispiece and figs. 1, 28–30).[84] Once again the Hieron, for centuries the goal of visitors to the island, assumed a dominant role in the Sanctuary.

By 1952, the plan and sections of the building, largely the work of Alec Daykin,[85] had been finished. The following year, Mr. Jones began investigation of the blocks of the superstructure. By the late summer of 1956, each block had been measured and recorded, and the preliminary field drawings had been completed. They included well preserved samples or key examples of typical categories of blocks, like the members of the entablature, as well as every atypical or unique block or fragment and every block or fragment belonging to a category of crucial significance for the reconstruction of the building—the rear corner blocks of

---

80. Below, p. 86, n. 126.

81. See below, p. 41, n. 19.

82. Small molded fragments were collected in an upper field east of the southeast block field and north of the path leading toward the South Nekropolis and the Ptolemaion.

83. *Guide*², pp. 80 ff., 88, 90 ff., 104.

84. For this anastelosis, which was effected between June 20 and August 29, 1956, see text II, pp. 132 ff. It was briefly reported in *Archaeology,* 10 (1957), 63 f., and *BCH,* 81 (1957), 609 f. In the course of this work, the extant stylobate blocks which had become damaged and dislodged by vegetation in the years following the Austrian excavation were mended and reset. The numerous lesser repairs made to the building or its blocks and to the adjacent stepping-stones

from 1948–63 are specified in chaps. I and V in notes to the particular areas or categories of blocks involved. The only additional work carried on in connection with the excavation and protection of the Hieron took place in the summer of 1955, when the slope to the east of the cella was graded and retained by low wattle fences to prevent the annual washing down of soil which had plagued the ruin following our excavation of this area in 1953. This simple device has proved effective—see figs. 29, 360.

85. The plan was begun by Stuart M. Shaw and carried on for a brief interlude by Roy Fraser, who was prevented by illness from continuing to work on it. Mr. Daykin was assisted for part of one season by Denys Spittle. Both plan and sections were ultimately emended and partially redrawn by Mr. Jones.

31. Plaster reconstruction of the central floral akroterion

the cella wall, the drums and capitals of the columns, the elements of the doors, to cite but a few examples. The next year, Mr. Jones and I began our joint effort to establish the reconstruction of the building. At the same time, Miss Love began to study the ceramic finds from the fills. Since then, we have had repeated opportunity to reconsider in the field and in the Museum whatever problems have arisen during the years in which this volume has been in preparation. In the meantime, Miss Loeffler and Mrs. Hadzi, who had originally taken part in the excavation of the building, completed their contributions to the Catalogue of Finds.

In 1959, I prevailed upon Professor Lehmann to interrupt his work on the Altar Court and the Temenos long enough to contribute to the volume a chapter on the *epopteia* and the function of the Hieron. Written that summer, it stands as Chapter IV. He had previously published the inscribed ceramics from the building in Volume 2, Part II.[86] Finally, in 1960,

86. See text II, pp. 211 ff., for further consideration of this material and cross-reference to the specific items in that volume which come from the Hieron.

Mr. Oliver-Smith and I joined forces to work out the reconstruction of the floral akroteria of the Hieron, first dealing with the fragments of the Hellenistic akroteria in the Museum in Samothrace and later, in 1963, with the fragments of the Roman replacement of the southern akroterion in the Kunsthistorisches Museum in Vienna. A by-product of this work has been the production of a plaster reconstruction of the Hellenistic akroterion (fig. 31) which now, in the summer of 1965, will be placed on exhibition in Hall A of the Samothrace Museum. Based on drawings by Mr. Oliver-Smith, it has been made by our restorer, Triandophyllos Kontogeorgis of the National Archaeological Museum in Athens.

Brief discussions of the Hieron have repeatedly appeared in our preliminary reports, *Guides,* and miscellaneous articles.[87] They are superseded by the present volume, in which the results of all earlier investigations of this remarkable building have been co-ordinated with the fruits of our own long labor.

87. I have incorporated in the notes to the following chapters all our previously published statements and opinions wherever they are at variance with the conclusions presented in this volume in order to correct any factual errors and to explain every re-evaluation of evidence.

32. Air view of the Sanctuary, 1957

I. Description and Reconstruction

THE Hellenistic Doric building known as the Hieron, in which initiation into the higher degree of the Samothracian mysteries took place, is situated in the southernmost part of the Sanctuary (fig. 32). It is oriented approximately toward the north, having a deviation toward the west of 20° 7′, and was accessible primarily on its northern side. Here it faced the oblique line of the older Temenos, while on the west it was flanked by the venerable Hall of Votive Gifts and the nearly contemporary Altar Court. The polygonal terrace wall of crystalline porphyry to its south almost parallels both the Hieron and the Altar Court, suggesting that the two Doric marble structures were conceived as part of one building program, however individual their character and style. The narrow interval between the Hieron and the terrace wall evidently served as a road leading eastward toward the ancient city or westward to the Theater via a stairway opposite the southern flank of the Altar

34

33. Detail of the abaton, showing the apse of the Hieron and the foundations for the apses of its predecessors

34. View of the Hellenistic apse, showing the foundations for the apses of its predecessors

Court. Confined on three sides,[1] the building was totally exposed to the east, where the ascending hillside may reflect a now vanished sacred grove.

The congestion of this quarter of the Sanctuary in the late fourth century was rooted in its archaic past. The archaic Hall of Votive Gifts was still upright; the position of the Altar Court had been determined by the hallowed place of worship contained within it; and the Hieron, too, preserved the orientation and location of two early predecessors. Their traces are still visible at the bottom of the wide opening in the Hellenistic apse (Pl. I; figs. 21, 33, 34).

Like the later marble building, the earlier structures were both apsidal. The curving line of the field-stone foundation for the apse of the first building on the site is visible ca. 0.82 m. north of the inner face of the Hellenistic apse wall, approximately at the level of the later marble euthynteria. Built of both green porphyry and gray crystalline porphyry, its average width is ca. 0.67 m. It was succeeded by a second building, the apse of which appears directly to its south. The apse of this immediate predecessor of the Hieron had a foundation at least 1.25 m. wide, constructed of porous limestone binders, and a wall of fine marine limestone.[2] Six of the regularly-cut foundation blocks of this apse and three of its limestone wall blocks may be seen in fig. 34, incorporated in the foundation and wall of the Hellenistic apse which rises over them. The three limestone wall blocks evidently

1. The Hieron is virtually parallel to both the Altar Court and the Hall of Votive Gifts but not to the line of the terrace wall, which diverges from it as it approaches the southern flank of the Altar Court and runs slightly farther to the north. The interval between the terrace wall and the rear foundation of the Hieron is 2.96 m. at the southeast corner of the building but 2.70 m. at a point 5.65 m. east of the southwest corner, where its original polygonal masonry has been altered. At the same southwest corner, the interval between the Hieron and the Altar Court is 1.10 m., and this narrow passageway between the buildings is essentially maintained, contracting only to 0.85 m. at the northeast corner of the Altar Court. A somewhat greater average interval of 3.45 m. separates the Hieron from the Hall of Votive Gifts; but, again, at its northeast corner, it comes within 2.96 m. of the adjacent rear corner of the Temenos at a point 1.20 m. west of that corner. For the terrace wall, see text II, pp. 71 f.

2. The total width of this foundation cannot be determined, given its present position within the foundation of the Hellenistic apse. The combination of materials found in it recurs in the enclosure wall of the Temenos.

belonged to the outer face of the wall; the inner face has disappeared. Just as traces of the first building were included in the second, so the second served as the actual base of the third, the three wall blocks becoming part of the lowest course of the apse wall at the level of the later euthynteria, while the foundation course beneath them lies at the same level as the uppermost foundation course of the Hellenistic building. The immediate predecessor of the Hieron must, therefore, have extended virtually as far to the south as the present structure; and, since the ritual installations of the latter were not only derived from those of its predecessors but literally placed on top of them,[3] it seems reasonable to assume that both earlier buildings were of essentially the same size as the Hellenistic cella. In view of the fact that at several points the native bedrock of the Sanctuary rises almost to the floor level of the present building, they, too, must have been built at the same level.

The apses of both earlier buildings were salient. This significant difference from their great marble successor is revealed by two groups of scale-shaped roof tiles, one black-glazed, the other red-glazed, that may be attributed to these buildings, since they long antedate the only other similar tiles—those employed on the Rotunda of Arsinoe, the single other building in the Sanctuary hitherto excavated on which such scale-shaped tiles could be used. Curved in their lower exposed parts and polygonal above, they are provided with raised ridges on their upper surfaces for the support of the overlapping tiles of the next tier (cf. Pl. LX.1, 3, 4). Other fragmentary tiles, both black- and red-glazed, may be attributed to the main roofs of these buildings (Pls. LVIII.3, LX.2). Inasmuch as several of these fragments were either incised before firing with a large square epsilon or stamped, they allow the black-glazed tiles to be dated in the fifth century—seemingly as repairs to the original archaic building[4]—and the red to be attributed to its successor,[5] the immediate predecessor of the existing early Hellenistic Hieron.[6]

No other certain elements of the two predecessors of the present Hieron have been found. But these eloquent fragments reveal both the form of those apsidal buildings and, as we shall see, their function.

---

3. For discussion of this point, see text II, pp. 56 ff.

4. 39.275, an unstratified fragment of a scale-shaped, black-glazed tile, incised before firing with a large square epsilon, and 48.723, a fragmentary black-glazed stroter of similar texture and glaze found in the fill of the pronaos of the present Hieron, provide key elements for the roof of the earliest building, although they are themselves repairs to it. 49.129, another un-stratified, fragmentary black-glazed stroter, incised on its upper surface with a large retrograde epsilon, evidently belongs to this same group. It is apparent from 48.723 that these tiles were set in stucco.

The epsilon inscribed on 39.275 has been dated in the fifth century: *Samothrace*, Vol. 2, pt. II, **276**. This

is a conservative date, since the same form of epsilon was used in the sixth century (ibid., p. 41). Whether sixth or fifth century in date, made when the building was constructed or repairs to it, the significance of these tiles is the same. For further discussion of the predecessors of the Hellenistic Hieron in the light of architectural and sculptural members that may be attributed to them and, therefore, more specific remarks about their probable date, see text II, pp. 51 ff. The present discussion is limited to the few facts that can be presented about them.

5. Comparable elements for the roof of the second building are provided by the following fragments: 53.162 C, two restored fragments of a red-glazed, scale-shaped tile found near the terrace wall slightly to the

Traces of burning on the lower surface of one of the red-glazed apse tiles of the immediate predecessor of the Hieron suggest that this structure intermediate between the archaic and early Hellenistic buildings was destroyed by fire. In any case, it was replaced late in the fourth century B.C. by one of the most remarkable buildings of ancient Greece, the present Hieron. Built of the same Thasian marble employed in the other classical and early Hellenistic buildings in the Sanctuary, it is Doric, 39.25 m. long, 14.03 m. wide at its façade, and 12.79 m. wide at its rear at the level of the euthynteria. It was intended to have a porch only slightly less deep than it now has and to be hexastyle prostyle, tetrastyle in antis, with a single column on each side of the porch between the corner column of the outer colonnade and the anta. But this projected porch remained incomplete, presumably owing to insufficient funds, until, in the second century B.C., the original plan was modified and the existing porch constructed.[7]

THE EARLY HELLENISTIC BUILDING

FOUNDATION (Pls. I, II; Figs. 35, 37, 58, 64)

When work on the early Hellenistic building ceased, its cella had been roofed, its pronaos partially finished, and the lower courses of its porch foundation built. The foundations of the cella and the original parts of the pronaos [8] are built of regular courses of gray porous limestone. The blocks of the uppermost course are laid as binders, as are the second course on the west and the third on the east, where the second course shows a mixture of binders and stretchers. The foundations vary in width from 1.16–1.50 m. and are composed

east of the southeastern corner of the later Hieron, as well as the smaller fragments 53.162 A–B; 54.155, a fragment of a red-glazed, scale-shaped tile of the same size found west of the Hieron and having a worn rectangular stamp on its upper surface, with traces of an epsilon preceded by a dot; 52.599, an unstratified fragment of a red-glazed stroter of similar texture and glaze, preserving part of a lambda, found near the Altar Court; and two fragmentary red-glazed ridge kalypters, 54.157 and 56.26, each bearing a rectangular stamp on its lower surface and being similar in texture to the preceding items. (The provenance of the latter two pieces is unknown, since their documentation was removed by the occupying Bulgarians during the war.) For further discussion of the incised or stamped fragments and their dates, consult Vol. 2, pt. II, **276–279, 281** and p. 115, where 54.157 is mistakenly printed as 54.153.

6. No pertinent stratigraphic observations regarding these structures could be made at the time of excavation, inasmuch as the Austrians had explored the interior of the apse to its lowest level. Hauser (*S,I,* pl. 17) clearly indicates the arcs of both the field-stone and limestone apses, in spite of the fact that they are

rendered in schematic fashion and not separated by the existing slight interval of space. But the section drawn on pl. 14 is totally inaccurate, especially in its false rendering of the irregular field-stone foundation for the earliest apse as a regularly built construction. It is all the more curious that this earliest foundation is nowhere mentioned in the text. In *S,I,* p. 60, the second limestone foundation is interpreted as a footing both for the present apse foundation and for the limestone blocks which the Austrians found edging the opening in the apse and which disappeared after their excavation. See below, p. 131. Fernand Chapouthier, not having reinvestigated the apse, ignored these earlier foundations in announcing ("Chronique des fouilles," *BCH,* 49 [1925], 466) that there was "nul vestige antérieur au IVᵉ siècle" beneath the building.

7. Evidence for the absolute chronology of the building and in support of these statements regarding the original plan of the early Hellenistic porch will be found on pp. 84 ff., below, and text II, pp. 70 ff.

8. The northern foundation under the inner colonnade and the adjacent northern parts of the two lateral foundations of the pronaos were rebuilt when the porch was completed. See below, pp. 85 ff.

35. View of the northwestern corner of the foundation

of courses having an average height of 0.35 m. The original courses of the porch are similar in height [9] but, like the later upper courses, were laid as stretchers. Since the sloping terrain of this region of the Sanctuary descends toward the north, the foundation of the porch was made considerably deeper than that of the rear south wall of the building, which may well consist simply of the one course now visible beneath the euthynteria, inasmuch as here the foundation ditch was cut into bedrock. At the façade, however, a foundation at least four courses high was planned to support the projected outer colonnade, for there the terrain was irregular and marked by outcroppings of rock. The transition to this greater depth had to take place in the lateral foundations.[10] The western lateral foundation of the projected porch was completed, as well as the northwestern corner, whereas its eastern and the greater part of its northern foundation still lacked the uppermost course when work on the building was interrupted. The second-century builders not only completed this unfinished course but also added still another, fifth course to the entire porch foundation in order to raise its level. Today only the upper four of the five or more courses of which the northern foundation was composed remain visible.

Obviously, the builders of the Hieron worked from south to north. Its lateral foundations must have been laid by two crews of masons who worked northward on each side of the building and met near the northwest corner of the façade foundation. The precise point at which these two crews met is still visible, because, as a result of careless workmanship, the individual courses proved not to be level with each other where the two sections of the

9. Except at the northwest corner, where they were mistakenly cut slightly too low.

10. It proved impractical to lower the hard, clay-like native earth around the building and to remove natural boulders immediately to the north of it in order to determine the number of courses of which the

foundation is built at different points. At the façade, we excavated to the level of the upper part of the present fifth foundation course. This fifth course is no longer visible now that the area to its north has been re-covered with earth and its level slightly raised.

northern foundation met. Figure 35 shows the northwest corner of the porch, where this juncture took place,[11] and the adjustment of one section of the foundation to the other.[12] In this view, only the lower three courses to the right of the irregular line of adjustment and the two to the left of it were laid in the fourth century; the entire upper course and the course beneath it at the left were added later when the porch was completed. The original levels of completion are easily discernible at the sides of the porch, owing to the fact that the fourth-century foundation projects beyond the slightly lower courses later built over it—the present third course beneath the euthynteria projecting at the east and the second course at the west. This structural procedure is confirmed by the evidence of the potsherds found in the foundation ditches.[13]

EUTHYNTERIA (Pls. I, II; Figs. 36–38)

The entire southern and a large part of the connecting eastern and western euthynteria of the cella were found *in situ*.[14] It consists of marble blocks having an average length of 1.18 m. (the variations range from 1.16 to 1.21 m.), except for the longer L-shaped blocks at the two corners, a width of 0.43–0.48 m., and an average height of 0.28 m. Actually, the blocks of the western euthynteria vary from 0.29 to 0.297 m., those of the eastern from 0.27 to 0.275 m. This unevenness in height between the blocks of a given course on the eastern and western sides of the building persisted throughout its construction and will be found in the wall entablature as well. The blocks of the euthynteria were doweled to the upper course of the limestone foundation, which projects slightly and irregularly beyond them (0.14–0.25 m.), by a pair of approximately square bronze dowels set in lead at one end of each block.[15] The corresponding dowel and pry holes cut in the foundation on every alternate block are visible on both sides of the building, where the euthynteria is no longer preserved. Each marble block was connected with the adjacent block at either end by a single bronze Π-clamp set in lead and with the limestone block or blocks at its rear by a pair

11. Ca. 4.45 m. east of the northwest corner of the building.

12. The quality of much of the limestone used at this corner is inferior to that of the remainder of the porch. The third and fourth courses below the euthynteria level of the present porch were mistakenly cut slightly too low. It was necessary, therefore, to cut down the regular, well-built third and fourth courses to the east in order to connect them with the faulty courses at the corner.

13. See text II, pp. 145 ff. It should be noted that the western foundation of the porch, in particular, has settled irregularly as a result of the destruction of the building by earthquake. See also n. 131, below.

14. Apart from the corner blocks, eleven are preserved on the east, nine on the west. The southern euthynteria, corners included, consists of ten blocks rather than the eleven indicated in *S,I*, pls. 11, 17. As always, these plans are highly schematic, indicating neither the rear clamps on each block nor their dowel or pry holes.

We have repaired several slightly damaged euthynteria blocks and replaced the first and third blocks north of the southeastern corner. The first block had been dislodged slightly by a tree. The third had been jerked upright, no doubt to be stolen; it proved to have three rather than the usual two dowel holes on its lower surface, one at the north and two at the south. Conceivably, the single northern dowel hole was a mistake, as, on the block nearest the corner, a Π-clamp was begun and abandoned.

15. The rear or southern end of the lateral euthynteria blocks. Both the dowels and the clamps used throughout the building were of bronze.

36. View of the southwestern corner, showing the foundation and euthynteria

37. Partial view of the southern foundation, euthynteria, and apse wall

38. Detail of the southwestern corner, showing the euthynteria, blocks of the stereobate, and the apse wall

of similar clamps.[16] The upper surface of the euthynteria was incised with two parallel setting lines for the placing of the next (or stereobate) course.[17] The inner line, 0.09 m. from the outer face of each block, indicates the position of the lower outer edge of the stereobate; the outer line, 0.07 m. from its face, corresponds to the projecting upper face of the stereo-

16. A few exceptions, where only one clamp was used at the rear of a block, may be noted on the plan (Pl. I). When the euthynteria was excavated in the summer of 1949, many of its dowel and clamp holes retained remnants of their lead casings. Upon our return to the island in 1950, we found that the euthynteria had been sadly defaced in the vicinity of dowel and clamp holes by a local resident in search of lead. This single defacement that the Hieron has suffered since its recent full excavation took place before the tenure of the present vigilant guard.

17. On the east, these lines have evidently worn off, but one must assume that originally they were present.

bate, which overhangs the lower part of each block. These guide lines imply that when a stereobate block was placed on the euthynteria the lower recess on its exposed face had already been cut, but that the overhanging upper portion of this face still retained its protective mantle. When that mantle was removed and the upper portion of the face trimmed to final smoothness, the outer guide line on the euthynteria was followed, with the result that the 0.02 m. interval between its setting lines determined the 0.02 m. overhang of the stereobate.[18]

Although the superstructure erected on this euthynteria is no longer *in situ*, it may be reconstructed with exceptional certainty, owing to the existence of hundreds of fully or partially preserved blocks found over or near the building.

STEREOBATE (Pls. III, IV, XCV.3, 4; Figs. 38, 44)

Fifteen blocks of the stereobate are preserved.[19] Apart from the corner block, their average length is 1.18 m. (the variations range from 1.167 m. to 1.19 m.), their height 0.296 m. (varying from 0.289 m. to 0.305 m.). They were doweled to the euthynteria but, being wider than it, rested partly on its porous backers.[20] A single Π-clamp at either end connects each block with the two adjacent to it, and two additional Π-clamps at its rear attach it to its backer.

As we have seen, the stereobate was set back 0.07 m. from the face of the euthynteria and was enlivened with two recesses, the upper 0.02 m. high, the lower 0.04 m. When the exposed face above these obliquely cut recesses was trimmed and aligned with the outer guide line on the euthynteria, it was given a slight slope to link it with their profile. This subtle device lends the course a lightness and animation it would have lacked had it been given an angular, vertical profile. The setting lines on the upper surfaces of these blocks indicate that the wall or, more precisely, the orthostates were set back ca. 0.08 m. from their outer face.

18. Mr. Jones has been unable to find conclusive evidence of the horizontal curvature detected in the euthynteria by Roy Fraser and reported in *Hesperia*, 20 (1951), 23.

19. Eleven blocks have been replaced on the euthynteria and grouped in such a fashion as to suggest the original appearance of this type of course. In the majority of cases, they were found at or near the very positions they now occupy; but since the precise original location of each block cannot be determined, given the incomplete preservation of the euthynteria, they have been provisionally placed on strips of wood, rather than let down directly upon the euthynteria, in order to remain easily movable. For blocks 387 and 432, which belonged to the original porch but were

recut for use in the second-century porch, see below, p. 94.

20. Their joints fell over the center of each euthynteria block. Lead channels were used at the corners, but not elsewhere, and there, too, the dowels were both approximately square and rectangular. On the western and nearly all the southern side, only one dowel was used at the rear end of the block, but on the east and at the southeast corner two were occasionally employed. This procedural difference between the two lateral sides of the building may be associated with the previously mentioned differing heights of identical courses on these flanks, and result from crews of masons working under different supervision on the east and west. The larger corner blocks had supplementary dowels.

Walls and Doors

(Pls. V–XLII, XC.1, XCV.1, 2, XCVI, CIII–CX;
Figs. 39–42; Cat. **160, 161**)

The several hundred marble and porous limestone blocks belonging to the cella wall found over the surface of the building and in its vicinity allow that wall to be reconstructed with absolute certainty (Pls. XXII, XXIII, CIII–CX). On the exterior, it was composed of nine courses of marble blocks having drafted margins rising above a smoothly dressed ortho-state and crowning string course. Six of these nine courses were high stretchers; three were low binders. They were laid in such a fashion that each course of binders alternated with two superimposed courses of stretchers; that is, the six courses of stretchers were arranged in three groups of two superimposed courses, separated from each other by single courses of binders. One of the low binding courses topped the wall, as a string course crowned the orthostate. The bold, ornamental pattern of the drafted masonry walls offered a rich contrast to the simplicity of their smooth dadoes. It was further enhanced by the unfluted pilasters terminating the walls on both the lateral and rear faces of the southern corners of the cella, which at once balanced and reiterated the antae at its north and, with them, provided at each end of the building powerful verticals that framed and united the horizontal courses of the wall.

Although the low binding courses of the cella walls and the string course above the orthostates penetrated the total thickness of the walls, the high stretchers and orthostates did not. On the contrary, these thinner blocks were clamped to limestone backers, the combined thickness of these blocks being equal to that of the binders. Hence, structurally speaking, the inner face of the cella walls consisted of three groups of two superimposed courses of porous blocks in alternation with the inner faces of the marble binders and the string course above the porous backing of the orthostates. Actually, this alternation of materials was invisible, since the interior of the cella was stuccoed and painted, as is attested by the innumerable fragments of painted and molded stucco described below[21] and the slightly roughened inner faces of the marble binders. The economical use of marble in the long cella walls greatly reduced the amount of marble that it was necessary to import from Thasos.

Turning from this general characterization of the cella walls to a detailed consideration of its courses, let us remark that the total height of the wall between the stereobate and the

---

21. Pp. 138 ff.

entablature was 5.665 m., the height, as we shall later see, of the columns of the porch. The thickness of the lateral and rear walls of the cella was 0.765 m., a figure dictated by the widths of the thickest marble binders and corroborated by the dimensions of the lateral thresholds on each side of the building. The door wall was slightly thinner, 0.733 m., as the main lintel indicates.

ORTHOSTATE (Pl.V.2)

Only one small fragment of this course is preserved, doubtless owing to the ease with which these thin, smooth blocks could be re-used in post-antique structures. But this single fragment is of prime significance, since it affords conclusive proof that the orthostates were smoothly dressed.[22] For it belonged to a corner block and thus retains a portion of the unfluted pilaster attached to the corner orthostate blocks, as well as a piece of the adjacent orthostate. Since all the remaining corner blocks, apart from the much lower string course corners, are characterized by sections of unfluted pilasters attached to wall blocks with drafted margins, this fragment can only come from a smoothly-dressed corner orthostate block. It is broken on all sides. Hence, the height of 1.202 m. given to this course in the reconstruction of the southeastern corner on Pl. XXIII may appear to be purely theoretical. In reality, it is not, having been obtained by subtracting the provable height of the remaining ten courses of the wall from its known total height, a figure established by the height of the columns of the Doric porch.

We must assume that the joints of these thin slabs fell over the centers of the stereobate blocks beneath them. The dowel and pry holes cut on the upper surface of this lower course indicate that each orthostate block was attached to the stereobate by two dowels, one at one end of the block, the other at some distance from the opposite end, thus set with the aid of a lead channel. The upper surfaces of the stereobate blocks also bear witness to the fact that the orthostate course was set back 0.08 m. from the outer face of the stereobate.

22. Conceivably, certain smoothly-dressed fragmentary blocks having a preserved height of as much as 0.79 m. and a thickness of ca. 0.28 m. are remnants of orthostates. But they could have served equally well as part of the facing of such monuments as altars or bases.

Hauser's reconstructions of a portion of the wall of the east flank of the Hieron (S,I, pl. 43) and of its rear wall (ibid., p. 75) are unfounded. They show a wall composed of thirteen smoothly-trimmed high courses above an orthostate with drafted margins. No reference to this imaginary orthostate appears in the Austrian text, nor can it ever have existed. The later reconstruction, presumably of the southeastern corner (S,II, pl. 13; cf. n. 33, below), as well as the wall blocks drawn on pl. 12, shows these courses correctly as having had drafted margins. Thus, the misleading longitudinal elevation of the building in S,II, p. 29, fig. 7, where the wall appears to be composed of sixteen alternatingly high and low courses of smoothly dressed masonry, is quite incomprehensible, unless we assume that it was intended as a rough sketch in which details were inconsequential. None of these reconstructions is rooted in fact.

In Hauser's second brief characterization of the nature of the cella wall, however (S,II, p. 27), he correctly described it as having been composed of marble stretchers backed by porous and marble binders, thus rectifying his earlier statement (S,I, p. 68) that it had had an outer face of marble but an inner face of limestone. His original mistake was repeated in Hesperia, 20 (1951), 23.

The thickness of the orthostate blocks, as well as the type of clamp used to link them to their porous backers, must remain uncertain. Although in both the marble courses beneath them, Π-clamps were employed to fasten marble blocks to their porous backers, in all the remaining, higher courses of the superstructure, swallow-tail clamps were used for this purpose, Π-clamps being reserved for the connection of marble with marble. Conceivably, this change in technical procedure could have taken place in the orthostate course. In any case, it implies that the builders of the Hieron decided that Π-clamps were a less satisfactory means of connection with the very porous limestone employed for backers throughout the building than the old-fashioned swallow tail, since the sponge-like irregularity of its surface precluded the cutting of the precisely shaped holes required for Π-clamps. Presumably, the blocks of the orthostate were connected with each other by Π-clamps.

STRING COURSE (Pl. VI.2)

Eleven blocks of the smoothly-trimmed string course capping the orthostate are preserved.[23] Their average height is 0.262 m. (they range from 0.249 to 0.275 m.), and they vary in length from 1.16 to 1.22 m. Their thickness fluctuates between 0.769 and 0.79 m., averaging about 0.78 m. The latter figures, coupled with the provable thickness of the wall (0.765 m.), the intentional roughness of its inner faces, and the existence of a setting line on the upper surface of two of the string course blocks [24] 0.03 m. behind the line of their faces, imply that the course of wall blocks resting on the string course was set back 0.03 m. from its outer face. Weathering has removed the comparable setting line on the worn surfaces of the remaining blocks. Presumably the string course overhung the orthostates to the same slight extent, and the outer face of the wall was flush with that of the orthostates.

The blocks of this course were doweled to the course below by a pair of dowels at one end—the outer one set into a dowel hole in the orthostate block, the inner one fitted into a hole cut in its porous backer—and connected with the adjacent blocks in their own course by a pair of Π-clamps at each end of every block. Like the other binding blocks of the wall, they were slightly roughened on their rear faces to receive a stucco coating.

23. Five additional blocks of apparently similar character have been eliminated from this category in spite of their correct dimensions, because extreme weathering of their faces or edges makes it impossible to be certain that they did not once have drafted margins and, hence, belong to the upper binding courses of the wall.

24. Blocks 175 and 776.

WALL BLOCKS AND LATERAL DOORS (Pls. V–XXXIV, XCVI, CVII; Figs. 39, 40)

Two hundred and forty-seven of the marble blocks of the cella wall remain, as well as scores of their porous backers.[25] One hundred and forty-seven are stretchers, ninety are binders,[26] and ten are corner blocks. The standard stretchers and binders have drafted margins 0.025 m. wide on all four sides of their outer faces, which thus seem to project 0.005–0.01 m. (Pls. VII, VIII). They vary in length from 1.17 to 1.20 m.; hence, the joints of a given course do not necessarily fall precisely over the centers of the blocks in the course below. The stretchers range from 0.53 to 0.60 m. in height; but, curiously enough, the courses characterized by these varied heights are scattered through the wall, rather than regularly decreasing in size as the wall mounts. This point is firmly established, owing to the fact that a number of blocks from the rear corners of the building can be shown to have actually fitted on top of one another (cf. Pl. XXII). However, the uppermost binding course is the lowest in height (ca. 0.24 m., with variations from 0.23 to 0.25 m.), while the remaining two binding courses average ca. 0.27 m. in height (variations from 0.26 to 0.28 m.). The lateral walls are marked by a second irregularity, namely, that a given course may vary in height as much as 0.05 m. in the long distance between the rear corners of the cella and the antae far to the north.

The stretchers range from 0.276 to 0.392 m. in thickness, the binders from 0.657 to 0.765 m. The latter figures indicate both that the lateral walls of the cella taper and that, at the bottom, they have a thickness of 0.765 m. This figure is in exact accord with the dimension of 0.765 m. dictated for the wall by the fully preserved western lateral threshold (Pl. XXXIII.1) and is confirmed by the further observation that addition of the thickness of the thinnest marble stretcher, 0.276 m., to that of the thickest porous backer, 0.49 m., yields the sum of 0.766 m.[27]

The binding courses were attached to the stretchers beneath them by a pair of dowels at one end of each block, the individual binders being linked to one another by a pair of Π-clamps at each end. Normally, the stretchers were doweled to the course below, whether it was another course of stretchers or a binding course, by two dowels, one placed at one end of

25. The over-all dimensions of all these blocks have been recorded, although not all of them have been drawn. The existence of this exceptional amount of evidence has made it possible to reconstruct the system of the cella walls with total certainty. It would be needless to describe the mathematical operations implicit in the general conclusions regarding the wall that are presented here, but, obviously, they have differed radically from the simple chart of eight varieties of

wall block published in *S,II*, p. 27.

26. This figure includes the five uncertain blocks mentioned above, n. 23. There are, of course, additional unmeasurable fragments of both types of wall block.

27. These specific figures apply to the eastern cella wall. Attribution of individual wall blocks to given courses in both lateral walls indicates that the western wall was slightly thinner than the eastern.

39. Southeastern corner block 284; view of bottom

the block, the other considerably farther in.[28] They were clamped to each other by a single Π-clamp at either end of each block and to their porous backers by a pair of swallow-tail clamps.

Twelve of the eighteen blocks of which the rear corners of the Hieron were built above the level of the string course are known, eleven extant in Samothrace, one reproduced by the Austrians but now lost.[29] It is largely owing to the existence of these crucial blocks that it has been possible to determine the character of the cella walls, for the majority of them can be precisely related to each other and fitted together, dowel hole over dowel hole, as Pls. IX–XIV, XVI–XXI suggest. Reconstruction of the lateral corners of the building has, in turn, carried with it and established the locations of the standard wall blocks.

Apart from their pilaster capitals, the rear corners of the cella were composed essen-

28. Block 331 (Pl. XXXII) is an exception to this rule. We have no explanation to offer either for the absence of clamps on one of its ends or for the singular dowel hole present on its upper surface. Conceivably, it is a repair or a re-used piece.

A group of binders, exemplified by block 197, is exceptional in that, unlike the normal blocks of this category, they lack the customary two dowel holes on their upper surfaces. Presumably, they belonged in the uppermost course of the rear wall beneath the extra long wall architrave blocks used on that side of the building.

29. The southeastern pilaster capital; see *S,II*, pl. 11, fig. II, where it is mistakenly called the anta capital. Three corner blocks were published on pl. 12 of the same volume. One, fig. III, can be identified with our block 229. The other two do not seem to tally with any of the extant blocks in Samothrace, although the inaccuracy of Hauser's plates in regard to the placing of dowel and clamp holes precludes absolute certainty in this matter.

Two additional fragmentary corner blocks exist in Samothrace but yield no supplementary information, owing to the nature of their breakage and damage.

46

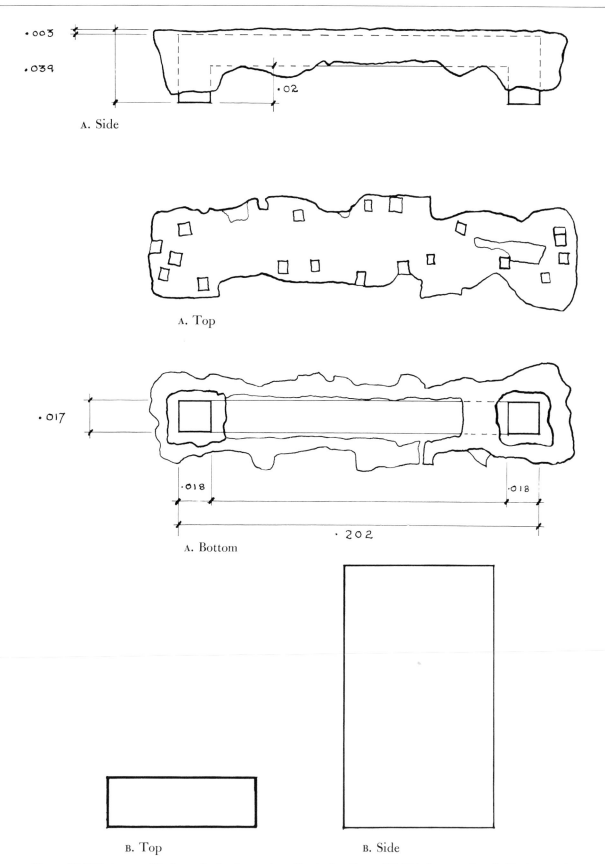

.003
.039
.02
A. Side

A. Top

.017
.018
.018
. 202
A. Bottom

B. Top
B. Side

40. A. 52.525, bronze Π-clamp in lead pouring (Scale 1 : 2). B. 53.584, bronze dowel (Scale 1 : 1).
Samothrace Museum

tially of two types of blocks, binders and L-shaped stretchers. Each type has two contiguous visible faces. With one exception, the preserved blocks always consist of a section of the unfluted corner pilaster on one face at right angles to the comparable section of pilaster on the other face, together with a wall block on one or the other end. The exception, block 229 (Pl. XIV), has a wall block attached to each end and fitted directly under the pilaster capital. The complicated fashion in which these blocks interlocked is visible in Pl. XXII. The pilasters taper slightly but lack entasis. They are set off from the wall blocks adjacent to them by a drafted margin slightly wider than normal (0.04 m.).[30]

As usual, the corner blocks are clamped to the adjacent marble wall blocks of a given course by Π-clamps, the binders having two at each end, the stretchers, one; the latter are connected with their backers by a pair of swallow-tail clamps. Inasmuch as all the corner blocks are reproduced, the variations in their doweling may be examined on Pls. IX–XIV, XVI–XXI. It will suffice to point out that these blocks differ from the standard blocks of the Hieron in their use of narrow, rectangular dowels like the example illustrated in fig. 40 B (cf. fig. 39). Wherever the wall block adjacent to a pilaster was an independent unit rather than being linked with it to form a corner block, it was somewhat longer than the standard binders or stretchers (cf. Pls. XV, XVI.2, XVII.1).[31]

On both corners, the pilaster capital was cut in one piece with the wall block adjacent to it on the rear, southern side of the building, thus constituting a kind of binder. On the other, lateral sides of the cella, the block adjoining the capital was an exceptionally long, separately cut binder. Both the wall blocks attached to the capitals and the independent binders adjacent to them were cut to receive the projecting moldings of the capital by contracting the drafted margin of the relevant corner and adjusting it to the boldly curving profiles of the capital (Pls. XVI.2, XVII, XCVI.2, 3). Although the eastern and western blocks differ markedly in execution (the former being far more assured and vigorous than the latter, which is an early Imperial replacement of the Hellenistic binder originally present in this later damaged and repaired corner), they are alike in their use of curving forms. On the south,

---

30. Again, there is a variation in dimension between the eastern and western sides of the building, the eastern pilaster being 0.705–0.729 m. wide at its widest, the western 0.771 m. We are at a loss to explain the narrow vertical cuttings found on the eastern face of the southeastern double pilaster blocks and on the rear, southern face of the southwestern. They seem to imply the attachment of some object or decoration, yet no means of attachment are visible. Equally enigmatic are the shallow horizontal cutting and deep narrow slit on the pilaster faces of block 746 (Pl. XVIII).

31. Two groups of abnormally long wall blocks were found, one near the rear corners of the building, the other in the vicinity of the pronaos. Those having a length of approximately 1.30 m. evidently belong to

the category mentioned above, since one of them (146) was doweled to the corner stretcher (283) and clamped to block 715, as Pl. XXII indicates. Together with the other preserved blocks of the southeastern corner and binder 904, block 146 establishes the jointing of the section of wall immediately adjacent to the pilaster. From this point northward, both varieties of wall block were of standard length except for those few, like block 297, which were adjusted to the lateral doors. The southern, rear wall followed the same system. The still longer blocks, ranging up to approximately 1.50 m. in length, occupied comparable positions in relation to the main door and the antae (see below, pp. 68, 100).

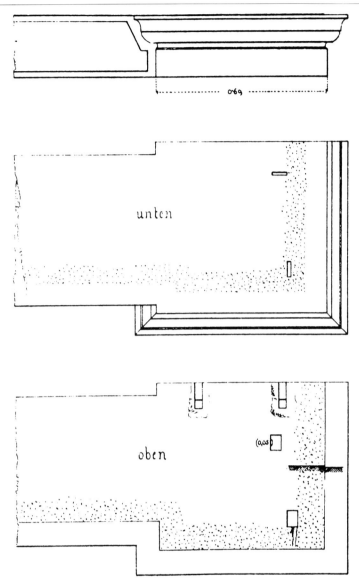

41. Southeastern pilaster capital and adjacent southern
    binder, after Hauser

however, the projecting face of the adjacent wall blocks was given a simplified, angular form. The broken southwestern capital and both adjacent lateral binders are preserved in Samothrace (Pls. XVI.1, XVII), while the southeastern capital, together with its differently-dressed connecting southern binder, was drawn by Hauser (fig. 41).[32] Fortunately, one

32. *S,II*, pl. 11, fig. 11. Cf. n. 29, above. Block 679 (Pl. XVII.1), the Roman replacement, differs from its Hellenistic counterpart at the southeast corner (904: Pl. XVI.2) not only in its reduction and simplification of the form of the drafted margin abutting the capital but also in the atypical cutting of one side, where the roughened surface within the anathyrosis has a pronounced setback, a technical detail not normally characteristic of the original wall blocks. For additional

details regarding the repairs made to this corner, see text II, pp. 79 ff.

A further difference between the two corners results from the fact that the lateral wall portion of the southwestern corner blocks is longer (ca. 1.10 m.) than the comparable portion of the southeastern corner blocks (ca. 0.74 m.). Whether this difference, too, reflects repairs to the corner or the slightly divergent practices of the different crews of masons working on the two sides of the building cannot be determined.

small but significant element of this now missing block has been rediscovered and confirms the angular forms of his rendering (930: Pl. XVII.2).

The two pilaster capitals were clamped and doweled to their neighboring blocks in the same fashion as the other corner blocks. They are characterized by bold, powerful moldings, the cavetto crown giving way to an ovolo hawk's beak above a high terminating fascia (Pl. XCVI.1).[33]

In addition to the corner blocks and the standard stretchers and binders of the cella wall, there are samples of two categories of wall blocks characterized by special features: the first consists of binders equipped with rear extensions to link the lateral cella walls with the returns of the apse wall (Pls. XXVI–XXIX); the second includes blocks placed in the vicinity of the doors (Pls. XXX.1, XXXI, XXXII).

The best preserved example of the first group, block 687 (Pl. XXVII),[34] was placed in the western wall, extending through it and the western return of the apse. The three-sided projection at its rear follows the shape of the right-angled return on two sides, while the third is mitered and, as its telltale swallow-tail clamp hole reveals, was connected with one of the curving porous blocks of which the face of the apse was constructed. The two right-angled faces of the extension and the short rear face of the binder proper were roughly dressed to receive the coating of painted stucco with which the apse, as well as the walls of the cella, was finished. These complicated blocks ensured the stability of the wall and obviated an undesirable joint between the lateral walls and the apse returns.

The very existence of this group of blocks would suffice to prove that the curving wall of the apse terminated on each side in an angular return instead of running directly to the lateral walls. But there is additional corroboration of this structural feature. Both the plan of the apse published by the Austrians and the photograph accompanying it [35] show two marble

33. Hauser's reconstruction of the southeastern corner (*S,II,* pl. 13) is misleading in its implication that the blocks of the entablature and the pilaster capital reproduced in the Austrian publication actually came from that corner and fitted together. This is not the case. For example, our southeastern corner architrave block (234) fitted the now lost Austrian southeastern capital (above, fig. 41), a fragment of which is preserved (our 930). Apart from the sima, all the blocks of the southeastern entablature are still at least partially preserved in Samothrace (234, 218, 348 A). Cf. nn. 106, 166, below, for further comment on Hauser's reconstruction.

34. Two of the three other, largely preserved blocks, 287 and 749, come from the eastern wall; the

third, 628, is from the western. Their rear extensions varied in shape and are in every case broken. Block 749 is closest in scheme to 687. Block 198, another binder equipped with a very small lateral extension at its rear, does not belong to this group of blocks. It is best understood as having been prepared to interlock with a neighboring block that had been damaged at its rear and cut back to create a small socket for such an interlocking extension, in analogy to the similar solution adopted for the re-used stereobate block 387. Cf. Pl. IV.3 and p. 94, below.

35. *S,I,* pls. 17, 18. After the Austrian excavation, several blocks which they had found and illustrated *in situ* were dislodged from their positions and thrown into the deep pit within the apse, where we recovered

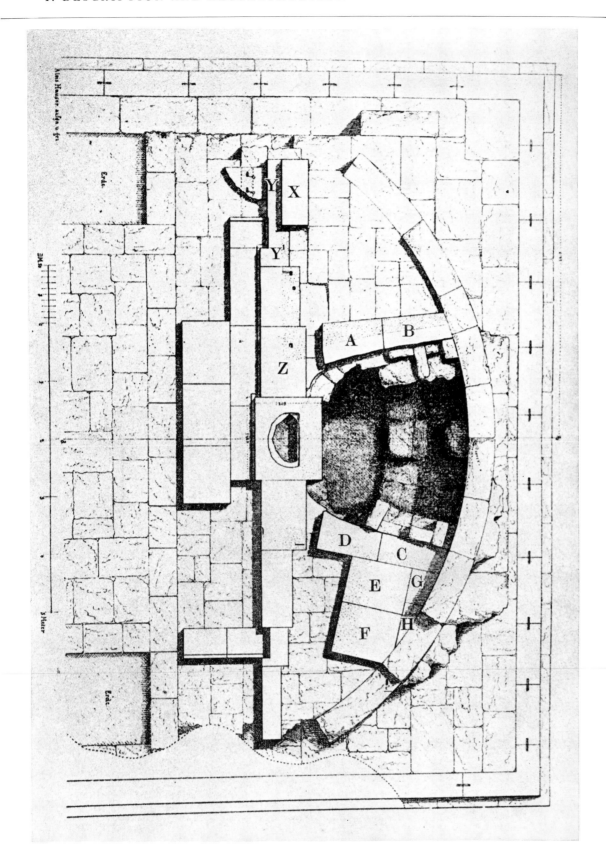

42. Plan of the abaton, after Hauser (letters added)

43. Partial view of the abaton after the excavation of 1873

blocks of the platform within the apse, one resting upon the other (figs. 42, 43; X and Y in fig. 42), which are interrelated in an unorthodox fashion: their eastern joints fall over each other. The abnormal placing of one joint over another was permissible and inevitable if both blocks abutted an eastern return and, in fact, provides independent evidence of the original presence of such a return.[36]

It has been pointed out that the apse of the Hellenistic Hieron was built directly over the salient apse of its immediate predecessor, incorporating six of the foundation blocks of this earlier building in its own foundation and three of its wall blocks in its own first course. Above this course, which is equivalent in level to the outer marble euthynteria, the apse was built exclusively of the gray porous limestone employed throughout the building for the inner, backing stretchers of the walls. Like them, it remained invisible, its inner surface

them in the course of our own re-excavation of this area (see pp. 20 f., above). Among them was block X, which we have replaced in approximately its original position. But Y, one of the two blocks (Y and Y¹) on which X once rested, had disappeared. In Hauser's plan (*S,I*, pl. 17), X appears to rest on one long thin marble block. This is an error, for Y¹ is still *in situ* and preserves the anathyrosis on its eastern face required for the adjacent block Y.

36. Curiously enough, Hauser cannot have seen the implication of these blocks or he would not have published the incorrectly restored ground plan in *S,II,* p. 29, fig. 6, which shows the apse wall merging with the lateral walls. The correct form of the apse was first observed by Roy Fraser, as cited in *Hesperia,* 20 (1951), 22.

44. View of the cella from the south

stuccoed and painted, its outer face concealed within the enclosing marble frame of the rear wall of the cella. The five irregularly preserved courses of this segmental apse are more than sufficient to indicate the precise curve of this most significant architectural feature of the Hieron, which, as will become evident, is the earliest large-scale building known to have contained a genuine apse, a form destined to achieve immense popularity some centuries later.[37] The introduction of this form of apse within a rectangular outer cella wall marked a radical departure from the salient apses of both predecessors of the Hellenistic Hieron.

The courses of this limestone wall are uneven in height, ranging from ca. 0.30 to 0.40 m., and are laid of a single series of stretchers from 0.50 to 0.60 m. thick at the uppermost preserved courses of the apse (cf. Pl. II.5 and figs. 34, 37, 38, 44).[38] The individual blocks vary from ca. 0.80 to 1.20 m. in length, causing the joints of a given course to fall irregularly over the blocks of the course below. They were clamped to each other by a single swallowtail clamp at both ends of every block; but, as the absence of clamp holes at the rear of these blocks indicates, the apse wall was not clamped to the porous backers of the outer rear

37. See below, pp. 155 ff. By the term "genuine apse," I mean one set off from the lateral walls of a rectangular building by just such returns as have been established in the Hieron, rather than a simple curving wall at the end of a cella.

38. As visible in fig. 87, one block is markedly shorter than the others.

marble wall. Instead it was bonded into that wall five times: once at the level of the second of the porous backers of the orthostate and four times, at its exact center, via the marble binders of the outer wall, which there—and there only—were enlarged to extend through both the exterior wall and the apse wall, as block 749 proves (Pl. XXVIII). Thus, the apse wall was bonded into the outer wall of the building at three points: at the center of its curve and at its returns (Pl. LVII); otherwise, the two walls were independent of each other. Obviously, the apse wall was carried only to the level of the top course of the outer wall. Two fragments of the porous backers of the marble orthostates that once separated the

45. Detail of the southwestern corner, showing packing between the cella and apse walls

straight outer wall from the curving apse are still *in situ* and discernible in figs. 37, 44. Only the upper two preserved courses of the apse were smoothly curved and dressed to receive stucco on their inner faces, since they alone remained visible above the irregular and projecting lower courses, as is most easily seen in the section on Pl. II.1.[39]

Finally, the small spandrel-like intervals at the two rear corners of the building between the inner face of the right-angled cella wall and the outer face of the apse were very probably filled with a packing of field stones throughout the total height of the cella. Theoretically, these invisible areas could have been left hollow. But the presence of field-stone packing set in earth in these portions of the building at the level of and behind the first foundation course of the outer wall and in the crevices between the apse wall and the porous backers of the orthostate (Pl. I; fig. 45) suggests that the former alternative was the more likely.

The second group of unorthodox wall blocks, consisting of blocks placed in the vicinity of the doors (Pls. XXX.1, XXXI, XXXII), includes two stretchers which, together with the evidence yielded by the lateral thresholds, allow the side doors of the Hieron to be reconstructed. One block (332: Pl. XXX.1) has been cut to fit against both a lintel and a jamb; that is, it has been notched to house the end of a lintel. The other (238: Pl. XXXI), as its

---

39. For further discussion of the interior of the apse and its segmental wooden half-dome, see below, pp. 78 ff.

abnormal length of 2.369 m. indicates, can only have been placed over a lintel and slightly overlapped the two small stretchers that framed it. The fully preserved western threshold (722: Pl. XXXIII.1) allows for a door 1.274 m. wide, as the carefully finished portion of its upper surface between the setting lines for the jambs reveals. The two stretchers fit a door of precisely this size; and, as the dimensions of the missing jambs may be deduced from the traces on the upper surface of the threshold, so the notching of block 332 provides the height of the equally missing lintel. That the jambs were of marble is apparent from the dowel holes on the threshold. Presumably they were monolithic like the lintel. In the restoration drawing on Pl. CVII these lost elements have been left unadorned, not only because there is no evidence to the contrary, but also because the effect of these smoothly dressed blocks framed by the drafted margins of the surrounding wall blocks is in accord with the relationship of the ornamental wall to its strong, severe base and emphatic pilasters, causing the door frame to stand out sharply and crisply from the wall as a bold edging for the door. The simplicity of the lateral door frames was, thus, in marked and appropriate contrast with the ornamental richness of the main door frame.

The fact that blocks 238 and 332 fit together and belonged to one of the three groups of superimposed stretchers of which the cella wall was partially composed forces them to be attributed to the central group in the middle of the wall and determines the height of the lateral doors as 2.986 m.[40] The existence of certain blocks of abnormal length—for example, the short binder (331: Pl. XXXII) and the extra long stretcher (297: 1.52 m.), which must be attributed to positions adjacent to a jamb, given their lack of clamps at one end—indicates that blocks of unusual size were placed in the immediate vicinity of the lateral doors, as proves to have been the case near the main door.

The lateral thresholds were placed on the stereobate (Pl. CIV). Their outer faces terminate in a cyma reversa molding over a base fascia (Pl. XCV.2); and these base fasciae were flush with the outer edge of that course, projecting outward 0.075 m. beyond the line of the wall (that is, of the orthostate). This relationship, implied by the setting lines on the stereobate blocks and the short returns of the better preserved western threshold, is confirmed by stereobate 387 (Pl. IV.3), which fits under the southern half of that threshold (Pl. XXXIII.1). The narrow inner treads of the thresholds were level with the pavement of the lateral cella aisles, which, unlike the wide central aisle, were paved not with marble but with *signinum* laid on a field-stone packing.[41] The roughened inner faces of the lateral thresholds establish the absence of marble paving in the lateral aisles, as the mark ΕΔΑ— (ἔδαφος, ground),[42] placed on the southern face of the incompletely preserved eastern threshold (714: Pl.

40. The fact that these two blocks differ slightly in height from those shown in the same course in Pl. CVII is the result, it will be recalled, of the standard irregularity pointed out above, p. 39.

41. For discussion of the cella pavement, see pp. 118 ff., below.

42. Cf. *Samothrace*, Vol. 2, pt. I, 87, where the lettering is described as "apparently Hellenistic." For the term ἔδαφος, see Friedrich Ebert, *Fachausdrücke des griechischen Bauhandwerks* (Würzburg, 1911), p. 12.

XXXIII.2), indicates the level to which the packing beneath the floor was carried. Thus the 0.06 m. interval between the upper surface of the inner tread and this guide line corresponds to the thickness of the *signinum* pavement. On the inner tread of threshold 722, cuttings for the two door pans and a vertical pin indicate that the doors had two leaves and opened inward (cf. Pls. XXXIII.1, CII). Presumably, like the main door, the lateral doors were hung in a wooden frame attached to the inner face of the marble lintel (cf. Pls. CIV, CV).[43] When closed, they were prevented from hitting the inner face of the higher main tread by the ingenious cutting of this face, which is not parallel to the outer face but slopes slightly and obliquely backward toward the center from both inner corners.[44]

The lateral doors were of wood. Their battens and meeting stile were attached by bronze-bossed iron nails of square or rectangular section. Inasmuch as two varieties of bosses or studs of different size and profile were recovered in the vicinity of the eastern door (Pl. XXXIV.1, 2; Cat. **160, 161**),[45] it is evident that they were arranged on the battens and stile in precisely the same manner as those on the outer wooden door of the well-known tomb at Langaza (fig. 149).[46] Conceivably, one leaf was further embellished with a bronze patera.[47]

My husband has called my attention to its use in reference to the foundation of a culvert in a building inscription from Oropos: *IG*, VII, 4255, line 13.

43. We are at a loss to explain the slight forward projection of the line of the main tread of the fully preserved threshold (722) to the right of one entering the door (cf. Pl. XXXIII.1). Given its position, it would have been invisible, concealed by the wooden door frame placed against it. But its existence would have slightly reduced the thickness of the frame on this side of the door—the side, curiously enough, that was subject to maximum use, since the off-center position of the cutting for the door pin indicates that the left wing of the door could be, and probably frequently was, kept closed when the right wing was opened. Conceivably, this slight variation between the left and right sides of the threshold affected the technical procedure of mounting the door in some fashion of which we are unaware. This inexplicable feature of the threshold cannot be dismissed as a meaningless irregularity in stonecutting, however, for it recurs on the threshold of the main door.

44. A subtlety probably more clearly visible in Pl. XXXIII.1 than in the restored plan, Pl. CII.

45. See text II, pp. 244 f., **160, 161**, for description and illustration of these studs, which are mentioned in *Guide*², pp. 67, 94. The recovery of the larger variety in the early Imperial fill near the southeastern corner of the building, which contained the damaged and replaced Hellenistic floral akroterion that had previously crowned the southern pediment, suggests that at least one of the lateral doors must have been repaired at the same time (cf. text II, pp. 81 ff.). But the additional fact that the smaller variety was found on the surface near the eastern lateral door indicates that these bronze-studded lateral doors were still in use in late antiquity.

46. T. Macridy, "Un tumulus macédonien à Langaza," *JDAI*, 26 (1911), 193 ff., and especially fig. 8 and pl. 4. Among the many representations of similarly studded doors on Attic red-figure vases, cf., for example, the very analogous ones on a fragmentary hydria in Braunschweig, At220: *CVA, Deutschland,* fasc. 4, by Adolf Greifenhagen (Munich, 1940), pp. 32 f. (with bibliography on the representation of doors on vases), pls. XXIV, 4–6; XXVI, 20; and on a pyxis in Vienna, 3719: ibid., *Austria,* Vienna, Kunsthistorisches Museum, I, by Fritz Eichler (Vienna, 1951), pl. XLIX, fig. 1. I am indebted to my husband for these references.

Ornamental bronze nail heads have been found, too, at Olynthos, Priene, and Delos. See David M. Robinson and J. Walter Graham, *The Hellenic House* (*Olynthus,* VIII), p. 257; *Priene,* p. 305, fig. 326; and Joseph Chamonard, *Le quartier du théâtre* (*Délos,* VIII), pp. 230 f., 286, and fig. 111.

47. See text II, pp. 254 f., **175**, for reference to the fragmentary patera and analogies thereto that Miss Loeffler suggests may be explained in this fashion.

The precise position of the lateral doors to which these thresholds belonged can be determined only theoretically, given the present state of the cella.[48] Clearly, they must have been south of the late Roman parapets that today separate the central from the lateral aisles, or they could not have functioned. Indeed, the very fact that these barriers were extended no farther to the south in itself implies that they were stopped just short of the doors. Other considerations resulting from the character and position of the benches introduced into the rear part of the cella and discussed below support this implication. Hence, the doors have been placed symmetrically in the restored plan (Pl. CII), one on each side of the building, at points corresponding to and opposite the interval visible on the actual plan (Pl. I) between the fifth and sixth bench foundations north of the apse on the western side of the building. These standard intervals recur throughout the length of the cella, and the size and position of the lateral doors were obviously correlated with them.[49]

The third of the unorthodox wall blocks that related to a door is the longest of the stretchers (414), which even in its present incomplete state has a length of 3.11 m. (Pl. VI.1). Both its size and its provenance indicate that it was placed in the northern wall of the cella directly above the lintel of the main door.[50] Coupled with that mighty block, it was inserted into the uppermost pair of high courses in the front wall; that is, it was laid in the second course below the wall architrave, the lintel falling in the third (Pl. XLII).[51] Its original length may be calculated as 3.478 m., given the positions of the dowel and clamp holes on its

48. The fragmentary threshold, block 714, was discovered by our predecessors near the southeast corner of the building (*S,II*, p. 30, and pl. 11, fig. III) but evidently later transported to the area above and behind the terrace wall south of the Hieron, where we rediscovered it in 1952. Curiously enough, the well preserved threshold, block 722, was discovered in the same general area more than twenty meters to the south. But it was not known to the Austrians, who restored the cella with two symmetrically placed doors purely on theoretical grounds (ibid. and p. 29). The door frame and lintel used in this restoration were equally hypothetical.

Given the Austrians' specific statement that 714 was found at the southeast corner of the cella, we assume that it originally belonged to the eastern door and that 722 must, therefore, be attributed to the western door. The crucial stretchers 238 and 332 were found lying over the eastern foundation in the very region to which we have ascribed the eastern door. Obviously, they had counterparts on the western side of the building. Hence, they have been combined with the fully preserved western threshold in the restoration of the lateral doors on Pl. CVII.

49. For further discussion of all points relating to the interior installation of the cella, see below, pp. 117 ff.

In spite of the proximity of the adjacent Altar Court and the awkwardness with which access to the western door was gained, the length of the parapets and the varieties of benches that must be included within the cella and placed according to some reasonable system preclude the otherwise conceivable possibility that both doors belonged to the eastern side of the building. The need for these doors was undoubtedly rooted in liturgical requirements rather than in physical convenience. For explanation of this point, see text II, pp. 21 ff.

50. It was found ca. 10 m. north of the northeast corner of the porch.

51. The height of the lintel, 0.522 m., is less than that of the other varieties of stretchers. But it is supplemented, at the ends, by the 0.056 m. projection of the mitered return of its meander border, thus reaching a normal dimension of 0.578 m. Hence, the notched wall blocks needed at the corners of the lateral lintels were unnecessary at the main door—a highly desirable feature, since such notched blocks would in this case have been awkwardly low, being binders. As it is, the binders adjacent to the doorjambs in this course fit neatly under the miter.

upper surface and the fortunate fact that it is preserved at one end (the right end in Pl. VI.1). The equally telltale dowel hole on its lower surface at that same end, one of a pair once cut in that surface, reveals in addition that at one time it was doweled to the lintel beneath it. Yet the three great fragments into which the existing lintel broke when it crashed to the ground—2, 2 A, 2 B, and the portion of 2 A now in Vienna (Pls. XXXV–XXXVIII, XLI) —show no trace of a dowel hole. Clearly, block 414 was designed to fit over another lintel, that of the original early Hellenistic door. But that lofty, relatively narrow door was replaced in later Roman times by a far wider door to which the extant lintel and the single preserved jamb block (55: Pl. XXXIX) belonged. Nonetheless, it may be accurately reconstructed with the aid of those Roman replacements and the Hellenistic threshold that remained *in situ*, if drastically altered.

THE MAIN DOOR (Pls. VI.1, XXXV–XLII, XCV.1, 2; Figs. 46–50)

Reconstruction of the original marble door frame is best preceded by discussion of the remodeled Roman door (fig. 46). Like its Hellenistic predecessor, it enclosed an opening 3.961 m. high, but it was far broader, having a width of 2.616 m. Its lintel was crowned by a boldly projecting series of moldings, the top cavetto giving way to a hawk's beak followed by an astragal carved with a bead and reel (Pl. XXXVIII.1; figs. 49, 439). The meander drilled beneath this crown was carried down the outer edges of the lintel and jambs to create an ornamental border for their otherwise unadorned surfaces. But the bead-and-reel pattern edging that meander was stopped abruptly at the outer edges of the lintel, in spite of the fact that space existed for it there and on the jambs. In all likelihood, these Roman blocks reflect the appearance of the original frame, save for their illogical and disturbing omission of this motif. The Hellenistic threshold supporting these blocks was similar in outer form and profiles to those of the lateral doors, except that it seemingly lacked the crowning molding once present on them. Actually, it, too, had originally been carved with such a molding, as the slight outward curve of the uppermost section of its preserved profile indicates (Pl. XCV.1).

The two-leaved door that once opened into the cella behind this remodeled marble door frame was hung in a wooden frame attached to the rear face of the marble lintel. Its appearance must remain hypothetical, like that of its wooden frame, since it was removed in late antiquity and evidently replaced by a heavy curtain. For the cuttings for door pans present on the low inner tread of the threshold have been enlarged, and the projecting inner face of the threshold adjacent to them, against which the wooden frame arose, has been rudely chiseled away in order to gain space for the mounting of a bulky object, presumably a leather curtain, to replace the dismantled door.[52] At the same time, the broad outer tread

52. Conceivably analogous to the great leather curtains hung in mosque doors. In connection with

58

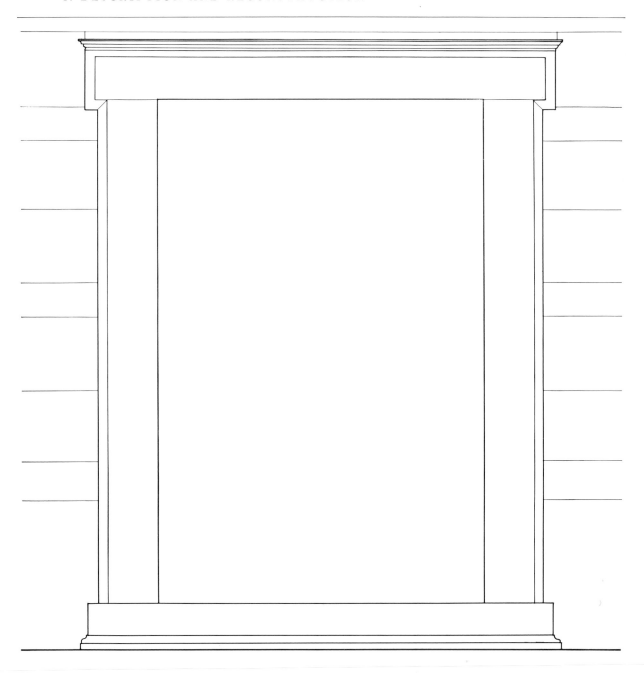

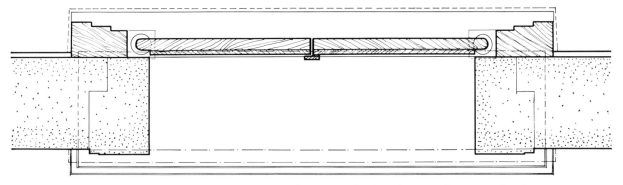

46. Remodeled Roman doorway. A. Diagrammatic elevation. B. Diagrammatic plan

47. Fragmentary eastern end of the main threshold, 36

48. Fragmentary western end of the main threshold, 62 A

of the threshold was lowered and the step that had always abutted its rear face was torn away. Hence, the holes for the door pins of both the Roman door and its Hellenistic forerunner have all disappeared, as have the wide arcs normally traced by the leaves of a door on the floor behind it but which, in this instance, were ground into the broad step level with the inner tread of the threshold.[53]

This twice remodeled threshold was found *in situ* by our Austrian predecessors but was willfully pried loose and smashed by local vandals between their first and second campaigns.[54] A large piece of its eastern half and a smaller fragment of its western end were recovered in 1948 and later replaced in approximately their original positions.[55] With the aid of the Austrian photographs and figures, this mutilated threshold may be fully reconstructed (Pls. XL, XCV.1; figs. 47, 48).[56] Its inner face was 3.94 m. long, the opening for the enlarged Roman door being 2.616 m. wide. It was doweled to the uppermost foundation course of the cross-wall separating the pronaos from the cella, a course level with the marble stylobate. Thus, although it was higher than the lateral thresholds—its tread, even in this period, rose 0.364 m. above the pronaos floor—it rested on the same level as they, its molded base projecting outward from the front wall as theirs did from the lateral walls.[57] The differ-

---

the replacement of this Roman door, see n. 45, above, and recall that its removal is implied not only by the alterations described above but also by the fact that no trace of the bronze decorations recovered in the general vicinity of the lateral doors was found in the region of the main door, obviously because it no longer existed when the building collapsed.

53. For evidence in support of these statements, see pp. 65 ff., below.

54. *S,II*, p. 10.

55. Blocks 36, the eastern end, and 62 A, the smaller western fragment, were restored to the cella in July, 1951. The limestone blocks on which they rest were intentionally set at different angles from those

of the now missing foundation courses on which the threshold was originally placed, in order to emphasize the fact that they are not actually *in situ*. When the threshold was smashed, or later, the two limestone courses immediately under it were also stolen. Hence, the preserved foundation for the door wall visible today is two courses lower than when it was first uncovered by the Austrians, as Hauser's section (*S,I*, pl. 11) makes clear. The plundered courses, like the upper courses beneath the preserved marble stylobate, were slightly lower than those still *in situ* for the door wall.

56. Ibid., pp. 52 ff., pls. 14–16, and 69, fig. I.

57. Hauser's suggestion (ibid., pp. 54 f., and fig.

ence in level still present at this time between its outer and inner treads has been eliminated from the broad area between the jambs by later recutting, but is visible at the outer extremities of the threshold, where the renewed jambs were doweled to it (Pl. XL; fig. 47).[58] The original Hellenistic level of the outer tread remains visible on the eastern extremity, where it survived as a rectangular slab 0.058 m. higher than the surrounding area and was contained within the L-shaped jamb block of the Roman door. An irregularly broken portion of this upstand is still discernible.

The frame of the wide Roman door erected on this altered threshold was composed of five blocks, two for each jamb, one for the lintel. Only the upper block of the western jamb is partially preserved, but virtually the entire lintel is extant, if in sadly damaged condition owing to breakage and mutilation (cf. Pl. XLI).[59] Together with the threshold, they allow the door to be reconstructed with exceptional precision (Pls. XXXV–XLII, CIII; fig. 46).

The exact relationship of the lintel to the threshold indicated in fig. 46 may be deduced from the cuttings on the inner face of the lintel. All three of its fragments have been notched either to receive the wooden frame in which the leaves of the door were hung or

---

18 on p. 57) that this molding might have continued along the pronaos walls as a base molding was hypothetical. We have not found any evidence of such a continuation.

58. Again, Hauser's assumption (ibid., p. 55) that this difference in level was reduced by the introduction of an intermediate step was entirely theoretical.

One of the two photographs of the threshold published in *S,I*, pl. 16, is misleading in conveying the impression that the recut tread slopes obliquely upward from front to back, retaining a higher level at the back. This is not the case, as examination of the actual fragments and Conze's other photograph, pl. 15, establish. Actually, the seemingly horizontal surface of the now roughly picked tread is slightly curved. The false impression created by pl. 16 results from the fact that its negative was obviously retouched to render more visible the far edges of the various blocks shown in the photograph.

59. Two of the three mighty fragments into which the lintel broke when it crashed to the ground, 2 and 2 A, were discovered by the Austrians (*S,I*, pp. 68 f., pl. 32). Although Hauser did not recognize their function, explicitly stating that no elements of the superstructure of the door had been discovered, he attributed these blocks to the outer face of the door wall and the inner face of the antae because of their provenance, interpreting them as members of an epikranitis and drawing the further conclusion that the pronaos wall, therefore, was divided into fields

framed by a carved bead-and-reel and meander border. (This suggestion was repeated in the *Guide*, p. 64, before the elements of the door frame had been correctly identified.) Blocks 2 (*S,I*, pl. 32, fig. 1), the central piece of the lintel, and 2 A, its eastern third, were rediscovered in 1948 along with 2 B, its western end, and 55, the sole preserved jamb block. But the tiny fragment that proved decisive for an accurate interpretation of these blocks—38.53, the return of the meander at the eastern end of the lintel—had been discovered on the surface of the ground east of the pronaos in 1938. In August, 1956, Mr. Jones observed this fragment in the storeroom of the Museum and recognized its significance. It was then possible to establish the correct relationship of 55 to 2, 2 A, and 2 B and to realize that they could have formed part of only one thing, the frame of a door. All four of these fragments were found in the vicinity of the door wall. Two additional small fragments of the molding of block 2 are preserved, one in the Museum in Samothrace, the other, according to information kindly provided by Jiří Frel, in the archaeological collection of the Charles University in Prague.

Following an unfortunate and now abandoned practice, the Austrians mutilated the eastern portion of the lintel (2 A) by sawing off a large part of its ornamental face and transporting it to Vienna, where it is now exhibited in the Kunsthistorisches Museum (No. 346 E; it lacks the vertical bead-and-reel molding erroneously added to its left edge, ibid., pl. 32, fig. 1). The remainder of block 2 A is in Samothrace.

49. Main lintel fragment 346 E. Kunsthistorisches Museum, Vienna

to partially house the circular bronze socket within which the pivots of the door revolved. Fragment 2 (Pl. XXXV) shows the cutting by means of which the frame was attached to the upper edge of the lintel at the center of this rear face; the two cuttings required for the partial housing of the bronze sockets appear on 2 A and 2 B (Pls. XXXVI, XXXVII). Inasmuch as one of the two cuttings on the latter fragments is a segment of a small circle in plan, the diameter of the bronze socket may theoretically be calculated as having been 0.165 m. This figure, in turn, is precisely the correct one for the circular depression in the door pans that once occupied the originally square cuttings on the inner tread of the threshold.[60] Hence, the correspondence of these two diameters conclusively establishes the relative positions of the lintel and threshold, a relationship corroborated by their respective lengths. The restored plan of the Roman door illustrated in fig. 46 B is not hypothetical, therefore, but indicates diagrammatically the actual interrelationship of its several parts, once the irregularities and damages caused by later alteration and destruction have been eliminated.

The jambs to which the lintel was doweled do not taper.[61] The lack of refinement implicit in this omission of a characteristic feature of monumental Greek doors is paralleled by the previously noted omission of the bead-and-reel edging from the jambs and the sloppy execution of the carved ornament on both jambs and lintel (figs. 49, 439). The scheme of the meander is basically similar to the system employed for the plastic meander on the sima of the mid-fourth-century Tholos in Epidauros (fig. 119)[62] or the painted meander on the

60. The relationship of this circular depression to the outer square of the door pan is identical with that of the preserved bronze door pans from the Anaktoron. Cf. *AJA*, 44 (1940), 352; *Guide*, p. 84; *Guide*[2], p. 87; Vol. 4, pt. I, p. 47.

61. The dowels used in connecting the upper and lower jamb blocks on each side of the door were

set parallel to their faces, rather than at right angles to them, whereas those used to attach them to both the lintel and threshold were placed in the opposite manner, at right angles to their faces; thus, block 55 may be identified as the upper western jamb block.

62. Cf. P. Cavvadias, *Fouilles d'Épidaure*, I (Athens, 1893), pl. 10.

later fourth-century terracotta sima of the South Stoa in Corinth (fig. 120) [63] and presumably reproduces the pattern on the original early Hellenistic door. Its execution, however, betrays the fact that it was carved centuries later, for the drill holes typical of Antonine and post-Antonine stonework are everywhere visible in the meander, as well as in the bead and reel. [64] The use of this technique affords evidence of the date of this remodeled door and, along with the lack of correlation between the lintel and the over-lintel and the recutting of the upper surface of the Hellenistic threshold, attests the Roman remodeling and widening of the original door ca. A.D. 200.

Both the height and width of the earlier door are established by the relationship between its lintel and over-lintel (a relationship, it will be recalled, that places them in the second and third courses below the wall architrave), by the length of the over-lintel, and by the position of the dowel holes on its lower surface, since logic as well as the analogy of the lateral doors implies that it must have been doweled to the wall blocks on each side of the lintel rather than directly to that block. Thus, the opening framed by the marble door was 3.91 m. high and 1.51 m. wide at its top. The degree to which it tapered can only be estimated on the analogy of contemporary doors, which suggest that its lower width was 1.59 m. —that is, that it tapered 0.04 m. on each side between the threshold and the lintel. [65] Presumably, the jambs themselves tapered 0.065 m. on their outer sides. This theoretical width yields an orthodox proportion of approximately 1:2.5 for the relationship between the width of the door and its height. [66]

Once the highly conventional dimensions of the original door have been established, it becomes apparent that its threshold projected 0.595 m. beyond its jambs, an unexpected, if not unparalleled feature. [67] Indeed, it was the very existence of this exceptionally wide threshold and its very projection beyond the door frame that made possible the Roman enlargement of the door. By taking advantage of its full width and placing the jambs for the remodeled door close to its lateral extremities, this far broader door could be introduced.

The unorthodox lateral extensions of the Hellenistic threshold are best understood as providing support or serving as bases for some object placed at the side of or flanking the

63. Oscar Broneer, *The South Stoa and Its Roman Successors* (*Corinth*, I, pt. 4), pls. 19, 20.

64. The central motif of the square is difficult to determine, owing to this drillwork. But its prototype was seemingly close to the examples cited, not yet replaced by the rosettes popular in later work, as at Ankara and Magnesia: cf., for example, Daniel Krencker and Martin Schede, *Der Tempel in Ankara* (*Denkmäler antiker Architektur*, III [Berlin and Leipzig, 1936]), pl. 23; *Magnesia*, fig. 65. Further discussion of the ornamental motifs of the door follows on pp. 191 ff., below.

65. Cf., for example, the die-wall and adyton doors at Didyma (*Didyma*, I, p. 55, pls. 81, 87, Z186–89; pp. 74 ff., Z311).

66. Or precisely 1 : 2.46. Again, compare the doors at Didyma, ibid.

67. Cf. the analogous situation at Mamurt-Kaleh: A. Conze and P. Schazmann, *Mamurt-Kaleh, Ein Tempel der Göttermutter unweit Pergamon* (*JDAI*, Suppl. 9 [Berlin, 1911]), p. 28, fig. 6, pl. 4, where the unduly wide threshold surely served a special purpose, too.

50. Fragmentary inscription prohibiting the uninitiated entrance to the Hieron. Samothrace Museum

door. It is tempting to attribute to this position the fragmentary inscribed marble stele found to the west of the pronaos in the narrow interval between the Hieron and the Hall of Votive Gifts (fig. 50).[68] Like the inscription found in the Anaktoron at the entrance to its rear chamber which forbids all but the initiated to pass into that room,[69] it proscribes entrance into the Hieron for the uninitiated, bearing the warning text: AMYHTON MH EIΣIENAI EIΣ TO IEPON ("He who is uninitiated may not enter the Hieron"). Obviously, it must have stood in the pronaos close to the door. During the last phases of the building's history, it stood in a marble base crudely fashioned to fit it from two re-used marble blocks, one of which is preserved, having been built into a post-antique enclosure over the southwestern corner of the Hall of Votive Gifts (Pl. XC.1).[70] The roughened faces of this base indicate

68. 51.501. Broken at the right and below. Preserved height 0.272 m.; preserved width 0.383 m.; thickness 0.086 m. Thasian marble. Found 4 m. west of the western foundation of the Hieron at a point ca. 20 m. south of the base for the granite monument at the northeast corner of the Hall of Votive Gifts. For further consideration of this inscription, see *Hesperia*, 22 (1953), 14 f.; *Samothrace*, Vol. 2, pt. I, **62**; and text II, pp. 4 ff.

69. See "Excavations in Samothrace," *AJA*, 43 1939), 138 f.; Vol. 2, pt. I, **63**.

70. Block 523. A cutting 0.095 m. wide and 0.069 m. deep has been made in what was originally the lower surface of this block to receive a stele. Given the dimensions and provenance of the two marbles, it seems reasonable to assume that 523 was recut to serve as the base for 51.501. The spacing of the cutting on 523 indicates that a second similar block must once have been clamped to it; this observation, coupled with the present width of the block, 0.66 m., suggests that the stele inserted into it must have been wider than the inscription now is to require a second such block. The

that it was set in earth or some type of floor other than a marble or stone pavement, neither of which could have been properly adjusted to it. Since other cogent arguments lead to the conclusion that the pronaos floor was paved with a variety of *signinum* or terrazzo,[71] the stele apparently stood on the floor near the door during the period when it was mounted in this improvised base. But in the second century B.C., when the porch was completed and its mighty coffered ceiling built, it is inconceivable that the inscription stood in so wretched a base. The fact that its dimensions accord so well with the space available on the upper surface of the projecting extremities of the threshold suggests, on the contrary, that when it was first erected, in the second century B.C., it was let into a threshold which had been expressly designed to accommodate a predecessor of identical size.[72] For the lettering of the preserved inscription dates it in the late Hellenistic age. That so vital a regulation as the prohibition of entrance into the building to the uninitiated was not part of the organization of the cult in the late fourth century, when the cella was constructed, is both improbable and belied by the very existence of this abnormally extended threshold.[73] The original inscription could easily have become injured or defaced in the course of the heavy structural work involved in the completion of the porch and the construction of its ceiling, and could have been replaced at that time by the present document. Whether a second sacred law stood on the opposite side of the door must remain uncertain. But once the threshold was lengthened to receive one such object, of necessity it was given a symmetrical extension at its other end.[74]

In any case, that one or more objects were actually let into the ends of the threshold is proven beyond doubt by the Roman removal of its original crowning molding. Only by taking advantage of the full length of the threshold could the door be enlarged. Only by placing the new jambs over the surfaces previously occupied by such objects could the enlarged door be constructed. And only by shearing off these surfaces and removing the slots cut into them to moor these objects—a process that unavoidably removed the molding, too— could an adequate footing be gained to which to dowel the new jambs. Had the threshold simply extended beyond the original jambs and not served as a base, it would have been

---

incomplete right side of the inscription accords with this assumption. The fact that its text is complete suggests that the otherwise blank and unnecessary space to its right was occupied by a cult symbol comparable to the kerykeion and snakes found on the Anaktoron stele. These considerations have determined the theoretical width adopted for the stele on Pls. XLII, CIII.

71. See below, pp. 95 f.

72. The space available was 0.595 m. in width, 0.141 m. in depth. For the date, see below, pp. 234 f., n. 229.

73. It will be recalled that the present Anaktoron stele is evidently a replacement, too, conceivably required because of the desirability, in the Imperial period, of adding a Latin equivalent to the Greek text.

74. The second stele introduced into the reconstruction drawing (Pls. XLII, CIII) is, thus, entirely hypothetical and may just as plausibly never have existed. The height of the text of the extant inscription is uncertain, too, but we have placed it at eye level on the general analogy of the known position of the text of the Anaktoron stele.

completely unnecessary to remove its crowning molding.[75] Hence, it became necessary to remove the inscription which in all probability once stood on the threshold, to provide it with a new, independent base, and to insert that improvised base in the earth floor of the pronaos, where it remained invisible.

The character of the original two-leaved Hellenistic door and of its wooden frame must remain hypothetical. Presumably, like the lateral doors, it was battened with bronze studs. Ample space existed for its wooden frame. That frame seems to have been stepped back in fasciae, ultimately facing the interior projection of the marble jamb visible in the restored plan of the Roman door (fig. 46 B), which was later chipped away when the door was replaced by a curtain in late antiquity. Doubtless the wooden door and its frame were attached to the original marble lintel in the same manner as their Roman successors, a manner similar in principle to the system employed in attaching a marble door to a marble lintel in the generally contemporary tomb at Palatitza in Macedonia (fig. 151).[76]

To recapitulate the intricate history of the main door of the Hieron, it was originally built in the late fourth century B.C., along with the outer fabric of the entire cella. Lofty, light, and elegant in proportion and membering, its frame enclosed an opening approximately two and one-half times as high as its lower width (Pl. XLII). In its lack of brackets or fasciae, it belonged to the category later classified by Vitruvius as Doric.[77] Essentially simple in scheme, it was sharply set off from the pattern of the surrounding wall and the texture of its courses of drafted masonry by the narrow border of delicate ornament that edged and enclosed its outer frame. The wide molded threshold on which it stood projected beyond its jambs, serving as base for a pair of objects, apparently inscriptions, that flanked it.

Centuries later, this early Hellenistic door was enlarged and remodeled. The Roman

75. The height (0.058 m.) and character of the crowning molding given to the threshold in Pls. XLII, CIII are based on the proportions of the preserved lateral threshold, block 714. The original height of the threshold was, therefore, 0.422 m.

76. From Léon Heuzey and H. Daumet, *Mission archéologique de Macédoine* (Paris, 1876), pl. 21 and pp. 230 f. Lacking evidence of the use of two varieties of studs for the main door, we have restored it in Pl. CIII with studs of uniform size on the basis of this model, assuming, too, that this system was better suited to the scale of the main door than the variation of it used for the smaller lateral doors. Cf. also the marble door from the more recently explored tomb at nearby Vergina: K. A. Rhomaios, Ὁ Μακεδονικὸς τάφος τῆς Βεργίνας (Μακεδονικὴ Βιβλιοθήκη, 14, Athens, 1951). For the similar door from Langaza, see T. Macridy, "Un tumulus macédonien à Langaza" (n. 46, above), pp. 193 ff., figs. 4, 5, pl. 5, and Gustave Mendel, *Catalogue des sculptures grecques, romaines et byzantines*

(Constantinople, 1912), I, no. 138, pp. 348 ff., as well as n. 46, above. The marble doors from Vergina and Langaza are discussed and illustrated by A. W. Lawrence, *Greek Architecture* (Pelican History of Art, Baltimore, 1957), pp. 211 f., pls. 103, 105. As far as I can see, the chronology of these Macedonian tombs has not yet been precisely or convincingly established. For a non-Macedonian example of this type of door and similar spacing of the studs, see E. Dyggve, F. Poulsen, and K. A. Rhomaios, *Das Heroon von Kalydon (Kgl. Danske Videnskabernes Selskab, Skrifter,* Historisk og Filosofisk Afdeling, 7 Raekke IV, 4 [Copenhagen, 1934]), pp. 337 ff.

77. 4.6.1–2. Cf. Heinrich Klenk, *Die antike Tür* (Giessen, 1924), pp. 2 f. and passim. For more recent discussion of Greek doors, see Robinson and Graham, *Olynthus,* VIII, 249–63; W. Kendrick Pritchett, "The Attic Stelai, Part II," *Hesperia,* 25 (1956), 233 ff. I am indebted to my husband for the latter reference.

door that replaced it retained its height but widened its opening (fig. 46). The proportion of the new opening, 1:1.5, was determined by the total width of the Hellenistic threshold. Stripped of the object or objects for which it had served as base and slightly lowered to eliminate the sockets into which these objects had been let, it was prepared to receive the new jambs. For the jambs, as well as the lintel of the original door, were replaced. Seemingly, these new members copied and repeated the ornamental motifs and moldings of the Hellenistic door. But the same lack of refinement that tolerated the necessary removal of the crowning molding of the threshold and the elimination of the slope of the jambs was insensitive to the omission of the bead and reel from their outer frames; and, while the venerable patterns of the model were reproduced in motif, they were executed in a later Roman technique at once sloppy, loose, and lifeless. New holes were cut on the inner tread of the threshold for the door pans of the new, wider door required for the enlarged opening, which must have been hung in a narrower wooden frame than was its predecessor.

Long before this first Roman remodeling of the door proved necessary, the original inscription barring entrance to the Hieron to all save the initiated had been replaced by a second-century replica, presumably at the time that work was resumed on the incomplete building and its porch finished. Now it was set in a hastily contrived base inserted in the pronaos floor and re-erected beside the door.

Once again, in late antiquity, before it became unlawful for even the initiated to seek entrance to the Hieron in pursuit of admission to the higher degree of the mysteries, the main door was altered. Traces of this last revision appear on the threshold and have rendered its interpretation exceedingly difficult. The original difference in level between the inner and outer treads was eliminated by roughly picking them throughout the entire door opening until that opening was lowered to a level only slightly above the molded base of the threshold. What had once been a steep step high above the pronaos floor was reduced to a slight elevation.[78] At the same time, the broad step abutting the inner tread at the entrance to the cella was also removed; the inner projections of the jambs that had reduced the amount of wood needed for the door frame were chiseled away; and the cuttings for the Roman door pans were hacked into and enlarged (Pl. XL). All trace of the door pin, even of the Roman door, vanished. The door itself was removed, evidently replaced by a curtain hung in a frame set in the recut extremities of the inner tread. Only the over-lintel and the twice recut threshold of the original Hellenistic door remained, the latter destined to suffer still more grievous mutilation in modern times.

The Roman remodeling of the main door is evidently to be associated with extensive alterations made in the interior of the cella, alterations affecting the marble platform in the

---

78. Hauser (*S,I*, p. 55) recognized that the treads of the threshold had been recut but offered no explanation of this fact.

apse and involving the introduction of new types of benches, as well as the heavy parapets that today separate the central from the lateral aisles of the building (fig. 44).[79] These structural changes imply a liturgical change and, given their character, appear to reflect an alteration in the ritual of the *epopteia* that made it necessary to bring animals into the Hieron.[80] This action would have been greatly facilitated by the widening of the door and, conversely, could have been accomplished only with difficulty through its original opening. Hence, it would seem that the desire to introduce new features into the cult at the end of the second century A.D. led to enlargement and revision of the main entrance to the cella.[81]

The last coarse remodeling of the door was again doubtless contemporary with the latest and poorest repairs made to the interior of the cella, including the sloppy rebuilding of the western parapet and the replacing of certain Roman bench supports.[82] Evidence gained elsewhere in the Sanctuary suggests that this final revision should be ascribed to the age of Constantine.[83] Once more, the drastic lowering of the threshold is probably to be connected with the need to lead animals into the cella. Now even large beasts could easily cross its low surface. Previously, it must have been necessary, on ceremonial occasions, to erect a temporary ramp on each side of the threshold, unless, as is possible, the animals required were different and smaller.[84]

At the level of the lintel, the front wall of the cella measured 0.733 m. in thickness—more than the comparable course of its other walls but less than their greatest thickness, because, unlike them, it did not taper. It was built according to the same system of low marble binders and high marble stretchers backed by limestone, as the anathyrosis on the sides of the threshold confirms. The joints of its blocks fell over the centers of the blocks in the course below with the regularity characteristic of the rear and lateral walls, except where they rested on the over-lintel and on the two extra long stretchers and the single long binder employed on each side of the door to obviate the less attractive use of very short blocks in the immediate vicinity of the jambs (cf. Pl. XLII).[85]

---

79. These alterations are described below, pp. 145 ff.

80. The liturgical changes alluded to here are considered in text II, pp. 42 ff.

81. See ibid., pp. 124 ff., for evidence in support of this date and discussion of the successive repairs and revisions of the cella.

82. See ibid., pp. 126 ff.

83. See ibid. and Vol. 4, pt. I, pp. 103 f.; *AJA*, 44 (1940), 348 f.

84. Text II, pp. 124 ff. What appears to be a fragment of such a ramp (53.607) was found near the northeastern corner of the porch among the shattered

remnants of the pedimental sculptures. Made of tufa, its surface has been scored with a series of parallel lines to produce a corrugated surface seemingly appropriate for this purpose. Unfortunately, neither the nature of the fragment nor its provenance allows it to be dated.

85. These six long blocks have been restored to the door wall on the analogy of stretcher 297, a block 1.524 m. long, which evidently occupied a similar position in relation to the eastern lateral door, and of the group of abnormally long wall blocks found at the rear corners of the building, which performed a similar function with regard to the pilasters. See above, p. 48.

INNER WALL ARCHITRAVE (Pl. XLIII)

The door wall, like the later anta walls, was crowned by a finely-profiled wall architrave on which the mighty marble beams of the coffered ceiling were laid. Five fragmentary blocks of this variety are preserved.[86] In so far as they were placed in the door wall, the blocks of the inner architrave were clamped to the normal porous backers characteristic of the cella walls. It is even possible that those used in the anta walls were similarly equipped with swallow-tail clamps at the rear to attach them to a porous backer intermediate between the marble blocks of the inner and outer architrave, since the lower courses of these walls are known to have been constructed in this fashion.[87] For this reason, it is impossible to ascertain whether the five remaining fragments originally belonged to the door wall or to the anta walls.

Whatever their position, the blocks in this course ranged in height from 0.635 to 0.65 m., in correlation with the height of the outer architrave. They varied in thickness from 0.263 to 0.305 m. The length of those built into the door wall may be deduced from the calculable positions of the ceiling beams that rested on them, and are established as averaging 1.20 m., with the customary variations from 1.16 to 1.20 m. They were connected with each other by a single clamp on each side and doweled to the uppermost binding course of the wall.

The upper fascia of this two-fasciaed course is crowned by a boldly projecting pair of moldings, an unadorned fillet followed by a cyma reversa carved with a vigorous leaf-and-dart pattern (fig. 181).[88] It provided a firm visual support for the richly membered ceiling above it, a clear separation of the vertical walls from the essentially horizontal ceiling, and a crowning at once simple and powerful for the richly textured wall.

Although the anta walls continued the scheme of the door wall, they were not completed in their extant form until the second century B.C., when work was resumed on the hitherto unfinished building. It will be well to postpone further consideration of the pronaos, therefore, and to return to description of the outer fabric of the early Hellenistic cella and, specifically, of the wall entablature.

WALL ARCHITRAVE (Pls. XLIV–XLVIII; Fig. 51)

Twenty-four blocks of the wall architrave are preserved, including the rear southeastern corner block (234: Pl. XLV; fig. 51). They have an average height of 0.64 m. and, apart from the corner block, an average length of 1.18 m. (variations range from 0.635 to

86. Blocks 53, 70, 436, 463, and 481. Two fragments of the inner architrave, 346 F 1 and 2, are in the Kunsthistorisches Museum in Vienna. It is impossible to say whether they belonged to columnar or wall blocks, because their lower surfaces are invisible.

87. Below, p. 100.

88. Hauser's suggestion (*S,I,* p. 64) that this Lesbian cyma was probably accompanied by a painted astragal is not convincing, in view of the absence of a molding on which to paint the customary bead and reel.

51. Southeastern corner architrave block 234

0.65 m. and from 1.174 to 1.187 m.). Like the euthynteria and stereobate blocks, they differ slightly on the eastern and western sides of the cella, the blocks found on the eastern side being 0.635 m. high, those from the west 0.645 m. That the southern blocks provided the necessary transition between the eastern and western sides is proved by the fact that the corner block is 0.64 m. high. The fillet of the western blocks is invariably 0.07 m. high, that of the eastern, ca. 0.08 m. The majority of the preserved blocks terminated at each end in a low half-regula from which three correspondingly low guttae hang, except near the corners, where blocks transitional to the corner block and its two abutting full regulae are recognizable by their single full, centrally placed regula. There is also a fourth variety having a full regula at the center and a half-regula at each end. The blocks were doweled to the uppermost course of the wall beneath them [89] and connected with the adjacent architrave blocks by a single Π-clamp at each end and with their porous backers by a pair of swallow-tail clamps. For, apart from the bonding architraves, these blocks (like the high courses of the wall) are less wide than the wall, penetrating it only ca. 0.44 m. Their joints fell over the centers of the binders constituting the uppermost course of the wall.

Four of the preserved architrave blocks are binders (cf. Pls. XLVI–XLVIII). They range from 0.707 to 0.767 m. in width; thus, they are automatically excluded from a position in any but the rear wall of the cella or the two places in the lateral walls where they abut the returns of the apse. Doweled to the top binding course of the wall, they, like the standard architrave blocks, are clamped to the adjacent block on each side by a single Π-clamp; but, unlike them, these thicker blocks are equipped at the rear with cuttings for the reception of

89. The number of dowels used varied. Normally, two were placed internally, supplemented, at times, by one or two additional dowels placed at one or both ends of the block.

certain of the timbers forming the conical roof over the apse. Further consideration of these four blocks is best postponed until discussion of the roof construction of the building.

Finally, the upper surfaces of the architrave blocks are incised with a setting line to indicate the position of the frieze.

WALL FRIEZE (Pls. XLIX–LI)

There are twenty-two relatively well preserved frieze blocks, including the southeastern corner block (218: Pl. LI).[90] The majority are double blocks consisting either of a metope at the left and a triglyph at the right or of the reverse,[91] but two individual metopes are also extant. The corner block is composed of two abutting triglyphs and the adjacent metope belonging to the lateral wall of the building. Unfortunately, this important corner metope is not fully preserved.

The average height of the frieze is 0.745 m., but, like the architrave beneath it, it is divided into an eastern and a western group, the former 0.75 m. high, the latter 0.74 m. It would be tempting to conclude that this slight discrepancy of 0.01 m. was an intentional compensation for the identical deviation in the architrave, the higher eastern frieze resting on the lower eastern architrave, the lower western frieze on the higher western architrave, were it not for the previously noted irregularities in the euthynteria, the stereobate, and the wall. Apparently such minor and, ultimately, invisible irregularities occurred at every level. The fillet of each frieze block is of uniform height over both the triglyph and the metope. It averages 0.10 m. and ranges from 0.096 to 0.106 m.

The triglyphs average 0.48 m. in width but vary from 0.459 to 0.485 m., widening toward the corners of the cella. They are among the earliest preserved examples of the triglyph with a fully developed ear, a feature no doubt adopted from the neighboring Altar Court.[92] Their glyphs are invariably triangular in section; but on some blocks they are curved at the top, on others, straight. Again, this feature is characteristic of the frieze of the Altar Court, where the presence of both varieties of cutting on the same corner block[93] indicates that this difference in workmanship has no chronological significance but simply reflects the different training or taste of individual masons, some of whom employed the more traditional curved glyph, while others preferred the newer straight form.[94]

90. Apart from the numerous smaller fragments, six additional blocks offer some, but not all, of their measurements. Block 342 (Pl. XLIX.2) is unique in being cut back and reduced in thickness across the upper part of its rear surface.

91. Thirteen metope-triglyphs and six triglyph-metopes.

92. For the Altar Court and discussion of the origin of this type of triglyph, see Vol. 4, pt. II, pp. 82 f.

and nn. 86–92, Pls. XXVI–XXIX. To the comments made in n. 88 add the fact that the hypothetical triglyphs restored to the late-fifth-century Temple of the Athenians in Delos (*Délos*, XII, 122, fig. 136) have also been incorrectly provided with ears.

93. Straight on one face, curved on the other. Cf. Vol. 4, pt. II, p. 54 and Pl. XXIX.

94. The straight variety occurs, for example, on the Thersilion at Megalopolis, on both the temples of

The triglyph of each block slightly overlaps the metope of the adjacent block. The metopes themselves average 0.72 m. in width and vary from 0.70 to 0.75 m. This variation in width of both the metopes and the triglyphs implies that at the rear corners of the cella the wall entablature echoed the spatial adjustment of the columnar entablature of the porch necessitated by the angular contraction of its columns.

The thin frieze blocks (ca. 0.25 m.) were doweled onto the wider architrave in the normal fashion, the face of the triglyph rising ever so slightly behind the face of the architrave, rather than being aligned with that of the projecting fillet beneath it. They had two dowels, one at one end of each block, the other, set with lead, farther in. Their joints fell in line with one or the other end of the regula beneath them. A single Π-clamp at either end connected each block with the adjacent frieze blocks, and two swallow-tail clamps attached it to its thick backer.

LATERAL GEISON (Pls. LII–LIV, LXXIII.3, XCVIII.1; Figs. 52, 54)

Twenty-nine geison blocks are sufficiently preserved to be partially or wholly measurable, among them both the southeastern and the southwestern corner blocks (348 A and 630: Pls. LIV, LIII.2; fig. 54).[95] They formed a low binding course somewhat wider than the total width of the wall, providing the necessary surface on which the transverse wooden beams of the cella roof rested, as well as the sima blocks into which these beams were set. They again average 1.18 m. in length (varying from 1.17 to 1.198 m.), are 0.225 m. in height (varying from 0.209 to 0.233 m.), and have a width or thickness of 0.70 to 0.88 m. Their total overhang from crown to soffit is ca. 0.37 m. The low mutules are separated from each other by viae 0.10–0.11 m. long; their own slightly variable lengths are co-ordinated with, but slightly greater than, the widths of the triglyphs and regulae beneath them.[96] Each mutule has the customary eighteen guttae. The geison crown has a firm hawk's-beak molding with an ovolo corona, while its soffit is formed by a vigorous cyma reversa over a base fascia (Pl. XCVIII). Finally, the drip profile terminates in line with the slope of the overhang and with the upper line of the mutule.[97]

Asklepios and of Artemis at Epidauros, and on the Temple of Zeus at Stratos. Both forms continued to be used throughout the subsequent Hellenistic age. The presence of straight as well as curved glyphs on the Temple of the Mother of the Gods at Mamurt-Kaleh (Conze and Schazmann, *Mamurt-Kaleh* [n. 67, above], pp. 22 f.) offers an additional third-century example of the mixed procedure and varied workshop tradition found in Samothrace in the previous century both in the Hieron and the Altar Court.

95. In addition, there are numerous fragments in Samothrace and one, 346 D 2, in the Kunsthistorisches Museum.

96. Judging especially by the evidence of the southeastern corner entablature blocks, all of which, unquestionably, fit on top of one another. The fragmentary preservation of the overhang of most of the geison blocks precludes any statement about the position of the mutules and viae of individual blocks.

97. In the majority of cases, this fragile profile is

52. Setting marks

The geison blocks were doweled onto the course below by a pair of dowels placed at one end of each block, one fitted to the marble frieze block, the other to its porous backer; their joints fell in line with one or the other end of the triglyph beneath them. A pair of Π-clamps at either end of each block linked it to the adjacent blocks. Some but not all of the blocks bear a setting mark on their lower surface, evidently indicative of the position of a given block within this course (fig. 52). Presumably, such blocks had special significance in connection with the building procedure.[98]

Inasmuch as the lateral geisa overhung the wall beneath them from 0.04 to 0.23 m. and, at the same time, were not dressed to be visible at the rear, they clearly imply the existence of a wooden ceiling beneath and between them. That ceiling must have been supported on beams notched into the porous backers of the frieze immediately below the undersurface of the geison. Finally, the space available between the projecting undersurfaces of the geisa, which the ceiling overlapped and concealed, and the transverse beams of the roof above them resting on the geisa is ample for the introduction of a coffered ceiling. As we shall see, there is tangible proof that such a ceiling existed.

broken, but fortunately it is preserved on several fragments. Therefore, the "reconstructed" block 243, illustrated on Pl. XCVIII.1, has been completed on the basis of existing elements. This block is atypical in one respect: the three guttae adjacent to the soffit overlap the inner line of the mutule rather than being aligned with it in the normal manner.

98. Only two other blocks, 128 and 671 (Pl. LXXV), also connected with the roof construction, bear such setting marks, which apparently were not used in the other courses of the Hieron. Blocks 704, 290, 680, 723, and 664, respectively, offer the following sequence: E, H, ΘE, K, X. Cf. fig. 52.

Our nineteenth-century predecessors recovered only one block from the Hieron bearing a setting mark—again, a geison block marked with a Θ (see *S,I*, p. 24). It has disappeared in the meantime. For the setting mark on block 128, see below, p. 228, n. 202.

53. Fragmentary lateral sima block, including waterspout 49.544

LATERAL SIMA (Pl. LV; Fig. 53)

Eighteen sima blocks are preserved, in addition to a large number of the lion's-head waterspouts and fragmentary ornamental gutters that once drained them. They are very slightly trapezoidal in shape (being alternately longer on the front than on the rear, and vice versa) in order to be wedged tightly against each other, since they were not clamped.[99] A pair of dowels at one end of every block attached it to the geison, each joint coinciding with the center of a mutule.

These blocks indicate the slope and construction of the roof, for each is notched at the rear with three holes cut into its lower surface to receive the horizontal wooden beams of the roof, in addition to being slightly cut down on its rear upper surface to form a continuous ledge, on which rested the thick boarding nailed to and connecting the rafters. The close-set beams were 0.20 m. square and were placed at intervals, center to center, of 0.585–0.614 m. Each block has three beam holes, a full-sized one in the center and a half-sized one at each end, since every second beam fell at the joint of two blocks. Obviously, the rafters abutted the rear of the sima and were notched into the beams.

The sima blocks constituted great marble stroters approximately 1.22 m. wide. Their sloping upper surfaces have been irregularly grooved by the rain of centuries pouring down over the terracotta stroters above them to splash from the lion's-head waterspout in the center of every block. Each lion's head was inserted in an acanthus calyx from which sprang two animated rinceaux, one to the right, one to the left; and each smooth, unfluted rinceau, in turn, sprouted curling stems. Both the three tendrils issuing from these shoots and the shoots themselves emerge from acanthus calyxes (cf. figs. 53, 116, 117), and between each pair

99. For example, 1.204 m. on the front, 1.235 m. at the rear.

of shoots there grows a lancet-shaped leaf. The background of these sculptured reliefs has a cyma recta profile terminating at top and bottom in a fascia (Pl. XCIX.1).[100]

REAR PEDIMENT (Pls. LII.2, LIII.2, LIV, XCIX, C, CIX; Figs. 54, 55, 131)

The rear corner geison blocks are sufficiently preserved to indicate the essential features of the rear pediment, including its slope. The southeastern block, 348 A, which was fully preserved in the nineteenth century, is still largely intact, but only a fragment remains of its southwestern counterpart, 630 (Pls. LIII.2, LIV, XCVIII.4, 5; fig. 54).[101] These complex blocks, in which the lateral, horizontal, and raking geisa meet, were doweled to the corner frieze blocks; they were connected by one pair of Π-clamps to the adjacent lateral geison and by a second pair to the adjacent horizontal geison. Their flat upper surfaces were prepared to receive a lateral sima block on the side, a corner tympanum block on the front. Their sloping upper surfaces, in turn, in addition to being abutted by these two blocks, were clamped to the adjacent raking geison block on the front and prepared to receive the corner sima block. The latter must have been equipped with a shallow socket into which the narrow rectangular projection on the sloping surfaces of the corner geison block locked (fig. 54).

No separate blocks of the raking geison were found at the rear of the building. However, on their lateral faces, both the corner block from the façade in Vienna and the rear corner blocks in Samothrace have moldings identical with those of the lateral geison, while the crown of the raking geison offers a slight variation on the hawk's beak of the latter (Pl. XCVIII.4, 5).

Similarly, no tympanum blocks from the rear pediment exist, although three belonging to the façade are known.[102] Two of them, along with the corner geison block, testify that the

---

100. The total height of the gutter, including the base fillet (0.043 m.), is 0.18 m. For discussion of the ornamental motifs of the gutter, including the style and execution of the lion's-head waterspouts, see below, pp. 170 ff. In addition to the fragments of the lateral sima in Samothrace and Vienna, there are three others among the marbles from Samothrace collected in the lower garden of the Ottoman Museum in Istanbul. The fragmentary lion's head tentatively ascribed to the Hieron in *Hesperia*, 21 (1952), 40 and pl. 10 e, was later correctly identified as belonging to the Altar Court.

101. The lower surface of this southwestern corner block has been sheared off, rendering it unusable. It is difficult to determine whether this revamping is

the result of an abandoned modern attempt to reshape and re-use the block or, given the provable replacement of the original blocks above and below it, the effect of a similarly intended and abandoned Roman effort to repair the original Hellenistic corner geison. In the latter case, this severely damaged block must have been cast aside and replaced by a now missing Roman counterpart. This alternative is not inconceivable, since other discarded marbles—including, of course, the replaced akroteria—have been recovered in the excavation of the Hieron. See text II, pp. 79 ff., for further reference to the extensive early Imperial repair made to this corner. The original state of the southeastern block may be seen in *S,II*, pl. 11.

102. See below, pp. 106 ff., for discussion of the porch pediment.

54. Fragmentary southeastern corner geison block 348 A

angle of the pediment was 14° 30′, and all three, together with the lost crowning block of the raking geison recorded by our predecessors, allow the tympanum of the front pediment to be reconstructed with a slope of 1:3.9 in the manner illustrated in Pl. CVIII. Presumably the rear pediment was similarly built.

One revealing fragment of a horizontal geison block found at this end of the cella (243: Pl. LII.2) implies that the rear pediment was sufficiently deep to receive some form of sculptural decoration subsequent to its original completion. For at least one dowel hole on its upper surface has been leaded from the front of the block, a procedure intelligible only if the object attached to it was added as an afterthought or a revision of the early Hellenistic pediment, when its tympanum wall had already been built. The recovery of fragmentary sculptures from this region of the building points in the same direction.[103] Although this important fragment confirms the fact that the horizontal geison reiterated the forms of the lateral geison, it is not sufficiently complete to indicate the precise depth of the rear pediment or the character of its floor.

Unfortunately, too, the southwestern corner sima block found and photographed by our predecessors was not drawn and, in the meantime, has disappeared (fig. 55).[104] Its general shape can be deduced from the upper surface of the corner geison block to which it was doweled; but the precise structural form of this important block, which carried the lateral akroterion, cannot be determined. Its two faces show the last of the rinceaux adorning the lateral sima and the first of the triad of motifs employed on the raking sima.

103. For consideration of these sculptures, see below, pp. 318 ff. Block 243 was found in the apse. The location of the dowel hole on its upper surface, discussed above, precludes its classification as a lateral geison block, since it cannot be correlated with the system of doweling used on the lateral sima blocks. A second horizontal geison block from the rear pediment, 655, found south of the Altar Court, also retains dowel holes.

104. *S,II,* pl. 14.

55. Lost southwestern corner sima block

The nineteen small fragments of the raking sima found at both ends of the building allow its ornamental pattern to be reconstructed with certainty, in spite of the fact that no single block is fully preserved (cf. fig. 131). It consists of three elements: a palmette; a lotus flower springing from an acanthus calyx; and a blossom which, like the palmette, is supported by two coiled tendrils. Each such tendril is overhung by a leaf, and the three vertical elements are linked by fluent curving stems. The seven-petaled palmettes, unlike those on the antefixes, are almost rectangular, being composed of petals that are pulled to the side and turned inward in crisp, elegant arcs.[105] Between every pair of lotus flowers there is, alternately, a palmette or a blossom and a palmette, except at the corners, where the terminal lotus was carved half on the lateral sima, half on the raking sima.[106] Both the cyma recta and the base fascia of the raking sima are somewhat less vigorous in profile than the comparable forms of the lateral sima (Pl. XCIX).[107]

105. Cf. p. 178, below.

106. Apparently, the Austrians found only the incomplete southwestern corner sima block, which preserves this corner feature but lacks both the normal lotus flower and the full sequence of motifs. Therefore, they assumed that the raking sima was composed of two rather than three alternating motifs, apart from its corner palmettes. The various fragments in Samothrace make it possible to ascertain the correct succession of motifs.

The lost corner sima block belonged to the southwestern corner of the Hieron, as both the photograph (S,II, pl. 4) and the text (p. 27) indicate; for during the second Austrian campaign, work was carried on to the east and south of the building. Thus, as has been pointed out in n. 33, above, the so-called reconstruction of the southeastern corner (S,II, pl. 13) in which this block figures is misleading, being schematic in character rather than a reconstruction of excavated

blocks belonging to that corner. Actually, the lost block was a Roman replacement of the early Hellenistic corner sima, as its debasement of the original motifs makes clear: the acanthus calyx of the lotus has been omitted; the blossom has been elongated, simplified, and devitalized; the palmette has been widened, thereby losing its characteristic angular verticality; and the bold curving stems that link the three motifs have been partially replaced by inert stems trailing lifelessly on the base fascia. Unfortunately, the atypical forms of this incomplete block served as the unavoidable basis for Hauser's reconstruction, hence reappearing in Martin Schede's widely quoted *Antikes Traufleisten-Ornament* (Strassburg, 1909), pl. 9, no. 58. For further reference to repairs made to the southwestern corner, see text II, pp. 79 ff.

107. The total height of the raking sima, 0.177 m., and the height of the base fillet, 0.035 m., are also slightly less than those of the lateral sima.

Inasmuch as the raking sima blocks occasionally end in different motifs, they must have been of varying lengths. They seem to have been interlocked, either having a projecting tang at the rear of one end in order to overlap the next block or being cut at the rear to receive an overlapping adjacent block (cf. Pls. XCIX, C). The exceedingly fragmentary state of these blocks precludes any further statement concerning the manner in which they were connected with each other or placed on the raking geison.

ROOF CONSTRUCTION (Pls. XXVII, XLVI–XLVIII, LV, LVII, CIV)

Throughout its entire length, the cella was crossed at intervals of ca. 0.60 m. by wooden beams 0.20 m. square, having a clear span of 10.72 m. (Pl. CIV). These strong horizontal timbers rested on the inner upper surface of the lateral geisa and were held in position by being set in square openings cut to receive them at the rear of the sima (Pl. LV). The diagonal rafters were notched into the beams and made to abut the inner face of the sima. A strong boarding or series of battens ca. 0.05 m. thick was nailed from rafter to rafter to support the terracotta tiles. The lowest section of this boarding or battening fitted into the shallow ledge cut across the back of the sima at the rear of its oblique upper surface. These timbers may be deduced from the character of the sima blocks and their relationship to the geison. Hence, the Hieron had a trussed roof—a conclusion implicit, too, in the fact that its transverse beams rested on the geison rather than, as normally, on the architrave. The use of a truss, in turn, implies the existence of a kingpost at the center of each beam. Only the pair of shorter, flanking posts introduced between the rafters and the beams in Pl. CIV is hypothetical. But some such lateral props, whether upright or diagonal and attached to the kingpost, were doubtless present.[108] Finally, as has been pointed out, a coffered wooden ceiling must have been introduced beneath and between the beams.

The roofing of the shallow, segmental apse in which the cella terminates can be reconstructed from the four previously mentioned bonding architrave blocks (cf. Pls. XLVI–XLVIII). It will be recalled that, owing to their abnormal thickness (0.707–0.767 m.), they can have been placed only in the rear wall of the cella, where it abuts the limestone wall of the apse, or in the two places in the lateral walls, one in each, where they abut the returns of the apse. What is more, none of these blocks can have been adjacent to another, since each is equipped with a slight lateral tang at its rear, generally on both sides, which prevents any two from being coupled. It follows that two may be attributed to a position over one of the apse returns, two to positions on each side of the pair of standard architrave blocks located behind the center of the apse (Pl. LVII).[109]

108. For further discussion of the roof, see below, pp. 198 ff.

109. From their provenance, blocks 744 and 754 may be attributed to positions over the eastern and

All four of these binders are characterized by two types of cutting at their rear, one a horizontal ledge produced by cutting back the upper half of the rear face, the other a narrow vertical notch cut in the lower half of this same face. The rough dressing of these cuttings indicates that they were for the reception of wood rather than stone. This fact and the combined size and section of the notch holes can be explained only by the assumption that narrow beams or rafters were inserted in these notch holes and pegged or nailed to wooden bearers projected from the timber wall plate. The latter, in turn, was housed in the previously mentioned horizontal ledge and clamped to the rear of the cut-back upper surface of the bonding architrave blocks.

The arched beam notched into the binders over the apse returns rested on the rear part of the upper surface of the top binding course of the wall, that is, on blocks like 687 (Pl. XXVII), which were provided with rear extensions allowing them to stretch over the returns. Hence, it was ca. 0.60 m. × 0.30 m. in size and must have tapered to ca. 0.30 m. × 0.30 m. at the highest point of its curve, since it could not rise higher than the top of the normal transverse beams of the cella, to the rear of one of which it had to be attached, or drop lower than the surface of the coffered ceiling of the cella. As a result, the 9.87 m. wide opening of the apse was spanned by a low segmental arch (Pl. LVII). Inasmuch as this arch rested only on the rear half of each return, the front half of the return probably either supported an upright porous block equivalent in height to the outer entablature or served as a pedestal on which an object or figure could be placed.

The rafters radiating from the rear face of this arched beam were similarly notched into the narrower vertical cuttings in the rear faces of the two binding architraves of the rear wall and, elsewhere, into the curving porous wall of the apse. Given the curve of the transverse beam framing the opening of the apse and the truncated radii between that beam and its curving periphery, these rafters must have been straight, if obliquely set, except for the slight curve at their base. The interstices between the radiating rafters must have been closed by boarding nailed to them. Additional invisible timbers or struts may have been used in constructing the false roof over the apse. In fact, the existence of enigmatic oblique cuttings at the lower edge of the rear face of the bonding architrave blocks implies as much. But it is impossible to suggest their character. Only the primary members of this roof may be established with certainty.

Hence, the segmental apse of the Hieron was covered by a wooden roof of tent-like shape in the form of a section of a cone. In basic scheme, it appears to be the sole monumental

western returns, respectively, blocks 524 and 826 to the rear wall. No more than the four preserved binding architraves can ever have existed, given their location. The lumbering shape of these blocks, which makes them at once impossible to re-use in a different position and awkward to transport even to a limekiln, is doubtless responsible for this rare preservation of a whole category of blocks.

example extant of a traditional form of archaic timber construction otherwise known from its reflection in certain rock-cut tombs of Etruria.[110]

MARBLE KALYPTERS (Figs. 56, 134, 178–180, 389–391)

Although the roof of the Hieron was essentially tiled with red-glazed kalypters and stroters, the lowest tier of kalypters, those visible over the joints of the marble sima blocks, was of marble. Triangular in section, like the Corinthian kalypters from the two predecessors of the present building, these marble kalypters terminate in carved antefixes that rested on the gutter and appeared above the joints of the sima blocks. Their undersurfaces are curved to fit the upper surface of the sloping sima and hollowed to allow them to be placed over the pair of parallel lips found on this surface wherever one block adjoins another; at the rear, their upper surfaces are reduced from a triangular to a curved section, in order to provide an extension on which the overlapping terracotta kalypter of the next tier once rested. Apart from its antefix, each kalypter was ca. 0.58 m. long. Beyond this point, the marble sima blocks were covered with terracotta kalypters and stroters, as is indicated by the cessation of grooves created by running water pouring off the terracotta stroters.

Fifteen such marble kalypters with relatively well preserved antefixes exist—six in Samothrace, seven in Vienna, and two in Prague (figs. 56, 178–180, 389–391).[111] Most of them are repairs, but they repeat the scheme of the original antefixes, if with variations.[112] Each antefix terminates in a low base fillet that makes it an independent unit visually, as it is structurally; each is decorated with an oval palmette that springs from a lancet-shaped member and is supported by a pair of coiled tendrils emerging from acanthus leaves. An indented leaf overhangs each tendril—a motif that recurs on the raking sima (figs. 131, 172). The lower two petals of each nine-petaled palmette are drawn down into a horizontal

110. Cf. the examples at Vulci, Cerveteri, and S. Giuliano discussed by A. Åckerström, *Studien über die etruskischen Gräber* (Lund, 1934), pp. 25 ff., 68, 88, under the term "Fächer-Decke" or "tetto a ventaglio." For more recent comment on the character of the structural forms imitated in these monuments, see Paola Zancani Montuoro and U. Zanotti-Bianco, *Heraion alla foce del Sele*, II (Rome, 1954), 58, n. 1, and Karl Lehmann, "The Dome of Heaven," *The Art Bulletin*, 27 (1945), 20, n. 176.

It may be worth remarking that a modern wooden ceiling of essentially the same type is to be seen in the eastern tower of the Porta Nigra at Trier.

111. In addition to numerous fragments on which the antefix is no longer preserved. The examples catalogued in Samothrace are 48.578, 49.514 A–B, 49.515,

51.219, 52.494, and 62.14; those in the Kunsthistorisches Museum are numbered 346 L 1–7, the first having been reproduced by Conze, *S,I*, pl. 31, fig. 1; the two in Prague belong to the Institute of Classical Archaeology of the Charles University.

Kalypters of similar structural form, though with painted antefixes, were used on the Philippeion at Olympia: *Olympia*, II, pl. 82, fig. 4.

112. For discussion of these repairs and analysis of the style and execution of the preserved antefixes, see text II, pp. 81 ff. 49.514 (fig. 391) is a late Roman replacement belonging to the western wall of the cella near the southern corner; 48.578 (fig. 134) comes from the original, early Hellenistic building period and belonged over the northeast corner of the cella.

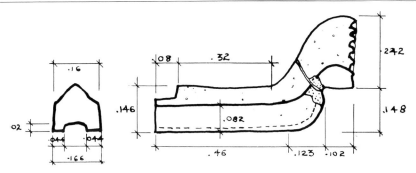

56. Lateral elevation and section of marble kalypter 49.514

position, and their tips turn upward. Otherwise, the round-tipped lateral petals droop slightly outward.[113]

ROOF TILES (Pls. LVIII–LXII; Figs. 141, 142)

The numerous fragmentary stroters, kalypters and ridge kalypters found over and around the ruins of the Hieron allow its red-tiled roof to be reconstructed with precision. Like the main roofs of its predecessors, it was Corinthian in form; yet, since its traditional apse was no longer salient but contained within the rectangle of the cella, it did not require their scale-shaped apsidal tiles.

The lowest tier of terracotta stroters partly overlapped the sloping upper surface of the marble sima, two such tiles being placed on each block (cf. Pl. LV). The outer, visible line of this lowest row of stroters was parallel to the gutter and ran immediately behind the two roughly circular hollows gouged in their upper surfaces. These hollows, like the grooves linking them with the gutter, are not man-made but carved by the rainfall of centuries, which streamed down the stroters, collecting in the depression in the center of each tile before pitching onto the marble stroters, flowing into the gutter, and being spewed forth by the lion's-head waterspouts. Endlessly dropping down from the centers of this slightly higher row of stroters and running over the slightly steeper pitch of the sima, the water gouged an irregular hollow where it fell and grooved an uneven channel to the gutter. The steeper pitch of the sima increased the momentum with which rain was forced through the narrow openings of the spouts, causing it to splash even beyond the line of the overhanging upper courses of the entablature. The central portion of one otherwise fragmentary stroter (Pl. LVIII.2) [114] confirms the evidence of these telltale traces on the marble sima.

113. The genesis and local character of this type of antefix are presented in Vol. 4, pt. II, pp. 87 ff. See also below, pp. 180 ff.

114. 48.559 contains a group of fragmentary tiles and potsherds found over the northern part of the cella and includes the small fragment illustrated here. It is similar in character to the larger fragment, 49.492 (Pl. LVIII.1), which retains faint traces of red glaze on its lower surface. A third fragment, also from 48.559, is the rear of such a stroter. All three were later repairs to the early Hellenistic cella.

81

The tiles of this lowest row of stroters, like the lowest kalypters resting on them, were somewhat shorter than the standard stroters. Two such tiles fitted snugly between the low lips edging each sima block at the sides and rear, and were prevented from slipping out of position by the marble kalypters which they abutted. They differed from the standard tiles, too, in lacking the overhanging lip normally present at the front of each tile. Otherwise, they were equipped with the same raised lip at the rear and with raised, notched lips at the sides (Pls. LVIII.1, LXII). The overhanging front edge of each standard stroter was inserted into the notched lateral lips of the tile below, overlapping its rear upstand. In addition to holding the stroter above it in place, its raised lateral lips, together with those of the two adjacent tiles, provided a ridge over which were placed the kalypters covering the open joints between neighboring tiles. Forced down the overlapping stroters between parallel rows of kalypters and, whenever the rainfall was light, coerced into their shallow central channels, water was led off the sloping roof in a fashion designed to protect the joints of the kalypters and to prevent seepage.

The standard kalypters were polygonal on the exterior but curved on the interior (Pls. LIX, LXII). Each tile was equipped at its rear with a short, raised extension that overlapped the front edge of the pair of stroters immediately above and behind it, their lateral ridges being curved and lowered at this point to receive it. The upper surface of this horizontal tang was curved and elevated above the polygonal forepart of the tile to form a ridge over which the kalypter of the tier above it could be fitted. The underside of each kalypter was thus hollowed, toward the front of the tile, to create a socket into which the curved, raised tang locked. The lowest row of terracotta kalypters—those resting over the curving extensions at the rear of the marble kalypters—was shorter than the standard length; it fitted against the rear face of the marble kalypters in such a manner as to be level with its upper surface, rather than being stepped up, as in the other tiers. Only the uppermost tier of kalypters was identical with the marble tiles in having a low collar-like extension at its rear, over which the ridge kalypters could be set (Pl. LXI.1, 2; upper tile, Pl. LXII).[115]

The ridge kalypters (Pl. LX.5), of necessity, were larger than the others and curving in section, since they covered the joints between the two uppermost tiers of stroters and kalypters, one at the summit of the eastern slope of the roof, the other at the top of the western. They fitted over the rounded rear extensions of these two uppermost tiers of kalypters, presumably

115. 49.312 and 48.487 exemplify this type of red-glazed kalypter. Both belonged to the original building period. The former was found on the surface south of the rear wall of the cella; the latter was recovered from the fill of the pronaos, into which it must have been thrown in the second century B.C., when the earlier building was completed—an operation obviously involving work on the original, as well as on the new, roof. It bears a rectangular stamp but lacks preserved letters. Two identical smaller fragments are accessioned with 48.559. For the date of these fragments, see below, n. 119. 50.216, a fragment of a dark-brown glazed kalypter of coarse clay found on the surface close to the northeast corner of the porch, evidently comes from a late repair of the roof. Whether it was a standard tile or came from the uppermost tier cannot now be determined. The same is true of 53.469, a brownish-red glazed fragment found on the surface east of the building, which reflects another such repair.

stretching from center to center of the uppermost stroters and overlapping each other in such a fashion as to create a continuous horizontal line along the ridge (Pls. CIV, CVII).[116] Like the marble kalypters, they were embellished with antefixes (Pl. LXI.3, 4; figs. 141, 142).[117] But, in view of their position, these crowning members were adorned on each face with an identical palmette and, in accord with normal practice, were placed in line with the complicated tiles to which they were attached, rather than at right angles to them, like the antefixes attached to the front of the marble kalypters. Their animated patterns enlivened the otherwise unbroken horizontal of the long ridge, reiterating the basic form of the marble antefixes below but providing variations on their essential theme, owing to the changed character of their palmettes and their quickened rhythm. For every row of kalypters was crowned at the ridge by such a terracotta antefix, in contrast with the wider spacing of the marble antefixes which alternated along the sima with lion's-head waterspouts, recurring at wider intervals and establishing a quieter rhythm (Pl. CVII).[118]

Portions of all three basic varieties of tile exist. Some are venerable relics of the early Hellenistic building, others, later Hellenistic or Roman repairs to its roof. Still other fragments of the original tiling found their way into the fill of the pronaos, when it was revamped and completed in the second century B.C. They bear witness both to periodic repair of the roof and to retention of its original system of tiling until late antiquity.[119] Broken though these typical tiles may be, they retain or imply key elements of the lost terracottas of the roof. For instance, no fragment preserves the specific form of the rear end of the standard kalypters. But it is implicit in the undersurface of kalypter 53.469 and its relationship to stroter 49.492 (Pls. LIX.1; LVIII.1), in addition to being confirmed by the related scheme of the Anaktoron kalypters.[120]

116. 48.754, found at the bottom of the pronaos fill and coming from the original marble building. When restored, the ridge kalypter proved to be semicircular, 0.69 m. in diameter and 0.60 m. long.

117. 53.152 and 53.210, both found in the debris near the southeastern corner of the cella and exhibited in Hall B of the Museum (*Guide*, pp. 66, 85; *Guide²*, pp. 67, 88).

118. The character of the ridge tiles in Hauser's restored lateral elevation in *S,I*, pl. 43, is hypothetical and incorrect both in the polygonal form of the tiles and in the omission of the intermediate antefixes. The Austrians found no whole roof tiles (ibid., p. 67) and obviously, in their generation, did not observe the revealing fragments of such tiles as must have been visible.

119. 49.312, for example, a fragmentary kalypter from the original building period of the cella, fits neatly onto the upper surface of the later stroter, 49.492, itself a repair. It is possible that 55.74, a small fragment of a stroter found on the surface to the east of

the building which is identical in texture and glaze with 48.754, belonged to the original roof, although it is slightly thinner than the normal stroter. It bears on its upper surface part of an oblong stamp with the retrograde inscription ΩN, which, it was suggested (Vol. 2, pt. II, **280**), might be restored: IEPA ΘE]ΩN. In connection with these stamped tiles, it is interesting to note that the Austrians found a roof tile somewhere in the vicinity of the building bearing a square stamp containing the letters ΠP (ΠP[ονάου?) in Hellenistic shape. Cf. *S,II*, p. 10, fig. 2, and Vol. 2, pt. II, p. 115, where the stamp is misprinted as ΠΠP.

120. Although the fragments of the ridge kalypter are sufficient to indicate the nature of its curve (hence, its diameter), they do not reveal the precise form of the rounded extensions which must have allowed one tile to overlap another. This tile, therefore, has not been included in Pl. LXII, since all the elements of the roof shown there may be reconstructed with certainty.

The standard stroters must have been 0.55 m.

Although the ridge antefix is incompletely preserved (Pl. LXI.3, 4; figs. 141, 142), it may be restored on the basis both of Samothracian tradition and of contemporary usage.[121] Its palmette is composed of two abutting half-palmettes, each growing from a stalk. The acanthus calyx from which the five fluttering petals of each half-palmette emerge also sends forth a curling tendril (see fig. 141 B), and the interval between the two half-palmettes is adorned with a rosette-like disk. This much of the design is certain. It has been completed in the restored elevation on Pl. CVII with the triple-leaved acanthus calyx at the base that logic and convention demand.

INTERRUPTION AND ALTERATION OF THE ORIGINAL BUILDING PROJECT

(Pls. I, II.1, 3; Figs. 57–64)

Some time after the completion of the cella, when the lower courses of the porch foundation had been laid and the pronaos at least partially constructed, work ceased on the porch of the Hieron. For nearly two centuries it remained incomplete.[122] When work was resumed on the building, the original fourth-century project was altered. Time had passed and taste had changed, turning from the proportions and forms of the early Hellenistic age to the revived classicism of the day. Originally, the porch of the Hieron had been planned as hexastyle prostyle, tetrastyle in antis, with an intermediate column on each side between the outer colonnade and the antae (fig. 57). The inner colonnade was to stand a step above the floor of the outer porch. As a result, it was slightly shorter than the outer colonnade, and its proportions were somewhat less radical than the advanced Hellenistic ratios of the latter. Evidently, the slender proportions of the late fourth and early third centuries no longer pleased the eyes of the classical revivalists responsible for the completion of the building, who reverted to the heavier forms of the late Classical age from which the original architect had intentionally deviated. The proportions of the entablature could not be altered; but the outer colonnade could be adjusted to the preferences of contemporary taste by the simple device of eliminating the difference in level between the outer porch and the inner pronaos. Once the forepart of the porch was raised to the level of the pronaos, the height of the projected outer colon-

---

wide and 0.60 m. deep, the overlapping standard kalypters, 0.60 m. long. Each slope was composed of eleven tiers of tiles. The preserved fragments, especially those of the kalypters, are characterized by variations in texture of clay, quality of glaze, and degree of slope that doubtless reflect the long centuries over which innumerable minor repairs must have been made to the roof with tiles of varying refinement. Thus, the

flaring profile of the original kalypters is not always present.

121. See below, pp. 184 ff., for discussion of this antefix and of the local traditions that underlie the design of a long series of Samothracian antefixes, as well as of their relationships to contemporary practice elsewhere.

122. For consideration of the circumstances that probably caused this interruption, see text II, pp. 74 f.

nade was automatically lowered, and the columns themselves acquired the firmer proportions admired by the proponents of the Classical Revival. At the same time, the anta walls were shortened to allow the inner colonnade to be made prostyle, an alteration in plan that required the respacing of the lateral columns in relationship to both the antae and the corner columns of the outer colonnade.

These revisions of the original plan were accompanied by the construction of a splendid marble coffered ceiling in the pronaos and outer porch and by the addition of pedimental and akroterial sculptures to the building. Whether such sculptures had formed part of the original project cannot be determined. But given the disappearance of traditional forms of architec-

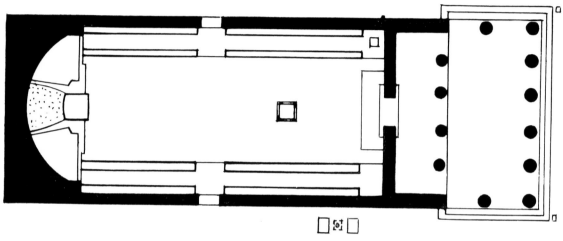

57. Projected plan of the early Hellenistic Hieron

tural sculpture in Greece between the early third and the mid-second centuries B.C., its presence in the executed porch of the Hieron constitutes the ultimate expression of the classicistic attitude of its builders and accorded with their modification of its formerly ultra-progressive Hellenistic proportions.[123]

The building history outlined here and the character of the original project are documented by certain singular features of the extant, late Hellenistic porch. It will be recalled that the western and northwestern foundations of the projected porch were completed in the late fourth century, as the ceramic material found in the western foundation ditch attests.[124] When work on the porch ceased, the eastern and the greater part of the northern foundations had been carried one course less high than the western and the northwestern. Both these original levels of completion—the present second course on the west and the third course on the

123. Further discussion of these general points follows on pp. 315 ff., below. The completion of the Hieron in the second century B.C. proves to have been a more limited task than we at first assumed (cf. *Hesperia*, 20 [1951], 23).

124. No potsherds later than glazed and coarse ware antedating the last quarter of the fourth century B.C. were found in the western foundation ditch at the level of the original top, but now second, course. For analysis of the fill of the foundation ditches, see text II, pp. 145 f.

58. View of the pronaos from the west, showing the juncture of the earlier and later foundations

east—are easily discernible, since they project slightly beyond the foundation courses later built over them. The precise point at which the two crews of masons responsible for the laying of the foundation met near the northwest corner of the porch has already been indicated, as have the slight discrepancy in the level of a given course at this juncture, caused by their careless workmanship, and the compensation for this unevenness by the adjustment of one course to another (fig. 35).[125] Thus, the original project for the Hieron evidently called for a porch of approximately the same size as the extant porch.

But the pronaos of the original project was slightly less deep, as its telltale foundation walls reveal.[126] The rear, southern foundation and the original portions of the lateral founda-

125. Cf. pp. 38 f. That this irregularity is the result of a procedural variation rather than of a chronological difference between these two portions of the lower foundation course of the porch is proved by the character of the ceramic material found in the eastern and the eastern part of the northern foundation ditches, which, again, includes no potsherds necessarily later than the third quarter of the fourth century B.C.

126. The photographs reproduced in figs. 19, 58–62, 64, 66 show the appearance of the pronaos after it had been fully excavated in 1949. In 1951, this sizable area was largely filled in with earth (retained at the east and west by two field-stone walls) in order to provide an appropriate field on which the great ceiling beams and some of the coffers of the marble ceiling of the pronaos could be placed and made conveniently available for inspection. An interval sufficient to allow the visitor

59. View of the northwestern corner of the pronaos foundation

60. View of the northern foundation of the pronaos, seen from the south

61. View of the pronaos, showing the western foundation

62. Detail of the pronaos, showing the eastern foundation

tions are both higher and more regular than the northern foundation and the northernmost parts of the lateral foundations (cf. Pl. II.1, 3; figs. 19, 58–63). The latter are composed of five irregularly laid courses of variable height and materials, while an equivalent height of the foundation beneath the door wall and the larger part of the lateral foundations are built of four regular courses of limestone.[127] As figs. 19, 58, 59, 61, 62 will make clear, both regular lateral foundations have been cut back to receive the interlocking lower courses now present at their northern extremities and bonded into the similarly-coursed northern foundation.[128] Both lateral foundations thus originally extended farther to the north before being widened to sup-

to study and compare all four foundations was left on the eastern and western sides of the pronaos, where both lateral walls are fully exposed, as are their junctions with the radically different northern and southern foundations.

127. This fourth course is preserved only on the western and the western half of the southern founda-

tions (figs. 58, 59, 61); hence, it is not visible in all views of the pronaos.

128. The junction of these interlocking sections of foundation occurs 1.065 m. south of the inner northeastern corner of the pronaos, at the lowest visible course in the eastern wall, and 2.07 m. south of the northwestern corner, at the same lowest course.

port steps; that is, they ran beneath anta walls longer than those of the extant building. Two of the additional binders by means of which this increased length of 1.22 m. was achieved may be seen on the eastern side of the pronaos both in the plan and in fig. 63.[129] They indicate the point at which the lateral steps of the projected porch were intended to stop but are now contained within the slightly lengthened foundation of the extant porch. The foundation of the inner colonnade (the northern foundation of the pronaos) was thus originally

63. Detail of the eastern foundation of the pronaos

bonded into the lateral walls south of the present cross-wall, and, at one point, must have included within it a portion of the great outcropping of rock in the northeastern corner of the pronaos.

The two building periods implicit in this alteration and rebuilding of the pronaos foundations are confirmed by the character of the pronaos fill, the ceramic material found beneath the floor of the porch, and the condition of the stylobate blocks laid on the rebuilt northern foundation. For although the extensive ceramic material found in the pronaos fill largely antedates the last quarter of the fourth century B.C.—that is, reflects the original building period—the additional fill required when the pronaos was enlarged and the porch completed contained a sparse amount of later material, and the stylobate blocks have plainly been re-used.[130]

At first sight, the two westernmost blocks of the incompletely preserved marble stylobate beneath the inner colonnade of the present porch are bewilderingly unlike their neighbors to

129. Now that the original southeastern corner euthynteria block of the porch (which was not found *in situ* but was recovered in the course of excavation) has been replaced on the building, these blocks are no longer wholly visible. (Our original statement, *Hesperia*, 19 [1950], 5, repeated ibid., 20 [1951], 21, that the present remodeled porch is wider than the projected early Hellenistic porch, was not correct, as further investigation of the exterior of its foundation courses later revealed.)

130. For description and analysis of the pronaos fill and potsherds extracted from the interstices of the underpavement of the porch, see text II, pp. 165 ff., 173 ff.

64. View of the northern foundation of the pronaos and the inner stylobate,
seen from the south

the east (Pl. I; fig. 64).[131] The outermost of the pair is considerably shorter than the other
blocks, and its northern face, which the marble pavement slabs of the finished building abutted, is dressed with lateral anathyrosis—unlike all the other blocks, which are logically
dressed to abut marble pavement slabs. Its original northern or front face is now placed
against the block to its east. If it were swung into its original position, not only would that
hidden face once more become visible and the present front face again become a side, but it
would also have the correct length. Similarly, the block to its east has a finely-dressed smooth
face at its present rear, the invisible side which abutted the pronaos floor of the existing
building; but the remaining blocks to the east still retain the rough picking and lifting bosses that it was unnecessary to remove, given the fact that the pronaos floor was at no time
paved with marble. If this second block, too, were swung into its original position, its
smoothly finished face would look toward the north. Clearly, the faces of all the blocks of

131. The ninth (then westernmost) preserved
block excavated by the Austrians and indicated in
Hauser's plans (*S,I,* pls. 11, 12) had vanished when we
re-excavated the stylobate. Harmful vegetation had
further altered the appearance of these blocks, splitting
and wrecking several of them badly, as our plan (Pl. I)
shows. But at no time can they have been characterized
by the rhythmical alternation in size found in Hauser's
drawings. Faced with a discrepancy in measurements
when he prepared these plans and unable to check
with the far-away blocks, he evidently regularized
them, as he resolved the similar difficulty resulting

from seemingly divergent frieze heights by fabricating
a figure inapplicable to any such block in the Sanctuary
(above, pp. 9 ff.). The diagrammatic rear elevation of
the stylobate (*S,I,* p. 51) is also completely inaccurate
in its depiction of the varying rear faces of these blocks.

When the porch was partially reconstructed in
1956 and properly skilled workmen and tools were at
hand, the opportunity was seized to remove the earth
which had washed under these blocks and to repair and
reset them in level and correct position, so far as is
now possible, given the derangement of the foundation
produced in the last mighty earthquake in which the
building collapsed. See text II, p. 138, n. 19.

the stylobate were once similarly dressed to be visible; that is, they were intended to rise a step above the pavement of the outer porch, rather than to be level with it as they now are. Exposure of the face of the stylobate of an inner colonnade is normal when columns are placed in antis. That the stylobate blocks were originally cut and laid for a colonnade in antis is confirmed by the narrow dowel hole now visible on the surface of this same second block from the west. If it were swung into proper position, this hole would be appropriate in size and position to contain a dowel for the lowest block of an anta.[132] Finally, although the stylobate blocks were certainly doweled to the course beneath them when they were first laid and, in certain instances, were again doweled to the new, lower top course of the extant foundation beneath them, toward the west they were relaid without the use of dowels, as the absence of dowel holes in the westernmost blocks of this foundation attests.[133]

The combined evidence of the unfinished northern and eastern foundations of the porch, of the altered and rebuilt foundations of the pronaos, and of the re-used marble stylobate blocks indicates that the original plan for the Hieron called for a porch that was hexastyle prostyle, tetrastyle in antis, with an intermediate column placed between the outer colonnade and the anta on each side (fig. 57). The inner colonnade and the pronaos were to be one step above the level of the outer porch. The setting marks incised on the stylobate to aid the masons in placing the lowest drums of the inner colonnade in correct position, together with the known height of the wall, allow the proportions of the projected colonnades to be calculated.[134] Both the inner and outer colonnades were to be 6.99 lower diameters in height. The height of the outer columns would have been 4.3 times the combined height of architrave

132. Cf. the line indicated for the original inner colonnade by the circular setting marks on the stylobate.

133. The easternmost preserved block of the stylobate had already been pried somewhat out of position when the Austrians uncovered it, as they observed (*S,I*, p. 51 and pl. 12). It had been pulled still further out of place and propped up on stones when we found it in 1948. When we cleaned and repaired the stylobate in 1956, we were able to see the dowel holes cut in the lower surface of the two easternmost blocks and the corresponding holes in the foundation blocks below them. But the dowels themselves had been removed in post-Austrian times, as the revealing presence of a modern horseshoe between the second and third blocks proved. The stone-robbers who removed the ninth, westernmost block of the stylobate and pried loose the two easternmost blocks evidently ripped out both dowels and lead casings, leaving only a few scraps of lead behind them.

Both the second and fourth preserved stylobate blocks from the east bear a graffito close to their southern edges: the former, a rough X; the latter, an A. The

fifth block, which had become cracked and broken through the intrusion of vegetation to the point of losing a large portion of its northern half after the Austrian excavation, was repaired in 1956 in the course of the anastelosis.

134. The ratios given here and elsewhere in the text are based on lower diameter measurements taken from center of flute to center of flute, since figures taken from arris to arris are less accurate, given their less perfect preservation. In so far as the extant outer colonnade is concerned, where three sizes of columns were used, the lower diameter of the central smallest pair is taken. Approximately 0.05 m. should be added to these figures if they are to be converted to arris-to-arris measurements.

The original inner colonnade had a lower diameter of 0.81 m. (cf. Pl. I). The height of the projected outer colonnade may be determined as 5.96 m. by adding the height of one step (ca. 0.30 m.) to the known height of the extant columns (5.66 m.). The unknown lower diameter of the projected outer colonnade may then be calculated as 0.85 m. (x:5.96 :: 0.81:5.66).

and frieze; the latter, 1.63 lower diameters of the same outer colonnade. These proportions draw the original project closest to the Temple of Athena at Pergamon, for which the comparable figures are 6.96, 4.3, and 1.6, and reveal the fact that the late-fourth-century building was characterized by exceedingly advanced early Hellenistic proportions.[135]

How far work on the pronaos had progressed when the construction of the Hieron was interrupted must remain uncertain. During the long period when the porch stood incomplete, its unfinished foundation must have been buried and the pronaos made accessible by a ramp. When work was resumed on the porch, two centuries later, the original project was modified. Although the outer colonnade and a pair of intermediate columns were retained, the inner colonnade was liberated from the confining antae and extended to the present prostyle row of six columns.[136] More important, the proportions of the façade were altered by shortening its columns and thereby converting its lighter, early Hellenistic façade into the firmer forms demanded by the classicistic taste of the day. The height of the revised columns now equaled 6.28 lower diameters and was 4.07 times the combined height of architrave and frieze, while the relationship between these two courses and the lower diameter of the column was 1.54. By thus reverting to the general proportions of Tegea, Nemea, Stratos, and the neighboring Altar Court, the builders of the second-century porch reshaped the original project in a fashion pleasing to contemporary eyes.[137]

These aesthetic changes were achieved and the façade was completed by raising the level of the porch one course to eliminate the difference in level originally planned between the outer part of the porch and the pronaos, hence lowering the outer colonnade by the height of one step; by shortening the anta walls in order to add two columns to the inner colonnade; by moving the line of that colonnade farther to the north; and, finally, by respacing the intermediate columns and centering them between the two colonnades.

More specifically, the foundation of the porch was completed by finishing the present second course on the eastern and the greater part of the northern sides[138] and adding another (the present top) course to the entire foundation. Addition of this course and, with it, elimi-

135. Cf. Richard Bohn, *Das Heiligtum der Athena Polias Nikephoros (Pergamon,* II), pp. 13 f., pl. 12. For further discussion of the proportions of the Hieron in comparison with other Greek buildings, see p. 214, below.

136. My suggestion, repeated in *Hesperia,* 19 (1950), 5, and 20 (1951), 23, that the executed forepart of the Hieron was a platform rather than a porch and supported six rather than fourteen columns was completely mistaken. At the time, I was unaware that the smaller coffers and beams belonged to the ceiling of the outer porch and, more important, of the number of drums used per column, as well as of the precise number of fragmentary drums preserved. Still more

recently, through a painful oversight, I have repeatedly published a schematic version of the restored plan, intended simply to convey its main features, in which the relationship between the lower two steps of the porch and the antae is shown incorrectly (e.g., *Pedimental Sculptures,* fig. 4; *Balkan Studies,* 5 [1964], fig. 2. It also appears in Vol. 4, pt. II, fig. 117). All versions of the restored plan previously reported or reproduced are superseded by Pl. CII of this volume.

137. For more detailed consideration of these relationships, see below, pp. 219 f.; Vol. 4, pt. II, pp. 76 ff.

138. If course two had ever actually served as course one, as had originally been planned, it would, of

nation of the original difference in level between the pronaos and the forepart of the porch (since both the projected and executed porches had a normal crepidoma of three steps) shortened the height of the front colonnade of the porch and the pair of lateral columns behind it. The foundation for the inner colonnade was dismantled, and the northern extremities of the lateral pronaos foundations were cut back to allow the rebuilt northern foundation to be bonded into them.[139] By moving that foundation to the north of its previous position and shortening the anta walls, space was gained for the addition of two lateral columns to the inner colonnade and for an appropriate interval between it and the antae. The antae now terminated 1.22 m. south of their original position; that is, they were shortened the length of one frieze block, as the original northerly extension of the eastern foundation of the pronaos proves. The shortened anta walls, in turn, slightly altered the length required for the lateral steps of the porch, forcing it to be lengthened ca. 0.46 m. at the southeastern, rear corner.[140] On this side, it was extended by the simple device of adding two blocks to the projecting end of the corner. Placed one above the other at the level of the upper two courses, they are easily recognizable (Pl. I; fig. 63). Unlike all the adjacent foundation blocks, the upper of the two is not a binder but runs parallel to the pronaos wall, thus widening it. Like the block beneath it, this upper block was not bonded into the pronaos wall.[141] The marble blocks of the inner stylobate were relaid on the rebuilt northern foundation of the pronaos.[142] Shuffled out of sequence, sloppily placed, and, toward the west, unattached to the foundation beneath them, they betray a degree of haste or negligence of procedure not found elsewhere in either the older or the contemporary parts of the marble superstructure. The no longer visible faces of these re-used blocks were now dressed to abut

---

necessity, have been level. But where the two sections of the foundation join near the northwestern corner, the eastern part of course two has been chipped down —proof that it was not laid in the original building period.

139. Several foundation blocks, both of the variety of soft yellow limestone used in the third course of the rebuilt northern foundation and of the normal type of porous limestone, as well as a narrow rectangular marble slab, were found lying in scattered positions at the bottom of the pronaos. Obviously, they were leftovers from the cutting back and rebuilding of the pronaos walls, which no one had bothered to remove.

140. The present higher ground level at the southwestern corner of the porch and the better preservation of that corner, where the southernmost euthynteria block was found *in situ,* make its foundation less easily examined. Inasmuch as it had origi-

nally been laid considerably farther to the south than the eastern foundation, it was unnecessary to extend it. Thus the present second course, the original top course of the completed western foundation, still extends 0.35 m. beyond the line of the present top course —a graphic illustration of the frequently mentioned differences in workmanship characteristic of the crews working on the eastern and western sides of the building.

141. Block 869, an unfinished euthynteria block found ca. 7 m. northeast of the northeast corner of the porch, probably comes from the original porch and was discarded when it was completed according to a revised plan.

142. Presumably, this stylobate had originally rested on a low euthynteria-like course of the variety used under analogous colonnades in antis as, for example, at Tegea (Dugas, pls. 9–11, 12–14). If so, it was removed at this time.

the marble pavement laid in the outer porch. Last of all, the lateral columns between the outer and inner colonnades, like the outer colonnade itself, were respaced the length of one frieze block to the north of their original position. Such activity alone can account for the singular features of the extant porch.

THE LATE HELLENISTIC PORCH

When the foundation for the original porch had been completed and amended by laying the unfinished portion of its top course and adding to it still another, the present top, course, the marble euthynteria was doweled to it.

EUTHYNTERIA (Pl. I; Fig. 65)

Only two blocks of this course are preserved, the southwestern corner euthynteria, which was found *in situ,* and its counterpart on the east.[143] The latter, too, has now been restored to its original position. These blocks indicate that, at the porch, this course was left unfinished, never having had its protective mantle chiseled away except at the joints and along the lower face, where technical procedure required it to be smooth. It was slightly less high than the euthynteria of the cella (0.256 m., as opposed to 0.28 m.) and two courses lower. A single setting line incised on its upper surface 0.07 m. within the line of the finished face determined the position of the lowest step above it. Like the euthynteria of the cella, it

65. Detail of the porch foundation, showing the
southwestern corner block of the euthynteria

143. *S,I,* pl. 12, shows the southwestern corner block *in situ,* together with two narrow standard blocks to its north. The latter had disappeared when we uncovered the porch in 1948. The southerly continuation of the foundation implied by this plate is actually nothing but the previously mentioned greater extension of the present second foundation course. The southeastern corner block which the Austrians found *in situ* (cf. ibid., pl. 13) was later removed from the foundation by the usual local robbers, but, fortunately, they abandoned it nearby.

was clamped to its porous backers with Π-clamps, as its individual blocks were connected to their neighbors by a single Π-clamp at each end.

STEPS AND PRONAOS STEREOBATE (Pls. XXX.2, CVII, CVIII)

Only one fragmentary block is preserved of the three steps of which the crepidoma was composed (Pl. XXX.2).[144] But their essential character and dimensions may be reconstructed from their porous backers and from the stereobate. For stylobate and stereobate were on the same level, proof that the former, too, was enlivened with two recesses. On the analogy of such a related and generally contemporary building as Temple A at Kos, we have assumed that the two lower steps were similarly dressed.[145] The height of the stylobate, therefore, was determined by the stereobate, but the two lower steps were slightly less high (0.28 m., as opposed to 0.295 m.). The tread in each case was 0.365 m. Each block was doweled to the course below by a pair of dowels at one end, one set in the step or euthynteria beneath it, the other in its porous backer. The blocks of a given course were linked to the adjacent blocks by a single Π-clamp at each end, and to their porous backers by a pair of Π-clamps at the rear of each block. As usual, their joints fell approximately over the center of the course below.

Two blocks previously used or prepared for use as steps in the original porch were recut and placed below the western anta (Pl. IV).[146] One, block 432, had served as a corner block and retains traces of its once visible lateral face; the other, block 387, although still usable, had been damaged on its bottom, which was recut to provide a socket for a specially-prepared interlocking block next to it. They give a hint of the degree to which the early Hellenistic building had been completed when work on the porch was interrupted.

FLOOR (Pls. I, II.1; Figs. 64, 66)

The forepart of the porch was paved with marble slabs 0.19 m. thick. None is preserved, but their presence may be deduced from the front faces of the six extant blocks of the inner stylobate that were re-used in correct position and dressed to abut marble. The underpavement of this portion of the porch was composed of narrow rails of the same porous limestone used throughout the foundation, set roughly at a right angle to the porous backers of the second step, on which the outer stylobate rested. These backers were equipped at the rear with an upstand against which the rear face of the higher outer stylobate blocks fitted; the inner stylobate, too, rested on a course provided with a similar upstand (cf. Pls. I, II.1).

144. Block 412, found close to the northern foundation.

145. *Kos*, I, 7, pl. 4, no. 4. For discussion of our partial reconstruction of the porch in 1956, see text II, pp. 132 ff.

146. Both were found northwest of the northwestern corner of the porch.

66. Detail of the pronaos after refilling in 1951, showing part of the
northern foundation and inner
stylobate, seen from the south

The intervals between the rails set within this framing upstand were filled with blocks of soft yellow limestone, which, like the rails themselves, were supported by a packing of field stones and earth.[147] Obviously, the marble pavement slabs were set from center to center of the parallel rails.

The roughly-picked rear faces of the same inner stylobate blocks, together with their projecting bosses, prove with equal certainty that the floor of the inner pronaos can never have been paved with marble. Inasmuch as an exceptional amount of chips and small frag-

147. Only one regular block of this easily de-
stroyed material was *in situ* when we re-excavated the porch, but many fragments and crumbled traces of it were still visible. The interstices between the lime-stone rails were explored to the level of their under-surfaces.

Neither the limestone foundation of the porch nor the underpavement described above at any time re-sembled their appearance in *S,I,* pls. 11, 12, which give a totally false picture of their character. They bear witness to the fact that the Austrian excavation was a sounding rather than a full exploration, especially in so far as all non-marble portions of the building were concerned. Hence, the size and shape of individual

foundation or underpavement blocks were fabricated from field notes over a distant drawing board; the rails, structurally the most significant and typical element of the underpavement, were completely omitted. Neither plate should be considered a faithful portrayal or re-liable document of the appearance of the Hieron in the nineteenth century, despite their giving the calculated impression of being precisely that; nor should either be regarded as an accurate indication of areas which were fully explored at the time, as they are explicitly said to have been (ibid., p. 51). The ease with which individual features of the foundation could be over-looked will be apparent to anyone examining ibid., pl. 13, a photograph of the northeastern corner of the porch which was construed to show it fully cleaned.

67. Capital 43

ments of marble was observed on top of the pronaos fill, it seems reasonable to assume that this floor was coated with a variety of terrazzo consisting of chips and splinters of marble set in a bedding of marble stucco.[148]

COLUMNS (Pls. LXIII, LXIV, XCVII; Figs. 67, 68, 443–447)

Thirty-three of the sixty-four preserved drums or fragments of drums are sufficiently intact to allow the prostyle Doric porch of the Hieron to be reconstructed with exactitude.[149] It consisted of two rows of six columns, separated from each other by a single intermediate column on each side of the porch. Each column was composed of four drums which, together with the capital, gave it a height of 5.66 m.; each shaft had twenty flutes.[150] Drums and capitals alike were lifted into position by a lewis inserted in a carefully prepared slit off center of the centrally-placed dowel hole and were doweled into position without the use of

148. Theoretically, the pronaos floor could as well have been covered with a mosaic pavement. But of the enormous number of tesserae or pebbles that would have been required in a mosaic pavement, not a single one was found. To be sure, they could have been present in the nineteenth century and overlooked. But it seems far more likely that our predecessors would not have observed chips or splinters of marble which would have been difficult, if not impossible, to distinguish from fragments of shattered blocks. No portion of such a terrazzo floor could have survived the shattering impact of the heavy beams and coffers of the marble ceiling, as well as the blocks of the door wall and timbers of the roof that crashed upon it in late antiquity.

149. That is, two of their three major dimensions (height and upper and lower diameters) may be measured with reasonable accuracy, in spite of weathering.

150. Hauser (*S,I,* pp. 72 ff.), working, evidently, with only eight specific drums, considered the possibility of a four-drum column but rejected it as producing too classical an effect for the Hellenistic proportions of the entablature. His five-drum reconstruction was frankly hypothetical (cf., too, pp. 62 ff., fig. 21, and pls. 42, 43).

68. Detail of the inner stylobate

lead channels (Pls. LXIII, LXIV). The central intercolumniation was 2.39 m. wide, the outer and lateral intercolumniations contracting to 2.18 m.

Although the individual drums may be said to average 1.31 m. in height, actually they range from 1.286 to 1.352 m., a fact which proved of prime importance in our re-erection of five columns. Coupled with the additional fact that the fourteen columns were graded into three sizes, this variation in height allowed the blocks of a given column to be reassembled with absolute certainty.[151] For the two central columns have an upper diameter of 0.722–3 m. and an average lower diameter of 0.895 m., while the shafts of the two corner columns taper from 0.753 to 0.918 m., and the remaining pair, as well as the two intermediate lateral columns, are ever so slightly smaller than the outermost pair. They follow good classical practice in having entasis. The central columns are 6.32 lower diameters high, measured from center of flute to center of flute, or 6.28 from arris to arris.

Seven of the original capitals are preserved.[152] They, too, fall into essentially two sizes, the larger of which rested on the corner shafts and those adjacent to them. They show a

151. For further discussion of the columns and specific description of the anastelosis undertaken in 1956, see text II, pp. 132 ff.; above, pp. 28 ff.

152. 28 B, 405, and 43 have been replaced, respectively, on the first, second, and third shafts to the west of the corner column in the anastelosis. 441 lies on the eastern foundation of the cella; 862, which was partially recut in post-antique times, may be found north of the building. Two capitals, one from the northeastern corner column, 346 A 1, and a second fragment, 346 A 2, were taken to Vienna. The former was returned to Samothrace in 1956 with the kind permission of the Austrian government and replaced in its original position on the northeastern corner column. Cf. below, nn. 166, 168. This corner capital was illustrated in *S,I*, pl. 22, fig. II, and correctly shown to lack a lewis hole. Figure I on this plate is our No. 405.

straight, oblique echinus slightly set back from the face of the abacus and set off from the fluting beneath by four annuli (Pls. LXIV, XCVII; figs. 67, 443). Including those terminal rings, the echinus is approximately two-thirds the height of the abacus. Two scamilli, a square one on the upper surface and a round one on the lower, set off each capital from both the architrave above and the top drum below. The former prevented the weight of the architrave from falling on the overhanging edge of the abacus; the latter must have been designed to protect the already executed fluting on the lower portion of the capital, when it was placed on the as yet unfluted upper drum. This lower scamillus also provided a field on which radii were incised to indicate the precise position and spacing of the arrises. Four intermediate radii, placed, as it were, at the cardinal points of the capital, served to align it with four similarly-placed setting marks on the stylobate below (fig. 68). On both the capital and the better preserved blocks of the stylobate, north-south is indicated by a double, east-west by a single, line. These rarely preserved or visible features of Greek stonecutting are recorded in Pl. LXIV, where they appear within a double-lined square presumably incised in order to facilitate correct calculation of the radii.[153]

In all probability, the diameters of the inner colonnade repeated those of the outer, once the originally intended difference in level between them had been eliminated. If so, the circles inscribed on the inner stylobate to guide the workmen responsible for placing the shafts of the projected columns were ignored when the stylobate was relaid, and these smaller columns, having a lower diameter of 0.81 m., were replaced. The suggestion that these circles —by no means ever-present or essential—were disregarded when the porch was at length completed is supported by the character of the preserved drums, as well as by the negligence with which the inner stylobate was relaid. For none of the large proportion of drums extant from the fifty-six required for the fourteen columns of the porch combines an appropriate taper with an upper or lower diameter of any of the sizes that would have been required in the original colonnade. It is doubtful whether the inner columns of the projected porch were ever fully erected, although it is conceivable, given the guide lines incised for them, that the lowest drums were actually placed on the stylobate prepared for them. Indeed, the weathering of the stylobate, which is more severe at the north than at the south, seems to imply this conclusion. As long as the porch remained roofless, the surface of the stylobate would weather in precisely this fashion, whereas later, when it had been roofed, this protected area would not have been subject to weathering. Hence, no telltale traces of larger columns would remain. But even had they been set up, they would no longer have been usable, once they had been dismantled and their drums pried apart. Inasmuch as it would have been necessary, in any

153. Lightly incised lines indicative of the four cardinal points and the position of the arrises occur on Doric capitals from the Temple of Athena Alea at Tegea (Dugas, p. 20 and pl. 36) and the lower story of the stoa in the precinct of Athena at Pergamon (*Pergamon*, II, 35 and pl. 22).

case, to replace them, there would have been no advantage or logic in retaining and duplicating their smaller dimensions in the interior of the modified porch. Therefore, inner and outer colonnades have been given identical diameters in the restored plan (Pl. CII), a solution in full accord with the extensive evidence of the preserved drums.[154]

ANTA WALLS (Pls. V.1, LXV–LXVIII)

Thirteen blocks of the antae and anta walls are known, twelve in Samothrace and one, a fragmentary capital, in Vienna.[155] They include the essential varieties of which the antae were composed.

The orthodox pilasters in which the anta walls terminated reiterated the forms of the rear corner pilasters and were wider on their inner than on their outer faces.[156] Presumably, their capitals were framed on each side by binders of the type adjacent to the rear pilasters, whose drafted margins have been adjusted to the overlapping capitals. Below the level of the capitals, the antae were built up of seven alternatingly high and low courses (Pls. CV, CVII). Three of the four high blocks of which they were constructed were equated in height and position with the three standard superimposed pairs of stretchers in the wall behind and abutting them (cf. Pl. LXV).[157] Like the column drums, they were lifted into place by means of a lewis. The fourth block was equivalent in height to the abutting orthostate. Two of the three low courses present in each pilaster not only were equivalent in height and position to the standard binders of the wall but were actually one with them, each double-faced block forming at once part of the smoothly-dressed, three-sided pilaster and part of the drafted masonry of the adjacent wall (Pl. LXVI.1).[158] The third binder lacked such drafting, since it united a portion of the pilaster with an adjacent section of the equally smoothly-dressed string course.[159]

The remaining binders of the anta walls were comparable, for the most part, to the

154. The alternative solution, that the inner colonnade consisted of smaller columns in both periods (whether they were leftovers from the projected porch or identical replacements), is ruled out both by the improbability that no single drum of these six columns would have been preserved and by the far more cogent argument that, under these circumstances, virtually no drum of the remaining eight columns would be missing today—a situation that clearly does not prevail, since among the preserved drums there are some that cannot be superimposed upon each other.

155. The capital in Vienna is numbered 346 E 2. It is too ill preserved to allow attribution to one rather than the other anta.

156. The anta capital and foot illustrated in *S,I*, pl. 43, were hypothetical, as Hauser stated, ibid., p. 74. The former is a simplification of the block that he mis-

interpreted as the epikranitis of the pronaos (which actually was the lintel of the main door); the latter is a repetition of the base profile of the main threshold, which he assumed continued along the pronaos walls. The coursing of the anta in this plate is equally and admittedly hypothetical. There is no need to assume the existence of an anta foot in such a Doric building. Given the additional fact that no trace of one has been found, we have eliminated this unnecessary member from the antae.

157. Two such blocks are partially preserved: 14, from the eastern anta, and 472, from the western.

158. Only a single precious fragment of one such block, 474, is preserved.

159. Since only two such blocks ever existed, one in each anta, it is not surprising that they are no longer extant.

standard binders used in the cella walls, except for the characteristic feature of being double-faced—that is, of being dressed with drafted margins on front and back, inasmuch as both faces were exposed (Pls. LXVI.2, LXVII). Evidently, occasional blocks of abnormal length were again used in the anta walls, as in the vicinity of the rear pilasters and the doors. One such fragmentary block is of special interest in that it exhibits a lewis hole (Pl. LXVI.2),[160] a cutting unknown on any of the hundreds of blocks of the original cella, regardless of their size or position. Conceivably, a lewis would have been used to lift drums and high anta blocks into position in the early Hellenistic building, had it been completed. But no trace of this technical device, employed repeatedly in placing other varieties of blocks in the later porch, is to be found in the fabric of the late-fourth-century cella.

The fact that the walls of the pronaos were identical in appearance with the exterior walls of the cella meant that the high courses of the anta walls had either to be designed as double-faced binding blocks or to be constructed of two contiguous marble blocks—one forming the inner, the other the outer, face—or to be built of three blocks, the outer two separated by a filler. That the latter two techniques were used, rather than the first, is evident both from the absence of double-faced binding blocks and the existence of certain atypical stretchers. Some may be distinguished from the standard stretchers of the cella wall because they are both thicker and obliquely cut at one end to compensate for the greater width of the inner than of the outer anta pilaster (cf. 518 and the similarly cut binder 407, Pls. LXVIII, LXVI.2).[161] They were placed back to back. Others, like 811 (Pl. V.1), are thinner at one end, having been partially separated from their marble backers by a thin filler.[162] The latter were inserted between the two faces of the wall after the marble stretchers had been doweled to the binding course below. This procedure is confirmed by binder 410 (Pl. LXVII.1), for lead can have been poured in the connecting channels leading to two of its dowel holes only if an interval existed between the marble stretchers doweled to its surface at this point.

160. The two other preserved binders, 410 and 496, lack this feature of 407 (Pl. LXVI.2).

161. Block 437, a stretcher having the abnormal length of 1.276 m. and lacking the customary Π-clamp on one end, obviously belonged to this group, too. Its provenance suggests that it abutted the pilaster of the western anta on its external face.

162. Three additional stretchers, 809, 810, and 827, have been partially cut back on their rear faces; blocks 809–811, at least, were left with only one usable swallow-tail clamp hole. The thinner, cut-back portion of their backs has been carefully smoothed, evidently to allow them to be backed by marble at this point. It seems likely that these otherwise inexplicable blocks were re-used (from the original anta walls) in the completed porch. If so, they might well have required alteration, like the stereobate blocks mentioned on p. 94, and the larger interval between them and the antithetical marble blocks behind them could have been filled by a thin marble backer, rather than by the customary porous limestone. Such an explanation is not implausible, since extra marble blocks or fragments were at hand from the originally longer antae, and Thasian marble is far more easily and accurately cut than the hard Samothracian porous limestone. The provenance and character of block 747 suggest that it may have been such an invisible block.

The use of intermediate fillers between the inner and outer marble faces of the anta walls in the Hieron also occurs in Samothrace in the Arsinoeion, where the two marble faces of the wall were separated from each other by porous blocks.

In their revised, shortened form, the anta walls were 2.356 m. long and separated from the outermost columns of the inner colonnade by an interval of 1.48 m. In width and taper, the antae were comparable to the corner columns of the outer colonnade, if not absolutely identical with them.[163]

OUTER AND INNER COLUMNAR ARCHITRAVE (Pls. LXIX–LXXI; Figs. 69 A, 181)

Of necessity, the entablature of the late Hellenistic porch repeated the forms of the early Hellenistic architrave, frieze, and geisa.[164] Eleven blocks were required for the outer columnar architrave—five for the façade, three for each side. Each was adjusted in length to the intercolumniation beneath it. Apart from the two corner blocks and the single block abutting each of these corner blocks on the façade, they bore a full regula at the center and a half-regula at each end. The corner blocks were provided with the required pair of full regulae at the exposed corner, with a third full regula at the center and a half-regula at their southerly ends, for they ran from the corner back to the intermediate columns on each side of the porch. Thus, the block adjacent to each corner block on the façade needed only one half-regula at its opposite end, in addition to its standard, centrally-placed full regula. Four of these outer columnar architrave blocks are known: the long block required for the central intercolumniation (Pl. LXIX) and a fragmentary block adjacent to it in Samothrace;[165] the equally fragmentary northwestern corner block in Vienna (fig. 69 A); and a last, now missing fragment recorded by the Austrians.[166]

163. They taper from 0.938 m. at the bottom to 0.87 m. at the capital, while the largest columns, measured now from arris to arris, have lower and upper diameters of 0.968 m. and 0.803 m., respectively.

164. Only information supplementary to the previous discussion of the entablature of the cella will be given in the following pages.

165. Blocks 406 and 444. The former, which was unknown to our predecessors, was sufficiently well preserved to be mended and replaced in its original position over the central intercolumniation in 1956 (cf. text II, p. 134). It affords conclusive proof that the Hieron bore no dedicatory inscription. Hence Antoine Salač' proposal ("Inscriptions inédites de Samothrace, I," BCH, 49 [1925], 245–53; repeated in slightly modified form, "La dédicace du nouveau temple des grands dieux à Samothrace," ibid., 70 [1946], 537–39) that a fragmentary inscribed block found near the northwest corner of the Altar Court should be ascribed to an otherwise hypothetical inscription on the architrave of the "New Temple" is invalid. Cf. above, pp. 13 ff. For discussion of this block, which ac-

tually forms part of the dedicatory inscription of the Altar Court, see Vols. 2, pt. I, pp. 41 ff.; 4, pt. II, pp. 120 ff. Block 720, a long but broken block, may conceivably have belonged to the columnar architrave, but its lower surface is too damaged to allow it to be assigned such a position with certainty.

166. The corner block is 346 B (S,I, pl. 23, fig. 1; fig. II on this plate has evidently been destroyed). No fully preserved blocks were found by the Austrians. Hauser reported (ibid., pp. 64 f.) that this block, together with the corner frieze and geison blocks in Vienna (346 C and 346 D 1), came from the northeastern corner of the building. But here, as in reconstructing the so-called southeastern corner of the cella, he either confused his notes or made a slip of the pen (cf. above, n. 33). For the Vienna corner geison block can have come only from the northwestern corner of the façade, as the junction of its raking and horizontal geisa proves (below, n. 180). The corner frieze and architrave blocks fit beneath it: the latter follows the system of the geison, stretching from corner to intermediate lateral column rather than resting on two of the

Like the blocks of the rear wall architrave, those on the façade were made 0.64 m. high to provide a transition between the slightly lower blocks on the eastern side of the building and the somewhat higher blocks on its western side.[167] They were lifted into position with the aid of a lewis; doweled onto the capitals beneath them by a single dowel near each end; and clamped to the adjacent outer architrave blocks by a single Π-clamp at each end, and to the inner architrave blocks at their rear by another pair of Π-clamps.[168] Their exposed lower faces were smoothly finished.

The inner columnar architrave, again, repeated the forms established in the pronaos by the inner wall architrave. It not only served as a backer for the entire outer columnar architrave, but also was placed back to back over the inner colonnade of the porch. Seven of its blocks are wholly or partially preserved in Samothrace, including the backer for the outer architrave block over the central intercolumniation of the porch (Pl. LXX).[169] Once more, these blocks were adjusted to the dimensions of the intercolumniations and the outer architrave. For the most part, their system of dowels and clamps was identical with that of the outer architrave,[170] and, like it, they were smoothly dressed to be visible from below. The twelve blocks having one end placed over one of the outer columns of the two colonnades were mitered at that end, as both fragment 385 (Pl. XLIII.3) and the dowel and pry holes on the upper surface of corner capital 346 A 1 indicate.

---

façade columns; the former, conversely, is longer on its façade face than on the short lateral face, which consists simply of the triglyph. In Hauser's reconstruction of the façade (*S,I,* pls. 33, 42, 43), the jointing of these courses is incorrect and follows no logical system based on the extant blocks. (The same system of coursing occurs in the entablature of the Temple of Athena at Lindos. Cf. *Lindos,* III, pt. 1, pp. 105, 150 f., fig. IV, 28, 29.)

Once these corner blocks are placed in proper position on the western side of the façade, a further important point can be established, namely, that the corner capital taken to Vienna, 346 A 1, for which no specific provenance was given, must have belonged to the northeastern corner column of the porch, since it cannot be fitted under the Vienna corner architrave, as examination of the dowel holes on the pertinent surfaces of these two blocks proves. Hence, it indubitably belonged to the corner to which it is now restored.

For reference to other instances in which Conze or Hauser confused the terms "east" and "west," see text II, pp. 102 f., n. 121, and p. 116; and note in *S,II,* p. 13, still another unequivocal instance of such confusion: reference to a foundation at the *south*east corner

of the "New Temple" instead of the *north*east, since allusion is made to the structure now called the Temenos, and there is, in any case, no foundation whatsoever at the southeast corner of the Hieron.

167. Above, p. 70.

168. Only the corner blocks were at times doweled to the corner capitals by more than one dowel, to judge from the upper surface of corner capital 346 A 1. Here two obliquely-placed dowel holes reflect the mitered ends of the two inner architrave blocks that rested on it and the three remaining holes related to the two outer architrave blocks that met over it.

169. Block 356, which was replaced in its original position in 1956 (cf. text II, p. 134). Block 18, too, is almost fully preserved, if sorely battered. The remaining fragments are incomplete: 15, 53, 66, 374, and 385. Cf. above, n. 86. Block 356 was known to the Austrians and illustrated in *S,I,* pls. 24; 69, fig. V. See also ibid., pp. 64 f.

170. Apart from the fact that the two fully preserved blocks were doweled to only one of the two capitals on which they rested. They, too, were lowered into position with the aid of a lewis.

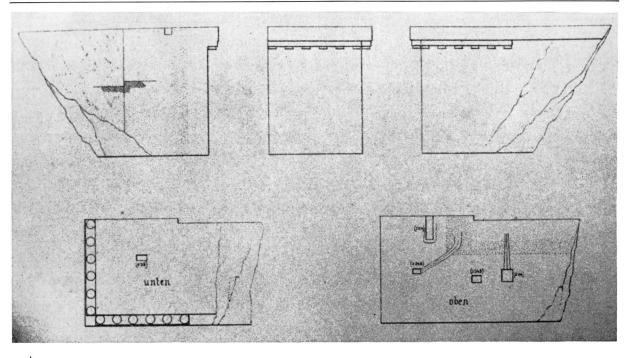

A

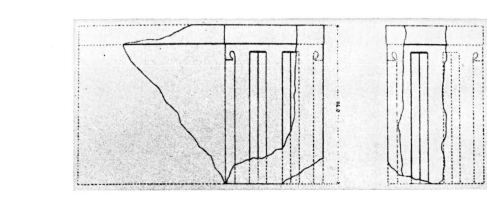

B

69. Fragmentary northwestern corner entablature blocks, after Hauser. A. Architrave. B. Frieze

FRIEZE AND LATERAL GEISON (Fig. 69 B)

Since neither the blocks of the porch frieze nor those of its lateral geisa exhibit any feature whereby they might be distinguished from the similar blocks of the cella, none of the frieze or lateral geison blocks extant in Samothrace may be attributed to the porch with absolute certainty.[171] However, both the sadly damaged northwestern corner frieze block and a second block reputedly found north of the building were recovered by the Austrians (fig. 69 B).[172] The former unites a metope at the left with the required pair of triglyphs at the

171. Not a single frieze block was found over or north of the porch. A very few fragments or damaged blocks of the lateral geisa were found considerably to the north of the building. But they yield no additional

information, because of their poor state of preservation.

172. The former, 346 C, is in Vienna. It was illustrated in *S,I*, pl. 25, fig. I, and pl. 69, fig. VI, along

right, its longer side having been visible on the façade.[173] The latter, too, combined a metope at the left with a triglyph at the right. But other combinations of triglyph and metope must have existed on the façade, as at the rear of the cella, to obviate joint falling over joint at the northeastern corner of the porch. Here, continuous use of one standard block of the type recovered by the Austrians would have created such a relationship between frieze and architrave, if the eastern corner frieze block was identical in form with the western. Doweled to the outer columnar architrave and clamped to their porous backers in the normal fashion, the frieze blocks constituted one of three contiguous sets of blocks resting on the porch architraves, which also supported the outer marble beams of the coffered ceiling.

LATERAL SIMA AND TILING (Pl. LXXII.1, 2)

The blocks of the lateral sima of the porch are immediately recognizable, unlike those of the geison and frieze beneath them, because the builders of the late Hellenistic porch modified the design of the cella sima, evidently with the intention of increasing the speed with which rain drained off the roof. Although they retain the basic character of the earlier sima blocks, the four examples known from the porch differ from the former in several respects (cf. Pls. LV, LXXII.1, 2).[174] No longer are they provided with a ledge at the rear on which to rest the boarding; on the contrary, the boarding was here nailed to purlins and abutted the rear face of each block which was, again, notched to receive the horizontal beams of the roof.[175] The upper surface of each block is equipped with three bosses, the central one polygonal in section and higher than the flat, squarish elevation cut at both of its rear corners. Furthermore, the interval between these raised surfaces is roughly picked and slightly hollowed. If the two lowest terracotta stroters placed on each block were set in hydraulic stucco poured into these depressions and fitted between and against the three bosses, in addition to being set within its lateral lips, they would have been held in place even more rigidly than previously, as a result of having been wedged into position and set in stucco. The rear lip present on the sima blocks of the cella, which would have impeded this

with the latter (pl. 25, fig. II), which has since disappeared, and is discussed on p. 65. See above, n. 166, for correction of Hauser's statement regarding the provenance of this block. 346 D 2, a small fragment of a geison block, cannot be attributed to a specific location in the building.

173. Cf. above, n. 166.

174. Blocks 359, 392, 394, and 398. Block 392 was also recorded by the Austrians (*S,I*, pp. 66 f., 72, and pl. 27, fig. I; cf. also pls. 34, 43). They assumed that it was typical of the standard sima blocks of the building, evidently not having found or observed the normal variety. The gutter had been broken off all

the examples known to them, but they recovered enough fragments to reconstruct it correctly. Cf. ibid., p. 28, and pls. 29; 30, fig. II; 70, fig. II. Apart from waterspouts, two fragments of the gutter were taken to Vienna. The larger one is the upper piece illustrated ibid., pl. 29. For further discussion of the ornamental gutters, see below, pp. 170 ff.

175. Block 398, illustrated on Pl. LXXII.1, is atypical of this group of sima blocks in that it lacks one of the lateral notches cut to receive these horizontal beams; i.e., it was placed over the southwestern corner of the pronaos, where no such beam existed, as its provenance confirms.

procedure, has, in fact, been removed. As a result, the crucial joint between each marble block and the timbers behind it was protected by the stucco from any water that might back up beneath the stroters in the course of a torrential rain. Finally, each block was hollowed directly behind the lion's-head spout to enable it to drain more quickly on such occasions.

These alterations in the original design of the cella sima suggest that the heavy rains of Samothrace had not always drained off the roof quickly enough, especially when they were attended by its proverbially strong winds; they imply, on the contrary, that water had been forced back under the lowest stroters and had seeped into the all-important timbers of the roof at their most vulnerable point. Whether the revised porch sima actually proved more satisfactory than its predecessor must remain uncertain.

Apart from requiring a change in the form of the lowest tier of stroters, this modification of the sima in no way affected the essential scheme of the tiling. The other tiers of tiles over the porch remained identical in size and shape with those of the cella. And, given the fact that the lowest intermediate kalypter now rested on a polygonal boss prepared to receive it, here, too, standard kalypters were employed, rather than the specially-prepared lowest intermediate kalypters of the cella, which differed from all others in having a closed face. But the lowest stroters must have been radically changed to adjust them to the more complicated field within which they were now placed and to allow the joints of neighboring tiles to be covered by the lowest terracotta kalypters, wherever they were contiguous. We do not venture to speculate on the precise form of this unorthodox tile.[176]

Only one fragmentary marble antefix was found in our excavation of the porch and its vicinity.[177] Damaged though it is, it is sufficiently preserved to indicate that it was identical in type and execution with several complete examples in Vienna (figs. 178, 180). Although it cannot be established with certainty that these antefixes date from the period when the porch was constructed rather than from one of the repairs to which the building was later subjected, they show that the porch antefixes repeat the basic type of the cella antefix but differ from it in detail and quality of workmanship. So, too, the tendrils and water-

176. Hauser (*S,I*, p. 67) reported that no whole or recognizable fragmentary tiles were found in the Austrian excavation apart from small bits, partly of marble, partly of clay. We found no trace of any marble stroter belonging to the Hieron. But the nearby Propylon did have marble stroters, a fact that probably accounts for the marble fragments mentioned by Hauser.

177. 51.219, found among a mass of fallen blocks at the northwest corner of the building. Presumably, some of the antefixes in Vienna came from the area of the porch, but no specific provenance is available for

them. For additional discussion of the antefixes, see pp. 226 ff., below. The example illustrated in *S,I*, pl. 31, fig. 1, is described in the text (p. 67) as the sole fully preserved example found. It is not in Vienna, nor has any antefix with a similar vertical rear end ever been recovered in our excavation. Invariably, their rear ends were shaped to allow the first terracotta kalypter to rest on them, as the example illustrated in our fig. 56 indicates. One wonders whether the atypical piece drawn by Hauser ever existed and suspects that it may have been incorrectly restored on the basis of incomplete information.

spouts of the ornamental sima reiterated the patterns of the cella gutter. But the bold, coarse workmanship of several lion's heads in Vienna differs from the firm, refined execution of the cella lions and betrays their later date.[178] Hence, on the exterior, the porch roof, like the entablature beneath it, preserved the basic visual forms of the early Hellenistic cella in spite of introducing minor variations. On the interior, however, its timbers appear to have been laid according to a wholly different system.[179]

PEDIMENT (Pls. LII.1, LXXII.3, LXXIII.1, 2, LXXIV.1, LXXV.2, XCVIII.2, 3, 6, 7, CV, CVIII; Figs. 70, 172)

The porch pediment repeated the ornamental forms and doubtless, too, the structural system of the rear pediment. Eleven of its blocks are known, in addition to numerous small fragments of the raking sima. Although only eight are still extant, they include such key elements as the northwestern corner geison block in Vienna, one of the two triangular blocks from the northeastern side of the tympanum in Samothrace, and six additional blocks recovered there: the central binder of the tympanum; a fragment of one of the blocks adjacent to it; two blocks of the raking, and two of the horizontal, geison.

The broken corner geison block [180] in Vienna differs from its counterparts at the south primarily in containing a rectangular bedding on its upper surface to enable the corner sima block, which in turn supported the lateral akroterion, to be more securely moored to it. At the south, where akroterial figures may not have been contemplated when the cella was built, this provision was not made.

The two preserved blocks of the horizontal geison yield valuable information regarding the installation of the pedimental sculptures (Pl. LXXIII.1, 2).[181] Apart from their upper surfaces, they are in every technical respect identical with the blocks of the lateral geison. But the forepart of their upper surfaces has been smoothly dressed to receive the low floor on which the pedimental sculptures stood, while the less finely-finished rear portions were

---

178. Specifically, 346 K 1, 2, and possibly 4. Inasmuch as the Austrians seem to have known only the porch sima blocks, it is probable that several of the lion's heads in Vienna were broken parts of those same fragmentary blocks, which in every instance are described as having lacked their gutters. Cf. n. 174, above. For discussion of the style and execution of the lion's-head waterspouts of both cella and porch, see below, pp. 174 ff., 223 ff.

179. Below, pp. 116 f.

180. It will be recalled that this block, 346 D 1, belonged to the northwestern corner, rather than the northeastern, as Hauser mistakenly stated (see above, n. 166). His drawing of this block (*S,I,* pl. 26, fig. i) is equally and incomprehensibly faulty, since the plan purportedly of the upper surface actually shows certain of its features superimposed on the contour of its

lower surface. The prime feature indicated—the large cutting referred to above—is not square but rectangular, measuring 0.575 m. on the side of the building and 0.19 m. along the front. Finally, the section is inaccurate, reversed, and totally misleading in regard to that cutting. Only the view of the lower surface of this block in fig. i should be heeded. For discussion of the akroterial and pedimental sculptures of the Hieron, see below, pp. 253 ff.

181. Blocks 783 and 784, found immediately to the east of the northeast corner of the porch. Presumably the block drawn by Hauser, *S,I,* pl. 26, fig. ii, was another such member of the horizontal geison of the pediment, given his specific reference to it on p. 65. Unfortunately, as far as discussion of the pedimental floor is concerned, he drew only its lower face.

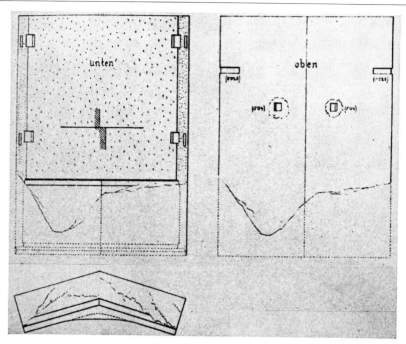

70. Ridge block of raking geison, after Hauser

evidently covered by porous slabs of identical height that were pried but not doweled into position. For the conventional dowel and pry holes on the foreparts of the horizontal geison imply the attachment of a course which, given its location, can only have been such a floor introduced within the gable to provide the pedimental sculptures with a slight elevation above the line and level of the horizontal geison. Such an elevation would have been desirable, since, for the most part, these sculptures were not provided with bases. Hence, whether the figures sit or recline, their draperies fall down to their lower edges, which would, thus, have been invisible had they been placed directly on the horizontal geison. The marble slabs of the pedimental floor, like their porous backers, have entirely disappeared; but, considering the height of the preserved figures, the floor may be estimated as having been ca. 0.05 m. high. Its depth, 0.635 m., considerably exceeded the depth available for sculptures in the finished pediment, inasmuch as the heavy binders, of which the lower course of the tympanum wall was largely built, rested partly on the rear portion of this marble floor, partly on its porous backing—an overlap that may have been devised in an effort to moor and stabilize the thin flooring beneath the sculptures standing on the most fragile part of the horizontal geison, its overhang (cf. the section, Pl. CV).

Although the preserved blocks of the horizontal geison have lost their crown and mutules, the extant block of the raking geison fortunately retains both a full section of its overhang and a telltale setting line on its undersurface that allow the depth of the pediment to be calculated accurately as ca. 0.47 m. (Pl. LII.1).[182] Both the ovolo corona and the hawk's beak

182. Block 895, measuring 1.031 m. in length. A second fragmentary block of this type, 428, is extant in Samothrace, but the fully preserved example recorded by Hauser (ibid., pl. 26, fig. IV, and pl. 70, fig. I) has disappeared. The preserved blocks were both found to the north of the façade.

of its crown present slight variations on the raking moldings of the corner blocks, while its soffit differs more markedly, terminating in a sloping rather than a vertical base fascia (Pl. XCVIII.2, 3). Its canonical lack of mutules has determined the altered contour of its overhang. To judge by this sole fully preserved example, the raking geison was composed of shorter blocks than the standard lengths employed elsewhere in the building. They were clamped to each other by a pair of Π-clamps at each end and doweled to the tympanum blocks beneath them by a pair of dowels at one end, one dowel connecting each block with the outer marble face of the upper course of the tympanum, the other attaching it to the porous backer of that block. For the small ridge block of the raking geison, recorded by our predecessors but evidently destroyed after their departure (fig. 70),[183] bears witness to the use of two faces for the upper course of the tympanum, the outer one thin, the inner thick, as the plan and section of its lower side indicate. This unique block was evidently doweled to the two blocks beneath it by a pair of dowels on each side.

The character of the tympanum wall is attested not only by this precious lost block but also by four others: two triangular blocks, 430 (Pl. LXXII.3) and a second, now lost, example documented by our predecessors; and 400 and 671, two of the at least five binding blocks placed in the lower course of that wall (Pls. LXXIV.1, LXXV.2).[184] Although block 400 is only partially preserved, its approximate length (1.96 m.) may be calculated from the position of the lewis hole on its upper surface. That same surface reveals the fact that two thin marble blocks were doweled over the forepart of its preserved right end and backed by a thick, doubtless porous, block doweled to the surface behind them. If a similar triad of dowel holes occurred on the now broken left end of this block, it must have been the central of the five binders of which the lower course of the wall was constructed; that is, it must have supported the thin outer marble block beneath the ridge geison block, one end of each of

183. Ibid., pl. 26, fig. III.

184. Block 430 was found lying slightly to the east of the corner of the building to which it belonged. It may well have been known to Hauser, who speaks (ibid., p. 66) of additional half-preserved *examples* apart from the one totally preserved piece he drew (pl. 27, fig. II), which has now vanished. It was 1.18 m. long, the length to which block 430 and the other two missing pieces required in the tympanum should be restored. Evidently the triangular blocks of the tympanum varied in thickness. Block 430 has a thickness of 0.215 m., a dimension compatible with that required for the central block over the single preserved binder from the lower course, block 400. But the lost Austrian piece was 0.39 m. thick.

The fact that Hauser referred to more than one such broken piece provides further confirmation of the pedimental system reconstructed in Pls. CVIII, CIX.

It also suggests that he discarded the evidence of these additional fragments in his own restoration of the tympanum (ibid., pl. 42); for, inasmuch as he mentioned them in the context of the façade, he cannot have attributed them to the rear pediment. In any case, his restoration must be abandoned.

The binder, block 400, was found to the northwest of the porch. We are at a loss to explain the small dowel hole present on the *rear* face of this block. Seemingly, it was a mistake. Does it imply that a similar hole, useful in connection with a pedimental figure, was present on the now vanished left face of the block?

Block 671 was found close to the western foundation of the building near the northeast corner of the Altar Court. It is inscribed with a large Δ on its upper surface, a setting mark no doubt indicative of its specific position in the tympanum. For further comment on this block, see below, p. 116 and n. 202.

the two marbles flanking that central block of the upper course of the tympanum, and the corresponding parts of their porous backers. In any case, this binder again implies that the tympanum wall was built of two courses: the lower composed of horizontal binders, probably five in number, flanked at each end by a triangular block, which may or may not have been a binder; the upper consisting of thin slabs of marble of varied size and shape backed by thick blocks of limestone. Block 671, which, as we shall see, provides important evidence for the roof construction of the porch (being smoothly dressed on its visible face and equipped at the rear to receive a purlin), is a fragment of one of the binders of the lower course. Given its provenance, it must come from the western side of the pediment. The two previously mentioned triangular blocks—430 and its lost counterpart—confirm this system in size, shape, and technique. The former comes from the eastern side of the pediment, the latter from the western. Whether these thin blocks belonged to the actual corners of the pediment or served as the outermost blocks of the upper course of the tympanum wall cannot be ascertained. They were clamped to the adjacent tympanum blocks and doweled to the courses above and below them, but they do not appear to have been clamped to their backers. Together with the lost ridge block of the raking geison, they imply the shape of the missing blocks of the upper course of the tympanum. For, weathered though it may have been in the nineteenth century, the originally straight lower line of its visible face eroded into a curve (fig. 70), this block is intelligible only if we assume that it united the crowning angle of the raking geison with a portion, however small, of the triangular tip or peak of the tympanum wall, in the manner of the analogous blocks from the Hephaisteion in Athens and the Treasury of Kyrene in Delphi—to cite but two familiar examples—and now known to have been followed in the pediment of the Stoa in Samothrace.[185]

The triangular field for pedimental sculptures created by the interrelationship between the raking and horizontal geisa and the outer face of the tympanum thus had an angle of 14° 30′ and a depth of ca. 0.47 m., the former corroborated by the triangular blocks of the tympanum, the latter by both the depth or thickness of the preserved binder, block 400 (0.661 m.; i.e., 1.132 m. [the depth of the raking geison] − 0.661 m. = 0.471 m.), and the dimensions of the largest of the pedimental figures. The space available for the pedimental figures was thus 1.47 m. high at the center of the pediment and 11.72 m. wide. The gable slope is 1:3.9.

Finally, the numerous extant fragments of the raking sima show that it repeated the three ornamental motifs crowning the rear pediment.[186] But the elegant, angular contour of

185. Herbert Koch, *Studien zum Theseustempel in Athen* (*Abh. sächs. Ak.*, Phil.-hist. Kl., 47, pt. 2 [Berlin, 1955]), figs. 57, 58, pp. 184 f.; Bousquet, pl. 25, fig. 19, and pl. 32; and block 855 of the recently excavated

Stoa. Hauser overlooked this detail in his incorrect reconstruction, *S,I*, pl. 42.

186. Fragments 50.70, 50.289, 50.422–423, 50.479, 50.482–483, 50.530, 50.542 A, B, 50.575, 51.100, and 51.172.

the original palmette has been lost by the introduction of an additional petal on each side, a slight but revealing reflection of the chronological difference between the two pediments (cf. figs. 131, 172).[187]

PORCH AND PRONAOS CEILINGS (Pls. LXXVI–LXXXV, CI, CIII, CV; Figs. 71–73)

Both the late Hellenistic porch and the pronaos were covered with marble coffered ceilings, but they were differentiated from each other in decorative system, as the character of their beams and coffers indicates. Among the eight fragments of beams found where they had crashed onto the floor beneath them, six belonged to the pronaos (Pls. LXXVII–LXXX, CI; fig. 71), two to the porch (Pls. LXXVI.2, CI).[188] The latter are smaller, in accord with the shorter span from the outer to the inner colonnade, having a calculated length of 4.60 m., and they lack the triangular extension surmounting the great beams stretching over the interval between the inner colonnade and the door wall, which may be calculated as having been 6.16 m. long. Otherwise, they are identical in system and profile. The upper surface of both types is equipped with two smoothly dressed strips running the length of each block on each longitudinal edge to receive the coffers resting upon it. Both types are adorned on the soffit with a narrow, shallow panel edged by a cyma reversa molding. Each lateral face of both varieties is crowned by a boldly projecting molding consisting of a hawk's beak topped by a fascia and followed by another still higher fascia. Viewed from below, these overhanging moldings, which actually frame the sections of coffering resting on each pair of beams, appeared as the outermost member of the richly profiled coffers.

Apart from its smoothly dressed edges, the invisible upper surface of the porch beams was left roughly picked, except for occasional transverse strips cut to facilitate accurate measurement and stonecutting. But the comparable area of the pronaos beams was occupied by a roughly-picked, approximately triangular, vertical extension reaching a height of ca. 0.50 m. over their centers. Obviously, these extensions were designed to strengthen the long stone beams at their weakest point, the center, and thus counteract their tendency to break at the point of greatest strain. Judging by block 56 (Pl. LXXVIII), each beam was moored

187. Hauser's statement (ibid., p. 66) that the two dowel holes on the upper surface of the ridge raking geison reflected the attachment to it of the central akroterion cannot be correct. Surely these holes were used in doweling the ridge raking sima block to it. Their position, as well as the two dowel holes on the upper surface of block 895, suggests that the raking sima blocks may have been fairly sizable and placed on the raking geison according to some interlocking system.

188. Conceivably, the single fragmentary beam

drawn by Hauser, ibid., pl. 27, fig. III, is identical with our block 56 (Pl. LXXVIII), since this variety of block does not lend itself to re-use, in addition to being awkward to handle. If so, it has been equipped with a theoretically logical but actually nonexistent second clamp hole at its left end. But it is also possible that his block was the larger part of the only full pronaos beam now entirely missing. For his discussion and typical restored beam, see ibid., p. 67. A fragment of the pronaos beam molding is stored in Vienna (346 G).

71. Fragmentary beam 40 from the pronaos ceiling

to the inner architrave by a pair of dowels at either end and clamped to the adjacent returns at each end by a single Π-clamp.[189] For although none of the returns linking these beams over both the inner colonnade and the door wall is preserved, the existence of such blocks is not only hypothetically necessary, but is also attested by the mitered termination of the molding on block 69 (Pl. LXXX).

Innumerable large and small fragments of the pronaos coffers are preserved in Samothrace, in addition to the sample piece taken to Vienna,[190] but only one incomplete section of the porch coffering is extant (442: Pl. LXXVI.1; fig. 72). Fortunately, it is sufficient to suggest the basic system employed in the outer ceiling (Pl. LXXXIII). Originally, it consisted of a strip of at least three contiguous rectangular coffers of which the central one is fully preserved, while the other two are broken. Each coffer is composed of two fluently profiled recesses, framed by a simple, unadorned border and set off both from its neighbors and from the molded beams on which it rested by a very slightly lower, equally unadorned panel (fig. 72). The longitudinal edges of the block which overlapped the beam on each side are roughly dressed. Finally, every coffer was closed by a separately worked lid resting on a frame 0.08 m. wide, prepared to receive it on the invisible upper surface of the block.[191] Inasmuch as two such blocks of three uniform coffers would have had the exact length re-

189. Actually, block 56 (Pl. LXXVIII) was clamped to only one of the two returns adjacent to its left end, as its well preserved upper surface proves. Whether it reflects a negligent omission or standard procedure cannot be determined, given the fragmentary preservation of the other blocks of this category. But that work on the beams was at times negligent is evident from block 69, where the soffit panel was cut too long and afterward shortened. The original faulty cutting is visible in Pl. LXXX. Later, the preserved end of the panel was chipped and roughened to receive stucco and provided with a properly-placed stucco termination.

190. 346 H, *S,I*, pl. 28, fig. IV. The other fragments illustrated on this plate (fig. V, for example) were left in Samothrace, being identical with the now broken but connecting pieces 30-33 (our Pl. LXXXI).

191. The upper surface of coffer 442 is too damaged to allow further description.

72. Fragmentary porch coffer 442

quired to span the porch from north to south, it is reasonable to assume that precisely this procedure was employed, rather than the use of so complicated a block as a continuous line of six coffers would produce.

Hence, the two fragmentary beams and the solitary partially preserved block of coffers attributable to the porch—if for no reasons other than their provenance [192] and the fact that they do not fit over the intervals of the pronaos ceiling—imply for all but the two outermost, lateral rows of coffering the scheme proposed in Pl. LXXXV,[193] consisting of six rows of six rectangular coffers set between seven full beams and running longitudinally from the outer to the inner colonnade of the porch. The narrowly spaced beams were set at intervals of 1.20 m. from center to center. In the outer rows, however, it was necessary to use coffers of another size, given the wider interval between the last full beam on each side of the porch and the adjacent half-beams resting on the anta walls. No fragment attributable to these outer rows is preserved. Thus, the coffers shown in these fields on Pl. LXXXV have been restored by coupling two standard single coffers of the porch.

The pronaos ceiling was far more elaborate in system. Its coffers were of three types: one a large square having a visible field between beams 1.632 m. square; the second similar

192. Beam 28 A was found at the northwest corner of the porch, coffer 442 slightly to the northwest of that same corner.

193. Plate LXXXIII illustrates the system em-

ployed in the six central intervals of the porch, not its actual appearance, presenting only one-third of this portion of its restored ceiling.

73. Fragmentary pronaos coffer 30-33

in size but subdivided into four parts; the third having a visible field of 0.80 m. (Pls. LXXXI, LXXXII; fig. 73).[194] All three are deeper than the standard porch coffers, having three rather than two recesses. Otherwise, they repeat its forms and profiles, apart from the inevitable slight flattening of the profiles introduced in the shallower porch coffers and the smaller compartments of the four-part pronaos blocks, in comparison with the fuller contours of the large single coffers (cf. Pl. CI). Again, they are framed by an unadorned border and set off from each other and from the beams by a second slightly lower frame. They, too, were closed by separately worked and attached lids resting on a surface dressed to receive them, but their upper surfaces were obliquely sheared to rid them of unnecessary weight (cf. Pls. LXXXI, LXXXII). It is owing to this feature that the four-part coffers can be reconstructed, for none is fully preserved. But that some of the extant fragments which appear to be two-part were originally four-part is established by the form of the upper, invisible surface of one fragment, 41 A, which lacks the slope requisite for a two-part coffer but is properly shaped for a fragment of a four-part coffer.

The dimensions of these blocks indicate that the pronaos ceiling was constructed of four beams (of which three are partially preserved), two half-beams (neither of which is extant), and, in the inner three zones, nine blocks of coffering, three set longitudinally in each of the three intervals between beams. The maximum distance of the beams from center

194. Fragments of all five of the first variety are preserved, as well as a small number of fragments of both the second and third types.

113

to center, 2.40 m., reflected the widest intercolumniation of the porch. That the first two varieties of coffering alternated in each row is indicated by the changing character both of the longitudinal or transverse edges of the large single coffers, which are designed to overlap the beams or returns on which they rested, and of the shallow depressed panels separating one coffer from another. Thus, the single coffer No. 30-33 (Pl. LXXXI) can only have been placed at one end of a given row, prepared, as it is, to rest on a return as well as on beams; a second variation of this type, coffer 68, equipped to overlap on only two of its sides, must have occupied the central position in its row. Similar variation occurred among the four-part coffers. Hence, the system of coffering proposed for the three central zones of the pronaos ceiling in the partial restored plan on Pl. LXXXIV is doubtless correct. It is in accord, as we shall see, with the testimony of the separately made lids of the large coffers, of which fragments of at least five are preserved.[195]

In the pronaos, as in the porch, the two outermost intervals differed from the central zones in width, this time requiring a coffer half the size of either the single or the four-part coffers employed in the central zones. Fortunately, fragments of this third variety of coffer exist (41: Pl. LXXXII). Thus, of the five types of coffer shown on Pl. LXXXV, only one —that used in the outer zones of the porch—is hypothetical. There the ingenious solution to the problem of the differing lengths and strengths of the beams required for the porch and the enlarged pronaos, as well as of providing certain coffers sufficiently large to receive lids sculptured in high relief, may be appreciated.

For each of these fields was embellished with a prancing or rearing centaur (fig. 187).[196]

195. Nine, conceivably ten, fragments of three or possibly four of the centaurs that once decorated these lids exist in Samothrace (the evidence in support of this statement follows in n. 196, below). The Samothracian fragments include: four forelegs, 48.573, 50.593, 51.368, 51.612 (provably, because of their type, from at least three, possibly four, different beasts); two rear legs, 50.387 and 51.413; two hooves, 39.558 and 51.708 (the former a rear hoof, the latter a forehoof, as Miss Bonnie Orr kindly informs me); one hand, 51.293; and possibly part of an arm, 51.441. In addition to the restored relief on exhibition in the Kunsthistorisches Museum, there are five fragments belonging to at least two other centaurs in the store-room of the collection (fragments of two forelegs, two rear legs, and one hand). For discussion and reconstruction of these sculptures, see below, pp. 237 ff. The additional fragments mentioned by Conze (S,I, p. 23: described as "Theile . . . von menschlichen Figuren, namentlich ein mit Aermel, wie barbarisch, bekleideter Arm . . .") and attributed to the restored centaur

relief can hardly have belonged to this series of reliefs. The sleeved arm specifically mentioned here proves to have belonged to one of the pedimental figures (see below, pp. 267 f.). In the context of his discussion, it is clear that Conze regarded all the additional fragments, the horse's legs included, as having belonged to a single high relief of which the restored figure (S,I, pl. 52) was but one section. For further reference to Zumbusch' restoration of the Vienna relief, see ibid., pp. 12, 27 f.

196. That the centaur relief in Vienna, if properly restored, fits the 0.816 m. square inner field of the large coffers and should be ascribed to them was proposed by Karl Lehmann in "Kallistratos Meets a Centaur," AJA, 61 (1957), 123 ff. It is needless to repeat his argument here, other than to remark that it is amply reinforced both by the number and character of the additional, repetitious fragments of similar reliefs and by their provenance. As is indicated above, n. 195, still more fragments of these centaurs have been recognized than had been remarked at the time of our

Very possibly it was the intention of decorating the inner ground of the coffers with reliefs that led to the use of separately worked lids for the coffering of the Hieron, a practice for which there was earlier Samothracian precedent in the Propylon of the Temenos.[197] The carving of the relatively high reliefs of the deep coffers of the pronaos was undoubtedly greatly facilitated by this procedure. All five of the centaurs moved toward the right, four prancing, the fifth rearing. Surely the rearing centaur occupied the central field of the ceiling and faced the initiates as they entered the pronaos. The others pranced about him.[198] Whether the four-part coffers, too, were decorated with a single repeated motif is impossible to state, since only one additional fragment that can be attributed to the pronaos lids has been recovered.[199] Appropriately enough, given the smaller scale of these coffers, the two leaves and cluster of grapes carved upon it are in lower relief (fig. 202).[200] The very presence

---

report in *Hesperia*, 21 (1952), 42, where it was first pointed out that more than one such relief must have existed. The following year, it was tentatively suggested (ibid., 22 [1953], 12) that the centaur reliefs might have belonged to the base of a monument standing to the northwest of the Hieron (later discussed in *Samothrace*, Vol. 4, pt. I, pp. 97 ff.), a suggestion still implicit in the phrasing of *Guide*, p. 87. But even then, the alternative possibility, that they might have "belonged to the interior decoration of the pronaos" was ventured, though discarded, because of their provenance. Re-examination of the problem, especially in the light of Kallistratos' allusion to a centaur in the pronaos of a ἱερόν and of the fact that the horse's body is too long in Zumbusch' restoration of the Vienna centaur relief, yielded the correct explanation for this series of reliefs. For Kallistratos' passage, see Vol. 1, **128** n. (Further examination of Zumbusch' restoration in Vienna in September, 1959, revealed that the centaur's head should be corrected to a less oblique, more vertical, position, since at present there is insufficient room for his raised left forearm, the general position of which is attested by the fragmentary shoulder. Needless to say, there is no longer any reason to assume that the fragments used in the restoration of this specific centaur actually came from one and the same beast. But together they do indicate the generic type of the figure.) For detailed discussion of these reliefs, see below, pp. 237 ff.

197. For discussion of the sculptured coffers of the Propylon, see Vol. 5, forthcoming. Unlike those of the Hieron, which simply rested on the surfaces prepared for them on the invisible tops of the coffers, the lids of the Propylon coffers were doweled into position in accordance with careful fourth-century workmanship. These coffers, which Hauser (*S,I*, p. 28) had correctly reported as too small to fit the coffers of the Hieron, were mistakenly attributed to it by Chapouthier, pp. 176–79.

198. It is reasonable to draw this conclusion from the fact that the forelegs of these centaurs, whether executed in the round or in relief, invariably move toward the right. Obviously, an arrangement of these figures forcing them all to move in one direction from the spectator's standpoint (namely, to *his* right) would be highly unsatisfactory aesthetically. But if the single coffers occupy the central field of the pronaos ceiling and the four corners of the total central group of nine coffers, and their axes are disposed in the fashion proposed on Pl. LXXXV, the centaurs not only move in the required direction but also form a closed, balanced composition almost identical and equally pleasing whether one entered or left the building. The sole invariable centaur—the one occupying the central field of the entire ceiling—would, thus, face the worshiper entering the pronaos. The special emphasis given him as a result of this position may partially account for Kallistratos' allusion to a single centaur (Vol. 1, **128** n.).

199. 48.579. For details about this fragment, which was found in the cella of the Hieron along with a centaur's foreleg (48.573), see below, pp. 243 f., *C(S)*10. The analogy between this piece and the relief leg fragment, 51.368, was noted by Martha Leeb Hadzi in 1953, even before its function and probable location had been discovered.

200. Inasmuch as the inner fields of the four-part coffers are 0.289 m. square, and the extant fragment has a preserved length of 0.185 m., it is probable that the entire original motif consisted simply of the completed bunch of grapes between leaves.

It is, of course, theoretically conceivable that this

of such a quiet pattern in the multiple fields of the smaller coffers would have intensified the dramatic effect of the turbulent figures boldly projecting from the innermost recesses of the deep single coffers. Tossing their shaggy heads, their skins and tails billowing behind them, they formed a *thiasos* endlessly encircling the spectator below. Finally, especially if the low reliefs of the smaller fields were to be adequately visible, the splendid coffered ceiling of the second-century pronaos must have been painted as well as carved.

ROOF CONSTRUCTION (Pls. LXXV, CIII, CV)

The timber roof over the marble ceilings of the porch and pronaos was constructed according to a system different from that followed in the cella, as consideration of the lateral sima blocks of this portion of the building has already suggested.[201] Although the transverse beams of the cella were retained and again housed in cuttings at the rear of the sima blocks, the rafters used in the interior of the building were omitted, the boarding resting instead on purlins supported by posts mounted on the transverse beams. Nine purlins, including the ridge piece, spanned the interval from the door wall to the inner colonnade and, again, from the latter to the tympanum wall. They were housed at each end in two of the three gable-shaped sections of wall above the door and the two colonnades in cuttings set at intervals of ca. 1.10 m. from center to center. Both the boarding supported on these purlins and the wall plate on which it rested on each side of the porch abutted the rear face of the sima blocks, the wall plate being set in the two outermost marble blocks in each gable-shaped field. Such is the implication of blocks 128 and 671 (Pl. LXXV).[202] Both are equipped with cuttings for sizable beams. They are best understood as having occupied positions either in one of the invisible tympanum-shaped walls required above both the inner colonnade of the porch and the door wall to receive the longitudinal timbers of the roof or in the tympanum itself. The fact that each was lifted into position with the aid of a lewis—a device used in the construction of the porch but not the cella—confirms their attribution to this

---

fragment came from the porch rather than the pronaos ceiling. Judging by the single preserved example, the coffering of that ceiling, too, was executed with separate lids, implying that some or all of its coffers were also adorned with reliefs. But considering that this fragment was found in the center of the cella together with another from one of the centaur reliefs, it is far more likely that it belonged to the pronaos ceiling, where its motif would by no means be inappropriate.

Hauser (*S,I*, p. 68) did not attempt to restore either ceiling but, observing that there were larger and smaller coffers, suggested that the former belonged to the pronaos, the latter to the porch. His statement (p. 72) that there was scarcely room beneath the transverse beams of the pronaos roof for marble lids to the coffers is entirely incorrect. The fully preserved thickness of fragment 51.368 (fig. 196), showing a left foreleg in relief, is 0.04 m. and would easily fit into the 0.10 m. space available in his restoration (*S,I*, pl. 34, fig. II). But it is not surprising that the Austrians did not recognize the function of the Vienna relief, since they were unaware of the numerous fragments of identical figures that we have now recovered, which, it must ironically be pointed out, in several cases were found in the course of our excavation of their dump.

201. Above, pp. 104 f.

202. Both blocks were found close to the western foundation of the building near the northeast corner of the Altar Court. For further comment on these blocks, see above, p. 108 and n. 184, and below, p. 228, n. 202.

later portion of the building. Since both blocks are rectangular and bear dowel holes on their upper surfaces attesting the presence of another course above them, neither can be placed in the summit of the triangular fields or associated with the ridge piece. On the contrary, they can be ascribed only to lateral positions within one of the three fields and identified as the recipients of purlins.

Inasmuch as neither face of block 128 is dressed to be seen and it has cuttings on both faces—on the front to receive the wall plate, on the rear to house a purlin—one may assume that it was the outermost block of the wall above the inner colonnade (cf. Pls. LXXV.1, CV). The additional fact that its lower surface is notched to fit over the slight projection of the geison block beneath it makes its position unequivocal, as that position, in turn, provides conclusive evidence that rafters cannot have been used over the pronaos or the porch. On the contrary, block 671, the front face of which is dressed to be visible, obviously comes from the tympanum wall. Each block was clamped to an adjacent block on either end, and its thickness was sufficiently great to obviate the necessity of a backer, whether it was placed over the inner colonnade, resting on a surface ca. 0.88–0.90 m. deep, or in the tympanum wall, the thickness of which may be determined from block 671.

The fact that both purlins and transverse beams were used to roof the porch and pronaos, although the distances spanned were far less than the clear span of the cella, suggests that the roof of this portion of the Hieron was considered subject to special stress. The weight of the pedimental and akroterial sculptures, and of the outer tympanum and the entablature beneath it, like that of the intermediate invisible tympanum and the courses below it, was borne by a colonnade, unlike the weight supported by the strong door wall. The porch also bore the brunt of the strong winds that sweep down into the Sanctuary from the north. The roof constructed to meet this stress followed an ultra-conservative design dependent upon an extravagant use of wood. The multiple timbers visible in Pl. CIII are at first sight surprising; but their use is unequivocally attested by the cuttings for transverse beams in the sima blocks—beams meaningless unless they supported posts on which the purlins rested.

THE INTERIOR OF THE CELLA

(Pls. CII, CIV–CVI; Figs. 42–44, 74–102, 159, 160)

The initiate entering the cella of the Hieron passed into a rectangular room 22.37 m. long and 10.90 m. wide, terminating in an apse covered by a wooden ceiling of conical form. The gleaming marble floor leading from door to apse was flanked on each side by a slightly raised platform occupied by marble benches running lengthwise to the lateral doors of the cella and continuing, beyond them, to the raised marble platform within the apse. Brilliantly-colored stuccoed walls and a coffered timber ceiling enclosed the rectangular space before the

117

mysterious curtained apse. Apart from these essential features, which characterized the cella throughout its long history, its installation was in other respects twice modified in late Roman times, once to adjust it to changes in the liturgy of the *epopteia* and once as a result of damage by earthquake. As initiates had originally passed through the lofty Hellenistic door but later entered the enlarged Roman door or the late antique leather curtain, so they and the witnesses present at their initiation took part in changing ceremonies in an altered interior.

Although it is the latest phase of the complicated building history of the cella that is visible today, its earlier chapters may be reconstructed from a variety of elements. Let us begin with the original, early Hellenistic interior, since it persisted unchanged at least until the late second century A.D. and remained fundamentally intact even after alteration.

PAVEMENT

Still less of the marble pavement that originally covered the central aisle [203] is preserved today than was in the nineteenth century. Traces of it exist immediately in front of the apse (Pl. I; figs. 44, 74), but only one slab of the then virtually intact section of paving adjacent to the main threshold is extant (Pl. LXXIV.2). Hence, the detailed plan of this area published by our predecessors and reproduced here (fig. 75) is an invaluable record.[204] It indicates that originally one stepped from the inner tread of the threshold onto a step presumably level with it and framed by a grille. The slightly roughened surface apparent in fig. 75 and described by Hauser reflects the area once covered by this step, which was composed of the kind of small slabs used for the floor itself, as the pry holes recorded on the plan show (the same technique may be observed in front of the apse, where the underpavement for the marble floor consisted largely of porphyry and tufa slabs). When these blocks had been pried into position, the step was doweled to the pavement on one side and corner, since, unlike the pavement itself, it was not contained by a structural frame.

The remaining dowel holes edging the lost step are smaller and lack the lead channels used for the step.[205] They imply the presence of a grille, which bordered the step and re-

203. Actually, the cella originally was not divided into central and lateral aisles but consisted of one unified space framed on three sides by very slightly elevated areas. But, for convenience, the terms "central" and "lateral" aisles will be used in the following discussion.

204. *S,I,* pl. 14. Cf. also the photograph, pl. 15, and Hauser's description, pp. 53 ff. Plate 15 is misleading, since it shows the now missing pavement seemingly *in situ* and abutting the lower edge of the

threshold. Originally, the pavement abutted the threshold higher up, but the entire northern part of the underpavement supporting these slabs has settled, as our section, Pl. II.1, indicates.

The sole preserved slab, recovered out of position to the east of the building in 1953, is the narrow bordered piece at the extreme left of Hauser's plate, i.e., at the west.

205. 0.03 m. square and deep, as opposed to 0.05 m. square and 0.04 m. deep. Hauser correctly

74. Detail of the cella, showing pavement and underpavement north of the abaton

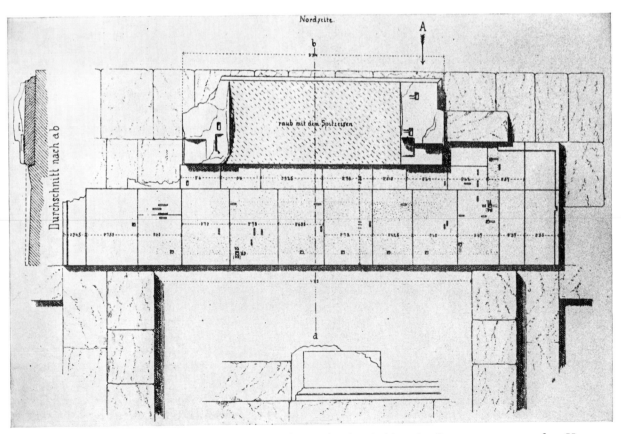

75. Plan of the northern end of the cella, showing main threshold and adjacent pavement, after Hauser

76. View of the cella looking south

turned to the door wall, as both logic and one revealing unleaded lateral dowel hole dictate. The off-center position of the two dowel holes required for the vertical posts of the grille door and the 0.60 m. interval between them indicate that it was a narrow, one-leaf door. Thus, admission to the cella via its main door must have been individual, since only one person could pass through the grille door at a time. Indeed, the function of the grille must have been precisely to regulate admission to the building in a manner that could not have been achieved by means of the great outer door. Once it was open, a group of people might look into the cella, but they could only enter it, and enter it singly, when the grille door was opened.

It was, of course, on the step behind the threshold that the leaves of the Hellenistic door would have ground their familiar arcs.[206] From it one stepped down 0.214 m.[207] onto

identified the grille holes but misinterpreted the pry holes as evidence of a bronze or wooden sheet over the grilled area (*S,I*, pp. 57 f.). Evidently he did not observe the pry holes present on the underpaving abutting the platform of the apse, which were unquestionably used to lay the marble pavement (cf. our Pl. I).

206. See above, pp. 58 ff., for discussion of the door.

207. This figure is calculated theoretically from the known level of the threshold, on the assumption that its inner tread was level with the surface (i.e., the step) behind it.

208. The marble slabs edged by this border which abut the apse, together with the lost section of pavement behind the door drawn by Hauser, indicate its existence on all sides of the floor. Conceivably, the large slab adjusted to the great block at the center of the lower step of the apse platform is a Roman replacement, made at the time that block was lifted and cut to serve as a pouring stone (see below, pp. 133 ff.), an action that could easily have damaged the slab adjacent to it. The fact that its border appears more coarsely cut than that of the little fragment to the east and that its surface has been left more roughly rasped near the bor-

77. Detail of the western aisle of the cella   78. Detail of the eastern aisle of the cella

the otherwise uniform surface of the central aisle, which was set off from the lateral plat-forms and apse both by its lower level and by the raised border edging its marble pavement on all sides (Pls. I, CII, CV; fig. 74).[208]

The underpavement supporting this floor was composed partly of porphyry and tufa blocks, partly of the same porous limestone used for the foundation (Pls. I, II.1, 2, 4; figs. 44, 74, 76–78).[208a] Presumably, the first two varieties were spoils from some earlier structure or structures, since both are found elsewhere in the Sanctuary. Although some-what irregular in shape and, at times, fragmentary, they are generally rectangular, except where they have been recut to fit around the foundations for benches in the side aisles. They bear traces of the setting lines and pry holes cut into them when the marble pavement slabs were laid upon them. Evidently they were employed throughout most of the southern part of the cella, along a great part of the line edging the western benches, and very sporadically elsewhere. In the remaining northern two-thirds of the cella, they gave way to narrow bars or strips of porous limestone, either because the supply was exhausted or the workmen laying the underpavement were drawing on different supplies simultaneously. The intervals between these limestone bars were packed with earth and small field stones and, inasmuch as their surfaces are naturally honeycombed with holes, it was unnecessary to cut pry holes in them. Unlike the smoothly-dressed re-used blocks of porphyry and tufa, these irregular porous strips were only roughly cut to receive the marble pavement slabs laid over them; these slabs, in turn, were roughly picked on their lower surfaces to adjust them to their irregular underpavement. As a result, the individual marble slabs must have varied some-what in thickness—unlike those cut for the more regular tufa and porphyry sections of the

der than elsewhere may imply that it is a replacement of the original slab. Yet the coarseness and pocking of this border may be explained equally well as the result of weathering.

208a. A few blocks of a denser variety of limestone occur among the porphyry and tufa blocks north of the abaton and in the side aisles.

underpavement, which were ca. 0.12 m. thick. In fact, the sole surviving slab from the northern section of paving documented by the Austrians is 0.087 m. thick. That the cella pavement to which it belonged was laid of slabs of varying size is borne out both by Hauser's plan and by the setting lines cut in the limestone underpavement (Pls. I, CII; fig. 75).

The entire underpavement, limestone and porphyry-tufa alike, rested on a packing of field stones itself supported by a fill of earth and boulders,[209] except where the porphyry bedrock rises close to the surface of the field-stone packing in the southern part of the cella and where, at its northern end, directly behind the threshold, the underpavement was laid primarily on earth and therefore has sunk. The character of the field-stone packing is most clearly visible in the southern part of the cella, where most of the underpavement indicated in Hauser's plans (cf. Pl. I; figs. 5, 42, 44) has now disappeared.[210]

The slightly raised lateral platforms running the full length of the cella on its eastern and western sides rose 0.069 m. above the surface of the marble-paved central aisle and were level with the inner treads of the lateral thresholds.[211] They are crossed by strips of porous limestone foundation placed at right angles to the lateral walls of the cella at approximately two-meter intervals from center to center of each foundation (cf. Pl. I). Nineteen of the originally twenty-two foundations, eleven to a side, are partially preserved.[212] The two blocks of which they are normally composed were connected by swallow-tail clamps; the inner block facing the central aisle is equipped with a projecting ledge containing two dowel holes

---

209. We ascertained this point when we excavated the areas where neither underpaving nor packing is preserved, in the hope of gaining information about the predecessors of the early Hellenistic building.

210. In view of the character of the preserved underpavement, it seems reasonable to assume that the underpavement Hauser indicated south of the late parapets in *S,I*, pl. 11, actually existed in his time, although other indications on this plan are highly inaccurate (for comment on the area immediately to the south of the parapets, see above, pp. 13 ff. and figs. 11–14.) The area marked "nicht vollständig aufgedeckt," for example, was actually considerably larger, as a glance at photographs of the building both after the Austrian excavation and at present reveals; for the area contiguous to the then preserved marble pavement behind the door is shown as fully excavated but hatched to indicate an earth floor precisely where the limestone underpavement is still *in situ*. Evidently, this diagrammatic plan was prepared away from the site. But the fact that the well-cut porphyry and tufa blocks of the underpavement are easy to transport and, unlike the limestone strips, lend themselves to modern re-use, suggests that they really existed in the nineteenth century to a far greater extent than they do today. Our sad experience with the partial destruction of the porphyry

adyton wall of the Anaktoron for re-use in a peasant's house in the early years of our work illustrates the degree to which these blocks are tempting to stone-robbers (cf. Karl Lehmann, "The State of Antiquities in Samothrace," *Archaeology*, 1 [1948], 47).

Granting that the interior of the cella had been incompletely explored, owing to insufficient time and funds, and never deeply excavated, Hauser (*S,I*, pp. 58 f.) concluded that the area between the late parapet walls, i.e., the larger part of the central aisle, was unpaved. The concept of an earth floor within the cella was disproved by Chapouthier when he uncovered a portion of the underpavement in 1925 (reported in *BCH*, 49 [1925], 466, and repeated in *Les Dioscures*, p. 163. See above, p. 13, figs. 11–14).

211. Again, we proceed on this normal assumption.

212. Several of these foundations were found slightly out of position or teetering in place or had tumbled out of position over a winter between excavation campaigns. Thus, the second, sixth, and seventh foundations from the north on the eastern side of the cella were replaced on the building on foundations constructed for them in June, 1950, as those on each side of the western lateral door had been replaced the previous July.

79. Detail of the packing in the eastern aisle

for attachment of the marble border edging the two low platforms throughout their entire length. For although none of the bars with which this border was constructed has survived, it may be deduced from both the projecting ledges of the limestone strips and the small blocks of limestone, also provided with two dowel holes apiece and aligned with them, introduced in the center of each interval between transverse foundations. Clearly, this border consisted of two bars per interval, each stretching from the center of a transverse foundation to the center of an intermediate block, and served to retain both the pavement and the limestone foundations of the platforms.

In these lateral areas, the pavement cannot have been of marble. This point is established by the fact that the inner tread of the lateral thresholds is not dressed to fit against marble and that the field-stone packing laid throughout these areas is continuous, running not only between but also under the transverse foundations (fig. 79); elsewhere in the cella, a genuine underpavement was invariably provided wherever marble flooring was laid. But this field-stone packing would have been entirely appropriate for a *signinum* or terrazzo floor of the variety we suggest and that has already been proposed for the pronaos (Pl. CII).[213]

The recovery of a substantial number of marble bench supports and fragments of such supports in the excavation of the Hieron indicates that the transverse foundations in the lateral platforms carried benches. Both the traces of dowel holes preserved on the bottoms of certain of these supports and another valuable document, recorded by Hauser but now lost, prove that these benches were attached to marble slabs placed over, and presumably having the same width as, the limestone strips beneath them. Figure 42 reveals the presence of a fragmentary marble block in the southeastern corner of the cella abutting the northern line of the apse, where today only a portion of a transverse foundation remains. The dowel holes and dressing on its upper surface bear witness to the marble bench once attached to it.

Thus, the slightly raised lateral areas of the cella were set off from the marble pavement

213. Above, pp. 95 f. The field-stone packing used in the platforms is precisely the same as the packing beneath the underpavement in the central aisle.

of the central aisle by a marble frame that gave visible articulation to the differences in level and function characterizing these parts of the building. Each platform was paved with eleven fields of *opus signinum* framed by the marble slabs covering the bench foundations and the marble border edging them. Only two of these fields on either side were fully visible—one at the northern end of each platform affording access to the benches from the front of the building, one farther to the south into which the lateral doors of the cella opened.

BENCHES (Pls. LXXXVI–LXXXVIII, CIV–CVI; Figs. 80, 95–102, 159, 160)

Twelve fragments of the early Hellenistic benches lining the cella walls are preserved (cf. Pls. LXXXVI, LXXXVII, LXXXVIII.2).[214] They were composed of two members, supports and covering slabs, none of which is extant.

The supports are in the form of naturalistically rendered lion's legs. A number of fragments are ornamented on both sides with concentric tendrils coiled beneath ragged overhanging acanthus leaves, a motif closely co-ordinated with that of the lateral sima in the lack of fluting on the tendrils (figs. 80, 159, 160). Evidently, three tendrils sprang from a calyx at the back of the support, two rising to antithetical positions toward its top, one falling toward its base. A shoot drooped between the upper front tendril and the lower tendril, to judge by the tip of a stem visible behind the lion's paw, and a half-palmette sprouted behind the upper rear tendril (Pl. LXXXVI.2; fig. 80 B). Presumably, these ornamental supports were used at each end of a row, that is, in the vicinity of the doors, where they would be most visible. One fragment lacks any trace of decoration, although it is sufficiently preserved to have shown it had it existed (Pl. LXXXVIII.2). It indicates the existence of a type of support identical with the ornamental variety in having the form of a lion's leg, but it is unadorned. In the restored perspective on Pl. CVI we have assumed, therefore, that the majority of the supports were of this simpler variety. The plinth in which these legs end was doweled to the marble slab covering the limestone foundation on which they stood, and further dowel holes on their upper surfaces attest the attachment of separate marble seats.

The depth of these supports (ca. 0.48 m.) and the width of the lateral platforms (1.62 m.) imply that two rows of benches ran the length of each platform, interrupted only to allow access to and from the lateral doors. This implication is confirmed by the existence of a number of examples of a third variety of bench support (Pl. LXXXVIII.1; fig. 95).

214. For the most part, they were found in or near the cella, even on the very lateral platforms. Nine fragments (48.580, 48.699, 48.719, 48.720, 49.538, 51.258, 52.154, 53.468, and an unnumbered connecting fragment A) come from the upper or rear part of a support; three are paws (48.639, 53.158, and 56.18). Their attribution to this variety of support is justified by the similarity of these paws and the fact that one, 56.18, bears a tip of the tendrils present on the upper part of each leg. This attribution is borne out by their dimensions. At its base, 56.18 measures 0.136 m., while the width of a thigh is 0.134 m. The three most revealing fragments are the literally connecting mended pieces, 52.154 and 53.468, and the unnumbered fragment A belonging to them.

A   B

80. Fragmentary Hellenistic bench support 56.18. A. Front. B. Side

Unadorned and lower than the other two, they evidently belonged to the front rows edging the central aisle. For when they are placed in that position, the difference in height between this type and the supports in the form of a lion's leg is compensated for by the marble border retaining each platform to which these plinthless supports were partially attached, inasmuch as the border itself stands 0.069 m. above the floor of the central aisle. As a result, the spectators sitting on these lower rows of benches sat at the same level above the marble floor on which their feet rested as did those in the higher rows above the *signinum* pavement beneath them. Hence, it seems reasonable to attribute the more ornamental supports to the two rear rows abutting the lateral walls of the cella (cf. Pl. CIV). Finally, the fact that the supports from the front rows are fragments of continuous benches, like those of a theater, suggests that the rear rows were similarly continuous.

The extant portions of the front rows are Roman replacements of the Hellenistic benches originally placed in this position, as will shortly be evident. Detailed consideration of them is best postponed to discussion of the modifications later made in the cella. But their very co-existence with the original benches abutting the walls when the building collapsed indicates that they had forerunners, as the dimensions of the platforms also attest. As we shall see, these forerunners had to be removed and were apparently no longer suitable for the changed liturgy of late antiquity. Their specific character remains unknown. Presumably they were continuous, like their successors; but whether they were slightly reduced, plinthless replicas of the rear benches or, like their replacements, unadorned cannot be determined. In either case, they were structurally identical with the rear row, being composed of narrow supports placed at two-meter intervals, on which the actual seat rested. Otherwise, had their supports been continuous, a correspondingly continuous limestone foundation would certainly have been provided for them in the original building period. A roomy interval of 0.75 m. separated the two rows from each other.

The maximum seating capacity of the Hieron was, therefore, one hundred and fifty. But somewhat fewer spectators would have sat in greater comfort.[215]

RITUAL INSTALLATIONS

Outlet (Pls. LXXXIX, XC; Figs. 81–84) : Some kind of receptacle for liquid must have been let into the *signinum* floor in the northwest corner of the cella immediately behind the door wall. For 12.42 m. south of the northwest corner of the porch, our predecessors found the marble outlet of a drain *in situ* in the face of a euthynteria block, which had been further hollowed to receive liquid pouring into it from a similar opening in the stereobate block immediately above it (figs. 81, 82).[216] From the adjacent debris, they also recovered a block containing a V-shaped channel that must have been inserted into or behind the orthostate just below the floor, and drained the now missing receptacle.[217]

Both of these blocks have been rediscovered; the latter has seemingly been hacked into and recut, the former smashed into a fragmentary but recognizable state (Pl. XC.2, 3; figs. 83 B, 84).[218] What is more, we unearthed a second such outlet, which, on examination, proved to be identical in scheme but far superior in workmanship (Pl. LXXXIX; fig. 83 A).[219] Curved at the sides and flat on the bottom, this trough is adorned on its surface with a modeled leaf and incised down the center with a narrow rib flaring toward the tip. The outlet found *in situ* by the Austrians is a crude simplification of this piece, lacking its modeling, heavier in proportions, and bearing a regular depression instead of a flaring rib. Clearly, it is a Roman replacement of the original Hellenistic outlet, as the akroteria excavated by our predecessors were renewals of earlier akroteria. Like them, it reflects damage to the building sufficiently serious to have necessitated extensive repair to it in the early Imperial age.[220]

215. Allowing 0.50 m. to a seat, 144 persons could have been accommodated.

216. *S,II*, p. 29, pls. 15, 16.

217. Mentioned ibid.; visible above the foundation in pl. 16 (here Pl. XC.1).

218. They were found on successive days, July 4–5, 1951, slightly to the west of the building in the vicinity of the Austrian dump. The outlet was taken to the Museum and later numbered 54.28. It is now exhibited in the southern wing of the courtyard. Comparison of the drain block (our Pl. XC.2; fig. 84) with the distant photograph of it in *S,II*, pl. 16, suggests that it was recut for some purpose after the Austrian excavation and then abandoned. In its present state, it is unintelligible. That it is a marble block can

be discerned even in the Austrian photograph. Hence, Hauser's rendering of it (ibid., pl. 15) in a technique different from that used for the marble euthynteria is both confusing and mistaken. Fragment Y (Pl. XC.3) may come from a vertical portion of the channel that must have led from the opening in the cella floor to the leaf outlet.

219. The two preserved fragments of this outlet were found in 1953 to the east of the building in line with the door wall. It was later mended, placed in the courtyard of the Museum near its counterpart, and accessioned 54.29.

220. Cf. text II, pp. 79 ff., for discussion of these repairs.

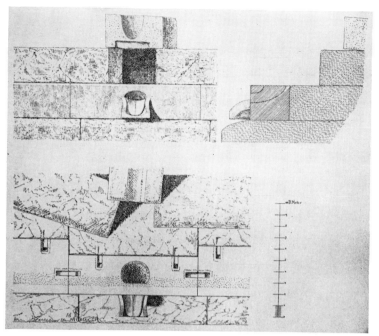

81. Plan and elevation of the drain below the northwestern corner of the cella, after Hauser

82. View of the western euthynteria in 1875, showing outlet; above, drain block

83. A. Fragmentary Hellenistic outlet 54.29. B. Roman replacement 54.28. Samothrace Museum

84. Recut drain block

127

Easily dislodged and broken, the projecting Hellenistic outlet was discarded, buried, and replaced, as were the southern akroteria.[221]

The form of the receptacle drained by this channel and outlet can only be surmised. Given its location at the northern end of the western lateral platform, it cannot have been so sizable an object as to have impeded access to the rear row of seats. Conceivably, it was simply let into the floor, providing a depressed area equipped with an outlet.[222] In any case, it must have emptied into a covered drain or piping running parallel to the porch until it reached the northwest corner and connected with the covered drain, which curves in a northeasterly direction from that corner of the building (figs. 369, 441). No trace of this channel was recovered farther to the south in the interval between the Hall of Votive Gifts and the porch.[223]

Eschara (Pls. I, II.1, 4; Fig. 85): Approximately in the middle of the central aisle but

85. View of the eschara in the central aisle

less than halfway between the main door and the apse, the marble floor was interrupted by a rectangular eschara, or hearth, set in the underpavement.[224] Its frame was composed of narrow rails of yellow limestone set upright in a shallow cutting prepared for them in the

221. Quite possibly, it was dislodged by the original northeastern corner geison block of the Altar Court, which was also later replaced. Cf. Vol. 4, pt. II, pp. 57, 142.

When the Hellenistic outlet was first recovered, we assumed that it implied the existence of a second outlet on the eastern side of the building. Later comparison of it with its counterpart, observation of their differences, and correlation of these observations with the numerous other analogous instances of damage and replacement in the building history of the Hieron provided the correct solution.

222. For interpretation of the installation in the northwest corner of the cella, see text II, pp. 23 ff.

223. See ibid., pp. 127 f., for discussion of the preserved drain. The lost section of drain parallel to the western foundation of the porch must have been

covered or below ground, given the narrow interval between the Hieron and the Hall of Votive Gifts through which it ran and which presumably remained traversable. The fact that we recovered a fragment of a drainpipe just outside the western foundation of the Hieron, very slightly to the south of the original position of the marble outlet, suggests that this portion of the drainage system may have been a line of terracotta piping rather than a channel. It would have been provided with some kind of mouth into which the marble outlet could drip.

224. Its northern edge is 7.50 m. from the inner face of the door wall, and it is slightly closer to the western than to the eastern wall of the cella (5.00 m., as opposed to 5.30 m.). Its outer dimensions are: length 1.10 m.; width 1.00 m.

86. View of the abaton from the east

limestone underpavement. The broken, western side of this frame is almost wholly preserved, and additional fragments of it were found within the eschara. Long exposure to fire has turned parts of it deep red. Although it emerges above the level of the limestone underpavement, it is unlikely that it rose above the surface of the surrounding marble floor if, as seems probable, it was sealed off in later antiquity.[225] A few bird's bones were found in the eschara, along with portions of its heat-resistant conglomerate floor.[226]

Abaton (Pls. I, II.1, 5, LVII, XCI, XCII, CII, CIV, CV; Figs. 42–44, 74, 86–88, 358): Throughout the history of the Hieron, the broad shallow apse in which the cella terminates contained a stepped platform. Slightly higher than the rows of benches before it and framed by the angular returns of the segmental apse wall, it was built of two marble steps nearly equal in height but differing in all other respects (Pls. I, II.1, 5, LVII, XCI, XCII, CII, CIV–CVI). In both the Hellenistic and Roman periods, this platform was divided into central and lateral areas both by the mighty block projecting from the center of the lower step

225. See below, p. 151. The present condition of the underpavement, which was badly wrenched by the earthquake that caused the Hieron's collapse, makes it difficult to ascertain this point, as does the variability in the thickness of the marble floor slabs. At the moment, the preserved western edge of the frame stands as much as 0.15 m. above the adjacent limestone underpavement.

226. For discussion of the function of the eschara, see text II, p. 30. Our original assumption (*Hesperia*, 19 [1950], 6) that the eschara remained in use as long as rites were celebrated in the Hieron now seems un

likely. Cf. below, p. 151. Our uncertainty regarding its original date (*Hesperia*, loc. cit.) no longer exists. It was, of course, contemporary with the early Hellenistic underpavement.

A better understanding of the varied character of the underpavement in the cella has also convinced us that the presumed second eschara mentioned (ibid., pp. 5 f.; 20 [1951], 20 f.; *Guide*, p. 65) never existed. At the time, we misinterpreted narrow fragments of certain of the tufa blocks of which the underpavement in the southern part of the building is partially composed as remnants of the frame of a large eschara. Actually, there never was a second eschara.

and by the character of the curved area behind that step, which at no time was paved with marble.

Originally, this curved central area was framed at the sides by the lower marble step (Pls. LVII, XCI, CIV, CV). Whether its floor was of earth or paved with some material other than marble cannot be ascertained, given the modern history of this portion of the apse, which was deeply excavated by our predecessors and so badly disturbed after their departure that we found that five of the marble blocks of which the platform is composed had been dislodged and thrown into their "pit" when we re-excavated it.[227] Fortunately, they could be replaced in correct position with the aid of the Austrian plans and photographs. Whatever its character, the level of the floor in the curved central area of the apse was presumably approximately the same as that of the lower marble step edging it at the sides. For this reason, only the upper two courses of the preserved limestone wall of the apse were smoothly dressed, since they (but not the courses beneath them) were wholly or partially stuccoed (Pl. II.1).

Actually, only the visible portions of the lower step were edged with marble, the invisible parts beneath the upper step consisting partly of field-stone packing, partly of porphyry and tufa blocks which served as the underpavement of the marble step above. Since the upper step was at once pavement and step, and the area so paved was small and supported no heavy attached objects, this economical construction was feasible.

The lower step projects slightly beyond the line of the apse, save at its extremities, which were concealed partly by the rows of benches contiguous with them, partly by the legs of the

227. Cf. *S,I*, pp. 13 f., 20 ff., 59 ff.; pls. 14, fig. 1; 17–21. When we re-excavated the central area of the apse in June, 1949, it presented a radically different appearance from that illustrated in Conze's plates. It was crammed with fragmentary blocks from the corners and rear wall which, after the departure of the Austrians, local vandals had thrown into the opening created by their excavation. Among these blocks, we recovered the two curving marbles belonging to the eastern side of the central area (A, B) and the two small, roughly triangular blocks flanking the great central pouring stone toward its back. They were replaced as nearly as possible in original position; but it was necessary to construct a stone foundation beneath blocks A and B, since the blocks originally supporting them had disappeared, along with all the late limestone foundation built within the curving marble blocks of this area and recorded by the Austrians and much of the footing supporting it. Block X, the easternmost marble of the upper step, was found at the southeastern corner of the building and likewise replaced in its original position. The easternmost of the two blocks on which it once rested was never recovered, nor were the two comparable westernmost blocks of the same step. Hauser's plan of this area (ibid., pl. 17) is incorrect in indicating one rather than two blocks beneath

X (cf. above, n. 35). Certain other errors in his plates of this area should be pointed out. The section (pl. 14, fig. 1) shows a kind of footing projecting far beyond the apse wall at the level of its fifth course. Actually, no such footing exists, an indication that the Austrians did not reach the bottom of this central area of the apse. Our recovery of a second fragment of the snake torch of which they had found one piece is another indication that they did not fully explore this region. The forms and character of the stones shown at the bottom of this portion of the apse in both these plates should be disregarded. Thus, the single stone seemingly present at the very bottom of the Austrian pit against the curving wall of the apse and referred to as a "sacred stone" in *AJA*, 44 (1940), 334, before our excavation of the Hieron, proved to be nonexistent. Finally, the regular underpavement indicated beneath the marble blocks in this area, as in the spandrel-shaped spaces behind the apse wall, is equally fictitious. The presence of porphyry and tufa blocks in the otherwise field-stone packing actually found in these areas, which were never completely exposed in the Austrian excavation, evidently led Hauser to assume that they formed part of a homogeneous underpavement.

very last person seated on each of the two lower benches. Since the benches were carried the full length of the available space, the upper ones abutting the returns of the apse, it was necessary to provide space for these two people. The little niche-like cutback in the lower step at these two points provided this necessary space. Indeed, its very existence confirms the suggestion that the Hellenistic benches literally abutted the apse, unlike their Roman successors. The line of the lower step thus projects forward twice—once immediately beyond these lateral spaces and a second time at the center, where the mighty block placed at that point projects forward into the central aisle, rises 0.10 m. above the remainder of its surface, and frames the central curved area of the abaton [228] on its northern or front side. Location, size, projection, and elevation all attest the unique importance of this block in the installation of the abaton. It was skillfully attuned to the curving wall of the apse by the curve of its own rear face. Finally, the animated contour of the lower step receives emphasis from the border edging the pavement of the central aisle which is carried around it.

The upper step was laid in such a fashion as to leave the lower step exposed not only across its full width, at the front and where it edged the central area, but especially on each side of the projecting central block, where it was cut back to create a niche-like space.

The original, early Hellenistic marble installation in the apse, described here and restored in Pl. XCI, is no longer fully preserved, having been altered in two essential respects in Roman times. But it can be reconstructed from telltale traces and indications on the extant marbles.

In its present form (Pl. I; figs. 44, 74, 86–88), the central area in the apse is no longer directly framed by marble. Although its size remains the same, it is edged by limestone blocks one course below the level of the lower marble step that served as a footing for limestone uprights, all of which have vanished today, as has the larger part of the footing. But both were drawn and photographed by our predecessors (figs. 4, 5, 42, 43, 88).[229] These uprights were set against the roughly-picked inner face of the marble blocks now edging the central area at the upper level—that is, against the four curiously shaped blocks preserved at the sides and the great block at the front.[230] That block, in turn, is both level with the other marbles of the lower step, though projecting beyond them, and rectangular in shape. Most important, it contains an opening hollowed through its entire thickness and roughly picked in two layers for the reception of a lid flush with the upper surface of the block (fig. 87). Obviously, that lid was of wood, since a marble lid could not be properly fitted onto this roughly chiseled ledge. Equally obviously, this lid allowed the block to retain its original function as a step and yet serve as an opening through which liquid could be poured onto

228. For the use of this term, see text II, pp. 33 ff. and n. 151.

229. *S,I,* pls. 14, fig. 1; 17–21.

230. The preserved portions of the footing con-structed for these porous uprights differ in level, the eastern being 0.655 m. below the surface of the cut-down marble blocks above it, the western 0.77 m. Probably the uprights standing upon them varied in height.

87. View of the abaton and the bema-pouring stone

the purple bedrock on which it now rests. And, presumably, the limestone blocks once edging the central area and rising slightly above the upper surface of the marble platform provided a foundation for a structure built over them. Otherwise they are unintelligible.

But, originally, both the pouring stone and the marble blocks edging the central area had a slightly different form. The latter are now mutilated, having been roughly picked on their inner faces, hence, reduced in width (figs. 44, 86–88). What is more, block A (cf. Pl. XCII) is clearly not in its original position. Its northern, front face has an obtuse angle dressed at the west to be visible, at the east with anathyrosis. If it were moved 0.20 m. farther to the north, it would fit behind the block once doweled to Z in such a fashion that the portion of its face having anathyrosis would abut that block but leave the remainder of its face exposed. That this was, indeed, its original position is confirmed by the dressing of the upper surface of Z. Moved forward into original position, its northwest corner would be aligned with the adjacent corner of the pouring stone.

When moved forward and widened into blocks having two parallel sides, as the preserved northwest corner of A implies that they did, the combined blocks A–B are 0.20 m. too short to extend to the curving wall of the apse. Investigation of the present rear face of B reveals that, unlike A, which retains its original anathyrosis, it has been roughly picked and trimmed. Originally, it must have been 0.20 m. longer. Similarly, blocks A–B would have overhung the central area before the present limestone footing was built, unless they had rested on a marble step. That such a step did, in fact, exist is proved by the rear face of block

88. Detail of the western side of the abaton

Z. It, too, has been roughly picked and shortened. Previously, it extended farther to the south, probably having a shape related to that of apse binder 687, and constituted one section of the curving lower step edging the central area on this side.

The pouring stone, too, has been recut at the rear, and, since the technique employed in recutting it is precisely like that used in shaping the hole inside it, it is evident that it acquired this hole at the same time that it was shortened.[231] Its original shape cannot be proved absolutely; but the alignment of its eastern rear corner with the adjacent corner of block A, once the latter has been put in original position, suggests that the corners themselves were not shortened and, thus, that it had a slightly curved rear face harmoniously co-ordinated with the curve of the apse wall. Doubtless the visible upper part of its rear face was smoothly dressed. In any case, it must have risen 0.10 m. above the level of the remaining blocks of the lower step, since it is unthinkable that it—the largest block in the step—was not provided with the same kind of foundation as they.[232] Once replaced on such a foundation, its lower surface level with theirs, its own greater height becomes apparent. It follows from these observations that this block singled out for special emphasis originally lacked an opening; instead, it provided an elevated step at the front of the apse facing the central axis of the building. When it was converted into a block through which liquid could be poured into

231. Both the rear face of the block and the hole inside it are picked below and obliquely chiseled above. Since it was necessary to cut the lower part of the hole from the bottom of the block but the overhanging lip

for the lid from the top, it was natural to employ the same technique simultaneously on its rear.

232. The face of this foundation was, of course, concealed by the marble pavement abutting this step.

133

the depths below, it was obviously necessary to remove the foundation beneath it in order to allow it to function in its new capacity. Hence, it dropped into a position level with the other blocks of the lower step.[233] At the same time, it was equipped with a lid which allowed it to retain its original function as well.

The paving system employed in the lateral parts of the platform when the early Hellenistic building was erected may be deduced by combining blocks A and B with counterparts to E, F, G, and the Austrian H (now in fragments) and adding to them the few slabs required to connect them with the three blocks facing the upper step-pavement on this side, one of which, X, is still *in situ*.

Centuries later, the central area of the apse was modified to adjust it to the requirements of a changed liturgy. The elevated step or bema at the front of the apse on which a hierophant may once have stood before the assembled company was converted into a pouring stone, but, at the same time, allowed to fulfill its original function, a circumstance implying that libations once poured in the interior of the apse could no longer be performed there and thus were transferred to the central step, which now served a double purpose. If so, the use of the central area of the apse for another and new purpose seems implicit. Be that as it may, the remodelers evidently wanted to introduce a new structure in the central area of the apse without reducing the space available within it. This project could be executed only by encroaching upon the lateral areas of the apse—and that is precisely what was done. In order to provide a foundation for some structure built over the original central area of the apse and to virtually retain its original dimensions, blocks A–D had to be reduced in width, the step-pouring stone trimmed, and the lower course of marbles originally edging the area removed at the sides and cut back at the front (Z and its counterpart). Only in this way could the required structure be built. These modifications were easily made, affecting only the original frame of the central area and the junction and interrelationship between its reduced and sheared-off members. In the course of this work, the relationships between A, the block it abutted to the north, and Z, as well as those of their counterparts at the west, were altered, for some reason impossible to establish. Either A or B was shortened 0.10 m. (or both were), requiring the introduction of a new little piece, A¹, at its north; and two irregular fragments of blocks were introduced on each side of the pouring stone to link it with A and D, now that Z and its counterpart had been shortened (and perhaps damaged) by the elimination of their rear extensions.

Although the majority of the marble blocks of which the two-stepped platform was originally composed remained in position and totally unaffected by the remodeling of the

233. The unusually wide anathyrosis or smooth dressing on the sides of this block is in accord with its special projection beyond the normal line of the step and elevation above its surface, being 0.272 m. at the front, 0.15 m. at the back, and 0.18 m. at the top.

central area of the apse, others, which it was theoretically unnecessary to replace or move, have in fact been replaced and moved. For example, blocks C, E, and F are re-used in their present positions, serving as replacements for their original predecessors, while G, H, and, conceivably, D are in original position.[234] As we shall see, the probable presence of a curtain across the entire apse would have concealed the upper step of the platform from view, rendering the appearance of its surface of no consequence. More important, the remodeling of the apse is surely to be associated with the other modifications made in the cella as a result of liturgical changes introduced in the cult around A.D. 200.[235] The sloppy execution of this revision parallels the careless workmanship of the other major alterations made in the cella at the same time.[236]

To recapitulate, throughout its history the apse of the Hieron was occupied by a two-stepped marble platform and divided into central and lateral areas. Obviously, the prime or culminating acts of the liturgy were performed in this, the culminating architectural feature of the building. The subdivision of the area into central and lateral parts and the emphasis given to the former, if by nothing else than the character of the great marble block before it, suggest that it was the locale of ritual acts.[237] If, as appears likely, that mighty block served as a bema or platform on which a hierophant stood and libations were poured, whether into a receptacle in the central area itself or into the later pouring hole, the lateral areas of the apse may well have been used for the storage of whatever cult objects were exhibited or employed in the liturgy. Surely they were concealed from public view, in all probability by a curtain [238] stretched across the entire width of the apse but, given the higher level of the bema and the niche-like spaces left on each side of it, divided into three parts: the lateral sections running straight from the returns to a pair of poles or standards set in these spaces; the central one, which could be parted, running from standard to standard. Apart from any inherent logic in this suggestion arising both from the probable need for such curtains and the necessity of explaining the spaces on each side of the apse, one piece of evidence points in this direction. Two fragments best understood as coming from the top and bottom of a marble torch were recovered in the excavation of the central area of the apse (figs. 89, 90). They show the head and tail of a snake wrapped around a ribbed object [239] and, judging by analogous

234. Block C cannot be in original position, since it lacks the obtuse-angled form required for the north face of the counterpart to A. E and F have the wrong anathyrosis for their present positions; they are smoothly dressed on the lower parts of their faces but chipped off above, in addition to being picked on top.

235. Text II, pp. 42 ff.

236. For the chronology of the Hieron, including the major repairs made to it, see text II, pp. 70 ff., 79 ff.

237. See text II, pp. 23 ff., for discussion of the specific rites that may have taken place in the Hieron.

238. For the use of curtains in pertinent cult buildings, see text II, pp. 34 f. The curtains shown in Pl. CVI have been hung on the analogy of the painted curtains in the cubiculum to the right of the colonnaded exedra in the House of the Labyrinth in Pompeii.

239. The tail, illustrated by Conze, *S,I,* p. 14, fig. 6, is specifically described as having been found in the "heiliges Loch." It seems to have disappeared, whether it was left in Samothrace or taken to Vienna. We recovered the head during our re-excavation of

A

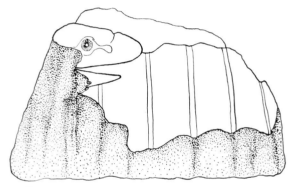

B

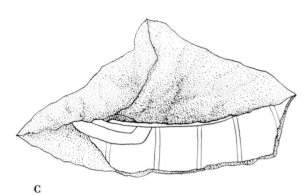

C

89. Fragment of marble torch 49.28 (Scale 1:1.67). A, B. Elevations. C. Plan. Samothrace Museum

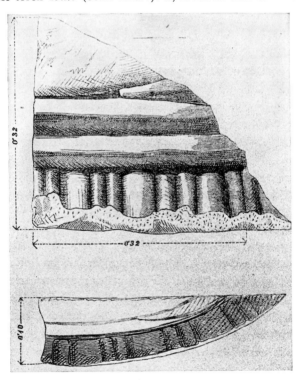

90. Lost fragment of a marble torch drawn by Hauser

monuments (cf. fig. 352),[240] probably belonging to a great marble torch entwined by a snake and bursting into flames at its summit. The provenance of this round torch, as well as its approximate diameter (ca. 0.54 m.), makes it ideally suited to stand in one of the spaces on each side of the bema as one of a pair of flaming torches. Strategically placed to emphasize the ritual center of the abaton, they could easily have served as poles to which the transverse curtain rods were attached.[241] They appear in this capacity in our restoration of the interior of the Hellenistic cella (Pls. CIV–CVI).

Inasmuch as the torch-poles were in use when the building collapsed, one may assume that the curtains were, too, and that when they were drawn the abaton presented the same appearance to the assembled company as it had in the early Hellenistic period when it was built. Only the very sharp-eyed might have noticed that a wooden lid had now been inserted in the center of the marble bema flush with its upper surface. But those to whom the abaton was accessible in late antiquity would have found that it differed from its original state in at least one major respect: the central area was no longer simply a space set apart for liturgical purposes but was occupied by a structure built on the curving porous foundation now edging that area. The precise form of that structure, as well as the material of which it was

---

the same area in 1949. It is exhibited in the Museum (*Guide*, p. 84; *Guide²*, pp. 67, 87) and accessioned 49.29. Thasian marble. Preserved height 0.163 m.; preserved width 0.255 m. Broken on all sides, including the back, except for the lower surface of the present fragment, which is roughly picked and regular, suggesting that the complete torch may have been built up of cylindrical sections or drums—unless this fragment reflects a repair to an originally monolithic object. Its worn surface retains faint traces of the snake's fangs. Cf. *Hesperia*, 20 (1951), 24 and pl. 14 b.

240. Figure 352, the important stele copied by Cyriacus of Ancona, shows a pair of torches entwined by snakes and presumably reflects the appearance of monumental torches having this form, rather than of actual torches encircled by living snakes. For reference to this stele, see text II, pp. 27 f., and Vol. 2, pt. I, **29**. Two other marble torches, one fragmentary but retaining simulated flames that flicker from its upper end, stand on the left side of the court between the entrance to the Museo Nazionale Romano in Rome and the Museum proper. The upper end of still another such marble torch has recently been found in the Later Stadium at Isthmia (Oscar Broneer, "Excavations at Isthmia, 1959–1960," *Hesperia*, 31 [1962], 193, pl. 9 c). We have used it as a model for the terminal flames restored to the marble torch shown in Pls. CIV–CVI.

The four marble fragments from the Dodekatheon that puzzled Ernest Will (*Délos*, XXII, 183, pl. 16, figs. 3–6) appear to come from another such snake-entwined torch.

241. It is tantalizing to note that Blau and Schlottmann, *Berl. Ber.*, 1855, p. 619, reported seeing a now vanished relief not far from the Sanctuary which seemingly showed an analogous installation: two candelabra-like objects before an adyton half-covered by a curtain.

On the lararium of Caecilius Jucundus in Pompeii, a pair of torches appears behind an altar and supports a canopy beneath which the image of a goddess stands. Presumably they are two of the four supports requisite for such a *baldacchino*: cf. the illustration in Inez Scott Ryberg, *Rites of the State Religion in Roman Art* (*Memoirs of the American Academy in Rome*, 22 [1955]), pl. 62, fig. 100. I owe this reference and knowledge of the torches in Rome cited in n. 240 to my husband.

The use of a pair of marble torches in Eleusis is documented by the great torches exhibited outside the Museum, the shafts of each of which were later incised with a Christian cross, as was pointed out in *Hesperia*, 20 (1951), 24, n. 91. See K. Kourouniotis, *Eleusis, A Guide to the Excavations and the Museum* (Athens, 1936), pp. 82 f.; Josef Durm, *Die Baukunst der Griechen* (*Handbuch der Architektur*, II, pt. 1 [3d edn., Leipzig, 1910]), p. 81.

built, cannot be determined, because of its total disappearance.[242] Only the character of the liturgy performed in the Hieron in its last centuries and the requirements of the cult yield clues in regard to its probable appearance. They suggest that it may have presented the appearance of a grotto and, inasmuch as the floor level within this cave-like structure was now considerably lower than the original floor in this area, it must have been accessible via a wooden stairway. Three steps would have sufficed to allow easy descent from the old bema into the new depths (cf. Pl. II.1, 5).[243]

Thus, the changes introduced in the installation of the abaton, like the alterations made to the main door, were motivated by new liturgical requirements.

WALL DECORATION (Pls. LVII, XCIII, XCIV, CV, CVI; Figs. 91, 92)

That the cella walls were stuccoed from top to bottom has been deduced from the character of the marble binders and stretchers of which they were built, the former slightly roughened on their inner faces, the latter backed by limestone. It is not surprising, therefore, that quantities of small fragments of the stucco coating that once adhered to these walls were recovered inside the cella.[244] The vast majority are painted a strong red or scarlet. Others, far fewer in number—indeed, only a small fraction of the preserved fragments—are black,[245] while a third group, the smallest in quantity, is white freely painted with faint, irregular, and curving lines of red to suggest the veining of marble.

Both the red and the white fragments are paneled, that is, characterized by raised surfaces

242. This fact and the very character of the foundation suggest that it may have been of concrete or wood. In the former case, it is very unlikely that our nineteenth-century predecessors would have recognized or recorded its fragments in the chaos of the ruined building; in the latter, it would, of course, have disappeared.

243. They can only have been of wood, since no structural traces of another type of stairway exist. Obviously, they would have disappeared.

Although the crypts in such varied structures as the Temple of Zeus at Nemea, the Doric Temple at Seleucia, the Serapeion in Miletos, and the Campus of Magna Mater at Ostia were entered via stone steps, the crypt in the Temple at Antioch-ad-Pisidiam must also have had a wooden stairway. For the crypt at Ostia, see text II, pp. 44 f.; for the other examples: Carl Blegen, "Excavations at Nemea, 1926," *AJA*, 31 (1927), 424 ff.; Richard Stillwell in *Antioch-on-the-Orontes*, III (Princeton, 1941), 34 and fig. 42; *Milet*, I, pt. 7 (H. Knackfuss, *Der Südmarkt und die benachbarten Anlagen* [Berlin, 1924]), pp. 184 ff. As far as I am aware, the crypt in the Temple at Antioch-ad-Pisidiam has not been previously mentioned (for example in the several reports

of Sir W. M. Ramsay and David M. Robinson). It is off center, its floor (which contains a channel) more than 2.20 m. below that of the cella, and it originally had a podium on three of its four sides. This brief statement reflects a visit to the site on April 28, 1953.

For discussion of the probable character of the liturgical acts performed in this "cave" and justification of the suggestion that the structure introduced into the central area of the abaton had this form, see text II, pp. 36 ff.

Previous writers have also assumed the existence of a grotto-like installation at this point in the apse. Cf. Otto Rubensohn on "Delische Kultstatten," *AA*, 46 (1931), cols. 377 ff.

244. They were also found in the immediate periphery of the cella and in the Austrian dump.

245. The black fragments, unlike the red, are unstable in color and tend to fade. Two (from 48.609) bear mottled traces of red, presumably indicative of veining. Conceivably, they belonged to the string course over the dado and slightly differentiated these two members from each other, as is suggested below, p. 140.

which stand 0.004 m. higher than their background or surrounding edge (cf. Pl. XCIII) .[246] They imply that the inner face of the cella walls imitated the effect of its outer face, seeming to be built up of painted blocks with drafted margins above the level of the string course over the outer marble orthostate. For the black fragments, which lack such drafted margins, are best understood as coming from a smooth black dado, given the prevalence of black dadoes in Hellenistic stuccoed walls [247] and the fact that they constitute the second largest group of fragments. The form of the painted dado, too, would then have echoed the dressing of the smooth orthostates.

The preponderance of paneled red fragments indicates that the walls were predominantly red.[248] At some point this color gave way to white, as the stripes of red paint preserved on the edges of certain fragments of white paneled stucco attest. These stripes of red pigment are similar in color to the red stucco but, unlike it, are created by the application of red pigment to the surface of the white stuccoed panel, rather than being bound into and actually constituting the surface of the stucco. They indicate that at least one white course was contiguous with a red course and imply that the inevitably slightly irregular joint between the two sections of stucco was corrected and straightened out by ruling over it a covering line or stripe of red paint of the same hue as the red stucco.

In addition to these paneled white fragments, a modest number of fragmentary white moldings is preserved.[249] Some belong to the type exemplified on Pl. XCIV.1 by 49.561 A, an incomplete molding related in profile to both the pilaster capitals of the Hieron and the inner face of the epikranitis of the Altar Court,[250] a type well suited to serve in similar capacity on the interior of the building. Other fragments appear to come from a strong, crowning molding (49.561 B and 49.476 B on the same plate), still others from engaged fluted columns

246. The stucco fragments found in the excavation were invariably taken to the Museum, accessioned, and stored. Those illustrated on Pl. XCIII were found together, along with other similar pieces and fragments from the interior of the raised panels, and accessioned as a group: 48.594. They come from the western side of the cella. The upper two fragments on Pl. XCIII are white, the lower two, red. One white fragment from 48.538 retains its red veining especially well. The use of yellow and green in the decoration of the cella reported in *Hesperia*, 19 (1950), 7, and *Guide*, p. 64, has not been confirmed by re-examination of the stucco fragments. A selection of the more revealing fragments is exhibited in Hall C of the Museum (*Guide*, p. 98; *Guide*², p. 103).

Conze and Hauser, too (*S,I*, pp. 11, 13, and p. 69, fig. 23), reported the discovery of similar fragments of paneled red stucco. A chemical analysis of the very fine stucco and its hair-thin line of color appears in n.

2, p. 69. Hauser interpreted the paneled pieces, which are sometimes composed of two layers, as evidence of two coats of stucco—i.e., as implying renewal of the original coat. But the 0.004 m. upstand on these fragments is by no means invariably created by the application to the background of a second layer of stucco. In the light of comparative material in Samothrace and elsewhere, it is clear that these fragments belonged to walls imitating the drafted margins of actual masonry. For analogous examples, see below, p. 206. The thickness of the stucco layer adhering to the wall, paneled upstand included, was +0.007 m., the upstand itself rising 0.004 m. above its 0.004 m. margin.

247. Cf., for instance, the black dadoes in Delian houses: Bulard, especially pp. 124 f.

248. As is most frequent, again, at Delos, ibid., p. 125.

249. Also found in the cella or along its walls.

250. Cf. Pl. XCVI.1 and *Samothrace*, Vol. 4, pt. ii, Pl. XXXVIII.5, 6 for illustrations of these moldings.

little greater in depth than pilasters (51.671). In view of the analogy between these elements and comparable architectural features in molded stucco known from Delos,[251] it is tempting to assign them to a similar position in the uppermost part of the wall, namely, to the zone equivalent in height to the combined architrave and the greater part of the frieze.

Although the exact appearance of the stuccoed walls of the Hieron cannot be established, especially the respective heights of the black, red, and white zones, the proportion of fragments of each variety preserved suggests that they were divided into three parts: a black dado surmounted by a central area largely of red paneled courses but topped by at least one, more probably by a second, paneled course of veined white, crowned by a white molded epikranitis, and terminating in still another white zone decorated with engaged colonnettes and bordered at the top by an appropriate entablature or crowning molding.[252] The last zone would be entirely suitable behind the outer architrave and frieze immediately below the wooden coffered ceiling. The wall proper would thus be crowned by an epikranitis occupying the very position internally that the pilaster and anta capitals do externally; it would itself be co-ordinated in height with the outer marble courses of drafted-margin masonry and, like them, rise above a smoothly dressed dado topped by an equally smoothly dressed string course. The precise nature of both this string course and the base course normally present in such walls cannot be determined, given the absence of any evidence in regard to the former, which often (for example, at Delos) appears to have been red;[253] but, since two of the black fragments show traces of red veining, it seems reasonable to assign them to the unmolded string course. Nor can the more significant problem of whether the main portion of the stuccoed wall literally echoed the structural system of its blocks be absolutely resolved—that is, whether its painted courses repeated the sequence of binders and stretchers characteristic of its outer face or, as in the majority of the preserved later Delian examples, were isodomic. But in view of the precedent for such a sequence of stuccoed binders and stretchers (cf. the Delian scheme reproduced in fig. 91)[254] and the fundamental logic of an interior decorative system which here, as elsewhere, would reflect an outer structural scheme, we have assumed in the restored section and perspective on Pls. CV, CVI that this was, indeed, the case.[255]

251. Cf. Bulard, pp. 152 f., figs. 52 c and 54, and the general discussion on pp. 149 ff., 158 ff., as well as F. Wirth, "Mittheilungen aus dem Kerameikos V. Wanddekorationen ersten Stils in Athen," *AM*, 56 (1931), 40, 56 ff.

No triglyphs were found among the stucco fragments recovered in the Hieron. They have been introduced into the restored wall on the analogy of the related tomb at Pydna (for which see below, p. 207) and of certain houses at Priene and Delos: *Priene*, pp. 310 ff.; Bulard, pp. 152 ff.

252. For an example of a similar sequence of red and white courses in which white not only serves as the uppermost course of a red wall but also appears to have been topped, above its crowning molding, by another white course, see Bulard, fig. 39 (= our fig. 92), from Room *a* of the Maison du Trident.

253. Ibid., p. 125.

254. Ibid., fig. 30, pp. 92 f., from Room 3 of the Maison de Kerdon, dated in the mid-third century (Chamonard, op. cit. [above, n. 46], pp. 126 f.).

255. Such simulated courses are normally separated by incised or black-painted lines. Since there is no trace of the former technique on our fragments, it

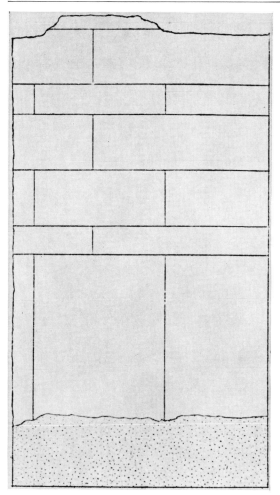
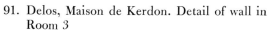

91. Delos, Maison de Kerdon. Detail of wall in Room 3

92. Delos, Maison du Trident. Detail of Room *a*

Ample fragments of red stucco found both in the nineteenth century and in our own excavation prove that the curving wall of the apse was stuccoed red. Our predecessors also found what they described as blackish, dark-green stucco in this area, particularly in the central portion which they hollowed out.[256] Conceivably, a low zone at the base of the scarlet wall above the floor level in this section of the abaton was painted green for some symbolic reason; but the instability of the black fragments that we have recovered elsewhere in the cella suggests that the fragments reported by the Austrians were originally black. Inasmuch as we are uncertain about this point, we have refrained from introducing this hypothetical zone into the restored isometric view of the apse or the restored longitudinal section on Pls. LVII, CV. Whether the conical wooden ceiling above the apse was also stuccoed and painted must remain uncertain. Nothing more can be said about the appearance of the apse wall,

---

is possible that the necessary lines separating courses and dividing them into blocks were painted. The fact that one fragmentary white molding, 48.467, has a

dark edge seems to confirm this suggestion.

256. *S,I*, p. 69. This is the only other color they observed, apart from the ubiquitous red.

save that it was surely smooth and lacked the drafted margins otherwise characteristic of the cella walls.

Although it cannot be established with absolute certainty that the wall decoration reconstructed here dates from the original building period of the Hieron, its stylistic character is such as to imply this date.[257] Even if the interior of the cella was renovated when the building was completed shortly after the mid-second century B.C. or, more than a century later, when it underwent repair in the early Imperial age, there is reason to assume that any refurbishing that may have been necessary at a later time involved restoration of the original decoration, rather than its revision.[258]

CEILING

Examination of the lateral geisa of the cella and of their relationship to the transverse beams of the roof has already revealed that its wooden ceiling was probably coffered.[259] That this was the case is attested by numerous fragments of bronze cymatia found in the excavation of the building. They are of two sizes (Pl. XXXIV.3, 4; Cat. **162–170**) [260] and appear to be rare examples of a technique documented by building inscriptions, notably those referring to the interior wooden ceilings of the Erechtheion and to the Temple of Asklepios at Epidauros.[261] The coffers of the eastern chamber of the former were decorated with two varieties of separately-carved wooden moldings, astragaloi and cymatia, the astragaloi being doweled to the coffers, the cymatia glued. Not only were several sizes of cymatia required for the individual "steps" of these coffers, but elsewhere, in the western chamber, the lids of the coffers were adorned with gilded bronze ornaments, as were the coffers at Epidauros.[262] The occurrence of precisely these moldings, carved with their canonical bead-and-reel and egg-and-dart patterns on the marble coffering of the Mausoleum at Halikarnassos (fig. 93) and

257. For analysis of this decoration and the wall paintings most closely related to it, see below, pp. 205 ff.

258. For discussion of these repairs, see text II, pp. 79 ff.

259. Above, p. 73.

260. Cf. text II, pp. 245 ff., for description and illustration of the individual fragments classified, according to size, as types 1 and 2. Their provenance indicates that they belonged to the early Hellenistic building period, since they were found either on the surface (i.e., remained attached to the coffers throughout the history of the building, until its collapse) or in the fill at the southeast corner of the cella, a fill containing both the damaged and replaced Hellenistic floral akroterion (that hence bears witness to a major Roman repair of the structure in the Augustan-Tiberian age) and material from the original building period.

In his discussion of the main door of the cella,

Hauser (*S,I*, p. 56) mentioned the discovery of many fragments of cymatia, implying, by the context of his statement, that they might have formed part of its decoration. But, as far as we can find, there is no analogy for the use of such moldings on Greek doors. In any case, his report is of interest in attesting the preservation, at one time, of still more remnants of what we have interpreted as decorative features of the coffers, also discovered, it would seem, in the cella.

261. Cf., especially, J. M. Paton, G. P. Stevens, et al., *The Erechtheum* (Cambridge, Mass., 1927), inscriptions VII, p. 321; X, XI, pp. 334 ff.; XIII, col. 1, lines 50–55, pp. 382 f.; XVII, col. 2, lines 1–8, 34–38, 69–85, pp. 394 ff.; XIX, lines 4–7, p. 399, as well as the discussion on pp. 364 ff., 408 f.; and Ebert, op. cit. (above, n. 42), pp. 51 f.

262. Surely the bosses of the west ceiling of the Erechtheion made from wax models and then gilded

93. Detail of coffering from the Mausoleum at Halikarnassos

the Temple of Athena at Priene[263]—to cite but two examples—coupled with this evidence for the decoration of wooden coffers with separately made and attached cymatia and bronze ornaments suggests that the most reasonable explanation of our recurrent bronze cymatia is that they are precious remnants of the gleaming moldings that once bordered the compartments of the dark timber ceiling. If so, its coffers had at least two steps or setbacks. The re-

were not of wood, as the authors propose (op. cit., p. 409), but, like the gilded stars at Epidauros, of bronze. For reference to such metallic ceiling ornaments here and elsewhere, see Roux, pp. 127 f.

263. Cf. A. S. Murray, "The Mausoleum at Halikarnassos," *Transactions of the Glasgow Archaeological Society*, n.s., 2 (1894), 10, pl. 3, reproduced above as fig. 93; and A. H. Smith, *A Catalogue of Sculpture in the Department of Greek and Roman Antiquities, British Museum* (London, 1900), II, p. 81, fig. 5, and p. 88, nos. 996–98; *Priene*, p. 99, fig. 68.

The repeated coupling of astragaloi and cymatia

in these documents and examples suggests the possibility that the wooden coffers of the Hieron's ceiling may also have been decorated with bronze astragaloi. If so, none of these still smaller, more fragile moldings has survived.

In this connection, it may be worth remarking that among the varieties of bronze nails found in the excavation of the cella, a number are of the same short size (0.04–0.045 m.), combining a big squarish head with a rectangular shank that tapers to a blunt point. Cf., for example, 48.614, 48.622, 49.326. Conceivably, they come from the coffered ceiling.

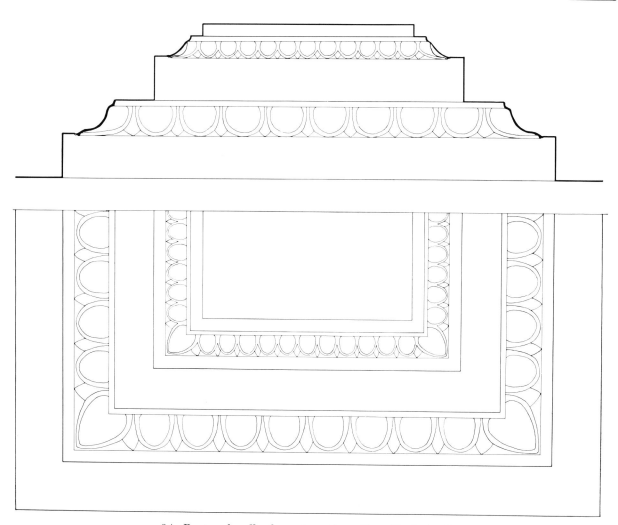

94. Restored coffer from the cella ceiling (Scale 1 : 3)

stored coffer illustrated in fig. 94 is based on that assumption and on the preserved fragments. Doubtless the lids of the coffers were adorned, too, but we refrain from proposing a specific ornament, since we lack tangible evidence of its nature. This restored coffer, in turn, has determined the size and system of the coffering shown in Pls. CIV–CVI, where units consisting of two coffers have been laid from beam to beam. Twenty-two such units would have been required to cover the full width of the cella from wall to wall in each interval between ceiling beams. When in position, they would have formed two parallel lines of coffering set between each pair of beams, creating a strong transverse rhythm within the longitudinal orientation of the cella.

Apart from repair or renovation, the cella of the early Hellenistic Hieron remained unchanged for centuries to come. But toward the turn of the second to the third century A.D., the venerable building was altered internally.

144

THE ROMAN REMODELING OF THE CELLA

(Pls. I, II, LXXXVIII.1, XCII; Figs. 44, 76–78, 95–100)

The Roman remodeling of the cella in no way affected its basic form or primary effect. It remained a richly colorful room, its brilliant walls set off both by the gleaming surfaces of the white marble benches and floor and by the dark coffered ceiling above it. The abaton continued to be the primary focal point of the liturgy performed within its walls, as the company assembled within them continued to sit on benches on the lateral platforms.

We have seen that both the abaton and the main door were altered ca. A.D. 200 as a result of changes in the liturgy of the *epopteia*, the former to accommodate a cave-like structure and to convert the bema into a block that served both as a platform and as a receptacle for libations, the latter to enlarge the door and allow the introduction of animals into the cella.[264] At the same time, heavy stone parapets were constructed in front of the two lower rows of benches on the lateral platforms to protect spectators seated on them from being injured by these animals (Pl. I, figs. 44, 76–78). Built of limestone blocks, they are ca. 0.45 m. high [265] and run from immediately behind the marble step level with the inner tread of the threshold to a point intermediate between the sixth and seventh foundations for bench supports—that is, approximately as far as the lateral doors. Their length implies both that these doors continued in use and still had to be kept accessible and that the worshipers seated beyond them at the back of the cella were not exposed to danger from the sacrificial animals.

When the parapets were built, the marble paving slabs in their line were taken up or hacked into, for they do not continue beneath the parapets. Although the slabs equipped with a raised border framing both sides of the central aisle may not have been lifted, those next to them certainly must have been removed, reduced in size, and relaid on each side of the parapets. Hence, the lower surfaces of the parapets were embedded in the marble pavement. Like the walls behind them, they were stuccoed and painted red, as fragments of stucco found adhering to their surfaces and in their vicinity attest.[266]

264. The present discussion naturally replaces our preliminary impressions in *Hesperia*, 19 (1950), 6 f.

265. In their present repaired state, they include heterogeneous material and are irregular in height, owing to the incomplete preservation of their upper surfaces. It is not possible to determine whether they were originally topped by a coping or simply stuccoed and painted on their upper surfaces, as they appear to have been in their last phase and as they certainly were on their sides. For their later repair, see text II, p. 126.

266. Although these fragments obviously come from the later restoration of the parapets, there is no reason to assume that the facing of the parapets in this later period did not reflect their original appearance.

The Roman parapets had no predecessors in the cella. The "thin parapets" referred to in the *Guide*, p. 64, were mistakenly deduced from the dowel holes at the edge of the transverse limestone foundations before the construction of the lateral parapets and the fashion in which the benches were attached to their foundations had been worked out in detail.

The western parapet rests, about in its center, on two underpavement slabs which are higher than usual;

145

95. Roman bench support

The construction of these parapets in turn entailed further modifications of the cella. Once they existed, it would no longer have been possible to reach the lustral area drained by the leaf outlet in the northwest corner of the cella if the grille behind the main door had not been removed (cf. Pls. CII, CV; fig. 75). Surely the rite performed in that corner continued to be part of the ritual of the *epopteia*.[267] An equally significant reason for taking down the grille was the fact that its narrow door provided an insuperable obstacle to the new phase of the liturgy requiring the admission of animals into the cella. Therefore, it must have been dismantled.

In addition to requiring the removal of the grille, the introduction of parapets in the central aisle forced removal and replacement of the front row of benches on each side of it by encroaching upon the space in front of them and rendering it insufficient for comfortable use of these benches. Conceivably, this necessity accorded with a desire to introduce a new kind of bench into the front rows. In any case, the original front row of benches was replaced on both sides of the cella by a new row of continuous, theater-like seats resting on an equally continuous support and provided with backs. The interval between front and back rows was now slightly contracted to 0.62 m.

Six sections of the continuous marble supports for these Roman benches are preserved (Pl. LXXXVIII.1; fig. 95).[268] For the most part broken at one end and somewhat diver-

but the discrepancy in level that the slight projection of these blocks would have created with the adjacent floor was concealed by the thickness of the stucco applied to its face.

Our preliminary discussion of the interior of the cella in *Hesperia*, 19 (1950), 4 ff., and ibid., 20 (1951), 21 f., reflects the fact that, like all our predecessors,

we did not at first realize that originally it had lacked parapets. For reference to the misinterpretation of these parapets as foundations for interior colonnades subdividing the cella into three aisles, see above, pp. 12 f.

267. See text II, pp. 23 ff., for discussion of it.
268. In addition to a fragment of the face of such

gent in length,[269] they usually retain a kind of rough picking or anathyrosis at one end, an indication that they formed part of a continuous support. Unlike the Hellenistic benches they replaced, whose supports had been carefully confined to the foundations prepared for them, the new supports were allowed to run over the *signinum* floor in the intervals between these foundations. The carelessness of this procedure is paralleled by the sloppy dressing of the backs of these Roman replacements, which are only roughly picked.

Like their predecessors, these new supports lacked lower plinths. They were evidently provided with backs, for their greater depth on top (0.584 m., as opposed to 0.48 m.) [270] can only be explained as allowing for marble cover slabs equipped with a back and doweled to them.[271] Thus, the new benches in the front rows resembled the proedria of the theater. Whether the two ends of these continuous benches were adorned with any ornamental pattern must remain uncertain.[272]

The provenance of these bench supports in itself implies that they were not installed in the rear part of the cella south of the lateral doors, for they were found exclusively in or at the periphery of the northern part of the cella into which the parapets were introduced. The discovery of fragments of a second variety of Roman bench confirms this implication and indicates, further, that the two rows of benches originally present on each side of the cella in the southern part of the building, too, were now replaced by a single row on each side.

Twelve fragments of the supports of this second variety of bench are preserved, including their lion's-foot paws and reeded legs (figs. 96–100).[273] They are similar in type to the

a block (48.574). All six were found in the cella or at the edge of its lateral foundations. They have been placed on the transverse limestone foundations at various points in the building to suggest the function of the lateral parts of the cella.

269. Only one, 96 A, is complete in length, measuring 0.602 m. It is by far the shortest of the preserved sections, which range up to 0.78 m. (713).

270. Their curving section causes them to narrow to 0.419 m. at the bottom.

271. The pair of dowels on the upper surface of the preserved sections of these bench supports imply that their heavy cover slabs were attached to them at frequent intervals; i.e., that these seats were very practically composed of shorter, more numerous sections of seating than were their backless predecessors, which ran from center to center of the transverse foundations beneath them. The preserved supports are sporadic fragments of originally continuous supports and cannot be interpreted as invariably having belonged over the transverse foundations, for which they are all considerably too wide, whatever their

length. The fact that one of these fragments—indeed the narrowest, 96 A—lacks dowel holes on its top is additional proof that the supports for the Roman benches were continuous and not restricted to the transverse foundations. Otherwise, it, too, would have had to be similarly equipped with dowel holes for the attachment of the cover slab.

272. As must the specific height of these benches. Their supports vary in height from 0.249 to 0.27 m. and must be supplemented, it will be recalled, both by the 0.069 m. difference in level between the lateral platforms and the central aisle and by the height of the cover slabs. The specific characterization of the benches in the *Guide*, p. 65, *Guide*², p. 66, should be disregarded since, again, it reflects a preliminary stage in our investigations.

273. Eight are fragments of paws: 49.536 A, B, C; 50.568; 51.265; 52.340; 53.464; 54.204. One preserves the lower part of the leg attached to a paw: 50.124; two are fragments of the paneled legs: 49.537 A and 51.200; the last, 49.537 B, combines part of the plinth, the fluting behind the paw, and a bit of leaf

147

96. Fragmentary foot of Roman bench support 49.536 B

97. Fragmentary foot of Roman bench support 49.536 B

98. Fragmentary foot of Roman bench support 50.124

99. Fragment of Roman bench support 51.200

100. Fragment of Roman bench support 49.537 A

comparable parts of a fully preserved late Hellenistic bench support that once stood on the outer terrace of the Temenos, by means of which their complete form may be reconstructed (figs. 101, 102).[274] Identically carved on both sides, it shows two boldly coiled volutes rising

from the central motif. They were all found in the cella. Still another fragmentary paw in Vienna seems to belong to this category (II, 9562). It appears to be the unmentioned fragment at the right of *S,I*, pl. 47.

274. 49.412 (*Guide,* p. 80; *Guide²,* p. 83). It stands 0.455 m. high without its actual seat, which must have been of wood, judging both by the character of its upper surface and the fact that it lacks any dowel hole for the attachment of a marble seat. It is 0.16 m. wide and 0.695 m. deep, in comparison with

the 0.48 m. depth of the original Hellenistic bench supports.

This support, seen by the Austrians in the school in Chora, where it was correctly reported to have come from Palaeopolis, had passed into the collection of marbles in the church of that village before we transferred it to Palaeopolis. Conze (*S,I,* pp. 23, 76, and pl. 47) had ascribed it to the pronaos of the "Dorischer Marmortempel," because of the discovery of related feet and volutes north of the building. In *Hesperia,* 20

101. Late Hellenistic bench support. Samothrace Museum

102. Detail of late Hellenistic bench support. Samothrace Museum

from two lion's paws, one at the front, one at the back. The legs of this support are no longer naturalistic but framed and subdivided or paneled by sharply-defined vertical fillets.

(1951), 25, where it was illustrated as pl. 13 d, it was tentatively attributed to the installation of the southern part of the cella, again, because of the recovery of related feet and volutes in that part of the building. Later, when it was remarked that all the feet found in or near the Hieron lacked the lower tang characteristic of this example and that the benches once standing in separately prepared bases on the lower terrace of the Temenos were evidently equipped with just such tangs for insertion into their bases, it became clear that this particular support belonged to the group of benches located on that terrace. It has since been mounted in one of those bases and placed in the center of Hall B of the Museum. Although the specific base in which it stands does not fit it to a centimeter (i.e., was not made for it), in type, the two belong together.

Theoretically, benches could have been placed in the pronaos of the Hieron, but there is no evidence whatever that any were actually installed there.

149

At the bottom, above the lion's paw, they are decorated with three tiny patera-like studs. In general, this support is an ornamental abstraction of the original Hellenistic benches, preserving their naturalistic paws and essential contour but developing their fluting into a linear pattern of vertical panels and fillets. The plump, naturalistic tendrils of the early supports have become abstract volutes; but they retain a vestigial remnant of their past in the form of an arrow-shaped shoot, which emerges from them and points toward the great upside-down acanthus calyx, from which leaves drop to the base of the support, that constitutes its central motif. The sole difference in type between this fully preserved support and the similar members found in the Hieron is that it was equipped with a tang for insertion into a separate base, inasmuch as it stood out-of-doors rather than being installed in a building; but however similar in scheme to this prototype, they differ from it in their sloppy execution. The lack of precision characteristic of all the replacements or alterations made in the cella at this time is observable in several respects—for example, in the shallow, irregular cutting of what were intended to be accurate horizontal terminations or borders in the base of each leg (cf. figs. 98, 102).

The paws of these dismembered Roman benches may be distinguished from those of their Hellenistic forebears in two respects: their less naturalistic toes adhere to each other at the tips and are separated by deep hollows; and their plinths are different in plan, resembling the support from the Temenos in this respect, too, rather than following the regular, rectangular form of the early benches.

If the upper edges of these Roman supports were similar in form to the example from the Temenos, as presumably they were, the seats which they supported must have been of wood. In any case, they were free-standing, as both their intrinsic shape and one of the slabs to which such supports were doweled prove. This important document, recorded by Hauser (cf. fig. 42) but later lost, has already been cited as proof of the fact that the marble bench supports of the Hieron were doweled to marble slabs the width of the limestone foundations they covered.[275] The support placed on this slab was attached to it by two dowels set with lead channels. These telltale traces indicate both that it did not abut the apse, like its Hellenistic predecessors, and that it stood in the center of the eastern lateral platform; that is, only one row of benches occupied the lateral platforms south of the side doors, where, previously, there had been two—a conclusion already implicit in the greater size of these benches. Whether this single row of free-standing benches running down the center of each lateral platform at the rear of the cella was continuous, like its predecessors, or consisted of individual benches approximately two meters long and separated from each other by an interval of similar length cannot be determined. In the latter case, they were placed in the first and third in-

275. See p. 123, above.

tervals north of the apse, since the form of their supports implies that they were placed over the transverse foundations, like their predecessors; and the lost block establishes the fact that such a bench did stand immediately to the north of the apse. In either case, the seating capacity of the rear part of the cella was drastically reduced, being either halved or quartered.[276]

When the Hieron collapsed in late antiquity, three varieties of bench thus coexisted in its interior. The rear rows in the larger, forepart of the cella retained their original, early Hellenistic benches supported on ornamental lions' legs. But, elsewhere, the original benches had been replaced. The lower rows in the forepart of the cella were filled with massive, theater-like seats of simple profile equipped with backs, while the portion of the cella closest to the mysterious abaton received the most elegant and elaborate of all the benches. Surely these diversities in form and location reflect some stratification in the congregation of *epoptai* during the last two centuries in which the rites were performed.

The desire to introduce animals into the cella, which, as we have seen, led to the enlarging of the main door, the removal of the grille, and the construction of parapets on each side of the central aisle suggests that the original eschara must have been sealed off at the same time, whether or not it was replaced by a differently located successor or a portable hearth. Its position in the center of the pavement would have impeded the new rites—quite apart from the further fact that these rites surely required the addition of new equipment to the central aisle, where the sacrificial animals were slaughtered. Two nearly square depressions in the limestone underpavement close to the western parapet, one near the door, the other parallel with the old eschara, are best interpreted as traces of such paraphernalia—whether altars, tables, or a new eschara—which must have been inserted in or moored to the floor in a manner requiring the underpavement to be slightly cut down in those places.[277]

To recapitulate, the Roman alteration of the cella involved enlargement of the main door, removal of the grille, covering over and replacing of the eschara, construction of parapets, and consequent shifting and replacing of the first row of benches in the forepart of the building, in addition to extensive rearrangement of the rear portion of the cella, where elaborate new benches, fewer in number than their predecessors, preceded the drastically

276. Originally it was sixty-four. Now only thirty-two or sixteen people could be accommodated. If there were four individual benches in this part of the cella, two on each side, they would have required sixteen feet. We have recovered fragments of precisely nine feet; i.e., even including the fragmentary paw in Vienna, not too many paws are preserved to exclude this solution.

277. The more northerly of these depressions, near the main door, may well have been an altar. Hauser (*S,II*, p. 28, fig. 4) reproduced a fragmentary corner block of small scale combining a Doric frieze 0.11 m. high with an architrave 0.09 m. high found in the cella, evidently toward its western side, which could have belonged to a conventional entablature appropriate in scale and type for the crowning of an altar. Its dimensions would fit the 0.72 × 0.97 m. cutting in the underpavement. Hauser, recognizing that its scale precluded attribution to the building itself, suggested that it might have come from a small aedicula in the cella. It did not reappear in the course of our excavation.

remodeled bema and abaton. These modifications, which reflect changes in or additions to the original liturgy of the *epopteia*, appear to have been made toward A.D. 200.[278] Nor were they the last changes or repairs to be made in the cella.

More than a century later, the main door was once again and brutally remodeled. The original difference in level between its inner and outer treads was eliminated by roughly picking them throughout the entire width of the door opening, until what had once been a high step above the pronaos floor was reduced to a slight elevation. At the same time, the low step abutting the original inner tread was dismantled, the inner face of the jambs and the Roman door pans were crudely recut, and the door itself was replaced by a curtain.[279] Now even large bovine animals could be led into the cella without benefit of a temporarily constructed ramp. Presumably, it was the desire to lead such animals into the building that motivated this second remodeling of the door, as a similar intention had lain behind the first.

This second alteration of the door should probably be linked with minor repairs to the building which suggest that it may have suffered from a tremor, if one less grievous than the earthquake that shook the Sanctuary early in the Imperial age and forced widespread repairs to its buildings and terrace walls, among them the replacing of the southern akroteria of the Hieron.[280] For the joints between the parapet blocks contain marble fragments and chips, and the western parapet has been repaired with large fragments of marble, including a piece of a geison block, toward its northern end. Scraps of marble have also been stuffed in beneath the parapets, suggesting that the underpavement had been wrenched into irregularity by an earthquake and its level beneath the sloppily rebuilt parapets corrected by this device. It is also probable that repairs were made to the front row of Roman seats at this time. The six sections of their continuous supports now preserved fall into two groups technically, one characterized by better workmanship and a more vigorous profile, the other by larger dowel holes provided with lead channels lacking in the former group, by slightly greater height (0.27 m., as opposed to 0.25 m.), and by a more angular profile.[281] Although, theoretically, these differences could simply reflect the varied procedure employed by different crews of stonecutters working contemporaneously, it seems more reasonable to interpret them

---

278. Cf. text II, pp. 42 ff., for discussion of this date.

The present slight irregularity in the width of the intervals between the transverse limestone foundations in the lateral platforms, especially at the very south of the cella, probably reflects similar slight shifts in position caused by earthquakes, whether at the time of the building's collapse or earlier. In any case, it does not seem to be meaningful.

279. Cf. above, pp. 67 f.

280. See text II, pp. 79 ff., 124 ff., for recapitula-

tion of the successive Roman repairs or revisions of the building.

281. The former group includes Nos. 150 and 713; the latter, Nos. 96 A, 119, 328, and 510.

Whether certain inconsistencies observable among the fragments of the ornamental Roman supports from the rear of the cella are to be similarly explained remains uncertain, given the so fragmentary nature of these pieces. But one, for example (50.124), lacks the little stud-like circles normally found above the paw, a circumstance that would fit such an explanation.

as indications that the better executed supports were carved at the time of the original Roman revision of the cella, the less well cut at the moment when the parapets were repaired.[282]

Obviously, both the first and second Roman revisions and repairs affected the marble pavement of the central aisle in the forepart of the cella. The construction of parapets and their later repair, as well as the rearrangement of the ritual installation between them and the introduction of new paraphernalia attached to the floor, must have necessitated considerable recutting or repairing of its marble pavement. Two fragments of a second-century-A.D. Roman inscription seemingly alluding to the abaton in the apse of the Hieron were found to the north of the building, one of them recut to serve as a paving slab.[283] In all likelihood, they reflect repairs made to its floor, whether during the revision of the cella ca. A.D. 200 or after the later earthquake.

The date of this tremor and of the repairs and changes subsequently made in the Hieron cannot be precisely defined on the basis of stylistic or documentary evidence. But the fact that there is evidence, elsewhere in the Sanctuary, of Constantinian building activity suggests that it was during the reign of that emperor that the Hieron received its last alterations. Before the century was out, the edict of his successor Theodosius the Great had put an end to the mysterious rites celebrated in this, the holiest of the Samothracian cult buildings. For more than another century, it stood upright and intact, if no longer the scene of nocturnal initiation, until in the mid-sixth century it succumbed to the last and most terrible of the earthquakes that had shaken it. Destroyed, deserted, plundered, and overgrown, its ruins retained the form of its last revision, the form now laid bare to the visitor's eye. Concealed by these Roman revisions, yet revealed through them, the early Hellenistic building onto which they were grafted emerges as one of the most significant creations of Greek architecture.

---

282. The bench support illustrated in *S,II,* p. 29, fig. 5, in the context of the discussion of the "New Temple"—although not specifically attributed to it— is similar to a support discovered in 1962 in a small late building abutting the western side of the Stoa. Both this newly recovered piece (62.893) and the lost support found in the nineteenth century are 0.32 m. high, i.e., slightly smaller than the otherwise identical Hellenistic bench supports found in the Sacristy, which have a height of 0.34 m. Presumably the smaller supports belonged to the same original context, the recently discovered one, at least, having been re-used in the building in which it was found. For the supports from the Sacristy, see *Guide,* pp. 48, 89; *Guide²,* pp. 48, 92; and *AJA,* 44 (1940), 345 and fig. 24, where it was assumed that the lost piece, too, had come from the Sacristy.

283. See text II, pp. 33 f. and n. 151, for discussion of these fragments published in Vol. 2, pt. I, as **78** (a), (b) and illustrated on Pl. XXVIII of that volume.

103. View of the Hieron and the Altar Court from the Theater, 1960

II. The Hellenistic Hieron: Structure and Style

THE *mystai* who passed from the columnar porch of the Hellenistic Hieron into a rectangular hall terminating in an apse entered a building unique in the history of Greek architecture. For although individual features of its plan and construction recur elsewhere, as a totality, it is without parallel. A hall for the performance of religious rites before a seated congregation rather than a temple, in external appearance it was nonetheless temple-like.

This coupling of an assembly hall with a columnar porch, a scheme familiar from the Telesterion at Eleusis,[1] may already have characterized one or both of the predecessors of the

1. For the Peisistratan and Periklean Telesteria, the latter equipped with its Philonian porch, see now

Hellenistic Hieron. Certainly in Samothrace, as at Eleusis, the basic plan of the later building was determined by the retention of architectural features of its forebears, features in themselves dictated by liturgical requirements and by the incorporation in a later structure of a hallowed place of worship. So in the adjacent Altar Court was the venerable archaic rock altar contained within the classical monument that superseded it; [2] thus was its location and orientation determined (fig. 103).

Our knowledge of the two predecessors of the Hellenistic Hieron is limited, it will be recalled, to their location, orientation, and approximate size, and to the fact that both buildings terminated in a salient apse (Pl. I).[3] This structural feature, common enough in Geometric and Archaic times for cult buildings,[4] is of the utmost rarity later.[5] Its retention in

---

George E. Mylonas, *Eleusis and the Eleusinian Mysteries* (Princeton, 1961), pp. 78 ff., 113 ff., 133 ff., and especially pls. 6, 20, 26, 27. It is obvious that the interiors of buildings like the Hieron and the Telesterion, both of them built to accommodate seated congregations, have more in common with the plans of such secular buildings as council houses than they do with temples. But their interior installations, including the disposition of their seats, are so individual, so conditioned by the character and requirements of the rites performed within them, as to make it profitless to cite examples of related features in civic buildings.

2. *Samothrace*, Vol. 4, pt. II, especially pp. 61 ff., 109 ff., and Pls. I–III.

3. Above, pp. 35 ff. These sparse facts may be supplemented by information obtained from architectural or sculptural members that may plausibly be attributed to both buildings. See text II, pp. 51 ff.

4. See, for example, the Geometric temples at Antissa, Perachora, Galataki, ancient Solygeia (the latter restored in the sixth century), and, possibly, at Eleusis: W. Lamb, "Antissa," *BSA*, 32 (1931/32), 42 ff., 45 ff.; Humfry Payne, *Perachora*, I (Oxford, 1940), 27 ff.; N. D. Verdelis, "A Sanctuary at Solygeia," *Archaeology*, 15 (1962), 186 ff.; Otto Rubensohn, "Das Weihehaus von Eleusis und sein Allerheiligstes," *JDAI*, 70 (1955), 31 f., and Mylonas, op. cit., pp. 57 ff.; and such archaic examples as Building B on the Akropolis (Theodor Wiegand et al., *Die archaische Poros-Architektur der Akropolis zu Athen* [Cassel and Leipzig, 1904], pp. 155 ff.); Temple B at Corinth (B. H. Hill, *The Springs, Peirene, Sacred Spring, Glauke* [*Corinth*, I, pt. 6], pp. 129 ff.; late archaic?); Building D at Kalydon (E. Dyggve, *Das Laphrion* [*Arkaeologisk-Kunsthistoriske Skrifter*, I, no. 2, Copenhagen, 1948], pp. 53, 271 ff., 331 ff.); at Larisa (*Larisa*, I, 75 ff., pl. 36, and figs. 3, 12); the Kabeirion at Thebes (*Kabirenheiligtum*, I, 11, fig. 1, and pls. 2,

3); and possibly a temple at Emporio on Chios (John Boardman, "Archaeology in Greece, "*JHS*, 76 [1956], 38).

For discussion of a number of these examples and evaluation of the evidence for others, see Carl Weickert, *Typen der archaischen Architektur in Griechenland und Kleinasien* (Augsburg, 1929), pp. 7 ff., 18 ff., 80 ff., 125 f.; and E. Gabrici, "Studi archeologici selinuntini," *MonAnt*, 43 (1956), cols. 340–41.

5. Dinsmoor (pp. 233 f.) refers to a "small marble temple-like structure with an apse" of fourth-century date on Paros, and Wiegand, op. cit., p. 162, to an unspecified Hellenistic sanctuary at Herakleia-on-the-Latmos (certainly not the Temple of Athena), where "die Wände verlaufen anfangs gerade, um sich dann in einer Apsis zu vereinigen." (I have been unable to obtain further information about the "small fourth century apsidal building found in Colophon" cited in *Hesperia*, 20 [1951], 23, n. 80, in spite of the kind assistance of Louise Adams Holland.)

Certain writers have drawn an analogy between the apsidal structure beneath the Great Altar at Pergamon and the Hieron (e.g., A. B. Cook, *Zeus*, I [Cambridge, 1914], 120; II [1925], 953 f., n. 3; and, recently, Gerda Bruns, "Umbaute Götterfelsen," *JDAI*, 75 [1960], 101 ff.). But until that structure has been more fully explored and explained, no satisfactory consideration of its function or form is possible. The character of its masonry, as recorded in *Pergamon*, III, pt. 1, 84, suggests that it does not antedate the period of Philetairos. As Erwin Ohlemutz pointed out in *Die Kulte und Heiligtümer der Götter in Pergamon* (Giessen, 1940), p. 196, n. 13, even the presumed formal analogy between this structure and the Hieron is doubtful. Hence I shall not comment on it further.

I do not refer to the presence of apsidal exedrae in such later buildings as the Great Stoa at Kalydon (Dyggve, op. cit., pp. 281 ff.).

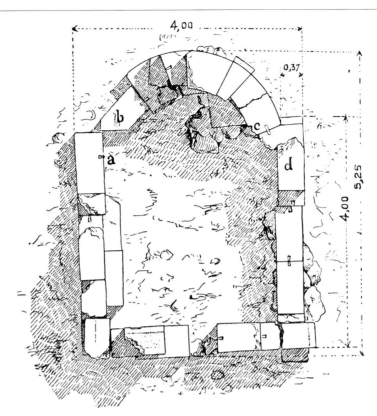

104. Delphi, Temple of Ge. Plan of the extant ruin

the immediate predecessor of the Hieron and the use of a variant form in the Hellenistic building imply that it had a special functional value for the performance of the rites of the *epopteia* that required the unknown architect of the third building to retain an apsidal termination for his cella (fig. 44; Pl. CII). Whether the salient apses of its predecessors also sprang from angular returns or emerged directly from the lines of the lateral walls must remain uncertain. Both the conscious use of a traditional form and the existence of at least one analogous archaic example, the little chapel of Ge at Delphi (fig. 104),[6] suggest that the salient apse of the first Hieron may have had a similar shape. In retaining this structural form, the early Hellenistic architect of the Hieron was evidently meeting an orthodox requirement. His innovation lay in inserting an apsidal interior into a rectangular frame, in concealing this evidently meaningful form within the neutral walls of the normal Greek cella. This prime architectural feature of the Hieron is seemingly unique among extant Greek cult buildings.[7] Equally without strict analogy is the installation of the apse—the abaton

6. Fernand Courby, *La terrasse du temple* (*Fd-Delphes*, II, pt. 1²), pp. 186–87, fig. 142.

7. I say "seemingly" because of the possibility that a second, still earlier example of the type exists in a small building at Nymphaia in the Crimea that has been interpreted as a Kabeirion, partly because of its analogies to the Hieron in Samothrace: M. M. Khu-

diak, "Two Sanctuaries on the Akropolis of Nymphaia," *Works of the State Hermitage*, 2 (1958), 83–93. But it is my impression from fig. 3 on p. 85 and John Boardman, "Greek Archaeology on the Shores of the Black Sea," *Archaeological Reports for 1962–63* (1963), p. 47, fig. 30, that the "apse" visible in this photograph and described as such by the author is neither set off

105. Dreros, Geometric Temple. Detail of eschara

with its stepped platform, its projecting bema, its subdivision into a central and two lateral areas. The design of this portion of the building must have been determined by the nature of the liturgical acts performed within it and, again, may have been inherited and prescribed.[8]

A second feature of the interior, the eschara, or hearth constructed in the underpavement of the wide central aisle (fig. 85), was doubtless retained, once again, from the original predecessor of the Hieron. Like the apse, it occurs almost exclusively in Archaic and pre-

from the lateral walls of this mid-fifth-century building nor structural—i.e., that it is an apsidal platform within the building over which no wall arose. The additional fact that the author describes the "apse" of the Hieron as constructed of ten marble blocks reinforces this impression, since although the precise figure is incorrect, it can refer only to the marble platform within the apse of the Hieron, the true apse itself being built of porous limestone. I am indebted to Virginia Grace for knowledge of this article.

The enormous unfinished Doric temple dedicated to Zeus Basileus by Antiochus IV Epiphanes at Lebadea also contained an apse within the cella. It differed from the earlier Hieron in being peripteral. Hence its plan, too, is unique among known cult buildings. Both the function of this apse and the nature of its covering are unknown. For the most re-

cent discussion of the inscription containing specifications for the construction of the temple—the sole source of information regarding its architectural form —see Georges Roux, "Le devis de Livadie et le temple de Zeus Basileus," *MusHelv*, 17 (1960), 175–84, where the most pertinent earlier bibliography is cited.

8. If I am correct in assuming that the "apse" in the sanctuary at Nymphaia discussed in n. 7, above, is a platform rather than a true apse, it constitutes a second example of the presence of a similar, if not an identical, ritual installation in a related cult building which also had an archaic predecessor. It is of interest, then, in providing further evidence of the meaningful character of the apsidal shape as such, which, it has been suggested, may symbolize a cave and be used in connection with the worship of chthonic divinities. For discussion of this point, see text II, pp. 36 ff.

106. Prinias, Temple A. View showing eschara

Archaic times (figs. 105, 106),[9] and its presence in the early Hellenistic Hieron implies a counterpart in the archaic *epopteion.*[10] Elsewhere in this traditional sanctuary, indeed in the nearby Temenos, a similar sequence of sacrificial hearths is documented.[11]

If we assume that the two other prime features of the plan of the Hellenistic cella, namely, the benches parallel to its lateral walls and the pair of symmetrically placed doors that penetrate those walls, were also present in the first Hieron—as is reasonable to suppose, in

9. For example, at Dreros: Spyridon Marinatos, "Le temple géométrique de Dreros," *BCH*, 60 (1936), 226 f., pl. 27; in the apsidal temple cited above (n. 4) at Antissa; in the Temple of Hera Limenia at Perachora: Payne, op. cit., pp. 111 f.; in Temples A and B at Prinias: Luigi Pernier, "Templi arcaici sulla patèla di Prinias," *Annuario,* 1 (1914), 33 f., 41 f., figs. 6, 7, 9, 10, 13, 14, 15, 17, and "New Elements for the Study of the Archaic Temple at Prinias," *AJA,* 38 (1934), 173 f.; in the Temple at Neandria: *Neandria,* p. 26 and fig. 55; in the Sanctuary of Herakles at Thasos: Marcel Launey, *Le sanctuaire et le culte d'Héraklès à Thasos* (*Études thasiennes,* I), pp. 36, 170 ff.; at Aliki on the southeast coast of that island: "Chronique des fouilles . . . en 1961," *BCH,* 86 (1962), 953, fig. 19, and p. 957; 88 (1964), 884 ff., figs. 1, 4, 5, 12; in Temple C at Selinus: K.P., p. 98; and possibly at Koressia on Keos: G. Welter, *AA,* 69 (1954), cols. 67 f. I do not include here the numerous examples of escharai found out-of-doors in sanctuaries or of the so-called circular eschara.

For comment on the meaning of the term "eschara" and discussion of the possible origin of the type, see Fernand Robert, *Thymélè* (Bibliothèque des Écoles françaises d'Athènes et de Rome, 147 [Paris, 1939]), pp. 185 ff., and M. Guarducci, "La 'eschara' del tempio greco arcaico," *Studi e materiali di storia della religioni,* 13 (1937), 159–65, as well as Marinatos and Launey, loc. cit. Although the type is essentially archaic, its retention in the Hellenistic Hieron and the occurrence in the fifth-century Ionic temple at Locri of what appears to be an eschara rather than, as it is described, a bothros (K.P., pp. 7 f., pl. 1) invalidates the statement of Constantine G. Yavis, *Greek Altars* (St. Louis, 1949), p. 208, that it does not occur in temples after the Archaic period.

10. For speculation on whether the slightly asymmetrical position of the eschara in the Hellenistic building results from retention of the exact location of such a sacrificial hearth in its first predecessor, see text II, p. 56.

11. See *Hesperia,* 21 (1952), 29 ff.; *Guide, Guide²,* p. 60; and, for illustration of these now destroyed escharai, *S,II,* pp. 21 ff., pls. 2, 4–7, where they are mistakenly interpreted as bothroi.

view of its function—what of the deep porch which preceded the Hellenistic cella? Was it, too, derived from a predecessor?

We have seen that although the plan of the Hieron called for a Doric porch, it was not completed until long after the construction of the cella, and then according to a slightly revised ground plan.[12] Both the projected and the executed porches were characterized by two features: their extension beyond the cella laterally and their use of two rows of columns separated by a pair of columns, one at each side. Although by no means standard practice, the use of a projecting porch or, rather, the omission of the lower two steps of the crepidoma beneath the antae and cella walls occurs in a number of classical or Hellenistic cult buildings. For the most part, they are tetrastyle prostyle in plan and have only a single row of columns;[13] but two are hexastyle,[14] and one, the presumably contemporary Temple of Zeus at Megalopolis, appears to have been identical in disposition with the projected porch of the Hieron, its inner row of columns numbering four and contained within the antae (fig. 107).[15]

The closest general analogy to the spacious porch-pronaos of the completed Hieron is to be found in a group of archaic Sicilian temples [16] characterized by what has been called a

12. Above, pp. 84 ff.

13. The later Temple of Dionysos in Athens: W. Dörpfeld and Emil Reisch, *Das griechische Theater* (Athens, 1896), pp. 19 ff.; the second Kabeirion at Thebes: *Kabirenheiligtum*, I, 12 f., pl. 3; the "temple en calcaire" in the Marmaria at Delphi: R. Demangel, *Le Sanctuaire d'Athèna Pronaia (Marmaria), Topographie du Sanctuaire* (*FdDelphes*, II, pt. 3), pp. 95, 109; Émile Bourget, *Les ruines de Delphes* (Paris, 1914), pp. 326–28; G. Karo, "En marge de quelques textes delphiques," *BCH*, 34 (1910), 217 f.; the Temple of Asklepios in Delos: Fernand Robert, *Trois sanctuaires sur le rivage occidental (Délos, XX)*, pp. 71 ff., figs. 48, 49; and, at least in its Hellenistic phase, the Temple of Artemis at Aulis: "Chronique des fouilles," *BCH*, 81 (1957), 586 ff.; 83 (1959), 682 ff.; and 84 (1960), 759 f. The small Bastion Temple at Delos and the North Market Temple at Miletos unavoidably fall into this category, too, because their cella walls are abutted by lateral stoai beyond which only their porches projected (for these buildings, see "Chronique des fouilles . . . en 1925," *BCH*, 49 [1925], 466–68; Armin von Gerkan, *Der Nordmarkt und der Hafen am der Löwenbucht* [*Milet*, I, pt. 6], pp. 30 ff.).

14. The temples of Zeus at Megalopolis and Despoina at Lykosoura (*Excavations at Megalopolis 1890–1891* [London, 1892], pp. 55 ff.; of the extensive bibliography on Lykosoura, it will suffice to cite B. Leonardos, «'Ανασκαφαὶ τοῦ ἐν Λυκοσούρᾳ ἱεροῦ τῆς Δεσποίνης,» *Praktika*, 1896, pp. 101 ff., pl. 2).

15. Roux, p. 215, seems skeptical about the correctness of the restored plan of the Temple at Megalopolis. Although no elements of the superstructure are preserved and the restored plan illustrated here is conjectural, I find it a reasonable solution in accord with the scant evidence available. However, the date of this temple, over which the nineteenth-century excavators puzzled, remains uncertain.

16. Particularly Temples C and F at Selinus, the Olympieion, and the Temple of Apollo on Ortygia at Syracuse: K.P., pp. 95 ff., especially p. 105, fig. 79, pl. 12; pp. 117 ff., pls. 16, 29; pp. 62 ff., pl. 7; pp. 66 ff., pl. 8, respectively. Temple G at Selinus (ibid., pp. 121 ff., pl. 17) and the Temple of Athena, formerly called of Ceres, at Paestum (Friedrich Krauss, *Die Tempel von Paestum*, I: *Der Athena Tempel* [Berlin, 1959], pls. 1, 3, 10, 11) offer further variations on this scheme. In the East, Robert Koldewey restored an extraordinary elaboration of this type to the later temple in Tarsus: "Das sogenannte Grab des Sardanapal zu Tarsus," *Aus der Anomia, Archäologische Beiträge Carl Robert . . . dargebracht* (Berlin, 1890), pp. 178 ff.

Dinsmoor (p. 269) has noted the similar disposition of columns in the porch of the Hieron and the archaic Sicilian temples cited above. However, his subsequent "description" of the plan of the Hieron is wholly incorrect, retaining the false suggestion (above, pp. 12 ff.) that the cella contained two rows of columns —a suggestion twice refuted by Chapouthier (*BCH*, 49 [1925], 466, and *Les Dioscures*, p. 163) on sound grounds that were later confirmed.

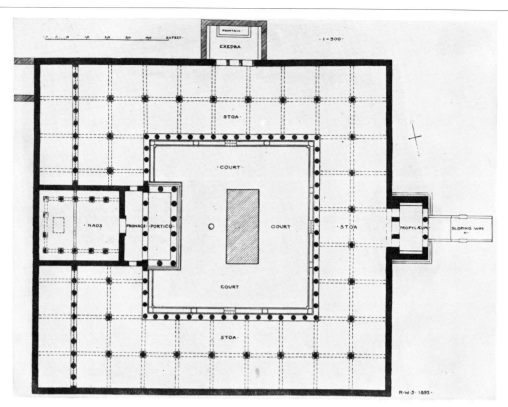

107. Megalopolis, Sanctuary of Zeus. Restored plan

peristyle porch[17]—that is, by the coupling of a deep hexastyle porch, containing two rows of columns set off from each other by a pair of intermediate columns, with an outer colonnade along the flanks and rear of the building to create a normal peristyle (cf. fig. 108). The location of the Hieron precluded the use of a peristyle throughout its history, given the tenacity with which specific cult spots were retained in the Sanctuary, for in all periods it was confined between a great altar at the west and the stepping-stones at which a rite preliminary to the *epopteia* took place at the east.[18] The fact that the Sicilian peristyle porch is an archaic architectural type suggests the possibility that the earliest Hieron, like its Hellenistic successor, may have been equipped with a deep porch-pronaos. But this point cannot be ascertained. The first *epopteion*, like the Anaktoron within which the initial rite of initiation was performed, may equally possibly have lacked any such feature. In that case, its addition to the building, whether in its second[19] or third phase, would imply the necessity of meeting

17. Robert L. Scranton, "Interior Design in Greek Temples," *AJA,* 50 (1946), 46 f. Instead of regarding the naos and pronaos of these buildings as preceded by "a room completely delineated by columns," I should be inclined to think of them in simpler fashion as prostyle temples that had been included within or surrounded by a peristasis, i.e., that they reflect the fusion of the developed prostyle type with the peripteral temple.

18. See text II, pp. 17 ff., 54 ff.

19. If we are correct in suggesting that the Early Classical pedimental sculptures discussed ibid., pp. 60 ff., may have come from the immediate predecessor of the Hellenistic Hieron, it is possible, if not obligatory, that that second Hieron had already acquired a columnar porch.

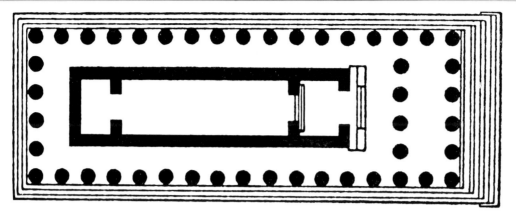

108. Selinus, Temple C. Restored plan

a liturgical need, perhaps the simple necessity of providing an appropriate place where a growing number of *mystai* could await their individual admission to the cella.[20]

The presence or absence of a porch before the main door of the forebears of the Hieron must remain a matter of speculation. But it is clear that the specific scheme adopted for both the projected and executed porches was not without antecedents and that the coupling of a projecting porch and a cella lacking an outer peristyle would not have looked novel to contemporary eyes.[21] A final feature of the plan, the fact that one stepped down into the interior of the building, though comparatively rare, is also not without precedent.[22]

Thus, with one exception, the characteristic features of the plan of the Hellenistic Hieron may all be found in archaic architecture. Their retention in the late-fourth-century building implies their derivation from its predecessors and their primary significance in the ritual of the *epopteia*. In incorporating these traditional elements in a rectangular edifice of temple-like exterior aspect, the architect of the third *epopteion* created a unique ground plan.

THE CELLA

The foundations of the cella are built of regular blocks of porous limestone for the most part laid as binders (Pl. I), a technique used extensively but not exclusively in the foundations of the neighboring Altar Court in the decade 340–330 B.C.[23] and, outside Samothrace, in certain structures dating from the last quarter of the century, among them the naiskos at

20. For evidence of individual admission into the cella, see above, p. 120, and, for its implications, text II, p. 21. It is interesting to recall that it has long been suggested that the divergences in plan of the Sicilian pronaoi are the result of cult requirements rather than of aesthetic considerations; see K.P., pp. 89, 201.

21. Cf. the date of the majority of the examples cited in n. 13, above.

22. For example, in the Temple at Neandria: *Neandria*, pp. 25 f.; and in the second Kabeirion at Thebes: *Kabirenheiligtum*, I, 12 f.

23. See Vol. 4, pt. II, pp. 70, 104 ff., Pls. I, III.

Didyma.[24] There, too, the width of the foundation is equivalent to the depth of the binders. The second course of the eastern cella foundation and all the foundation courses of the porch are laid as stretchers. A mixture of techniques also occurs in the Altar Court, there, however, in one and the same section of the foundation.

The stereobate-stylobate course is enlivened by two recesses (Pls. IV, XCV.3, 4, CIII, CIV, CVIII, CIX). Again, there was local precedent for the use of this device. The steps and step-elements of the Altar Court have a single recess,[25] those of the Propylon of the Temenos, dating from the same quarter of the century, both single and double recesses. But this device was popular throughout the century and later.[26] Its adoption by the architect of the Hieron was inevitable, given the character of the wall that he devised for the cella and the fact that the stereobate provided both the structural and the aesthetic basis for that wall. The firm, reiterated horizontals of the double-recessed stereobate establish an emphatic base for the wall and set it off sharply from the euthynteria and the smooth-faced dado. Equally important, they are attuned to the powerful rhythm of the wall supported by that dado. And it is precisely in his design for the cella walls that the unknown architect of the Hieron made one of his most effective and characteristic contributions to the building.

Confronted with the necessity to build a long cella and with the impossibility of enclosing it by a colonnade, he avoided the lifeless visual monotony that would have characterized the long flanks of the building had the walls been built of uniform courses of smoothly dressed masonry. By adopting a recently invented system of coursing and exploiting the aesthetic possibilities inherent in the technical procedures normally used in the cutting and laying of blocks, he enlivened the walls, creating subtle contrasts of surface, texture, and tone on a building stripped of the customary bold juxtaposition of forms, of gleaming surfaces and intense shadow, produced by framing a rectilinear cella with the animating forms of a colonnade (cf. Pls. CVII, CIX, CX).

The structural system employed for the walls of the Hieron, whereby two high courses

24. *Didyma*, I, 102 f., pl. 70, Z512. For discussion of the chronology of the Didymaion, including the execution of what was certainly an earlier plan, see C. C. van Essen, "Notes sur le deuxième Didymaion," *BCH*, 70 (1946), 607 ff. (Armin von Gerkan's proposed emendation of Knackfuss' reconstruction of the naiskos, "Der Naiskos im Tempel von Didyma," *JDAI*, 57 [1942], 183–98, even if wholly correct, does not necessarily affect its date. I find his arguments in support of a mid-third-century date inconclusive and unconvincing. Rehm, too [*Didyma*, II, 15], appears to have questioned his conclusion.) Among other examples, note the late-fourth-century temple at Kastraki near Karditsa in Boeotia: *BCH*, 60 (1936), 3 ff., pl. 2; and the Sanctuary of Asklepios at Troizen: G. Welter, *Troizen und Kalauria* (Berlin, 1941), pl. 11.

25. Vol. 4, pt. ii, Pls. IV, V, XXXV, XXXVI.

26. Steps with two recesses occur in the fourth century at Olympia in the Metroon, the Philippeion, and the Echo and South Stoai (*Olympia*, I, pls. 24, 51, 60); in the Thersilion at Megalopolis (op. cit. [above, n. 14], pl. 12); on the Tholos at Delphi (*FdDelphes*, II, pt. 2, pp. 2 f., pl. 3); in the temples at Tegea, Nemea, and Stratos (Dugas, pls. 12–17, 32; A. W. Lawrence, *Greek Architecture* [Pelican History of Art, Baltimore, 1957], pl. 97a; Courby-Picard, pls. 4, 7, 8); Roux, p. 91, suggests that the stylobate of the Temple of Asklepios at Epidauros may have been similarly recessed; but, judging by p. 206, fig. 44, and pl. 55, he does not accept the older restoration of such steps to the Temple of Artemis (*Praktika*, 1906, pl. Γ',fig. 1). For second-century examples, see below, p. 218.

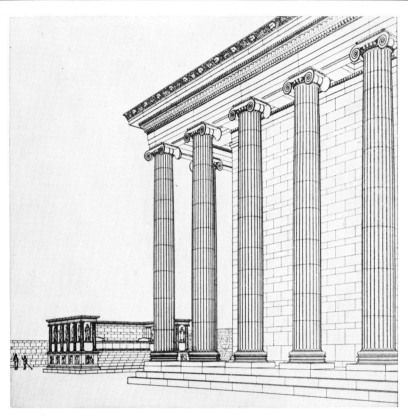

109. Priene, Temple of Athena. Restored elevation

alternate with a low binding course, appears to have been used for the first time in the Temple of Athena at Priene dedicated in 334 B.C. (fig. 109) [27] and, at a later date, in the Ionic Temple at Messa.[28] It was also retained for the Hiera Stoa in the Market of Priene,[29] is documented in Pergamon,[30] and very likely occurred elsewhere in Asia Minor in the Hellenistic period.[31] In Priene, the courses of stretchers are composed of an inner and an outer face separated by filling material of splinters of stone and clay; in the Hieron, the marble stretchers are backed by blocks of the same porous limestone used in the foundation—an economical

27. *Priene,* pp. 95 ff., fig. 66; Martin Schede, *Die Ruinen von Priene* (Berlin and Leipzig, 1934), pp. 30 ff. and fig. 32 (our fig. 109, above). There, too, some of the upper courses, both high and low, are slightly higher than their counterparts below.

28. Robert Koldewey, *Die antiken Baureste der Insel Lesbos* (Berlin, 1890), p. 56, pl. 22.

29. *Priene,* pp. 194, 201 f. Here the same number of nine wall courses used above the dado in the Hieron occurs.

30. In the Temple of Hera Basileia, *Pergamon,* VI, 104, pl. 33; and the so-called Theater Temple, ibid., IV, 45, pls. 30, 33.

31. I suspect that the Temple of Athena and the Upper Market Temple in Pergamon, the Artemision at Magnesia, the Smintheion, the Temple of Dionysos at Teos, and others, the walls of which have been restored with alternating courses of stretchers and binders, owing to the preservation of a few examples of both types of blocks on these sites, might well prove to have been constructed in the same fashion as the Hieron, had a sufficient number of their blocks been excavated and studied. Nineteenth-century investigators confronted with two varieties of wall blocks tended to assume, as did our predecessors in Samothrace, that they automatically implied a simple alternation of high and low courses.

110. Sardis, Temple of Artemis. Detail of the wall

technique that may have been suggested by the sparing use of marble on the Altar Court, to judge by the scant evidence preserved.[32] Furthermore, the walls of the Temple of Athena at Priene, unlike those of the Hieron, are smoothly dressed in the normal classical fashion.

The earliest example outside Samothrace of the use of drafted-margin masonry for the walls of a building is the late-fourth-century Temple of Artemis at Sardis (fig. 110).[33] The essential feature of this system, retention of the protective *Werkzoll* removed from smoothly dressed blocks, occurs earlier in Greek architecture only on unfinished buildings like the Mnesiklean Propylaea on the Akropolis in Athens (that is, accidentally, as a result of circumstances that have prevented its removal) or in the construction of terrace, fortification, and peribolos walls,[34] whether because it was considered unnecessary or undesirable to trim their extended surfaces to smoothness. Innumerable examples of such walls and unfinished portions of buildings must have arrested the gaze of any sharp-eyed individual interested in building in the fourth century and earlier. It remained for one to discern in this functional, procedural device its decorative potentialities and to exploit them for conscious

32. See Vol. 4, pt. ii, pp. 51 ff., 71 f. The fact that marble had to be imported and that the inner surface of the wall was stuccoed made this economical system the only reasonable one.

33. Howard Crosby Butler, *Sardis*, Vol. II, *Architecture*, pt. 1: *The Temple of Artemis* (Leiden, 1925), pp. 29 ff., figs. 25, 44, 52, 101 a, b. Here, too, the dado of the wall is smoothly dressed; the coursing is isodomic. For the date, see ibid., pp. 100 ff., 140 ff., and Gottfried Gruben, *AM*, 76 (1961), 180 f., 192.

34. For consideration of the sources of drafted-margin masonry, see Walter Wrede, *Attische Mauern* (Athens, 1933), p. 54 and figs. 37, 44, 52; Robert L. Scranton, *Greek Walls* (Cambridge, 1941), pp. 115, 129 ff.; and, most recently, Roland Martin, *Manuel d'architecture grecque*, I (Paris, 1965), 418 f. On the earlier examples of the occurrence on buildings of some form of drafting cited by Martin, the technique is limited to courses below the wall or to its inner face (e.g., the Doric stoa of the Asklepieion in Athens, where the raised surfaces of the incompletely drafted blocks are also not smoothly dressed panels as they are on the developed drafted-margin masonry of the Hieron).

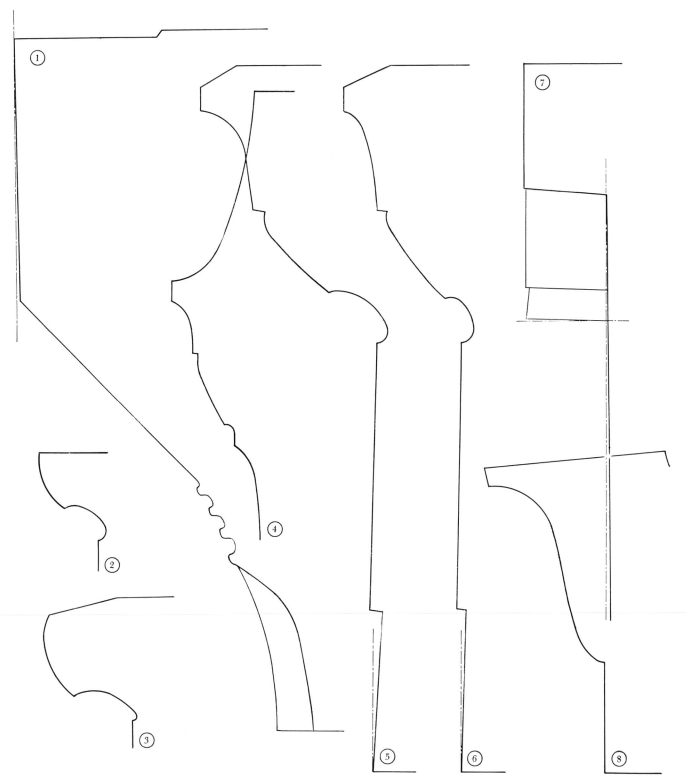

111. Samothrace, the Altar Court. Profiles of moldings. 5, 6: the epikranitis

ornamental purposes. Both the special nature of the aesthetic problem faced by the architect of the Hieron and the lack of any earlier example of the use of drafted-margin masonry for the exterior of a building would make it tempting to suggest that it was he who took this fateful step. Yet the fact that such masonry was imitated in stucco wall decoration in Olynthian houses antedating 348 B.C. precludes this suggestion.[35] In any case, whoever first employed the technique of drafted-margin masonry for ornamental purposes—and it proved a technique increasingly popular in the subsequent Hellenistic period, from which true rustication developed in Roman times[36]—the Hieron is the earliest preserved building in which that device was coupled with its particular system of alternating courses, a system not known before the third quarter of the fourth century B.C.

The use of this system meant that the wall was crowned by a low course related in function to the string course topping the orthostates, and that the drafting of the terminal blocks of this course was adjusted to the contours of the pilaster and anta capitals (Pls. XVI, XVII). Smoothly dressed, like the dado, the clear-cut verticals of the antae and pilasters provided a strong simple frame for the richly textured wall, uniting its multi-zoned surface into a broad base for the entablature. Like the pilasters at the rear corners of the Treasury of Kyrene in Delphi,[37] a building contemporary with the Altar Court in execution, the abutting pilasters of the Hieron were slightly narrower on the rear wall of the building than on its flanks, and their capitals must always have been identical with those of the antae (Pl. CVII).

It is not surprising, given the evident tact of our architect and his willingness to adjust to traditional forms, that he heeded the proximity of the Altar Court in designing these capitals and co-ordinated them with one of the most conspicuous and characteristic features of that structure, its epikranitis (fig. 111, nos. 5, 6).[38] For the cavetto crown and the blunt hawk's beak followed by a concave recess and high fascia are so similar to the profiles of the outer face of that member as obviously to have been modeled on it. This similarity is especially worthy of remark since the detailing of the two buildings is at times very dissimilar, reflecting the attitudes of two very different if, as we shall see, contemporary or near-con-

35. See above, pp. 140 ff., and below, pp. 205 ff., for discussion of this type of interior decoration.

36. It is needless to cite examples of the continuing use of this ornamental form for the walls of later buildings and monuments or for their dadoes and steps, but it is interesting to note that the conservative Vitruvius still recommended this technique because of its pleasing aesthetic effect: 4.4.4. (This passage has been misunderstood by English translators, hence mistranslated. It clearly refers to drafted-margin masonry, as the comparison with a picture—i.e., a framed field—indicates. Louise A. Holland calls my attention to the related phraseology of 7.3.10.)

37. Bousquet, pp. 41 f., pls. 16, 20, 30, 32–34. For the chronology of the building, see p. 29. Such rear corner pilasters also occur at Delos in the earlier Temple of the Athenians and the later Dodekatheon: *Délos*, XII, 145 ff., pls. 16, 19; XXII, 67 ff., pls. B, E. In both instances, the rear pilasters are the wider. On the early Hellenistic Temple of Zeus at Priene, the corner pilasters are equal in width on both the rear and lateral walls: *Priene*, p. 142, fig. 111.

38. Vol. 4, pt. II, Pl. XXXVIII.5. For analysis of this wall capital and its earlier fourth-century antecedents, see ibid., pp. 74 ff.

112. Partial reconstruction of the wall entablature of the Hieron. Samothrace Museum

113. Partial reconstruction of the wall entablature of the Altar Court.
Samothrace Museum

temporary architects. Nowhere are their divergences in taste more apparent than in the overall proportions of their entablatures or the features of their architraves and simas.

Like the Altar Court, the Hieron reflects the general fourth-century movement toward a lower architrave than frieze that culminated in the Hellenistic age (cf. figs. 112, 113). The relative proportion of architrave to frieze in the Hieron (1:1.16) is more conservative than that of the Altar Court (1:1.23).[39] The Temple of Zeus at Stratos, its nearest counterpart in this respect (1:1.15), is slightly later than the Altar Court.[40] But closely related to both the Hieron and Stratos are the general proportions of the considerably earlier temple at Tegea (1:1.14).[41] The height of the taenia in relation to the architrave as a whole on the Hieron (1:8.53) and of the regulae to the taenia (1:3.4) is paralleled on the Leonidaion at Olympia (1:9.25) and the Philonian Porch at Eleusis (1:3.5), respectively,[42] that is, on buildings completed slightly later than the Altar Court, where the heavy regulae preserve an old-fashioned relationship to the taenia of 1:1.21. It is, in fact, precisely in this detail, in its strong, firm regulae and conical guttae, that the entablature of the Altar Court differs most markedly from the lighter, more minute forms of the Hieron—there, and in the execution of its sima. As a result of this feature, the proportion of the combined height of the taenia and regulae to the height of the architrave on the Altar Court (1:5.42) is, again, *retardataire* for its date in comparison with that of the Hieron (1:8.28), which even exceeds the early-third-century Arsinoeion (1:7.5) in its exaggeration of these contrasts. So, too, the height of its guttae in relation to its taenia (1:6.2) is closer to the proportions of the Arsinoeion (1:7) than to those of the Altar Court (1:4).[43] Otherwise, the closest parallels for the architrave of the Hieron point to a date ca. 325 B.C. or, broadly speaking, very late in the third quarter of the century.

The classical norm of 2:3 for the proportion of triglyphs to metopes, a norm followed by the architect of the Altar Court, also governs the frieze of the Hieron. The triangular

39. For discussion of the entablature of the Altar Court, see ibid., pp. 78 ff., where pertinent statistics are also cited for other fourth-century Doric buildings in so far as published figures exist for them. I shall not repeat the general trend of this discussion, to which the reader may refer directly.

The occasional minor discrepancies between the figures cited for the Hieron in this discussion and those reported in the present volume result from the fact that the former were based on typical blocks, whereas those quoted here are median figures calculated on the basis of the extremes in the dimensions of the preserved blocks. For the variations in the size of the blocks in a given course on the several sides of the cella, see above, pp. 45, 70 f.

40. For the date, see Courby-Picard, pp. 85 ff.

41. For the date of this temple, see the bibliog-

raphy of P. E. Arias, *Skopas* (*Quaderni e guide di archeologia*, I [Rome, 1952]), pp. 116 ff.; and Vol. 4, pt. II, p. 74, n. 57.

42. For the date of the Leonidaion, see Emil Kunze and Hans Schleif, *IV. Bericht über die Ausgrabungen in Olympia, 1940–41* (Berlin, 1944), p. 14; and Franz Willemsen, *Die Löwenkopf-Wasserspeier vom Dach des Zeustempels* (*Olympische Forschungen*, IV [Berlin, 1959]), p. 50. For the Philonian Porch, see Noack, pp. 112 f.

43. The height of the guttae in relation to that of the combined taenia and regulae (1:6.1), a proportion recurring both at Nemea and on the Arsinoeion (1:6), does not illumine the chronological position of the Hieron, nor does that of the regulae to the architrave (1:28.1).

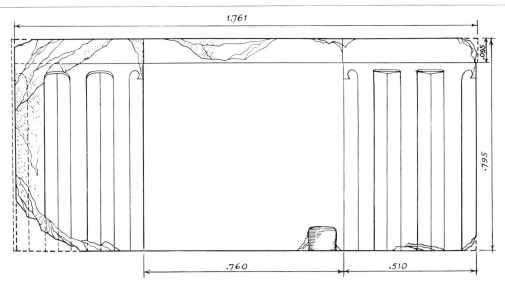

114. Samothrace, the Altar Court. Corner frieze block 586

cutting of the glyphs and the fully developed ears at the top of the outer half-glyphs, even the coexistence of both curved and straight-topped glyphs characteristic of the triglyphs of the Altar Court, recur on the Hieron (cf. Pl. XLIX; fig. 114).[44] The presence of both the new straight-topped glyphs and the older form of curving glyphs on the frieze of the Altar Court has been convincingly interpreted as evidence that crews of workmen of different origin were free to follow the practices with which they were familiar in the execution of such details—hence their lack of standardization.[45] The recurrence of this fluctuation a second time on a building adjacent to the Altar Court not only links the two in time but also implies the great likelihood that some of the workmen employed on the Altar Court were retained for the Hieron, that is, that the Hieron must have been in construction shortly after the Altar Court.[46]

The geisa of the two buildings are also interrelated (cf. Pl. XCVIII.1; fig. 115). Both exhibit the ovolo hawk's-beak crown, the blunt-tipped drip level with the viae, and the geison soffit equipped with a cyma reversa characteristic of fourth-century Doric cornices. Indeed, the very presence of the ovolo crown precludes a date for the Altar Court or the Hieron in any other century.[47] Although they differ in two respects, namely, in the contour of the hawk's beak and the spacing of the guttae, they have in common a further rare detail: the pointed oval section of the drip. The existence of this feature on both geisa again implies

44. For discussion of the genesis of such "ears" and their gradual adoption in the last decades of the fourth century, see Vol. 4, pt. II, pp. 82 f., and above, p. 71, n. 92. Schober's discussion of this form (pp. 5 f.) and assumption that it did not occur until the second century are strangely incorrect.

45. Vol. 4, pt. II, pp. 82 f.

46. A further implication of this detail, that the marble-cutters at work in the Sanctuary during the decades when a succession of marble buildings was being erected were, like the marble itself, imported, is probable, given the absence of marble on the island. No tradition for this craft can have existed locally.

47. See Shoe, p. 106.

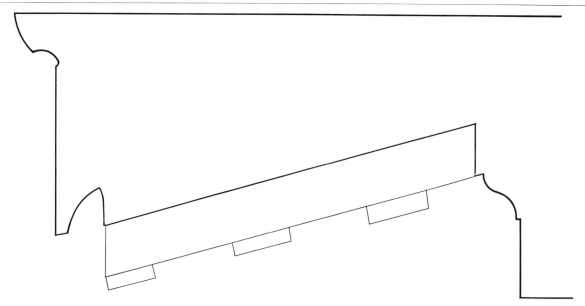

115. Samothrace, the Altar Court. Profile of geison (Scale 1 : 3)

the re-employment on the Hieron of workmen previously engaged on the Altar Court and the nearness in time, as well as space, of the two buildings.[48] The contour of the receding hawk's beak on the geison of the Altar Court, obviously designed to echo the recess on the continuous epikranitis beneath it, was replaced on the Hieron by a more conservative shape.[49] So, too, the spacing of the guttae on the geison of the Hieron is more conventional, the inner row being close to the cyma reversa of the soffit.[50]

Equally characteristic in type, proportion, and decoration are the forms of the Hieron's sima (Pls. LVI, XCIX.1, C; fig. 112). Its cyma recta profile between an upper and a lower fillet, its height in relation to that of the geison (1:1.2), and its carved ornament occur throughout the fourth century.[51] The slight notch between the cyma recta and the lower fillet that characterizes its profile, unlike that of the Altar Court, may be paralleled on a presumably late-fifth-century treasury in Delos and, toward the close and turn of the fourth century, on the Dodekatheon and the Monument of the Bulls in the same sanctuary.[52]

Although the basic ornamental scheme of this sima—its embellishment with lion's-head waterspouts and carved rinceaux—is dependent on mainland, especially Peloponnesian, practice,[53] the specific forms of these motifs are both individual and rooted in local tradition.[54]

48. This observation was made and its implication noted in Vol. 4, pt. II, p. 84.

49. The hawk's beak on the Doric geison of the Tholos at Epidauros overhangs the vertical face of the drip in a somewhat related manner: cf. Shoe, pl. 55, fig. 1.

50. Cf., for example, the geison from Tegea, ibid., pl. 44, Ad.

51. Ibid., pp. 90 f. For example, the proportion of the lower fillet to the cyma recta (1:3) occurs early in the century on the Metroon at Olympia (1:3.3) and at its very end on the Asklepieion at Delos (1:3).

52. Cf. ibid., pls. 41, fig. 5; 43, figs. 3 and 2, respectively. For the sima of the Altar Court, see Vol. 4, pt. II, pp. 84 ff., Pl. XXXVIII.8.

53. The generic type has been discussed by Mar-

116. Detail of lateral sima

117. Detail of lateral sima

118. Fragment of the lateral sima of the Propylon of the Temenos. Kunsthistorisches Museum, Vienna

The powerful lion's head at the center of each block emerges from a calyx of acanthus leaves from which two symmetrical stalks grow, one to the left, the other to the right margin of the block (figs. 116, 117). Each undulating, unfluted stalk sends forth shoots. Both these lesser stems and the three tendrils curling from them sprout from acanthus leaves, and between each pair of shoots there grows a lancet-shaped leaf.

The tripartite system peculiar to a series of Samothracian marble simas first appeared in still more elaborate form on the Ionic Propylon to the Temenos shortly after the mid-century (fig. 118).[55] In adopting this triple-tendril scheme rather than the otherwise standard two-tendril system of the period (cf. figs. 119, 120), the architect of the Hieron has simplified his model, eliminating the half-palmettes flanking its lion's head, converting its upright

tin Schede, *Antikes Traufleisten-Ornament* (Strassburg, 1909), chaps. 5 and 6, and more recently by Roux, pp. 328 ff. The suggestion made by G. Daux and A. Laumonier, "Fouilles de Thasos (1921–1922)," *BCH*, 47 (1923), 320, n. 2, that it was transmitted from the mainland to the northeastern Aegean via the Arsinoeion, reflects the incorrect chronology previously accepted for the buildings of the Sanctuary and must now be discarded.

54. As Schede pointed out, op. cit., pp. 83 ff.

55. For this Propylon, which will be published in Vol. 5 of this series, forthcoming, see, for the time being: *Hesperia*, 21 (1952), 21 ff.; *Guide*, pp. 57 ff.; *Guide*², pp. 58 ff.; Vol. 4, pt. II, pp. 85 f. It is worth noting that although Schede knew this building only in the incomplete and garbled form of the Austrians' "Old Temple," he recognized its sima as the first of the Samothracian examples: op. cit., pp. 86 ff. His emphasis on the contemporaneity of the "New Temple" and the Arsinoeion (p. 88) reflects both the customary earlier opinion and an inaccurate drawing of the anthemion frieze of the Arsinoeion in *S,I*, pl. 64, in which one of its recurrent palmettes seems so similar to the antefix of the Hieron as to have implied to him that they were the work of the same hand.

171

blossoms into lancet-shaped leaves, reducing the spiral coil of the terminal tendrils to the simple curl of the other tendrils, and sharpening the contrast between tendril and stem by hollowing the tendrils and eliminating the ribbed sheath normally used for stems and stalks. As a result of this last unusual detail,[56] the rinceaux of his sima retain an organic clarity of form lost on the sima of the Arsinoeion, where the tripartite Samothracian rinceau is presented in the customary fluted fashion (fig. 121).

In adopting this local variation on a popular contemporary pattern, our unknown architect has again revealed his visual tact, his willingness to adjust the ornamental details of his building to those of its immediate neighbors and thereby establish greater harmony between these otherwise disparate structures. No single feature of his long cella counted as heavily in the over-all effect of the exterior as the richly carved and, doubtless, painted sima (cf. Pl. CVII).[57] This thin course running the length of the building and crowning its walls gave final definition to its form, reiterating and balancing the unbroken lines of the recessed stereobate at its base, firmly weighting the wall by the very insistence of its repeated, long-drawn patterns and recurrent waterspouts, and provided a support for the vertical antefixes which, like the ridge antefixes cresting the roof above them, recall its triangular shape. In co-ordinating the details of his Doric entablature with the forms of its Doric neighbor, the Altar Court, and in echoing a feature of the only external ornamental member it had in common with its Ionic neighbor, the Propylon, he adjusted the Hieron to its visual setting to the maximum degree possible, given its own function and requirements.[58]

It is altogether possible that the painted sima of the Altar Court already echoed the tripartite scheme of the lateral sima of the Propylon.[59] In any case, it was retained on the next marble building constructed in the Sanctuary, the great rotunda dedicated by Arsinoe early in the third century, but abandoned in the later terracotta sima of the limestone Stoa.[60] Out-

---

56. It does recur on a few of the pilaster capitals from Didyma: cf. *Didyma*, I, pl. 114, F278, F271. The fact is not without interest, since these very capitals are also related in compositional scheme to the floral akroteria of the Hieron, for which see below, pp. 329 ff. Unfluted stalks appear again on the sima of the Market Temple in Pergamon.

57. See Roux, pp. 107 f., for payments made to a workman for painting the sculptured sima of the Temple of Asklepios at Epidauros according to a model provided by one of the leading masters, Hektoridas. For traces of paint on the sculptured sima of the naiskos at Didyma, see *Didyma*, I, 118. Given the frequent decoration of the lower fillet of analogous fourth-century simas with a carved or painted meander (e.g., the Tholos at Epidauros and the Leonidaion at Olympia), it is altogether likely that this molding of the

Hieron's sima was similarly painted.

58. Although the present porch of the Hieron is the work of a later period, it is tempting to think that the use of sculptured coffers for its ceiling was planned by the original architect of the Hieron and provided a second ornamental link with the Propylon. See above, pp. 114 ff.; below, pp. 232 f.

59. Vol. 4, pt. II, p. 86.

60. For the Arsinoeion, see *S,I*, pl. 59; for the Stoa, James R. McCredie, "Samothrace: Preliminary Report on the Campaigns of 1962–1964," *Hesperia*, 34 (1965), 108. Whether the local scheme had already been abandoned on the presumably painted marble sima of the Ptolemaion remains uncertain. [As this volume goes to press, blocks from still another Doric marble building are being discovered on the eastern hill of the Sanctuary. Although its function and many

119. Epidauros, Tholos. Detail of the sima

120. Corinth, South Stoa. Sima and antefix

121. Fragment of the sima of the Arsinoeion. Kunsthistorisches Museum, Vienna

side Samothrace, the triple-tendril sima has been found only in the Agora of Thasos.[61] Indeed, simas decorated solely with rinceaux of acanthus seem not to have been adopted elsewhere on the islands or along the coast of Asia Minor.[62]

It is not surprising that the powerful lion's-head waterspouts emerging from the acanthus calyx above each triglyph are stylistically linked with the mainland tradition from which the Samothracian rinceau sima stems.[63] These splendid heads (figs. 122–126) are characterized by eyes set deep beneath a scalloped, beetling brow; by a marked vertical furrow at the center of the brow; by prominent cheekbones over which the skin is tautly stretched; by the schematic, linear patterns which define the nose and muzzle; and by the double-rowed mane that frames each face. The very motif established sufficient visual connection with the waterspouts of the adjacent Altar Court to leave the designer of the Hieron free to depart from their specific form. For the little that is preserved of the Altar Court's waterspouts implies another standard variety [64] in which the head is ringed by a single row of locks, a type co-

of its features are not yet known, it is already apparent that it antedates the Arsinoeion, having been built by Philip III and Alexander IV, i.e., between 323 and 316 B.C.]

61. In the northwest stoa and the "édifice à paraskénia," the former dated at the end of the fourth century B.C., the latter somewhat earlier in the same century: Roland Martin, *L'Agora* (*Études thasiennes*, VI, pt. 1), p. 49, pls. 10, fig. 1, 26, fig. 1; and p. 74, pl. 22, fig. 5, respectively. (I am at a loss to understand Martin's retention of the long outmoded late-fourth-century date for the Victory of Samothrace, hence his still earlier date for the nearby Stoa: ibid., p. 49, n. 2.)

62. As Roux, pp. 329 ff., has noted. A variant form occurs on the naiskos at Didyma, where a ribbed stalk from which two tendrils uncoil springs from each side of each lion's head, and a third tendril droops directly from each side of the main acanthus calyx. See *Didyma*, I, pls. 200, 203, in particular.

63. Portions of twelve heads are preserved in the Samothrace Museum, five on exhibition either on the reconstruction of the entablature in Hall A (52.493) or on the south wall of the courtyard (49.452, 49.453, 49.544, 49.545). The remaining seven less well preserved fragments are in storage (49.568, 51.392, 51.692, 52.232, 53.555, 54.203, 56.66). There are, in addition, five fragmentary heads in the storeroom of the Kunsthistorisches Museum (346 K 1–5) and two in the Archaeological Museum of the Charles University in Prague. For the latter, see Jiří Frel, *Listy Filologické*, 74 (1950), 65 ff.; and *Fasti Archaeologici*, 5 (1952), 233, fig. 58.

The pieces in Samothrace show minor differences in execution that doubtless reflect the work of different hands, but provenance and style imply that they be-

longed to the cella. The majority of the fragments in Vienna appear to come from the later porch, but one (346 K 3) and possibly a second (346 K 5) are sufficiently related to 56.66 to suggest that they, too, may have belonged to the earlier cella. Although it is difficult to judge from the available photographs, in which the two heads in Prague have been taken in sharp light and at very different angles from those in Samothrace or Vienna, it is, again, conceivable that one (*Fasti Archaeologici*, loc. cit.) came from the cella, while the other is certainly later, as Frel proposed. The statement published in *Hesperia*, 21 (1952), 40, n. 85, should therefore be discarded. For further discussion of the porch sima and repairs to the sima of the cella, see below, pp. 223 ff.

64. See Vol. 4, pt. II, p. 41, fig. 51. It is a pity that in the valuable compendium by Franz Willemsen, op. cit. (above, n. 42), pp. 65 f., 126, both this fragmentary lion's head from a structure securely dated on the basis of architectural-epigraphic-ceramic evidence and the heads from the Hieron are misdated, the former being lumped with the later Hellenistic Stoa, the latter placed in the third century. Our own mistaken initial assumption that the fragmentary head from the adjacent Altar Court belonged to the Hieron (*Hesperia*, 21 [1952], 40, pl. 10 e) certainly contributed to this confusion. Again before the excavation of the Hieron was completed and full evidence had been obtained both for the superstructure of the building and its foundation fills, we, too, retained the traditional third-century date for it (e.g., ibid., 20 [1951], 21 ff., where the waterspout illustrated above in fig. 122 was incorrectly dated). But the correct late-fourth-century date of the Hieron proper has been available in print since 1955.

122. Detail of sima block 49.453. Samothrace Museum

123. Detail of sima block 49.544. Samothrace Museum

124. Detail of sima block 49.545. Samothrace Museum

125. Detail of sima block 49.452. Samothrace Museum

126. Detail of sima block 52.493. Samothrace Museum

existent with the double-rowed variety that was retained in the following century for the Arsinoeion (fig. 127). In their double-ringed manes and possibly, too, in the shape of their peaked ears, the lions of the Hieron and the Propylon have one or two features in common (cf. figs. 126, 118). Otherwise, they are wholly different in character and style, the latter wide-eyed and serene, the former tense and emotional. The dramatic contrasts of surface, the vigorous line by means of which the cheekbones of the Hieron lions are defined and emphasized (set off from the brow above by a bold horizontal furrow and from the muzzle below by a sharp indentation) or the looped brow and the tiered muzzle shaped are absent from the less powerfully conceived, more delicate features of the Propylon lions.

The closest relatives of the Hieron lions are the lions from the richly-carved marble sima of the Tholos at Epidauros (figs. 128, 129) [65] and from the painted terracotta sima of the Leonidaion at Olympia (fig. 130),[66] both completed in the third quarter of the century.[67] The snarling heads from the Tholos have in common with their less ferocious Samothracian counterparts their double-ringed mane and ridged locks, their looped, beetling brows and deep-set eyes, their knobby cheekbones again emphasized at the top by a violent horizontal, and their lean, taut faces stamped with linear patterns on the nose and muzzle.

In the shape and diagonal slashing of the nose and in the essentially tiered effect of the muzzle, the heads from the Leonidaion are somewhat more analogous to those of the Hieron, sharply as they differ in other basic respects. These connections are of interest chronologically, adding to the cumulative evidence that the immediate antecedents of the Hieron may all be found in the third quarter of the fourth century; they do not illumine the origin of the architect-sculptor [68] who devised the lions on the Hieron's sima. They remain individual in mood and style—in style primarily because of the curious, rippled surfaces of the muzzles with which the flaring nostrils are co-ordinated.

Happily, the raking sima does throw light on the artistic connections of our architect (cf. Pls. XCIX.2, C; figs. 55, 131). Essentially the same as the lateral sima in profile, if marked by a somewhat flatter cyma recta, it is decorated with a running pattern composed of three motifs: a palmette; a lotus flower springing from an acanthus calyx; and a blossom

65. For additional illustrations, see P. Cavvadias, *Fouilles d'Épidaure*, I (Athens, 1893), pl. 10; A. Defrasse and H. Lechat, *Épidaure* (Paris, 1895), pp. 111, 123; and Roux, pl. 43.

66. Willemsen, op. cit., pl. 60 and pp. 49 ff. Among the many heads from this sima in the Museum at Olympia are examples exhibiting the vertical furrow in the forehead characteristic of the lions from the Hieron but not visible in the piece from the Leonidaion illustrated above.

67. Cf. Ernst Pfuhl, "Bemerkungen zur Kunst des vierten Jahrhunderts," *JDAI*, 43 (1928), 30 f.; and Roux, p. 184.

68. Whether the architect created the model for these heads himself, as may well have been the case at this time, or it was the work of an associate cannot be determined. But as pointed out above (n. 57), Hektoridas, the sculptor responsible for the pedimental figures in the east gable of the Temple of Asklepios at Epidauros, also provided a painted model to be followed in the execution of the lion's-head waterspouts on the lateral sima of the temple.

127. Lion's-head waterspout from the Arsinoeion. Kunsthistorisches Museum, Vienna

128. Detail of the sima of the Tholos at Epidauros. National Archaeological Museum, Athens

129. Fragment of the sima of the Tholos at Epidauros. National Archaeological Museum, Athens

130. Olympia, Leonidaion. Waterspout

131. Fragment of the southern raking sima. Samothrace Museum

which, like the palmette, rises above a pair of symmetrical, coiled tendrils. Each tendril is overhung by a leaf, and it is the fluent curving stems from which the tendrils curl that link the vertical elements. Between every pair of lotus flowers there is, alternately, a palmette or a blossom and a palmette, save at the extremities, where the terminal lotus was carved half on the raking sima, half on the lateral sima.[69]

The use on a raking sima of a pattern composed of three rather than the more customary two motifs appears to have been introduced by Pytheos on the Temple of Athena at Priene.[70] Regardless of when its sima was actually executed, the fact that this scheme recurs in Priene both on the early Hellenistic Temple of Zeus (fig. 132) and on the later Stoa of Orophernes in the Agora [71] implies that it was a feature of the original design for the fourth-century temple. As an ornamental system, it became popular in Asia Minor, recurring on the frieze of the naiskos at Didyma,[72] as well as on certain of the richly carved bases of the later outer colonnade of the Temple,[73] on the raking sima of the Temple of Zeus at Magnesia,[74] and, at Pergamon, on a sima from an unidentified monument or building.[75]

69. Nineteen fragments of the raking sima of the Hieron were recovered, many of them small splinters. In addition to the two larger fragments illustrated on Pls. XCIX.2, C, the two most revealing pieces, each assembled from smaller fragments, are 49.194-49.363 A, B (fig. 131, above), found to the south of the building and now on exhibition in Hall A of the Museum, and 50.289 A, B–51.100, found to its north and now in storage. The former was published in *Hesperia*, 20 (1951), 23, pl. 13 c. For discussion of the latter and the slight but revealing differences between the northern and southern raking simas, see below, pp. 223 f.

70. See *Priene*, p. 108, fig. 78.

71. Ibid., pp. 145, fig. 116; 197, fig. 191. The triple scheme used in Priene employs a lotus flower and two varieties of palmettes; i.e., it lacks the Samothracian blossom.

72. *Didyma*, I, pl. 202, F548 e, again using a lotus flower and two varieties of palmette. For the chronology of this building, see above, n. 24.

73. Ibid., for example, pls. 151, F368; 152, F369; 154, F371.

74. *Magnesia*, pp. 147, fig. 158; 149, fig. 159.

75. *Pergamon*, VII, pt. 2, 378, no. 14. For an example outside this region, if close to Samothrace, see G. Bakalakis, Προανασκαφικὲς ᾿Ερευνες στὴ Θράκη (Thessaloniki, 1958), pl. 9, fig. ε. It reappears in Samothrace on the Arsinoeion: see below, pp. 223 f.

132. Priene, Temple of Zeus. Fragment of the raking sima

133. Priene, Temple of Athena. Anta capital

Thus, there was precedent for the use of a pattern composed of three ornamental motifs to decorate a raking sima. But the particular combination employed on the Hieron does not occur on its forebears. In replacing the open-petaled palmette that usually alternates with a "gesprengte" palmette by a ragged eight-petaled blossom, the architect of the Hieron introduced a new motif into the repertory of patterns used on raking simas.[76]

Again, it is the Temple of Athena at Priene that provides the closest prototype, if not an exact analogy, for this motif—the pair of flowers leaning toward the central palmette on its anta capitals (fig. 133).[77] There seems to be no earlier or contemporary example of the nearly rectangular palmette on our sima. Crisp and elegant in form like the sharp-leaved lotus beside it, it contrasts with the loose contour of the blossom in its angular precision. By grouping these uncommon shapes in an unusually intricate rhythmical sequence, the architect of the Hieron has designed a raking sima for which there is no precise parallel.

The fact that the basic system of the raking sima links the Hieron to the Temple of

76. As Schede noted, op. cit. (above, n. 53), p. 95.
77. *Die Ruinen,* fig. 36. A blossom similar to that on the Hieron's sima occurs, too, on the lateral face of the pilaster capital at the entrance to the northern vaulted passage at Didyma. Cf. *Didyma,* I, pl. 106, F209, and the additional examples, F207, F208. For further reference to this motif popular at Didyma, see below, pp. 358 f.

134. Antefix 48.578. Samothrace Museum

135. Antefix from the Altar Court. Samothrace Museum

Athena at Priene a second time, that these buildings have in common, therefore, both an unusual and largely regional ornamental feature and a new structural system for their walls, is of prime importance, for it implies a connection between the architect of the Hieron and one of the most famous of Greek architects: Pytheos, architect of the Mausoleum at Halikarnassos. To be sure, the elegant and seemingly so individual details of the Hieron's raking sima may have been derived from the raking sima of the Propylon, as was the equally tripartite system of its lateral sima. This possibility cannot be explored, since the raking sima of that richly decorated building was painted. Even if the raking simas of both buildings were similar in this respect, the link with Priene would remain.

Nowhere is our architect's willingness to adopt traditional Samothracian forms more apparent than in the marble antefixes that topped the lateral sima (fig. 134). Provided with a low fillet or base, hence divorced from the sima beneath them, they show a nine-petaled palmette rising from an arrow-shaped calyx and supported by two antithetical tendrils that curl from a pair of acanthus leaves. As on the raking sima, each curled-up tendril is overhung by a drooping leaf, and the arrow-shaped member from which the petals radiate is marked by a vertical ridge. All but the two lower petals of the compact fan-shaped palmette are blunt tipped. Hollow and widely separated from each other, they droop gently on each side

180

136. Antefix from the Propylon of the Temenos.
Kunsthistorisches Museum, Vienna

of the upright central petal. The lower petals, on the contrary, are drawn sharply down to a near horizontal position and flare into tips that point upward.[78]

The immediate forebear of this antefix in several basic respects is the antefix of the Altar Court (fig. 135).[79] There, too, as on most Samothracian antefixes, the classical separation of antefix and sima into two visually, as well as functionally, distinct entities has been retained; there, too, the widely spaced, hollow petals emerge from a lancet-shaped center, as they do on the earlier Propylon (fig. 136). But our architect has grafted onto the old-fashioned,

78. Fifteen antefixes are preserved from the Hieron: six in Samothrace (48.578, 49.514 A–B, 49.515, 51.219, 52.494, 62.14); seven in Vienna (346 L 1–7); and two in Prague. 48.578, illustrated above, fig. 134, and now exhibited on the restored entablature in Hall A of the Museum, is the only example of the original late-fourth-century type, all the others, with the possible exception of the pieces in Prague, being later variations on the original type. For discussion and illustration of representative examples of these later variations that reflect the several major repairs to which the Hieron was subjected over the centuries, see text II, pp. 81 f. and 49.514 A–B, the poorest and possibly the latest of these replacements, which is also exhibited on the reconstruction in Hall A. The remaining pieces in Samothrace and all those in Vienna are in storage.

79. As was pointed out in Vol. 4, pt. II, pp. 97 f. For discussion of the Samothracian antefixes extant from the Archaic to the late Hellenistic period, see pp. 87–99 of that volume.

137. Terracotta antefix from the Anaktoron, 39.657. Samothrace Museum

drooping-leaved palmette generally preferred in Samothrace a suggestion of the "gesprengte" palmette fashionable elsewhere at this time and present on his own raking sima and ridge antefixes. The remaining features of his design are again drawn from local models: the reduction to nine in the number of petals already characteristic of the late-fifth-century antefix type of the Anaktoron (fig. 137); the overhanging leaf, a classical detail present on the antefixes of the Temple of Apollo at Phigaleia [80] (fig. 138) and, in exaggerated, flourishing form, on the same antefix from the Anaktoron; and the tendrils coiling from individual acanthus calyxes above the fillet, in the manner of an Early Classical terracotta antefix from the Sanctuary (fig. 140).[81] It is this very type, as has been shown,[82] that served as the model

80. For reference to the antefixes from this temple and a general discussion of the development of palmettes, see Ilse Kleemann, *Der Satrapen-Sarkophag*

aus Sidon (*Istanbuler Forschungen,* XX [Berlin, 1958]), pp. 73 ff., 84.

81. 61.186, found in the fill brought into the nar-

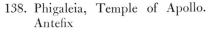

138. Phigaleia, Temple of Apollo. Antefix

139. Didyma, Temple of Apollo. Sima and antefix

for the antefixes of the Altar Court, where its fat, early-fifth-century petals and convex tendrils have been replaced by more up-to-date forms, but its basic scheme retained. The antefix of the Hieron is still more dependent upon this prototype in that the acanthus leaves from which the tendrils grow repeat its forms more precisely.

Thus, apart from their slight concession to the "gesprengte" palmette, the antefixes of the Hieron are a blend of traditional local forms. That they would nonetheless have been acceptable to contemporary eyes, at least in the eastern Aegean, is evident from the fact that they share with the antefixes from the naiskos at Didyma (fig. 139) [83] such basic forms as total separation from the sima and the older variety of palmette. Our architect has shown his customary tact in accepting and combining these Samothracian forms. His chief model (fig. 140), the Early Classical antefix that underlies the antefix of the Altar Court, has been modernized primarily by reducing the number of petals in its compact palmette, thereby creating the space between them that later classical taste demanded; by hollowing the petals

row interval between the west wall of the Anaktoron and the Proto-Anaktoron to its west when that wall of the Anaktoron was extensively repaired in the Hellenistic period. Four other less well preserved examples of the type have been found in the Sanctuary: 48.457, from the fill of the Arsinoeion; 49.460 and 57.435, both surface finds from widely separated parts of the Sanctuary; and a piece now in Prague, the specific provenance of which I am unaware. I owe my knowledge of it to a photograph showing miscellaneous fragments from Samothrace in the archaeological collection of the

Charles University, provided, in 1954, by Jiří Frel. On this example, comparable in extent of preservation to the larger fragment of 61.186 but far fresher in surface, the pair of disks or rosettes flanking the central petal is perfectly preserved.

82. Vol. 4, pt. II, pp. 93 ff.

83. *Didyma*, I, pls. 202, 203, and Vol. 4, pt. II, p. 90, where it is suggested that the type may have been used on the earlier Mausoleum and on the Temple of Athena at Priene—a suggestion of still greater interest and plausibility, in view of the interrelationships with Priene that emerge from the present study.

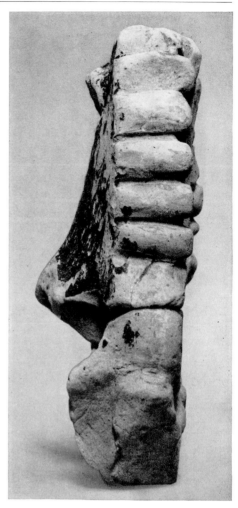

A   B

140. Terracotta antefix 61.186. Samothrace Museum

into concavity and turning up the tips of the lowest pair; and by intensifying the incipient naturalism of its tendril base. His retention and elaboration of this basic type resulted in the creation of an antefix compatible with the antefixes of the Altar Court, hence illustrative of his now familiar readiness to adjust the details of his building to those of its neighbors, and may, in addition, reflect his retention of the scheme of the antefixes of the immediate forerunner of that building, the Early Classical Hieron. For there is reason to propose that the terracotta model of this marble antefix should be attributed to that lost building.[84]

The most unusual feature of this palmette, its singular combination of two types of petal, was probably devised to link the marble antefixes with the terracotta ridge antefixes of the building (Pl. LXI.3, 4; figs. 141, 142). Although only two fragments of this double-faced member are preserved,[85] they suffice to establish its character. Its "gesprengte" palmette is

84. See text II, pp. 61 f.
85. 53.152 and 53.210, both exhibited in Case 3 of Hall B. They were found in the debris of the col-

lapsed building and may be replacements. The worn character of their surfaces makes it impossible to discern the period in which they were executed, but the

184

A   B

141. Fragmentary terracotta ridge antefix 53.210. Samothrace Museum

142. Fragmentary terracotta ridge antefix 53.152. Samothrace Museum

composed of two abutting half-palmettes whose ten undulating petals issue from a pair of acanthus leaves, each of which sends forth, too, a curling tendril. Like the very similar members of the flame-palmette antefixes from the Temple of Apollo at Delphi (fig. 143),[86] these half-palmettes must flower above short vertical stalks. They have been restored with a slightly projecting rectangular base decorated with a triple-leaved acanthus calyx, on the analogy of the antefixes from the naiskos at Didyma (fig. 144)—a temple that has proved to have a number of ornamental details in common with the Hieron and, in this respect, to stem from a common background.

When thus restored, the terracotta ridge antefix of the Hieron proves to resemble the marble antefix of the third-century Ptolemaion in organization[87]—confirmation of the probable correctness of this restoration, given the recurrence of traditional forms in Samothracian antefix designs. Still later in the Hellenistic age, a similar acanthus calyx was used to form the base of the terracotta antefixes of the Stoa (fig. 145),[88] as a related form appears on those from the Hellenistic roof of the Anaktoron (fig. 146).[89] Restored in this manner, the ridge antefix is strikingly analogous to the crowning finials or capitals of certain Attic grave stelai[90] which, like it, are decorated with a rosette-like disk placed in the upper field between the abutting half-palmettes. The fact that a pair of ornamental disks flanks the central petal of the Early Classical forebear of the marble antefixes of the Hieron provokes the thought that a similar prototype on the second Hieron may have provided the basic system used for the ridge antefixes of its successor. The popularity of this composition as a crowning motif in the fifth century adds to the likelihood of such a filiation. But it cannot be confirmed.

Two features of the outer fabric of the cella remain to be considered: the rear tympanum and the doors.

Although no blocks of the southern tympanum are preserved, it is reasonable to assume that its construction was identical with that of the northern. If so, it was built of two courses of marble blocks of varying size and shape, the lower composed of horizontal binders flanked at each extremity of the gable by a triangular block that may or may not have been a binder, the upper built of thin blocks of marble clamped to porous backers. The peak of the tympa-

---

variety of palmette makes it certain that they repeat the scheme of the original late-fourth-century ridge antefix.

86. Schede, op. cit. (above, n. 53), pl. 5, fig. 33.

87. *S,II*, pl. 43, fig. III.

88. For this building, now being excavated, see *Hesperia*, 34 (1965), 101 ff.

89. For the Anaktoron, see, for the time being, *Guide, Guide²*, pp. 45 ff.; "Chronique des fouilles . . .

en 1961," *BCH*, 86 (1962), 845.

90. For example, A. Conze, *Die attischen Grabreliefs* (Berlin, 1893), no. 1539, pl. 321; and Hans Möbius, *Die Ornamente der griechischen Grabstelen klassischer und nachklassischer Zeit* (Berlin-Wilmersdorf, 1929), pp. 42 f., pl. 29 a–b. The latest examples in this group, dating from the third quarter of the century to 317 B.C., are particularly relevant.

143. Delphi, Temple of Apollo. Sima and antefixes

144. Didyma, Temple of Apollo. Antefixes

145. Terracotta antefix from the Stoa. Samothrace Museum

146. Terracotta kalypter from the Anaktoron. Samothrace Museum

num was provided by the ridge raking geison block with which it was united (Pls. LXXII.3, LXXIII.1, LXXIV.1, LXXV, CVIII; fig. 70).

No exact parallel for this system appears to be preserved or published outside Samothrace, where it is likely that the tympana of the Stoa were constructed in a similar fashion.[91] Local tradition existed for building up a tympanum of several courses of blocks of varying size and shape, as the archaic Hall of Votive Gifts establishes.[92] Indeed, the use of this system for the venerable neighbor of the Hieron suggests that it may have been followed on the archaic *epopteion* and, like other features of the Hellenistic building, been carried over from its predecessors.

In any case, analogies exist both for constructing a tympanum of several horizontal courses rather than of a single series of graduated blocks adjusted to the slope of the raking geison, and for coupling the tip of the wall with the ridge geison block. The latter device occurs on those interrelated buildings, the Temple of Poseidon at Sounion and the Hephaisteion in Athens, as well as on the later Treasury of Kyrene in Delphi, to mention a few classical examples.[93] On these buildings, it is combined with the use of a single series of blocks rather than with the two courses of the Hieron's wall. A number of South Italian or Sicilian temples [94] show the use of the alternative system of two or more courses in the pediment wall, as do the temples of Athena Alea at Tegea and of Zeus at Nemea.[95] Closest of all to the Hieron, in a sense, is the later Temple of Artemis at Magnesia (fig. 147).[96] There the tympanum was built of five courses of varying height composed of blocks of differing length. Hence, the scheme followed on the Hieron is not as singular as it might at first sight seem.

With an angle of 14° 30′, the pediment has a pitch of 1 : 3.9, a proportion close to the classical norm of 1 : 4.[97] Its slightly greater steepness more than likely reflects conservative adherence to a proportion that experience had proved necessary to combat the snowfall and torrential rain of a Samothracian winter. The fact that the similar proportion of 1 : 3.8 occurs

91. A final statement on the tympanum of the Stoa must await completion of its excavation, now in progress. But it is already certain that the peak of the wall was provided by the same block as the ridge of the geison-sima and that the wall itself seems to have been built of three courses.

92. Vol. 4, pt. 1, pp. 43 f., Pl. XIII.

93. For this point, see, respectively: A. K. Orlandos, «Τὸ ἀέτωμα τοῦ ἐν Σουνίῳ ναοῦ τοῦ Ποσειδῶνος,» ArchDelt, 1 (1915), 4, fig. 3; Herbert Koch, *Studien zum Theseustempel in Athen* (Abh. sächs. Ak., Phil.-hist. Kl., 47, pt. 2 [Berlin, 1955]), figs. 57, 58, pp. 184 f.; Bousquet, pp. 55 f.; pl. 25, fig. 19, and pl. 32.

94. E.g., the temples of Athena (Ceres) and Poseidon at Paestum (see the illustrations in Friedrich Krauss, *Paestum* [Berlin, 1943], pls. 27–32, 42–45);

the Temple at Segesta and the Temple of Concord at Agrigento: K.P., p. 136, fig. 122, and pp. 174 f., fig. 155.

95. In the reconstruction proposed by Dugas, pp. 26 f., pls. 12–14, 49, 50. Charles K. Williams kindly informs me that the tympanum walls at Nemea are built of three horizontal courses, and their peaks are again coupled with the ridge raking geisa.

96. *Magnesia*, pp. 63 f., figs. 32, 48, 56, 59.

97. For comparative figures, cf. Orlandos, op. cit., p. 3, n. 4; and Etienne Lapalus, *Le fronton sculpté en Grèce des origines à la fin du IVe siècle* (Bibliothèque des Écoles françaises d'Athènes et de Rome, 165 [Paris, 1947]), pp. 234 f. The classical buildings for which such figures are available range from 1:4.031 to 1:4.210.

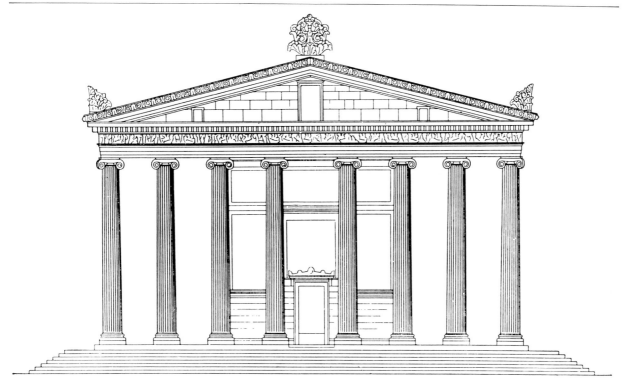

147. Magnesia, Temple of Artemis. Restored elevation

on the mid-second-century Temple of Hera Basileia on the exposed heights of Pergamon strengthens the thought that climatic conditions in the northeastern Aegean were probably responsible for the use of this somewhat steeper pitch.[98]

All three doors of the Hieron fall into the category later classified by Vitruvius as Doric and defined by the absence of brackets or fasciae.[99] The unadorned frames of the lateral doors appear to be edged by a narrow border in the fashion familiar from numerous examples, including the die-wall doors of the Temple of Apollo at Didyma [100] and certain Macedonian tombs (cf. figs. 148, 149).[101] Here, however, the effect is achieved not by a molding outlining the frame and setting off the smooth surfaces of jambs and lintel from the equally smoothly dressed wall, but by the drafted margins of the wall blocks, which border the entire lintel and the greater part of the jambs and separate them from the slightly raised surfaces of the adjacent wall blocks. By this simple device, a conventional-looking, eared frame has been effected for the standard two-leaved wooden doors, which were battened and bolted precisely like the outer wooden door in the Hellenistic Tomb at Langaza (fig. 149) and the doors reflected on earlier vases (cf. Pl. CVII).[102]

98. *Pergamon*, VI, 106.
99. See above, p. 66, n. 77.
100. *Didyma*, I, pls. 81, 87, Z186–89; pp. 74 ff., Z311.
101. For these doors, see above, p. 66, n. 76.
102. Above, p. 56, n. 46.

148. Didyma, Temple of Apollo. Die-wall door

149. Outer wooden door from the Tomb at Langaza

Although no comparable bronze bosses were recovered from the great two-leaved main door, owing to its removal in later antiquity, it has been restored in essentially identical form (Pls. CIII, CVII). The sole slight difference, the use of bolts of uniform size both for the battens and the stile, for which marble doors in the tombs at Palatitza, Langaza, and Vergina offer parallels (figs. 150, 151), is in accord with the scale of this door.[103]

Like the die-wall and adyton doors at Didyma,[104] the main door was approximately two and one-half times as high as its lower width (the comparable figure for the lateral doors being 1 : 2.3). The profiled base of its wide threshold, a cyma reversa molding above a simple

103. Above, p. 66, n. 76.
104. Above, p. 63, n. 65. The reader is reminded that the preserved frame of the main door of the Hieron is a late Roman replacement of the original frame in

which the essential form of that earlier frame was retained but its proportions altered. For proof of this point and the history of the door, see above, pp. 58 ff.

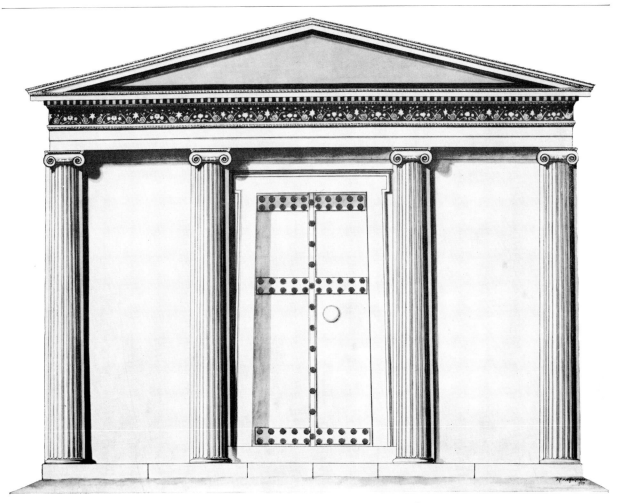

150. Marble door from the Tomb at Vergina

fascia, links it with the thresholds of the lateral doors (cf. Pls. XXXIII, XL, XCV.1, 2). It is related in type and contour to the molded toichobate of the Philippeion at Olympia.[105] The frame of the main door was again set off from the drafted-margin masonry of the surrounding wall by a narrow border. Appropriately enough, given the greater importance of this door, that border was ornamented with two carved moldings—an outer astragal and an inner meander—and its eared lintel was topped by a molded crown composed of a boldly projecting cavetto followed by a hawk's beak (Pls. XXXVIII, XLI, XLII; figs. 49, 439).[106]

The most conspicuous feature of this ornamental frame, the swastika-meander running

105. Shoe, pl. 37, fig. 11. Cf., too, the seemingly related, if later, profile on the threshold of the Temple of Zeus at Magnesia: *Magnesia,* pp. 150, 152, fig. 164. Mr. Jones reports that the threshold of the Temple of Artemis at Epidauros is also similar in form. The paucity of published profiles of molded thresholds makes it difficult to investigate their character.

106. Such a molded crown over an eared lintel is so orthodox a combination as to require no comment or analogy beyond that provided by the doors illustrated or referred to above. It is the absence of such a crown over the side doors that is less usual.

191

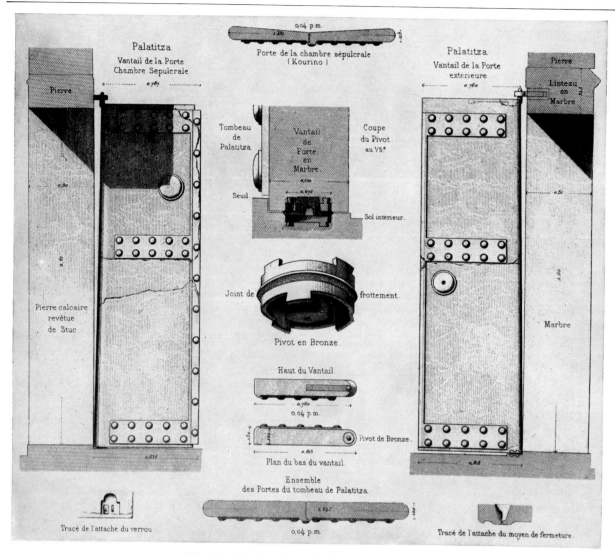

151. Marble door from the Tomb at Palatitza

about its edge, was a popular pattern in the fourth century B.C. It occurs in both carved and painted form on a wide variety of monuments.[107] Yet it appears to have been rarely used to decorate door frames. Hence, its occurrence a second time, at the entrance to Temple A at

107. For example, at Epidauros, above the frieze of the inner order of the Tholos and on the sima of the Temple of Asklepios (Defrasse and Lechat, op. cit., pl. 7; and Cavvadias, op. cit., pl. 10); on the simas of the Leonidaion at Olympia (*Olympia,* II, pl. 123) and of the South Stoa at Corinth (*Corinth,* I, pt. 4, pls. 19, 20); on the ceiling of the stairways at Didyma (*Didyma,* I, pl. 85, F327); on sarcophagi from the nekropolis at Sidon (O. Hamdy Bey and Théodore Reinach, *Une nécropole royale à Sidon* [Paris, 1892], pls. 25 ff., 40). It occurs, too, on Hellenistic tombstones (P. M. Fraser

and T. Rönne, *Boeotian and West Greek Tombstones* [Skrifter Utgivna av Svenska Institutet i Athen, 4°, VI, Lund, 1957], pp. 59 f., pl. 10, no. 44) and in Delian wall decoration (Bulard, pls. 6 a, b, d; 7 b, e, h; 8).

The square that alternates with the swastika figure in this running meander is at times empty, at times occupied by a dot or cross or checker. Inasmuch as the extant frame of the Hieron's door is a late Roman replacement marked by coarsely executed drillwork, it is not certain whether on the original frame this field contained a dot or a cross.

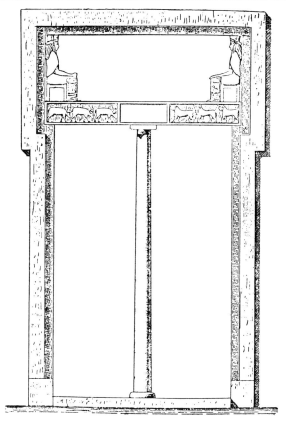

152. Prinias, Temple A. Restored entrance

Prinias (fig. 152),[108] and its acknowledged use in antiquity as a symbol for a labyrinth raise the question whether its selection to adorn the door frames of two unusual cult buildings was the result of purely aesthetic considerations or reflected its value as a meaningful pattern.

It has long been recognized that, in certain contexts, the meander is an allusion to and symbol of the legendary Palace of Minos, the Labyrinth at Knossos.[109] As such, it appears in varying form on the classical and Hellenistic coinage of Knossos [110] and on a group of vases, both black-figured and red-figured, on which Theseus' victory over the Minotaur is depicted.[111] On the finest of these vessels, an Attic kylix in Madrid signed by Aison (fig. 153),[112] the triumphant hero drags his defeated foe from a building identified as the Laby-

108. For this reconstruction, see Luigi Pernier, *Annuario*, 1 (1914), 62 f. and pl. 5.

109. For extensive discussion of this topic, see, in particular, Richard Eilmann, *Labyrinthos, Ein Beitrag zur Geschichte einer Vorstellung und eines Ornamentes* (Athens, 1931), where the earlier bibliography is cited.

110. For convenient illustration of the major types, see Barclay V. Head, *Historia Numorum* (2d edn., rev., Oxford, 1911), pp. 457 ff.; S. W. Grose, *Catalogue of the McClean Collection of Greek Coins* (Cambridge, 1926), II, pls. 237, 238; A. B. Cook, op. cit. (n. 5, above), pp. 476 f.

111. See especially P. Wolters, "Darstellung des Labyrinths," *SB bayer. Ak.*, Phil.-hist. Kl., 1907, pt. 1, pp. 113 ff.

112. *CVA, Espagne*, fasc. 2, Museo Arqueológico Nacional, fasc. 2, III, I D, no. 1, pl. II = our fig. 153; J. D. Beazley, *Attic Red-Figure Vase Painters* (2d edn., Oxford, 1963), p. 1174, no. 1; briefly mentioned and discussed by F. Hauser in A. Furtwängler and K. Reichhold, *Griechische Vasenmalerei*, III (Munich, 1910), pp. 48 ff.; and Charles Dugas, *Aison* (Paris, 1930), pp. 45 ff., 62 f., fig. 9; and discussed in greater detail by Wolters, Cook, and Eilmann, loc. cit.

153. Kylix by Aison. Museo Arqueológico Nacional, Madrid

154. Detail of a lekythos from Vari. National Archaeological Museum, Athens

rinth by a conspicuous vertical meander, a bold device repeated on related cups in the British Museum and at Harrow-on-the-Hill.[113] On the black-figured predecessors of these late-fifth-century Attic kylikes, the setting of the contest is indicated in still more concise and explicit form.[114] In the most intelligible of these compositions, the scene on a lekythos from

113. For the kylix from Vulci in the British Museum (E 84) attributed by Beazley (op. cit., p. 1269, no. 4) to the Codrus Painter, see Cecil Smith, "Kylix with Exploits of Theseus," *JHS,* 2 (1881), 60; Hauser, op. cit., p. 49; Cook, op. cit., pp. 473 ff.; C. Dugas and R. Flacelière, *Thésée, Images et récits* (Paris, 1958), p. 68, pls. 16, 17, as well as Wolters, op. cit., pp. 118 ff., fig. 2, and Eilmann, op. cit., pp. 56, 59 ff.

For the kylix from Nola in the School Museum at Harrow-on-the-Hill (no. 52) attributed to the Phiale Painter by Beazley (op. cit. [1st edn., 1942], p. 660), see Wolters, op. cit., pl. 1; and Eugénie Strong, *Burlington Fine Arts Club. Exhibition of Ancient Greek Art* (London, 1904), p. 114, no. 60, pl. 97, I 60.

114. I have discussed these vases, both red-figured and black-figured, in greater detail in "The

155. Didyma, Temple of Apollo. View of ceiling in southern stairwell

Vari in the National Museum in Athens (fig. 154),[115] the bearded archaic hero and his opponent emerge from the door to the Labyrinth, the all-important entrance-exit emphasized by ancient writers in their accounts of the contest.[116] Here that ἔξοδος, so difficult to find in the winding obscurity of the building, is represented by a sketchily drawn doorway identified as the entrance to the Labyrinth by a series of loosely painted meanders alluding to that other prime and related feature of the palace, its intricate ground plan. Here the meander is not a decorative pattern but an eloquent symbol of a specific place and its most characteristic feature. Here the meander-door is at once a symbol of the Labyrinth and of the experiences and episodes associated with it.

The equation meander = labyrinth is documented again at Didyma. In the late-third- and early-second-century building accounts from the Temple of Apollo, the term *labyrinthos* is repeatedly applied to the winding stairwells of the huge structure whose ceilings were adorned with carved and painted meanders.[117] On the well-preserved southern side of the building, one of these ceilings is still *in situ* (fig. 155).[118] The marble-colored swastika-

Meander Door: A Labyrinthine Symbol," *Studi in onore di Luisa Banti* (Rome, 1965), pp. 215–22. The reader is referred to this article for more extended analysis of their imagery and of the entire topic discussed here.

115. Wolters, op. cit., pp. 122 f., pl. 2; Cook, op. cit., pp. 474 f., fig. 330 (whence our fig. 154); and n. 112, above.

116. See "The Meander Door," pp. 218 ff.

117. *Didyma,* II: *Die Inschriften,* nos. 25 A, lines 9, 14; 26 B, lines 7, 14, 21 f.; 27 A, lines 81, 86, 88, 93,

118, 120, 123; 27 B, lines 2, 65; 29, line 11; 35, line 18. See the commentary on pp. 27 ff., 32 ff., 37 ff.

Fernand Robert, *Thymélè* (above, n. 9), pp. 323 f., mistakenly applied the term *labyrinthos* to the straight vaulted passages leading down to the adyton. It is obvious, both from their winding plan and their meander decoration, that the term refers to the stairwells above them.

118. *Didyma,* I, 79 ff., pl. 85, F327 (our fig. 155). The swastika-meander employed here is identical in form with that of the Hieron (and the London kylix).

195

meander standing out against its blue ground covers its entire surface, one with it in length and breadth. It is inconceivable that so elaborate a ceiling would have been placed above this dark, cramped passage had that stairway served merely to give access to the roof for the utilitarian purpose of repairing or caring for it, as has been proposed.[119] Whatever its function within the context of the oracular cult at Didyma, this passage and its counterpart clearly had a ritual use, and their splendid ceilings were carved to be seen by some, however few. In any case, at Didyma the term *labyrinthos* was applied to narrow, maze-like passages decorated with meanders. There the pattern has been used both to symbolize a labyrinth and to decorate it; there its association with both a spatial and a spiritual experience cannot be doubted.

The specific nature of that experience, like the ultimate significance of Theseus' encounter with the Minotaur, remains a matter of speculation. The testimony of the recently discovered Sanctuary of Hades at Ephyra is less obscure.[120] Immediately before reaching the symbolic Underworld at the center of this Hellenistic complex, the pilgrim had to pass through a dark labyrinth, individual sections of which were closed by doors (fig. 156). Thence, after previous purification and sacrifice, he might penetrate the Underworld. Here the meaningful character of the labyrinth and the symbolic value of the pattern which mirrors its plan are undeniable; here the labyrinth led to a ritual center in which the living confronted the dead.

Some common denominator of religious experience must have linked these antique labyrinths. The widespread occurrence of mazes of varied form and character in pagan and Christian Europe from prehistoric times onward [121] has led to the belief that they reflect an

119. By H. Knackfuss, ibid., p. 81. But he was surely right to reject the earlier suggestion of E. Pontremoli and B. Haussoullier, *Didymes* (Paris, 1904), pp. 92 ff., that these stairways led to two rooms which served as the *chresmographion* and the πρυτανικὸν οἴκημα of the sanctuary. The symbolic value of the meander at Didyma as "ein redendes Ornament" comparable to the pattern on the red-figured kylikes was recognized by Wolters in a later article ("Archäologische Bemerkungen," *SB bayer. Ak.*, Phil.-hist. Kl., 1913, 4. Abhandlung, pp. 18 f.), and by Eilmann, op. cit., p. 53.

120. For a convenient description of this building complex in use in the second half of the third and the first half of the second century B.C., see Sotiris I. Dakaris, "The Dark Palace of Hades," *Archaeology*, 15 (1962), 85–93, as well as "Das Taubenorakel von Dodona und das Totenorakel bei Ephyra," *Antike Kunst*, Beiheft I. *Neue Ausgrabungen in Griechenland*, 1963, pp. 35–54. Additional photographs of the excavation and finds appear in the successive "Chroniques des fouilles" for the years 1958, 1960, and 1961: *BCH*, 83 (1959), 665–69; 85 (1961), 729–33; 86 (1962), 767–72; 87 (1963), 771–74. For further reference to this sanctuary, see text II, p. 68 and n. 47.

In this context see, too, the narrow labyrinthine corridor beneath the Temple of Apollo at Klaros which leads from the pronaos to the subterranean inner sanctum, a distance of ca. 30 m., in the course of which it changes direction no less than seven times via abrupt, right-angle turns: Louis Robert, *Les fouilles de Claros* (Paris, 1954), pp. 13 ff.; idem, "Fouilles de Klaros et Mission Robert 1955," *Türk Arkeoloji Dergisi*, 7, no. 1 (1957), 7 f.; and, for a more accessible brief summary, Machteld Mellink, "Archaeology in Asia Minor," *AJA*, 60 (1956), 382.

121. See, for example, the varieties illustrated by W. H. Matthews, *Mazes and Labyrinths* (London, 1922); the note by John L. Heller, "A Labyrinth from Pylos?" *AJA*, 65 (1961), 57 ff.; and the recent illumi-

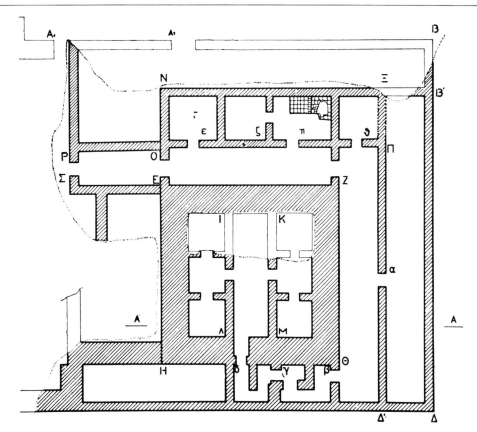

156. Ephyra, Sanctuary of Hades. Plan

almost universal search for ultimate reality. In varied metaphor, they give expression to the difficulty of the quest—to the confusion, the darkness, the struggle that precede the revelation or the triumph.[122]

It has been remarked that "the maze form habitually implies correlative notions of exclusion and conditional penetration," that mazes reflect the concept of "obstructed penetration."[123] These concentrated formulae apply not only to mazes but also to the Hieron. That it was difficult of access both physically and spiritually [124] is indicated by the fact that only those who had previously become *mystai* were admitted to its interior; that indeed only initiates who had been absolved of their most grievous sins in the nocturnal rite of confession which appears to have preceded admission to the *epopteia* were granted such admission; and, finally, that these select individuals were required to enter the building one by one. Did the

nating discussion of Heinz Ladendorf, "Das Labyrinth in Antike und neuerer Zeit," *AA*, 1963, cols. 762 ff.

122. The psychological and spiritual implications of legends revolving around passage through a labyrinth and the related themes of danger-ridden voyages and difficult pilgrimages are well stated by Mircea Eliade, *The Myth of the Eternal Return* (Bollingen Series XLVI [New York, 1954]), p. 18.

123. W. F. J. Knight, "Maze Symbolism and the Trojan Game," *Antiquity*, 6 (1932), 445 ff. The passages quoted occur on pp. 447, 457. Note, too, the definition of a maze on p. 446: "Its principle seems to be the provision of a difficult but possible access to some important point."

124. See above, pp. 64, 120, and text II, pp. 14 ff., for these proscriptions and requirements.

initiate who stood before the lofty main door awaiting admission to the secret rites of the *epopteia* see in the meander decorating that door a symbol of his entrance into a spiritual labyrinth, a realm of religious experience from which he, like Theseus, would emerge victorious? It is tempting to think so, given the standard equation meander = labyrinth, its established symbolism in the context of a door, and its evidently meaningful value at Didyma. If so, what was the nature of that victory? Did the mysterious rites through which the initiate became more pious and more just hold out to him the hope of immortality, the victory of life over death? [125] It may well be.

Whatever its specific content within the context of the Samothracian mysteries, the use of a meander to decorate the door of the Hieron appears to reflect the fact that, under certain circumstances, that pattern was meaningful as well as ornamental in Greek art. Its use in connection with the crucial entrance-exit to the Cretan Labyrinth in painting, the emphasis upon the door in antique references to the Labyrinth, and the resulting device of the meander door as a richly meaningful symbol for that Labyrinth and the experiences encountered within it justify the assumption that when the meander pattern was used to decorate the door of a Greek cult building, it had a dual function: to adorn it and, via its vivid visual symbolism, to allude to a spiritual concept. The specific content of the allusion may have varied to some extent from one religious context to another. But that the meander-bordered doorways through which the worshiper entered the Hieron in Samothrace and Temple A at Prinias [126] were meaningful as well as ornamental is hardly to be doubted. Finally, the existence of such a doorway in a seventh-century cult building containing an eschara and dedicated to the worship of the Lady of the Rocks suggests the likelihood that the meander pattern on the door frame of the early Hellenistic Hieron, like its apse and eschara, was carried over from its first forebear, the archaic *epopteion*.[127]

When the grille door admitting the individual initiate to the cella was opened, he stepped down into a rectangular hall lined on its long sides by low marble benches terminating in a stepped platform contained within a segmental apse (cf. Pls. CII, CV, CVI). However long and narrow in effect, this room is in fact the widest chamber known from Greece or the Greek

---

125. The eternal renewal of life implicit in the vibrant forms of the floral akroteria provokes the same query. See below, p. 204, n. 147, and pp. 386 f. and n. 236.

For the recurrent formula μύσται εὐσεβεῖς in the catalogues of *mystai*, see text II, pp. 8 ff.; Vol. 2, pt. I, p. 150, Index 1, E, e; *Guide*², p. 29. Cf. also Diodorus' statement, 5.49.6 (Vol. 1, **142**, lines 41–47).

126. Curiously enough, Robert, *Thymélè* (above, n. 9), p. 318, in reporting the theory that the frieze of horsemen at Prinias may represent the *ludus Troiae*,

drew attention to the interest, in this connection, of the meander border above the frieze and hinted at its meaningful character in this context without remarking that the very same pattern occurred again on the door frame.

127. One cannot fail to wonder, too, whether the *labyrinthos* of the Hellenistic Didymaion was derived from *its* archaic forebear, like other features of that unorthodox building. (See also below, p. 236, the addendum to n. 127.)

East up to its day to have been spanned without the aid of an interior colonnade. With a clear span of 10.72 m., it exceeds all earlier buildings outside Samothrace and Sicily in its breadth of undivided space.[128] In Samothrace, it was nearly equaled by the older Anaktoron with its clear span of 10.58 m.[129] There is, thus, every likelihood that in this respect, too, the architect of the Hieron followed a structural system already employed in the archaic and classical buildings that preceded it and that the use of a trussed roof was traditional in Samothrace. That the roof of the Hieron was trussed is, in any case, certain, given the form of its sima blocks (Pl. LV), which, together with the geison, housed and supported the roof timbers at a level higher than the normal one. The multiple-purpose sima blocks fulfill the function of the wedge-shaped blocks placed on the geison in certain Attic buildings of the later fifth century in providing abutment for the rafters and support for tiles,[130] in addition to themselves serving as eaves tiles and housing the transverse beams. Designed to discharge this variety of functions, they are seemingly unique in form.

The undeniable presence of a trussed roof over the cella of the Hieron and the likelihood that the use of this structural system here was the outgrowth of traditional practice imply that the current view that the Greeks of the Classical period did not know or use the truss is at fault.[131] When and where this system was invented remains uncertain.[132] But there is no reason to assume either that the architect of the Hieron adopted it directly from archaic Sicilian models or that he invented it independently. It must have been known and used for a long time somewhere in the northeastern Aegean region, where the evident availability of excellent tim-

128. See the chart of cella spans published by A. Trevor Hodge, *The Woodwork of Greek Roofs* (Cambridge, 1960), p. 39. The figure 10.72 is conservative, since some geison blocks overhang the cella wall more than others. The interior width of the cella is 10.92 m.

129. *AJA*, 44 (1940), 331; *Guide, Guide*², p. 46. The piers used in this building reduce the interior width by 1.0 m.

130. Cf. Hodge, op. cit., pp. 85 f.

131. See Hodge's statements, ibid., pp. 38 ff.: "One thing is clear: when the Greeks had to roof a cella wider than 6.5 m. they broke the span up by the insertion of a colonnade; the Sicilians did not. . . . This can only mean that the Sicilians knew of some easy way of spanning a cella and the Greeks did not." The author's arbitrary elimination of the Temple of Athena Alea at Tegea (clear span 8.94 m.) from his consideration of this problem because "it is very advanced in technique in many ways; and late in our period" (p. 133) scarcely contributes to the solution of a difficult problem.

I assume that it was the "late" date of the Hieron and reliance on Dinsmoor's handbook that led to its omission from this discussion, too. Unfortunately, Dinsmoor's retention (p. 269) of a long disproved and totally unfounded proposal that the cella of the Hieron was subdivided by two colonnades appears to have contributed to the spread of a theory refuted by Chapouthier in 1925 (see above, p. 159, n. 16, for these references).

132. Hodge's suggestion (op. cit., pp. 42, 135) that the "uninventive" Sicilians may have derived their knowledge of the truss from the Carthaginians is hardly supported by reference to Carthaginian dependence on Greek prototypes (e.g., their coinage)! The Greeks as well as the Phoenicians were a maritime people, and there may, indeed, have been a connection between ship-building and the development of roof construction in antiquity, as there obviously was in medieval northwestern Europe. Nonetheless, technical knowledge derived from such experience need not have remained confined to its place of origin.

The geographical and cultural implications of Rodney Young's assumption that an eighth-century

ber would have fostered its acceptance.[133] Its use in the Hieron was obligatory if the segmental apse in the abaton was to be fully visible and not overlapped at the summit by the coffered ceiling of the cella. Only by raising the main ceiling and the transverse beams above it to the unorthodox level of the geison could this result be achieved; and, once the beams were elevated to that course, no construction other than the truss was possible for this roof. In the Hieron, then, its use was motivated by aesthetic considerations in themselves doubtless rooted in liturgical requirements or practice.

The wooden coffered ceiling introduced below these great timbers was orthodox in material and general scheme, but it was marked, as we have seen,[134] by one technical feature as yet undocumented outside Samothrace: the decoration of its two-stepped coffers with two sizes of cast bronze cymatia (Pl. XXXIV.3, 4; Cat. **162–170**). The continuing popularity of this molding long used to decorate coffers is attested by its presence, in carved form, on the outer, marble ceiling of the slightly earlier Temple of Athena at Priene. Conceivably, its lost cella ceiling was similarly embellished by cast, nailed-on bronze moldings. If so, one more link would exist between the two buildings. But the fact that at least one other building in the Sanctuary of the Great Gods had such ceiling decorations [135] and that separately-made wooden moldings and bronze attachments are documented for the ceilings of the Erechtheion and the Temple of Asklepios at Epidauros [136] suggests that the use of bronze moldings on coffered ceilings may have been more widespread and customary than the sparse evidence now available can establish.

Still another feature of the timberwork in the cella of the Hieron is unique among extant buildings—the tent-like roof over its segmental apse. Again, the sole analogies for this structural form are to be found in the West, this time in Etruria, where the ceilings of certain archaic rock-cut tombs clearly reflect similar constructions.[137] But the salient apses of the

---

megaron at Gordion (clear span 9.74 m.) was roofed with a truss are more to the point in this connection. See *AJA*, 61 (1957), 322, and, in particular, "Gordion: Phrygian Construction and Architecture: II," *Expedition*, 4 (1962), 6 ff., where (p. 9) a simple truss is plausibly predicated for this so-called "Mosaic Building." In a previous installment of this discussion, ibid., 2 (1960), 3 f., the author has pointed out the provable abundance of good local timber at Gordion, the use of beams 20–30 feet long in the Royal Tomb there, and the extreme conservatism of building technique in country districts. I am indebted to Professor Young for drawing my attention to this convincing and fascinating pair of articles.

133. On the excellence of Macedonian timber and its export to other regions, see Stanley Casson, *Mace-*

donia, Thrace and Illyria (Oxford, 1926), pp. 52 f., and Roland Martin, op. cit. (above, n. 34), pp. 30 f. Theophrastus' statements are of special interest, in view of his date (*Historia plantarum* 4.5.5 and 5.2.1): "Some indeed . . . say that the best of the timber which comes into Hellas for the carpenter's purposes is the Macedonian, for it is smooth and of straight grain, and it contains resin. . . ." (Tr. Sir Arthur Hort, Loeb edn., I, 427.)

134. Above, pp. 142 ff.

135. It is not yet clear to which building the additional fragments of bronze cymatia mentioned in text II, pp. 248 f., n. 4, belong.

136. See above, pp. 142 f.

137. See above, pp. 79 f., n. 110.

157. Delos, Thesmophorion. Outlet in the western foundation

predecessors of the present building may also have been roofed in a similar fashion and, given their less shallow form, have looked still more tent-like.

The introduction of a stepped platform within the apse and its probable separation from the rest of the hall by a curtain made of it a kind of rear chamber (cf. Pls. CII, CIV–CVI). Analogies for such a raised adyton and for its separation from the main hall by a curtain or screen exist outside Samothrace,[138] but its use in the early Hellenistic Hieron was in all probability dictated by its presence in the predecessors of that building and by the requirements of the liturgy. The existence of a prominent raised, screened rear chamber in the Anaktoron strengthens the likelihood that these features of the interior installation of the Hieron were traditional.

So, too, the eschara in the forepart of the cella and the outlet near its entrance, the two other centers of ritual activity within the building, met liturgical requirements. We have seen that the eschara, like the apse, was a feature of numerous archaic cult buildings.[139] There is no

138. See text II, pp. 31 ff. and nn. 146 f., 153, for specific examples of such chambers and of the use of curtains in cult buildings. For the marble torches to which the curtains in the Hieron were attached, see above, pp. 135 ff.; text II, pp. 31 ff.

139. Above, pp. 155, 158, nn. 4, 9.

exact analogy for its particular form in the present Hieron—a limestone frame set in a rectangular cutting in the underpavement and level with the marble floor—as no such hearth is otherwise known in a building of this period. Again, there are numerous parallel instances of the presence of a drain in cult buildings where, as in the Hieron, some lustral or sacrificial rite must have been performed.[140] Normally, such drains are equipped with an outlet in the form of a simple channeled block built into and projecting from a wall or euthynteria in the manner illustrated in fig. 157, a detail of the west foundation of the south room in the Thesmophorion at Delos. The architect of the Hieron has elaborated the requisite outlet; flaring its contour and decorating its channel with a slightly-raised leaf pattern (fig. 83 A), he has once again exhibited the taste for fresh ornamental detail that marked his raking sima pattern.

The two rows of marble benches lining the long wall of the Hieron were a prime feature of its interior installation (Pls. CII, CIV–CVI). Placed on lateral platforms only slightly higher than the main floor of the cella and set off from that marble pavement by a low border of the same material, these benches were continuous and accessible either from the main door or from the lateral doors. The *mystai* admitted through the great bronze-studded door and the grille-gate behind it stepped down into the cella—an unusual but not unparalleled feature of the Hieron [141] that recurs in Samothrace in the Anaktoron. But the difference in level between the main "aisle" and the lateral platforms was scarcely more than that needed to articulate them visually and to provide them with a retaining frame. For the *signinum* pavement of the aisles required such a border. The use of two kinds of pavement, one for the center of the cella, the other for the aisles, another unusual feature of the interior,[142] gave visual expression to the different functions of these areas of the building—one occupied by witnesses, the other animated by the participants in ritual acts. It reflects the same concern for the subtle adjustment of the parts to the whole that underlies the correlation of the ornamental detail of the building with that of its neighbors.

The two rows of benches on each lateral platform were, again, differentiated, doubtless

---

140. For example, in the rear wall of the cella of the Temple in Neandria (*Neandria*, pp. 24 f., fig. 55); in the door wall of the Temple in Larisa (*Larisa*, I, 80); in the pronaos of the Kabeirion at Thebes (*Kabirenheiligtum*, I, XI); below the euthynteria in the west wall of the south room of the Thesmophorion in Delos (René Vallois, "Topographie délienne, II," *BCH*, 53 [1929], 277, n. 3, where, however, it is suggested that this outlet implies "qu'on lavait à grande eau le sol de cette salle"); and in the south wall of the Naxian Oikos in the same sanctuary: cf. Vallois, *Les constructions antiques de Délos. Documents* (Bibliothèque des Écoles françaises d'Athènes et de Rome, 157 bis [Paris, 1953]), fig. 13. For discussion of the rites requiring

such outlets, see text II, pp. 23 ff.

141. The venerable Temple in Neandria that shares so many features with the Hieron is similar in this respect, too: see *Neandria*, pp. 25 f.

142. The slightly later temple on the middle terrace of the Asklepieion at Kos, Temple B, shows a related differentiation between the marble pavement of the pronaos and the mosaic floor of the cella: *Kos*, I, 37, pl. 17. The kind of *signinum* or terrazzo floor that we have restored in the aisles was used for the entire pavement in the small late-second-century Bastion Temple at Delos. I can vouch for this fact, which is not mentioned in *BCH*, 49 (1925), 466–68, or ibid., 53 (1929), 209.

for some ritual reason.[143] Both were backless and consisted of simple plinths resting on recurrent supports (Pls. LXXXVI–LXXXVIII, CIV–CVI; figs. 80, 159, 160). The supports of the front row were presumably unadorned and without base, characterized only by a curving front contour. Those of the rear row abutting the walls were more elaborate. Their supports, shaped at the front in the form of a lion's hind leg and paw and, at the ends of each section, decorated on both sides with ornament carved in low relief, terminate in a low base.

This form of bench appears to have been especially popular in mystery cults. It occurs repeatedly on monuments connected with the mysteries, both in scenes representing an initiate seated on such a bench and, coupled with telltale objects, as a symbol of such a

158. Delos, Serapeion A. Bench support

cult.[144] Hence, it is not surprising that the closest parallels to the benches in the Hieron outside the Sanctuary of the Great Gods are to be found in Serapeion A and Serapeion B on Delos and in the late-fourth-century Aphrodision on that island (fig. 158).[145]

None of these examples is adorned with carving like the terminal supports from the Hieron, which were embellished with a plant motif reminiscent of the rinceaux on the lateral simas (cf. figs. 159, 160, 116, 117). Although the ill-preserved fragments of this ornamental support do not allow the motif to be fully reconstructed, it included the familiar elements of unfluted stems overhung by ragged acanthus leaves, from which hollowed tendrils coil and an occasional half-palmette or arrow-shaped shoot springs. An impression of the original

143. See text II, pp. 31 f., for discussion of this point. For description of the extant fragments and explanation of their relationship to each other, see above, pp. 124 ff. and n. 214.

144. For examples of paintings and reliefs, ranging from Arretine ware to sarcophagi, see the references cited in text II, p. 31, nn. 142 f.; for the use of benches in a hall for initiation, ibid., pp. 21 f., n. 99.

Both the benches depicted and the preserved examples are at times individual seats, at times continuous.

145. For the examples from Serapeion A, see W. Deonna, *Le mobilier délien* (*Délos*, XVIII), p. 13, fig. 11, and pl. 7, fig. 61. Those in Serapeion B and the Aphrodision are, as far as I know, unpublished. I do not include the related type equipped with a more complicated seat found in the Agora of the Italians and the Inner Propylaea at Eleusis, nor do I mean to imply that the use of this type of bench was restricted to mystery cults. On the reverse of the silver tetradrachms of Philetairos and his successors, Athena sits on precisely such a seat. See Hans von Fritze, *Die Münzen von Pergamon* (Berlin, 1910), pp. 38 f., pl. 2.

159. Fragmentary Hellenistic bench support 52.154-53.568. Samothrace
Museum

effect of this luxuriant floral pattern may be gained from the similar composition on a marble
bench from the Gymnasium in Pergamon (fig. 161).[146] This bench is Roman in execution
and its support differs from those of the Hieron in its cumbersome frame and in the fact that
its stalks spring from the bulky lion's leg rather than issue from the frame; but it is evidently
dependent upon an earlier Hellenistic prototype related in scheme to the supports of the
Hieron. On the latter, the concentric tendrils and overhanging leaves echo the curves of the
linear frame into which the inner contour of the lion's leg is converted—a refinement worthy
of its designer, whose pleasure in ornamental detail is again apparent, as is the harmonious
reiteration of decorative motifs that characterized his work.[147]

No feature of the interior of the Hieron can have played as important a part in its total decorative effect as its wall decoration (Pls. CIV, CV, CVI). The stuccoed painted walls, predominantly scarlet and white above a black dado, must have created an effect at once rich
and powerful, set off as they were against the white marble floor and benches and the dark

146. Published by P. Schazmann, "Bankfüsse in
Pergamon," AM, 36 (1911), 110 ff. The drawing reproduced in our fig. 161 is incorrect in showing two
rows of toes rather than a normal paw. See the photograph in Pergamon, VII, pt. 2, 387, pl. 48 A.

We observed a fragment of such a lion's-foot
bench support decorated with foliage in the guard's
house at Ialysos in May, 1953. See Lindos, III, pt. 2,
p. 310, pl. 7, N (bench J), for another example.

147. One wonders whether, within the context

of the Hieron, the use of plant forms to adorn benches
on which epoptai sat and the outlet draining the lustral
area was purely decorative in intention or whether,
like the meander pattern on the door frame, they were
selected because of their inherent symbolic value. The
recurrence of such motifs in the epopteion—for the
bench supports and outlet as well as for the sima and
central akroteria—suggests that this may be the case,
and that this use of living forms implies a conscious
emphasis upon life and the renewal of life.

204

Side A   Side B

160. Fragmentary Hellenistic bench support A. Samothrace Museum

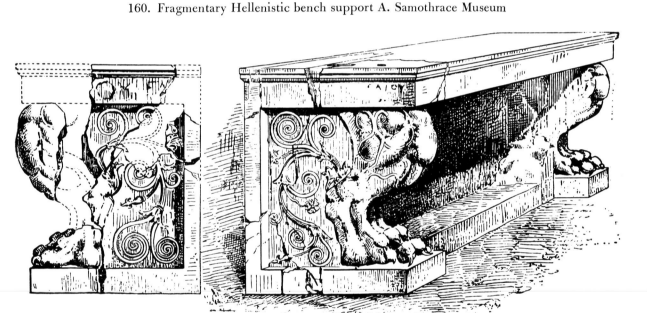

161. Roman bench support from the Gymnasium at Pergamon

timbered ceiling with its gold-colored, metallic moldings. Lit by flickering lamplight during the nocturnal rites, the cella must have been rich in contrasts, now gleaming, as light fell on the pavement and the white upper wall or picked out the bronze edges of the shadowy coffers, now muted as it struck the full, firm colors of the lower wall.

If the ornamental wall system restored in Pl. CV is correct, as there is good reason to suppose,[148] we may detect behind its design the same mentality that we have discerned in the

148. For justification of this reconstruction, see above, pp. 138 ff.

solution of other aesthetic problems posed by this building—in the clear articulation of the inner floor levels, for example, or of the outer walls, their textured surfaces framed by smooth pilasters, dado, and entablature. Strict co-ordination of the decorative system of the inner plaster surface of the wall with its actual construction and outer face, that is, correlation of the primary zones of dado, wall, and entablature on the exterior of the building with identical zones of painted decoration on the interior, and simulation there in stucco of the coursing and drafting of the marble wall are precisely what we should expect of this mentality.

To what extent this decorative system was original must remain a matter of speculation. No other cult building known from the Greek world appears to have had similar decoration. But the Hieron is not a temple, strictly speaking, and the fact that analogies to the wall decoration of this building for congregational worship occur exclusively in domestic or funerary architecture is probably not accidental. Granting the widespread use of scarlet stuccoed walls in cult buildings, the simulation of drafted-margin masonry in plaster in the Hieron and the subdivision of its walls into three primary zones—a dado, a central area, and an ornamental crowning section—may be paralleled in earlier or near-contemporary monuments only in those two traditionally interrelated spheres.[149] Imitation of drafted-margin masonry in stucco, a feature of later Hellenistic houses in Sicily, Priene, and Delos, occurred in Olynthian houses before 348 B.C.[150] Nor is it likely that the subdivision of the

149. The wall decoration of the later heroa at Kalydon and Assos should doubtless be associated with the same domestic-funerary tradition. For illustration of these stuccoed walls, see E. Dyggve, F. Poulsen, K. A. Rhomaios, *Das Heroon von Kalydon (Kgl. Danske Videnskabernes Selskab, Skrifter,* Historisk og Filosofisk Afdeling, 7 Raekke IV, 4 [Copenhagen, 1934]), p. 384, fig. 104, and p. 391; and J. T. Clarke, F. H. Bacon, R. Koldewey, *Investigations at Assos* (Cambridge, 1902), pp. 109 ff.; 111, fig. 1; 113, fig. 2.

By the later Hellenistic age, this style of wall decoration had, in any case, been adopted for other types of building; witness the Prytaneion in Magnesia: *Magnesia,* p. 138, fig. 150.

150. For example, in the House of Many Colors and the House of Asklepios. Cf. David M. Robinson, *Domestic and Public Architecture (Olynthus,* XII), pp. 191 ff., 201; 139, n. 96.

Examples of stucco wall decoration imitating drafted-margin masonry have been discovered in recent years in the House of Ganymede at Morgantina dating from the period 250–211 B.C. (Erik Sjöqvist, "Excavations at Morgantina [Serra Orlando], 1959, Preliminary Report IV," *AJA,* 64 [1960], 131 f.), and in the apparently still earlier third-century houses at Villa Jacona. The latter are exhibited on the wall near

Case 23 in the Museum at Gela (Piero Orlandini and Dinu Adamesteanu, *Guida di Gela* [Milan, n.d.], p. 36; Pietro Griffo, *Sulle orme della civiltà gelese* [Agrigento, 1958], p. 21).

For examples from Priene and Delos, see *Priene,* pp. 308 f., figs. 333 f.; and Bulard, pp. 98 ff., 129 ff. For further discussion of the background and development behind the Delian system of wall decoration, see Joseph Chamonard, *Le quartier du théâtre (Délos,* VIII, pt. 2), pp. 367 ff., 387 f.; and F. Wirth, "Mittheilungen aus dem Kerameikos V. Wanddekorationen ersten Stils in Athen," *AM,* 56 (1931), 35–42. The latter's assumption that the use of incision antedated the appearance of plastically modeled paneled courses simulating drafted-margin masonry and constituted an earlier phase in the development of the First Style was disputed by Achille Adriani, *La nécropole de Moustafa Pacha (Annuaire du Musée gréco-romain,* 1933/34–1934/35 [Alexandria, 1936]), p. 129, and has, of course, been invalidated by these later discoveries.

Simulated drafted masonry appears, too, in the vaulted tomb illustrated by M. Rostovtzeff, *Ancient Decorative Painting in South Russia* (in Russian; St. Petersburg, 1913), pls. 29–31.

162. Pydna. Entrance to tomb chamber

wall into three primary zones, including the introduction of an ornamental architectural motif in the uppermost zone, that was to remain a feature of later wall painting and that is found in the princely Macedonian tumulus at Pydna was devised for that tomb (fig. 162).[151] Evidently, the basic ingredients of the wall decoration of the Hieron had already come into use when the building was constructed, although it is conceivable that its degree of correlation of the outer and inner faces of the wall was exceptional. In any case, this system of decoration appears to stem from domestic architecture. Were the residential quarters of the Macedonian princes decorated in this manner? The occurrence of simulated drafted-margin masonry at Olynthos and the character of Macedonian tomb decoration in the third century, coupled with Macedonian patronage of the Sanctuary of the Great Gods in the third quarter

151. Léon Heuzey and H. Daumet, *Mission archéologique de Macédoine* (Paris, 1876), pp. 246 ff. and pl. 18 (partially reproduced above, fig. 162). Cf., too, the related scheme in an early Ptolemaic tomb near Sidi-Gaber published by Hermann Thiersch, *Zwei antike Grabanlagen bei Alexandria* (Berlin, 1904), pp. 2 ff., pls. 1, 2, which the author suggests may have belonged to a Macedonian.

163. Delos, Maison de la Colline. Restored section

of the fourth century and the nature of the interior decoration of the Hieron, provoke this thought. But it must remain a matter for speculation until our knowledge of Macedonian architecture is greater.[152]

The building history of the Hieron precludes a conclusive statement about the date at which its wall decoration was devised or when the remnants of that decoration recovered within the cella were actually executed.[153] Theoretically, they could date from the original early Hellenistic building period of the cella; from the third quarter of the second century, when work was resumed on the unfinished building; or, more than a century later, in the early Imperial age, when repairs were made to one portion of the cella. Indeed, at first sight, the painted stuccoed walls of the cella, with their black dado, their predominantly scarlet paneled courses, their white moldings, and their miniature crowning colonnade, are so strikingly analogous to Delian houses in their decorative system (figs. 163, 164) [154] as to imply that they were executed in the second century B.C., when the porch was com-

152. I have raised this question in "The Wall Decoration of the Hieron in Samothrace," *Balkan Studies*, 5 (1964), 293–303. For Macedonian patronage in the Sanctuary, see text II, pp. 74 f.; *Guide, Guide²*, pp. 14 f.; Vol. 4, pt. II, pp. 131 ff.

As this volume goes to press, Martin's volume (cited above, n. 34) on the materials and techniques of Greek architecture has just appeared. On pp. 433 ff., some of the same monuments and problems considered in the article cited are also discussed—I am glad to see,

from a basically similar point of view.

153. For recapitulation of the building history of the Hieron, see text II, pp. 69 ff., 74 ff., 79 ff.

154. Cf., for example, Chamonard, op. cit., pt. 2, pl. 18, and Bulard, fig. 41 and pl. 6 A, a, from the Maison de la Colline and the Maison de Dionysos. Note, too, the related system restored by Wirth, op. cit., Beilage XIV–XV, from the Kerameikos fragments.

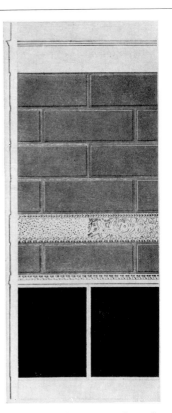

164. Delos, Maison de Dionysos. Partial restoration of a wall

165. Partial restoration of a wall in Delos

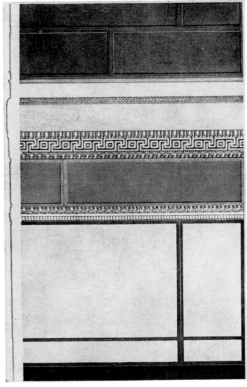

166. Delos, Maison du Trident. Partial restoration of a wall

167. Partial restoration of a wall in Delos

pleted and the building embellished by the addition of pedimental sculptures, akroteria, and carved coffered ceilings. Surely, it would have been a natural moment to refurbish the then nearly two-century-old interior. Yet the absence of that conspicuous and characteristic Delian feature, an elaborately painted, molded, and ornamented zone between the ortho-states and the wall proper,[155] lends to the walls of the Hieron a far greater simplicity, especially since it is coupled with the use of a severely unadorned dado (cf. figs. 92, 163–167). The more advanced Delian walls appear to be elaborations of a basic scheme they share with the Hieron. This fact, together with the long established earlier tradition of red stuccoed walls both in Samothrace and elsewhere,[156] with the previously mentioned imitation of drafted masonry at least as early as the mid-fourth century in painted, stuccoed walls at Olynthos, and with the decorative system used at Pydna (fig. 162), suggests, on the contrary, that the walls of the Hieron may already have received their permanent decoration late in the fourth century, when the cella was constructed. Not only are the walls at Pydna divided into three primary zones consisting of a dado, a central field of red, and an ornamental crowning section, but the dado of this princely tomb is still more elaborate and varied in coloration than is the dado of the Hieron. If both this tripartite division of the wall into dado, scarlet central area, and a more richly decorated crowning zone and the use of simulated drafted masonry are provable in the early Hellenistic period, only the engaged order in the uppermost zone of the Hieron's cella remains without positive parallel at that date. Yet the fact that the great rotunda dedicated to the Megaloi Theoi by Arsinoe only a few decades later was adorned by an engaged gallery in the uppermost tier of its interior (fig. 168) [157] indicates that this ornamental feature existed in Greek architecture long before its stucco surrogates in Delian houses and implies the possibility that a similar decorative device may already have been used in the slightly earlier Hieron. The very fact that a course of drafted-margin masonry topped by a pair of profiled courses has been introduced between the smoothly dressed dado of the Arsinoeion and the main drafted-margin masonry of its interior walls again illustrates the degree to which motifs characteristic of late Hellenistic

155. For example, see Chamonard, op. cit., pt. 1, fig. 83; pt. 2, pls. 18, 49; and Bulard, figs. 39, 43, 45, and pl. 6 A, a–c.

156. Red stucco fragments have been recovered in numerous places in the Sanctuary and in more than one fill, including that of the pronaos of the Hieron itself. They include paneled fragments, an indication that before the period in which the porch was completed, stuccoed walls reflecting drafted-margin masonry were already in use in Samothrace.

157. In this royal dedication, both the outer and inner faces of the wall were built of marble; hence, the interior of the building was neither stuccoed nor painted. On the exterior, the massive drum was

smoothly dressed between the two ornamental courses that define its top and bottom, the upper a binding course that supported the gallery at the summit of both the inner and outer walls, the lower a richly carved base restricted to the outer wall.

I am indebted to Stuart M. Shaw for the drawing illustrated in fig. 168. It and the brief description of the wall of the Arsinoeion given here reflect Mr. Shaw's exhaustive study of the superstructure of the Arsinoeion in recent years. His re-examination of the extant building blocks has yielded a reconstruction of the building differing from that of Niemann (S,I, pl. 55) in a number of respects. It will appear in Vol. 7 of this series.

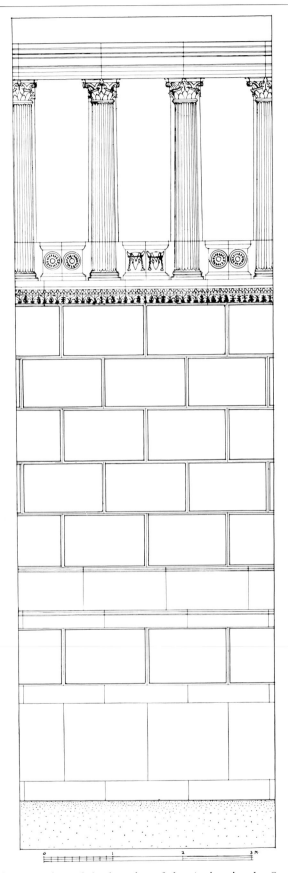

168. Partial restoration of the interior of the Arsinoeion by Stuart M. Shaw

wall decoration were anticipated at least as early as the beginning of the third century (cf. figs. 165–168). Conversely, the absence of this element in the far simpler decoration of the Hieron provides another argument for considering that decoration part of the original design for the late-fourth-century building.

Hence, it is tempting to attribute the design of the wall decoration of the Hieron to its original period. It is possible, indeed likely, that that decoration was renewed or repaired either in the late Hellenistic period or in the early Imperial age—or at both times.[158] But the relative simplicity of the Hieron's decoration in comparison with the character of the wall painting popular in these later periods suggests that such renewal or repair as was necessary for the maintenance of this decoration was achieved by repeating a late-fourth-century scheme rather than replacing or redesigning it.

THE PORCH

On the contrary, the porch originally planned to precede this hall differed in plan and proportion from the one actually constructed when the building was completed. Its twelve columns were disposed in an outer row of six, separated by a pair of intermediate lateral columns from an inner row of four columns between antae (fig. 57). The outer eight columns were taller than the inner four, since the floor level of the pronaos was a step higher than that of the outer porch.[159] Hence, they were taller, too, than the columns of the extant porch.

Only a few prime proportional relationships may be deduced for this projected porch, apart from those previously established for the members of the wall entablature which, obviously, were identical with those of the columnar entablature. In both the inner and the outer colonnades, the relationship of the lower diameter to the height of the column was 1:6.99. The nearest parallels to this slender proportion are offered by those of the Treasury of Kyrene at Delphi (1:6.94), built in the third quarter of the fourth century; the Temple of Artemis at Epidauros (ca. 1:7), now dated at the end of the fourth or the beginning of the third century;[160] and the Temple of Athena at Pergamon (1:6.96),

158. For the completion of the building in the second century B.C. and major repairs made to it in the early Imperial and later ages, see text II, pp. 75 ff., 79 ff., 124 ff.

If the wall decoration of the cella was, in fact, renewed or repaired when the porch was completed, it is conceivable that the scarlet fragments found in the pronaos fill and mentioned in n. 156, above, came from the original decoration of the cella, having been thrown into it, along with other material, when the

pronaos was enlarged; more probably, they came from another deposit drawn on for fill.

159. For evidence in support of these statements, see above, pp. 84 ff.

160. For the figures given here and below, see Vol. 4, pt. II, pp. 76 ff., and the charts assembled by Ernest Will, *Le Dôdékathéon* (*Délos*, XXII [Paris, 1955]), p. 150; and Roux, pp. 129 f., 177 f., 410 ff. For the proportions (1:6.8–1:7) and date of the Temple of Artemis cited above, ibid., pp. 208, 221 f., 320, pl. 55.

variously dated in the early years of the third century.[161] The relationship of the combined height of the architrave and frieze to the height of the column (1:4.3), somewhat lighter in effect than the comparable proportions of both the Treasury of Kyrene and the Altar Court (1:4), recurs again in the Temple of Athena at Pergamon, where the combined height of architrave and frieze in relation to the lower diameter of the columns, 1:1.6 (as it was in the earlier Temple of Zeus at Stratos, ca. 330–320 B.C.), again offers the closest analogy to the Hieron's 1:1.63. These slender proportions, lighter than those of late classical buildings, indicate that the design for the projected porch of the Hieron was decidedly advanced, anticipating an aesthetic preference characteristic of later Hellenistic architecture.

It is impossible to define the precise point at which construction of the superstructure of the porch was interrupted.[162] Conceivably, the original plan called for a sculptured, coffered ceiling and the kind of roof that were ultimately built. In its present form, however, the porch is the product of a later period and, as such, requires separate consideration. The date of the original project and the stylistic affiliations of its architect may be established only on the evidence provided by the cella and implicit in the original lower parts of the porch.

As to chronology, analysis of that evidence has repeatedly pointed to a date ca. 325 B.C. for the cella and the projected porch—a date emphatically confirmed by the supplementary evidence of the ceramic finds from all four foundation ditches of the building and from its interior.[163] Certain features of the Hieron, more especially of its plan, are so rooted in liturgical requirements and so obviously retained from its archaic predecessor as to afford little help in determining its date.[164] Others, like the use of a double recess on the stereobate, reflect a practice popular throughout the fourth century. But still others have proved highly revealing —in particular, the character of the walls and the proportions and ornamental detail of the entablature. Let us briefly summarize this evidence.

The walls were built according to a system first documented for the Temple of Athena

161. Since the original publication of this temple by Richard Bohn, *Das Heiligtum der Athena Polias Nikephoros* (*Pergamon*, II [Berlin, 1885]), where a fourth-century date was proposed for it, there has been an increasing tendency to date it in the third century. Cf. D. S. Robertson, *A Handbook of Greek and Roman Architecture* (2d edn., rev., Cambridge, 1945), pp. 146, 330: ca. 290 B.C. (?); Will, loc. cit.: 290 B.C.; Lawrence, op. cit. (above, n. 26), p. 208: "a date rather early in the third century seems most likely"; most extreme: Dinsmoor, chart opposite p. 340, and Roux, p. 327, n. 5: ca. 250 B.C.; most recently, Helmut Berve and Gottfried Gruben, *Griechische Tempel und Heiligtümer* (Munich, 1961), p. 268: first quarter of

the third century. The varied evidence in favor of a date in the first decade of the third century has been presented, in my opinion convincingly, by Ohlemutz, op. cit. (above, n. 5), pp. 17–23. (Andreas Rumpf, *Griechische und römische Kunst* [A. Gercke and E. Norden, *Einleitung in die Altertumswissenschaft*, II, 3, Berlin and Leipzig, 1931], p. 65, retained the original fourth-century date. But his opinion may reflect the erroneous statement [ibid.] that the temple still exhibited the forms and number of triglyphs characteristic of older classical architecture.)

162. See above, p. 91.

163. See text II, pp. 145 ff., 165 ff.

164. See above, pp. 154 ff., for more detailed presentation of this and subsequent points.

at Priene, in construction when Alexander's benefactions to it were recorded in 334 B.C. They were enlivened by the use of drafted-margin masonry, an ornamental device also applied to the late-fourth-century Temple of Artemis at Sardis but not found on the walls of earlier buildings. The coupling of this device with the system of bonding used at Priene seems to have occurred for the first time on the Hieron. This prime feature of the building implies a date neither earlier nor necessarily later than the third quarter of the century. Repetition on the anta and pilaster capitals framing the walls of the Hieron of profiles characteristic of the epikranitis of the adjacent Altar Court, erected in the decade 340–330 B.C., confirms this implication and suggests, in addition, that the Hieron was contemporary with or slightly later than the Altar Court.

Turning to the entablature, we may classify its features in two categories: those for which the closest parallels have been found on the neighboring Altar Court and the slightly earlier Propylon to the Temenos; and those which link the Hieron to buildings outside Samothrace.

The proportion of architrave to frieze on the Hieron (1 : 1.16) falls in the latter category, being closest to that of the Temple of Zeus at Stratos (1 : 1.15), a building perhaps a decade later than the Altar Court; but the same general proportions had occurred a generation earlier on the Temple of Athena Alea at Tegea (1 : 1.14) and do not in themselves afford a narrowly defined date within the century. On the other hand, the more detailed proportional relationships within the architrave between the heights of the taenia and the total block (1 : 8.53) and of the regulae to the taenia (1 : 3.4) on the Hieron are approximately paralleled on the Leonidaion at Olympia (1 : 9.25) and the Philonian Porch at Eleusis (1 : 3.5), respectively, that is, on buildings slightly later than the Altar Court. Analysis of the architrave thus reinforces the testimony of the wall and contributes to the mounting evidence pointing toward a date close to but later than the Altar Court.

That evidence is augmented and the relationship between the two structures illumined by the character of their friezes and geisa. The recurrence of such singular details as the presence of both curved and straight glyphs on the triglyphs of both friezes and the pointed oval section of the drip on both geisa has led to the suggestion that these blocks were shaped by the same masons; that is, that some of the stonecutters at work on the Altar Court were retained for the subsequent construction of the Hieron which must, therefore, have followed soon after the completion of the great Doric enclosure.

The lateral simas of the two structures may well have been similar in pattern, although one was painted, the other carved. In any case, the triple-tendril rinceau of the Hieron is a variation on the scheme devised for the Propylon shortly after the mid-century. And it is to the waterspouts on a contemporary monument, the Tholos at Epidauros, constructed during the third quarter of the century, that the lions of the Hieron's sima are most akin. Finally,

214

the use of a triple motif on the raking sima in place of the conventional alternation of two motifs has proved another link with the Temple of Athena at Priene.[165]

On the basis of its architectural features, both structural and ornamental, the cella of the Hieron and its projected porch must, therefore, be dated ca. 325 B.C.[166] The character of the ceramic material from its interior, pronaos, and foundation ditches strongly reinforces this date, for in type, fabric, glaze, and profile it repeats the forms characteristic of the pottery found in the rich fill of the Altar Court.[167]

The sole stylistic feature of this very early Hellenistic building that may evoke surprise, the lightness of proportion of its projected Doric order, suggests that the unknown architect of the Hieron was among the architectural *avant-garde* of his day. His use of drafted-margin masonry again anticipated the widespread popularity of this ornamental device in later Hellenistic architecture. His readiness to adopt or create new forms, whether structural or ornamental, is most strikingly apparent in his ground plan, a plan unique in the history of Greek architecture. Yet that plan, born of the coupling of two types in themselves traditional—the rectilinear cella and the cella with a salient apse—reveals another marked characteristic of his artistic personality: the acceptance of traditional forms when liturgical requirements or visual tact dictated them. The individual ingredients of his plan and the detailing of his entablature reflect this point of view. Indeed, apart from the novel aspects of its plan, walls, and proportions, the majority of the structural or ornamental features of the Hieron—whether the use of a trussed roof or of a particular form of antefix, to recall but two examples—have proved to be the outgrowth of local tradition.

In so far as the structural or ornamental features of the Hieron are alien to Samothracian tradition, their sources or parallels have been found in Asia Minor or Macedonia. In two such diverse respects as the structural system of its walls and the decorative system of its raking sima, the Hieron has proved to be closely related to the Temple of Athena at Priene. Furthermore, like Pytheos, the architect of the Hieron employed a foot approximately

---

165. Certain other features of the building, both ornamental and structural, appear to stem from its immediate forebear or to reflect usage for which contemporary analogies exist but whose application was not restricted to one period: e.g., its antefixes and its tympanum wall. Although they are entirely appropriate features of a building constructed around 325 B.C., they do not contribute materially to the definition of that date.

166. As late as 1952, before excavation of the Hieron had been completed—therefore, before it could be reconstructed and investigated or its ceramic material properly studied—we, too, continued to labor under the mistaken assumption that it was built in the mid-third century. Only after the final campaign of 1953 could its complicated sequence of building periods and repairs be established. For reference to our previous faulty conclusions and to the equally erroneous assumptions of earlier scholars, see above, pp. 11 ff., 24 and n. 64.

167. See text II, pp. 145 ff., 165 ff., 173 ff., and Vol. 4, pt. II, pp. 151 ff., especially 8 ff., and 217–24.

Setting marks were rarely cut on the blocks of the Hieron (see fig. 52). For the most part, they cannot be narrowly dated as letter-forms, but the kappa on geison block 723 is of a variety used only in the fourth century in Samothracian ceramic inscriptions (cf. the chart in Vol. 2, pt. II, p. 41), and the ΘΕ in ligature found on another such block, 680, appears to have been restricted to the same century.

0.295 m. in length.[168] If the unorthodox decoration of the coffered ceilings of the two buildings with lids separately made and carved in high relief, characteristic of both buildings in their completed state, formed part of their original design—as is more than likely, given the occurrence of this device on both the Mausoleum at Halikarnassos and the Propylon to the Temenos in Samothrace—they were linked in still another respect.[169] This affiliation is the more remarkable when one considers the scant opportunity for analogies between a Doric and an Ionic building. Were it not for Pytheos' known injunction against the use of the Doric order for temples,[170] it would be tempting to attribute the Hieron to him. To be sure, the Hieron is not a temple; but it is sufficiently temple-like in exterior effect to make one reluctant to propose an attribution that cannot be further substantiated, given the Ionic forms of the master's two documented works.[171] Whatever his relationship to Pytheos—as apprentice, associate, or admirer—whatever his homeland or training, the anonymous architect of the Hieron was evidently familiar with architectural practice in Asia Minor, since it is to monuments of that region, rather than the Peloponnesos or Attica, that his work shows the closest affinity.[172] In this respect, as in others, he differed from the architect of the Altar Court, whose range of affiliations was broader, even though they included dependence on Anatolian tradition.[173]

The interior decoration of the Hieron offers another clue to the associations and activity of our architect. Its relationship to Macedonian prototypes reveals his second regional affiliation. For it is hardly possible that one unfamiliar with Macedonian wall painting could have devised the interior decoration of the Hieron. Was the architect of the Hieron a Macedonian trained in Asia Minor? If, as is not inconceivable, the Hieron, like the Altar Court, was a gift of Arrhidaios, its architect may well have been a Macedonian.[174] Or was he a Samothracian who grafted knowledge of contemporary architectural practice in the nearest cultural centers onto traditional local forms? Such questions cannot be answered at the present time. But two conclusions may be drawn about this unknown architect, whatever

168. *Priene*, pp. 86, 104, 118. I say "approximately" because, as the measurements on these pages indicate, there are repeated minor divergences from the exact figure 0.295 m. that is normally cited as the length of the foot used by Pytheos (Dinsmoor, p. 222, n. 2, calculates this "Ionic" foot as 0.294 m.). Conceivably, they reflect the weathering of blocks, shifts in a foundation caused by damage to its superstructure, or faulty measuring, to mention a few possible explanatory factors.

169. See below, pp. 233 f. The beams on which these coffers rested in both buildings have in common another unusual feature: the use of a paneled soffit. The additional fact that Π-clamps were used on both buildings simply reflects widespread contemporary practice.

170. Vitruvius 4.3.1.

171. For a lengthy discussion of Pytheos and his works and full bibliography on this thorny subject, see H. Riemann, s.v. *Pytheos, RE*, XXIV, 1963, cols. 371–513.

172. Although the closest analogies to the lion's-head waterspouts of the Hieron occur on Peloponnesian monuments, they are of value only for its chronology and do not imply dependence on Peloponnesian style or personal acquaintance with the monuments of that region on the part of our architect, as has been pointed out above, p. 176.

173. See Vol. 4, pt. II, pp. 106 f.

174. For the argument establishing Arrhidaios as donor of the Altar Court, see ibid., pp. 120–33; for speculation on the possibility that he also provided funds for the construction of the Hieron, see text II, pp. 74 f.

his origin or training: he was clearly familiar with architectural practice in Asia Minor and Macedonia and equally clearly ready to observe local Samothracian tradition when the function of the Hieron or its proximity to its neighbors made the retention of earlier forms desirable. Analysis of the structure and style of the Hieron has shown his artistic mentality to have been a rare blend of originality and tact, of the progressive and the conservative, a turn of mind that enabled him to design a building notable both for its originality and for its harmonious adjustment to an architectural setting marked by extreme diversity.

How long it took to complete the cella and begin construction of the porch, when and why work on the Hieron was interrupted—these are questions to which no certain answer may be given and about which speculation is best postponed until the history of the building is reviewed.[175] Still more uncertain are the circumstances that led to its completion. But the character of the porch, hence, the period in which it was erected, may be established.

The architect responsible for completing the older Doric building had little opportunity to alter its original design, given the necessity of retaining in his porch the proportions and basic forms of the cella entablature. Fortunately, that older cella cannot have looked old-fashioned or displeasing to his eyes, for its most unusual external feature when it was built in the late fourth century, the character of its wall—both its structural system and its drafted-margin masonry—had remained in fashion in Samothrace and elsewhere.[176] On the contrary, the original design for the porch was apparently no longer pleasing aesthetically; otherwise, it would not have been revised. Fortunately, again, revision of the original project was easily effected, since the obligatory proportions of the cella entablature could be retained and coupled with columns different in proportion from those originally planned, with the result that the over-all proportions of the façade could be altered to suit the taste of a later day. This, as we have seen, is precisely what was done.[177]

As it was ultimately constructed, the prostyle porch of the Hieron was provided with two rows of six columns separated from each other by a pair of intermediate columns, one on each side of the building, and rested on a crepidoma of three steps (Pls. CII, CVII, CVIII). In completing the foundations of the porch and providing for the support of the marble pavement laid in its forepart, the second architect of the Hieron followed a system

---

175. Ibid.

176. To cite but a few examples: for the wall system, see the mid-second-century Temple of Hera Basileia at Pergamon (*Pergamon*, VI, 104 and pl. 33) and the Hiera Stoa at Priene of the same date (*Priene*, pp. 201 f.); for drafted-margin masonry, the third-century Ptolemaion in Samothrace (*S,II*, pls. 31–33) and the second-century Temple of Artemis at Magnesia (*Magnesia*, p. 74, and fig. 71 on p. 79, although this feature is not shown in the general reconstruc-

tion drawings of the building).

177. Above, pp. 93 ff. It has been suggested that when the Early Classical Temple of Apollo in Delos was completed toward the end of the fourth century, its proportions were similarly altered to adjust it to the taste of a later day—in this case, by the introduction of an unorthodox ornamental course between the frieze and the geison that produced an entablature more open in effect than the projected, partially built entablature would otherwise have had: *Délos*, XII, 105.

long used in Samothrace and other regions of the Greek world.[178] Narrow rails of the porous limestone used throughout the foundations were set roughly at a right angle to the porous backers of the second step, the intervals between them being filled with blocks of soft yellow limestone, which, like the rails themselves, were laid on a packing of field stones and earth (Pls. I, II.1, 2). This technique, which may or may not have been intended for the original porch, and the use in its forepart of a marble pavement composed of slabs set from rail to rail afford no chronological indications. Neither, in a limited sense, does the terrazzo floor laid in the pronaos.

The crepidoma itself is scarcely more revealing. Of necessity, the stylobate was enlivened by two recesses, since it continued the line of the stereobate (cf. Pls. IV, CVII, CVIII). On the analogy of Temple A at Kos—a building with which the porch of the Hieron proves to be related[179]—we have restored such recesses to the lower two steps, neither of which is preserved, although theoretically the lowest step may have had only one, as did the nearby Propylon to the Temenos.[180] In any case, the use of this device on all the marble buildings in the Sanctuary means that its presence here has no chronological implications but simply reflects its continuing popularity in the Hellenistic age in Samothrace and elsewhere. This ornamental detail of the fourth-century cella could be retained in the later porch without difficulty. The blocks of the euthynteria on which these steps rested were not smoothly dressed like those of the cella but were allowed to retain their protective mantle. As a result, this sequence of rusticated blocks provided a firm horizontal accent at the base of the façade, emphasizing its stability. Whether this effect was achieved by accident or intention is uncertain; yet the use of rustication at the base of the Altar Court and still more conspicuously at the entrances of the barrel-vaulted passage beneath the Ptolemaion not only indicates that there was local precedent for this practice, but also suggests that rustication in the true ornamental sense was consciously used on this course.[181]

The porch erected on this triple-stepped base was radically classicistic. The slender

178. In Samothrace it occurs in the earlier Ptolemaion (*S,II*, p. 37 and pls. 17, 18, 31–33), but it is also found in such widespread random monuments as the Peisistratan Telesterion at Eleusis (Noack, pp. 48 ff. and pl. 3); the porches of the Temple of Asklepios at Epidauros (Roux, pls. 27, 29), the Temple of Zeus at Megalopolis (*Excavations at Megalopolis* [above, n. 14], pl. 14), the Temple of Zeus at Nemea (Mogens Clemmensen, "Le temple de Zeus à Nemée," *BCH*, 49 [1925], pls. 1, 2), and the "temple en calcaire" in the Marmaria at Delphi (*FdDelphes*, II, pt. 3, pl. 1, better illustrated in the older article by Frederik Poulsen, "Recherches sur quelques questions relatives à la topographie de Delphes," *Oversigt over det Kongelige Danske Videnskabernes Selskab, Forhandlinger*, 1908, pp. 363

ff.); the Doric Temple at Seleucia (Richard Stillwell in *Antioch-on-the-Orontes*, III [Princeton, 1941], pl. 9, p. 260); the Pythion at Delos (Vallois, *Les constructions antiques de Délos*, pl. 5; and the Great Altar at Pergamon (*Pergamon*, III, p. 12 and pls. 2, 3), to cite a few examples.

179. See below, pp. 221 f. For this feature of the temple, see *Kos*, I, 4, pl. 3 a, b.

180. For this building, see Vol. 5 of this series, forthcoming.

181. Cf. the similar effect on the Temple to the Mother of the Gods in her mountain fastness at Mamurt-Kaleh: A. Conze and P. Schazmann, *Mamurt-Kaleh, Ein Tempel der Göttermutter unweit Pergamon* (*JDAI*, Suppl. 9 [Berlin, 1911]), pls. 5, 6.

169. View of the Hieron after the anastelosis of 1956

columns and light proportions of Hellenistic Doric architecture were abandoned in favor
of the heavier, stronger forms of an earlier day (Pl. CVIII; fig. 169). Analysis of the proportional relationships of the colonnade and its entablature reveals a revival of classical, in
particular, fourth-century, relationships. The proportion of the lower diameter to the height
of the columns (1:6.28) is exactly that of the north wing of the late-fourth-century Harbor
Stoa at Miletos and, among more analogous buildings, is closest to that of the earlier temples
of Asklepios at Epidauros (1:6.2) and of Zeus at Nemea (1:6.5).[182] The comparable figure
for the third-century Temple of Athena at Pergamon is 1:6.9. The central columns taper at a
ratio of 1:0.81, the slightly larger outer columns of 1:0.82, thus falling within the range
of 1:0.7–1:0.9 characteristic of the century. The relationship between the lower diameter
and the length of the abacus on these columns (1:1.10) occurs almost exactly at Tegea
(1:1.11), as does the relationship between the upper diameter of the shaft and the length
of the abacus (1:1.41) earlier in the century on the Temple of Asklepios at Epidauros
(1:1.4). In one important respect, however, the internal relationships of the column strike

182. For these and other proportional statistics, see Fernand Courby, *Les temples d'Apollon (Délos,*
XII), p. 99, and the references cited above, n. 160.

a note alien to the classical tradition: in the height of the echinus in comparison with the height of the abacus (1:1.9). The lowness of the echinus reflects the later date of the porch.[183]

The relationship of column to entablature is again classicizing. Like other features of the entablature, its height (geison included) in comparison with that of the column (1:3.5) links the Hieron to its neighbor the Altar Court (1:3.4), as does the identical relationship on both buildings between the combined heights of the architrave and frieze and the height of the column (1:4), a proportion recurring at Lindos and not unlike that in the earlier temple at Tegea (1:4.03). So, too, the ratio of lower diameter to the combined height of architrave and frieze (1:1.55) is hardly to be distinguished from the comparable figures for the same temples (Lindos, 1:1.56; Tegea, 1:1.51). Finally, the spacing of the columns as expressed in the relationship of lower diameter to axial intercolumniation (1:2.6) is virtually the same as that found on the Temple of Athena at Lindos (1:2.66). Nor are these relationships surprising, since the new colonnade designed for the porch was adjusted to the requirements of a late-fourth-century entablature by an architect who was consciously reverting to proportions characteristic of that age in general, if no longer acceptable to the *avant-garde* taste of his predecessor.

Apart from their unclassical proportion of echinus to abacus, his capitals, too, reflect this point of view (Pls. LXIV, XCVII). The contours of the echinus, which ends in a slight curve beneath and behind the abacus, and of the annuli are closer to normal late classical forms than are the profiles of the capitals of the Altar Court, on which the oblique line of the echinus runs directly to the abacus, as it commonly does on later Hellenistic capitals.

Judged only on the basis of its proportional interrelationships, the façade of the Hieron might almost pass for a fourth-century building. But such a date is precluded by the evidence provided by the structural history of the pronaos and porch,[184] the pronaos fill [185] and the sculptured coffered ceiling of the pronaos,[186] and by such telltale features as the use of building techniques not employed on the cella and the alteration in style and pattern of its ornamental detail[187]—quite apart from the testimony of its pedimental and akroterial sculptures,[188] which theoretically could have been added later. On the contrary, they bear witness to the later date of the porch, as will shortly become apparent.

183. The proportions cited for the capitals of the Hieron by W. Wilberg, "Die Entwicklung des dorischen Kapitells," *JÖAI*, 19/20 (1919), 177, are incorrect, as is his description of it and, naturally, given the date of this article, his date for it. For the latter point, see below, pp. 234 f.; text II, pp. 75 ff.

184. See above, pp. 84 ff.
185. See text II, pp. 173 ff.
186. See below, pp. 246 ff.
187. See below, pp. 223 ff.
188. See below, pp. 302, 360 ff., 381 ff.

For the proportions of the porch link it not only with the fourth-century buildings cited above, but also with two others: the Temple of Despoina at Lykosoura and Temple A at Kos, both dated shortly before the mid-second century B.C.[189] The significant proportion of lower diameter of the column to size of the intercolumniation, 1 : 2.6 on the Hieron, recurs exactly at Lykosoura and is nearly paralleled at Kos (1 : 2.3). The relationship between that same lower diameter and the combined height of architrave and frieze, 1 : 1.55 on the Hieron, is 1 : 1.59 at Lykosoura, and the proportion of architrave to frieze, 1 : 0.86 on the Hieron, is close to that at Kos (1 : 0.84). Lack of evidence for the heights of the colonnades at Kos and Lykosoura forbids other comparisons.

The three buildings are linked in a still more important respect: they constitute a small group in which the three-triglyph system that replaced the classical two-triglyph system on Hellenistic Doric temples in the third century and the first decades of the second [190] was abandoned and the classical solution revived (cf. Pl. CVIII; figs. 170, 171).[191] Despite this primary relationship, the three façades are sufficiently dissimilar in detail (for example, in the design of their triglyphs) to imply that they are not the work of one architect. It would be tempting to ascribe this revival of classical—more especially, fourth-century—proportions

189. For the Temple of Despoina, see especially Leonardos, op. cit. (above, n. 14), pp. 93–126. I have recently discussed certain other aspects of this temple in "The Technique of the Mosaic at Lykosoura," *Essays in Memory of Karl Lehmann* (*Marsyas*, Suppl. I [Locust Valley, N.Y., 1964]), pp. 190–97, where the full bibliography for it may be found in nn. 1, 3, 4. For the date, ca. 160 B.C., see ibid., p. 196, n. 33.

For Temple A at Kos, see Schazmann, *Kos,* I, 72 f., where it is dated ca. 160–150 B.C. primarily on the basis of its relationship to the Temple of Hera Basileia at Pergamon, a dedication of Attalos II, who reigned from 159–138 B.C.

190. The Temple of Demeter and Kore at Aegae actually had a four-triglyph system: R. Bohn and C. Schuchhardt, *Altertümer von Aegae* (*JDAI,* Suppl. 2 [Berlin, 1889]), p. 41. The Doric temples of the Hellenistic age, often of modest size, have been largely overlooked in general architectural discussions, with the erroneous result that a popular misconception has arisen to the effect that for temples the Doric order was "virtually abandoned" in the Hellenistic age, and the few examples discussed are characterized as Doric intruders: Dinsmoor, p. 267. Louis Robert, too, has expressed surprise at the fact that the great third-century Temple of Apollo at Klaros was Doric: "C'est une surprise en Ionie, sur la terre classique de l'architecture ionique" (*Les fouilles de Claros* [above, n. 120],

p. 12, a statement reiterated by Günther Klaffenbach, "Die Ausgrabungen in Klaros," *Das Altertum,* 1 [1955], 218 f.).

Recently, this misconception has been attacked by R. A. Tomlinson, "The Doric Order: Hellenistic Critics and Criticism," *JHS,* 83 (1963), 133–45, who has correctly pointed out that the Doric temples extant from this period are more numerous than the Ionic. Unfortunately, his own chart of late classical and Hellenistic temples, being based on Dinsmoor's, again omits many small but typical Doric temples in or near such prime centers as Pergamon and Delos— to mention but two. His refutation of the orthodox view is, therefore, far less effective than it could have been. It is marred, in addition, by his advocacy of unprovable theories, such as the "royal prestige attached to the Doric order" (p. 141), and a total lack of appreciation of the conscious juxtaposition of the two orders in innumerable architectural ensembles, especially in the clearly intentional use of a contrasting order in the framework of stoai, which provide the setting for so many Hellenistic temples. These flaws are the more regrettable since they obscure the basic and welcome premise of the article: the continuing use of the Doric order for temples, as well as other structures, in the Hellenistic age.

191. Leonardos, op. cit. (above, n. 14), pl. 4; *Kos,* I, pl. 6.

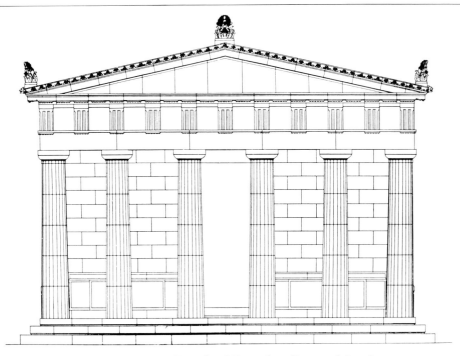

170. Lykosoura, Temple of Despoina. Restored façade

171. Kos, Temple A. Restored façade

to the second architect of the Hieron and to suggest that in adjusting his porch to the late-fourth-century cella and reverting to late classical proportions he had inaugurated a new aesthetic movement in Hellenistic art, were it not for the relative dates of the Hieron and the Temple of Despoina [192] and the greater probability, therefore, that the movement was launched by Damophon, fresh from his work on the chryselephantine statue of Zeus at Olympia.[193] In any case, the use of the two-triglyph system and the proportional relationships established above would in themselves imply that the porch of the Hieron was constructed close to the mid-second century B.C.

An interval in time between the construction of the cella and the completion of the porch is further attested by certain divergences in motif or style between the simas and antefixes of the porch and those of the cella. Although the three motifs of the southern raking sima were retained at the north, the crisp, angular form of its highly individual palmette was altered by the addition of two petals, one on each side (cf. figs. 131, 172).[194] The resulting nine-petaled palmette is less vigorous and more commonplace than its seven-petaled predecessor and related in type, if not in execution, to the palmettes on the ornamental, binding wall course of the early-third-century Arsinoeion (fig. 173). This type of palmette occurs elsewhere in the second century, for example, on the raking sima of the Temple of Artemis at Magnesia [195] and the entablature of the Ionic niches in the lower story of the stoa in the precinct of Athena at Pergamon (fig. 174).[196]

The provenance of the sparse fragments of the northern raking sima assures their attribution to the porch. Unfortunately, no lion's-head waterspouts were recovered in our excavation of the porch and its vicinity, although several of the big sima-stroter blocks from its roof—all lacking their gutters—are preserved. But three of the lion's-head waterspouts from the Hieron stored in the Kunsthistorisches Museum in Vienna (figs. 175, 176) differ in style so markedly from their counterparts found toward the southern end of the cella that it is reasonable to attribute them to the porch, in spite of the fact that their specific provenance was not recorded in the nineteenth century.[197] Although they repeat the basic type of the cella lions (cf. fig. 126), they differ from them in detail, and their loose, coarse execution contrasts sharply with the precise, firm workmanship of the earlier heads. The locks of their double-rowed manes are fewer and more widely spaced; their cheekbones, unlike the powerfully modeled, knobby forms of the cella lions, are flat and unemphasized; nose and muzzle, while shaped according to the same linear patterns, are carved in a superficial style wholly lacking the grasp of organic structure, the clarity of form, of the original

---

192. See below, p. 234.

193. For Damophon see, among others, the references cited in "The Technique of the Mosaic at Lykosoura," loc. cit., p. 190, n. 4; p. 196, n. 33.

194. This detail was overlooked in *Hesperia*, 21 (1952), 40.

195. *Magnesia*, p. 63, fig. 51.

196. *Pergamon*, II, 46 and pl. 28.

197. Inv. nos. 346 K 1, 2, and 4.

172. Fragment of the northern raking sima

173. Detail from the wall of the Arsinoeion

174. Pergamon, Precinct of Athena. Entablature of an Ionic niche in the Stoa

175. Lion's-head waterspout 346 K 2. Kunsthistorisches Museum, Vienna

176. Lion's-head waterspout 346 K 1. Kunsthistorisches Museum, Vienna

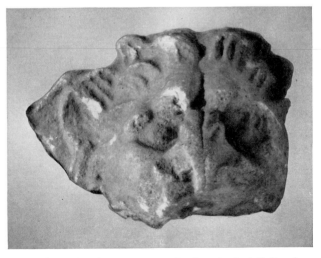

177. Lion's-head waterspout. Archaeological Collection
of the Charles University, Prague

heads. A fourth head in Prague (fig. 177) exhibits the same crude variations on the original type and clearly belongs to this same group.[198]

Only one of the six antefixes recovered in our excavation of the Hieron was found in the vicinity of the porch.[199] Badly shattered though it is, enough remains of the lower part of the face to link it with at least two of the seven antefixes stored in the Kunsthistorisches Museum (fig. 178) [200] and to suggest that they, too, come from the porch. The probability that the lateral sima fragments taken to Vienna belonged to the porch strengthens the likelihood of this suggestion. Like the waterspouts, they follow the basic scheme of their prototype on the cella but differ from it in detail and in quality of execution (cf. figs. 134, 179). The lateral petals of these antefixes droop more limply than the firm, blunt-tipped petals of their forebear, quite apart from being less finely hollowed, and the leaves from which their supporting tendrils emerge are no longer modeled to suggest the ragged acanthus. The remaining examples in Vienna and Samothrace are still more crudely executed (cf. fig. 180),[201] the lower acanthus leaves, coiled-up tendrils, and overhanging leaves of the original design being reduced to clumsy abstractions. Inasmuch as the Hieron was subjected to repair or remodeling no less than three times in the Imperial age, it is probable that among the extant antefixes in both collections there are examples from all three periods, but it would be arbitrary to

198. Jiří Frel, *Listy Filologické*, 74 (1950), 65 ff. (reported, too, in *Fasti Archaeologici*, 5 [1952], 233), has correctly distinguished between the two heads in Prague, attributing the one illustrated above to the later porch. In misdating the other head, he simply followed Salač's argument, for which see above, p. 17; but in attributing one of these heads to the cella and the other to the porch, Frel was correct. Our own first interpretation of the Prague heads, *Hesperia*, 21 (1952), 40, n. 85, has proved to be erroneous.

Willemsen, too, op. cit. (above, n. 42), pp. 65 f., has noted the connection between this later Prague head and the Vienna heads and assumed that they could hardly antedate the early first century B.C. While the cella of the Hieron was damaged and underwent extensive repair in the early Imperial age (see text II, pp. 79 ff.), and easily dislodged objects like the kalypters can also have been damaged and replaced at the same time, the fact that the second-century akroteria of the porch remained in position throughout antiquity makes it highly improbable that the original lateral simas of the porch were replaced at that time. The gulf in quality that separates the porch lions from the akroteria implies not so much a difference in date as that the former were carved by nondescript stonecutters, whereas the latter were the work of a virtuoso master of the first order, to judge from their counterparts at the south. Comparison of these lions with the

second-century waterspouts from the Artemision at Magnesia, different as they are in style, reveals a similar coarseness of execution in the same century (cf. *Magnesia*, p. 65, fig. 53). How careless work on the porch could be is shown by the character of the relaid inner stylobate (above, p. 92).

One of the Vienna lions' heads, 346 K 1, probably comes from the same block as one of the two extant fragments of the rinceaux from the lateral sima of the porch in the same collection, although the two fragments do not fit break on break. This fact may have contributed to Willemsen's opinion that the sima of the Hieron, hence the building, postdates the Arsinoeion. Actually, these fragments from the porch were executed later than the rotunda, but they differ not at all in motif from the sima of the cella. Hence, the fact that the rinceaux of the Hieron are smooth, unlike the ribbed stems of the Arsinoeion, does not provide a criterion for its date, as he assumed, op. cit., p. 66. For comment on Willemsen's retention of a third-century date for the Hieron (ibid., p. 65, n. 3, and p. 126), see above, n. 64.

199. 51.219, found among the fallen debris at the northwest corner of the building.

200. 346 L 1 and 2.

201. 346 L 3–7 in Vienna; 49.514 A–B, 49.515, 51.219, 52.494, and 62.14 in Samothrace.

178. Antefixes 346 L 1, 2. Kunsthistorisches Museum, Vienna

179. Antefixes from the Hieron in the Archaeological Collection of the Charles University, Prague

180. Antefixes 346 L 4, 6. Kunsthistorisches Museum, Vienna

227

assign them to one or another restoration. Nevertheless, the similarity between the fragment found at the northwest corner of the porch and the better preserved pieces in Vienna implies that the design of the cella antefix was slightly simplified when the porch antefixes were made, as the waterspouts of the porch show deviation from their model.

Although these divergences in motif or style between the ornamental details of the porch and cella are of little value in establishing the absolute chronology of the porch, their very existence reflects the difference in date between cella and porch that can be established on other grounds. So, too, do certain divergences in building technique that differentiate the porch and the cella.

No matter how high their position or how unwieldy their shape, the blocks of the cella were placed without the use of a lewis. The presence of lewis holes on the drums and capitals of the columns, on the columnar architrave blocks, the anta blocks, and the binding blocks of the tympana (both the outer tympanum and the invisible triangular fields above the inner colonnade and door wall) attest the use of this lifting device in the porch. It had been used long earlier in the construction of both the Propylon to the Temenos and the Altar Court; hence, its use in building the porch carries no chronological implications. But it does reflect a difference in procedure in the construction of the cella and porch that presumably would not have occurred had they been built at one time by one contractor.[202]

The anta walls, unlike those of the cella, had both an inner and an outer face of marble.[203] Following a system used still more extensively in the Arsinoeion, limestone fillers were introduced between the two faces of the wall at various points—an economical system in accord with the substitution of limestone for marble wherever it was feasible in the cella. Probably it would have been employed for the anta walls of the projected porch as well; but it does constitute one of the technical differences between the two parts of the building.

More significant of the difference in period between porch and cella is the alteration in the design of the porch sima blocks (cf. Pls. LV, LXXII.1, 2). It has been suggested that this change implies correction of the earlier design to enable the roof to drain more quickly.[204]

202. Block 128, one of the inner tympanum blocks mentioned above, not only has a lewis hole but also bears a setting mark which appears to be a Latin R (see fig. 52). I am indebted to Herbert Bloch for his comment that if this mark is, indeed, a letter and not a personal *sigla*, its shape, although unusual, is not inconsistent with a date in the second century B.C. If so, this mark again reflects the later date at which the porch was completed.

203. See above, pp. 99 f.; Pl. CIII. The antae proper were built of marble blocks equivalent in height to the recurring pairs of stretchers in the adjacent wall that abutted them in alternation with binders in themselves part pilaster, part wall block.

Similar systems occur, for example, on the Temple of Zeus at Magnesia, on Temple B at Kos, and at Lagina. The interior pilasters were wider than the exterior, as, again, in Temple B at Kos and still earlier at Tegea.

The structural system described above and ascribed to the Arsinoeion, too, has been recently established for the latter building by Stuart M. Shaw.

204. Above, pp. 104 ff. The provision of a polygonal boss to support the lowest kalypter in the center of each block is not without analogy: e.g., on the Temple of Apollo and the Temple of the Athenians at Delos (*Délos*, XII, pp. 39 ff., figs. 53–57, and pp. 136 ff., fig. 158, respectively); on the northwest stoa in

The fact that the system whereby the corner geison blocks were attached to the pair of sima blocks that supported the lateral akroteria was also revised implies either a similar correction to provide greater stability for these figures than was afforded at the rear corners of the building, or that no such sculptures were planned for the fourth-century Hieron. The former alternative is the more likely. In any case, the northern akroteria remained in place until the building collapsed, unlike their counterparts at the south, which fell to the ground little more than a century after they had been mounted[205]—proof of the superiority of the revised system.

The porch sima blocks also reflect the difference in structural system between the porch and cella roofs (cf. Pls. CIII, CIV).[206] The replacing of the simple truss used over the cella by an elaborate construction of purlins supported by posts resting on transverse beams implies both extreme structural conservatism and the view that this portion of the roof required exceptional stability.[207] Whether the plan for the projected porch called for a similar roof cannot be determined, but it is entirely possible that it did. In any case, the use of two differing systems of roof construction over the cella and porch of a building is not without parallel. The Temple of Concord at Agrigento is marked by a similar divergence, although the specific systems employed are not those of the Hieron.[208] Indeed, the roof construction implied for the porch by its sima and the extant blocks of its tympana (both visible and invisible) seems to be without parallel. Like the roof over the porch in the Temple of Concord, it involved the use of a number of purlins on each side of the ridge beam between the outer and inner tympana over the colonnades and the door wall; but, whereas at Agrigento the purlins were tilted and attached to rafters, in the Hieron they were upright and supported by props mounted on the cross-beams. Both systems reflect an almost profligate use of wood in strange contrast with the economical use of marble in the Hieron and the re-use of older building material commonly encountered in Greek buildings.[209]

---

the Agora at Thasos (*Études thasiennes*, VI, pt. 1, figs. 15–17); and on the Temple of Artemis at Magnesia (*Magnesia*, p. 64 and fig. 46 on p. 59). The sima of the latter is of particular interest, since it is designed to allow water in the gutter of an individual block to flow into the gutters of the adjacent blocks if the waterspout of that block becomes stopped up—an even superior system.

205. See text II, pp. 81 ff.

206. Hauser's comparison between the sima blocks of the Ptolemaion and those of the Hieron (*S,II*, p. 42) is misleading. He knew only the porch variety with which the block from the Ptolemaion has certain features in common. But judging by his pl. 41, fig. I, the cuttings at the rear of this block housed the oblique rafters rather than the horizontal beams, in which case the roof of the Ptolemaion differed in con-

struction from both the cella and the porch of the Hieron. In our current re-excavation of the Ptolemaion, we have not yet recovered a sima block.

Hauser records the discovery of a roof tile stamped ΠΡ (*S,II*, p. 10, fig. 2), which, it has been suggested (Vol. 2, pt. II, p. 115), might stand for Πρ(ονάου). The form ΠΠΡ in the latter citation is a misprint.

207. See above, pp. 116 f., for description of these blocks and deduction of this system. Hauser's hypothetical reconstruction of the pronaos timbers (*S,I*, pl. 34, fig. II), based only on the character of the sima blocks, is incorrect.

208. See Hodge, op. cit. (above, n. 128), pp. 25 ff., for discussion of this temple and pp. 50 ff. for other examples of his so-called Gaggera roof.

209. For example, in the underpavement of the

181. Inner architrave block 53

182. Detail of inner architrave block 260 from the Ptolemaion

The mighty beams of the marble coffered ceilings beneath these invisible timbers rested on the inner architrave of the porch and pronaos (Pls. XLIII, LXX, LXXI; fig. 181). This two-fasciaed Ionicizing course crowned by a boldly-projecting carved Lesbian cymation beneath a fascia is an unusual feature in a Doric building. Its rare forebears, with painted rather than carved ornament, occur in buildings like the Hephaisteion at Athens and the Temple of Poseidon at Sounion, where they are coupled with an unorthodox Ionic frieze.[210]

cella and the rebuilt northern foundation of the pronaos of the Hieron and the foundation of the peristasis at Didyma (*Didyma*, I, 49).

210. See Carl Weickert, *Das lesbische Kymation* (Leipzig, 1913), pp. 80 f.; and Shoe, p. 58. Weickert's proposed chronological sequence for the Samothracian examples discussed is correct, given the date of the porch, although his specific date for the "New Temple" is wrong.

230

183. Magnesia, Temple of Artemis. Detail of column capital

184. Magnesia, Temple of Artemis. Detail of anta capital

A similar inner architrave, whether carved or painted, backed the outer Doric architrave in the Temple of Athena at Pergamon.[211] The presence of this uncommon feature in both the Hieron and the Temple of Athena provides another link between the two structures and reinforces the logical assumption that it must have formed part of the original late-fourth-century design for the Hieron, since obviously the door wall of the cella was completed, however provisional the arrangements may have been to roof some portion of the unfinished porch.

The broad leaf and projecting profile of this molding recur on the Lesbian cymatia of the Arsinoeion and the Ptolemaion (cf. figs. 181, 173, 182), which were doubtless derived from it.[212] But the cymatia on the former two buildings are closer to each other in detail than to the Lesbian cymation of the Hieron, especially in the more oblique, angular contour of their leaves and in their proportionately greater depth. The shallower, gently curving leaves on the inner architrave of the Hieron are more analogous to those on columnar and anta capitals from the Temple of Artemis at Magnesia (figs. 183, 184),[213] a relationship that is not surprising, since the majority of the blocks from this course in the Hieron come from the columnar architraves of the later porch.

The marble beams resting on this unusual Ionicizing course in both the porch and

211. *Pergamon*, II, 9 and pl. 9. The same form was retained on the mid-second-century Temple of Hera Basileia: ibid., VI, 105, pl. 34, figs. 11, 24. The inner architrave of Temple A at Kos offers another example of this scheme; but the order of fillet and cyma reversa is reversed, and it was evidently not carved: *Kos*, I, 9, pl. 4.

212. Cf. *S,II*, pl. 37. On the Arsinoeion, the pattern appears on the richly-carved binding course beneath the gallery; on the Ptolemaion, it was used on both the inner architrave and the abacus of the capitals.

213. *Magnesia*, p. 50, fig. 34; p. 74, fig. 64. Cf., too, the profile of the latter (Shoe, pl. 11, fig. 8) and our Pl. XLIII.2.

185. Coffer lid from the Propylon of the Temenos, 55.149. Samothrace Museum

the pronaos are also characterized by an equally rare feature: the decoration of their soffits with a narrow, shallow panel edged by a cyma reversa molding (Pls. LXXVI.2–LXXX, CI.1).[214] Like other ornamental details on the Hieron, it has local precedent in the beams of the Ionic Propylon to the Temenos, which also supported coffers with sculptured lids,[215] and, outside Samothrace, it recurs on the beams of the Temple of Athena at Priene.[216]

The richly profiled coffers supported on these beams were also provided with paneled soffits, and both beams and coffers, whether the two-stepped coffers of the porch or the three-stepped coffers of the pronaos, were articulated by hawk's-beak moldings of varied projection (cf. Pl. CI.2–6).[217] Only the crown of the porch coffers shows a simple cyma reversa beneath a fascia. These elaborate hawk's-beak moldings are wholly different in their cyma reversa profiles from the bold simple cavetto-and-ovolo contours of the fourth-century pilaster capitals that were reiterated on the antae (cf. Pl. XCVI.1). Far more analogous to them are the profiled anta capitals on certain Delian houses of the second century B.C.[218]

214. On the comparative rarity of this ornamentation, see Shoe, p. 86. Miss Shoe's statement that all the extant cyma reversa moldings on such panels occur on Asiatic Ionic buildings must be revised, given their presence in the Hieron.

215. See Vol. 5 of this series, forthcoming.

216. *Priene,* p. 109. The ceiling beams of the Athenian Temple at Delos are equally exceptional in their paneled soffits which, however, lack a profiled border (*Délos,* XII, fig. 163).

217. Again, Miss Shoe's statement (p. 116) that this molding is never used to decorate the steps of a coffer except at Tegea is in need of revision.

218. Ibid., pl. 60, fig. 3 (House III K); pl. 60, fig. 5 (Maison du Trident). Unfortunately, the comparative material available for beams and coffers is limited. The analogies cited in this note are general rather than precise, but, such as they are, they illustrate Miss Shoe's distinction (p. 106) between the ovolo hawk's beak of the fourth century used on the pilaster capitals and the characteristically later cyma reversa hawk's-beak moldings of the coffers, as they are in accord with the tangible date provided for these moldings by the style of the sculptured coffer lids.

186. Fragmentary coffer lid from the Temple of Athena at Priene, No. 1171.
The British Museum, London

The use of separately-worked sculptured coffer lids in the pronaos ceiling again links the decorative forms of the porch with Ionic buildings.[219] In the nearby Propylon to the Temenos, built shortly after the mid-fourth century, this decoration took the form of sculptured busts (fig. 185),[220] an ornamental scheme for which there was precedent in the painted busts on the coffered ceiling of the Nereid Monument.[221] But on the Mausoleum at Halikarnassos and its descendent the Mausoleum at Belevi, as well as on the Temple of Athena at Priene (fig. 186), the lids of the coffers were carved with figural compositions.[222]

219. See below, p. 245, n. 12, for other examples of the use of separately-made coffer lids.

220. For the Propylon, see Vol. 5 of this series and, until its publication, the brief description in the *Guide, Guide²*, pp. 57 ff.

221. See A. H. Smith, *A Catalogue of Sculp-*

ture in the Department of Greek and Roman Antiquities, British Museum (London, 1900), II, no. 934, 3, where traces of a painted head in the center of one of the fragmentary coffers are recorded.

222. See below, pp. 245 f. and nn. 14–16, for bibliography on these monuments.

Although the ceiling at Priene was not completed until the mid-second century, the fact that Pytheos used such sculptured coffers at Halikarnassos makes it probable that they were included in his design for Priene. The combined evidence of the coffers in the Propylon and at Halikarnassos suggests that the coffered ceiling of the Hieron, too, reflects the intention of its first architect to provide such sculptural decoration in his projected porch. If so, the ceiling of the porch affords still another example of his tact in adjusting the ornamental forms of the Doric Hieron to the decorative features of its Ionic neighbor and adds significant testimony to his connection with Pytheos, whether direct or indirect.[223]

Whoever devised the coffered ceiling of the pronaos, its blocks were not cut or carved until the porch was constructed. The well-preserved coffer lid in Vienna cannot be dated far from the mid-second century,[224] a date in accord with the chronological implications of the most revealing and characteristic features of the porch: its over-all proportions and the two-triglyph system of its intercolumnia.[225] These features, which link the Hieron with the Temple of Despoina at Lykosoura and Temple A at Kos, indicate that on purely architectural grounds its porch could be dated shortly before the mid-century. For conservative dating of the Temple of Despoina places it ca. 160 B.C., and Temple A cannot have followed it by much more than a decade.[226] Yet the additional evidence afforded by the pedimental and akroterial sculptures with which both the new porch and the old cella were decorated suggests that the Hieron should probably be dated somewhat later than these temples in the early years of the third quarter of the century.[227] Theoretically, the porch and its coffered ceiling could have been completed slightly earlier, and time could have passed before its sculptural decoration was finished. But the scant year required for the execution of the pedimental sculptures[228] and the likelihood that once the not very extensive task of completing the building was undertaken it was carried through make it more reasonable to assume that the porch of the Hieron was built shortly after the mid-second century B.C.[229]

223. See above, pp. 215 f.

224. See below, pp. 247 ff.

225. The numerous other differences between the porch and the cella that have been pointed out above—whether structural, technical, or stylistic—confirm the difference in period between the two parts of the building and are in accord with the date now proposed for the porch, but they do not in themselves establish it.

226. For these dates, see above, n. 189, and the references cited therein. If Dinsmoor's date (175–170 B.C.) for Damophon's cult group at Lykosoura were accepted, this group of buildings might be antedated. But in view of their complicated relationships with each other and with the Temple of Hera Basileia at Pergamon (which was certainly built between 159 and 138 B.C., probably earlier rather than later in the reign

of Attalos II, given the nature of this tutelary divinity), the later date is the more likely. Margarete Bieber, *Hommages à Joseph Bidez et à Franz Cumont* (*Collection Latomus*, II [Brussels, 1949]), pp. 39 ff., also assumes that Damophon's work at Olympia preceded his cult group for Lykosoura, by implication dating the latter after 165 B.C.

227. See below, pp. 312 f., 327 f., 381 ff.

228. See below, p. 307, for this suggestion.

229. Although the contents of the pronaos fill do not yield as specific a date for the porch as its architectural and sculptural members, they, too, are in accord with a date in the second century B.C. (see text II, pp. 173 ff.).

In all probability, the stele forbidding the uninitiated to enter the cella, which was originally mounted on the threshold of the main door, dates from this pe-

Like his early Hellenistic predecessor, the architect who reshaped the late-fourth-century design for the porch of the Hieron worked in the most up-to-date contemporary architectural idiom. However different their tastes and outlook, they had this quality in common. For in abandoning the established forms of earlier Hellenistic Doric architecture and joining the group of second-century architects and sculptors who created the Classical Revival of later Hellenistic art—the first major classicistic movement of the many that were to follow in European art—he, too, was one of an *avant-garde* who turned away from the aesthetic traditions on which they had been reared and inaugurated a new artistic movement.

So much and no more may be said of this later architect, whose origin and training cannot be deduced from his completion of an older building that to a large extent determined his own work. Nor does his revival of classical forms necessarily imply specific regional connections, but rather association with a larger movement embracing the Greek mainland, the islands, and Asia Minor; for Teos, Alabanda, the Smintheion, Magnesia, and Lagina bear witness to the second-century revival on Ionic and Corinthian temples, too, of that prime feature of the classical tradition, architectural sculpture. Yet the very strength of the movement in Anatolia and the style of the sculptures with which the porch of the Hieron was embellished [230] suggest that the architect who directed its completion, like his fourth-century predecessor, was primarily in touch with artistic developments in Asia Minor.

No other Doric building exemplifies the Classical Revival as fully as the Hieron, since it alone, among extant monuments of the period, retains both its pedimental and akroterial sculptures, fragmentary though their preservation may be.[231] But the uniqueness of the

---

riod, too, as was proposed immediately after its discovery (see above, p. 64, for description and bibliography). Fraser's view (Vol. 2, pt. i, **62**) that "the large round lettering suggests a date in the first century B.C." is evidently based on a general impression rather than any binding objective criteria. Acceptance of this date would entail the unlikely conclusion that the inscription previously placed in this position—for there must always have been such an inscription—either dated from the original fourth-century period of the threshold or was itself a renewal dating from the time when the pronaos was rearranged. Theoretically, these alternatives are possible. But there is no evidence to support the next obligatory conclusion, namely, that one or the other of these hypothetical earlier inscriptions was damaged and replaced in the first century B.C. On the contrary, although the rear part of the cella was repaired in the early Imperial age, there is no trace of any damage or alteration to the second-century porch until the late Imperial remodeling of the door

that led to the transfer of this inscription from its original position on the threshold to a crudely-made base fashioned of re-used marbles. Hence, it is reasonable to assume that it should be dated in the second rather than the first century B.C. and that it replaced an earlier inscription damaged during the dismantling and rebuilding of the pronaos.

For reference to previous theories about the date of the Hieron, including the porch and its sculptures, and for bibliography in support of these views, see above, pp. 12 ff.; below, p. 302. It is needless to repeat or refute them here, especially since prior to our re-excavation of the building, the fact that the cella and the porch were constructed in different periods had not been conclusively established.

230. See below, pp. 247 ff., 309 ff., 381 ff.

231. It is impossible to determine from their present state of preservation and publication whether the temples at Lykosoura and Kos were intended to have pedimental sculptures. They, of course, did have or were intended to have akroteria.

Hieron is not primarily the product of historical accident. Although analogies exist for its individual features and forms, as a totality it stands without parallel in the history of architecture—a building designed for a special liturgy, hence conditioned by the requirements of that liturgy, a building in which the traditional in architectural expression commingles with the new.

Begun about 325 B.C. and completed nearly two centuries later, the Hellenistic Hieron was subjected to successive repairs and minor alterations during the Empire, but its essential appearance remained unchanged.[232] As the centuries passed and a new faith emerged in the ancient world—that triumphant faith which, like the rite of the Samothracian Gods, welcomed men and women, slaves and free men, Greek and non-Greek—the once unorthodox interior of the *epopteion* must have become less and less unusual in appearance. For to a remarkable degree such a significant aesthetic feature of the interiors of both the secular and the nonsecular basilica in later antiquity [233] as their apsidal terminations was anticipated in its interior, as were certain other features that link it with forms that became traditional in the Greek Orthodox Church.[234] Unorthodox in form as in function, the Hellenistic Hieron is a monument to the importance of the atypical in Greek architecture.

232. See text II, pp. 79 ff., 123 ff.

233. The analogy between the apsidal plan of the Hieron and a variety of later Roman buildings, both pagan and Christian, has long been noted: e.g., Hans Lietzmann, "Der unterirdische Kultraum von Porta Maggiore in Rom," *Vorträge der Bibliothek Warburg,* 1922/23, II (1925), 70; Karl Lehmann, "Samothrace: Fourth Preliminary Report," *Hesperia,* 20 (1951), 22; and, recently, Hugh Plommer, *Ancient and Classical Architecture* (London, 1956), p. 325. The wide acceptance of a faulty restored plan of the Hieron (above, p. 12) has even led to the theory that the Hieron was one of the prototypes of the earliest Christian basilicas: Émile Mâle, *The Early Churches of Rome,* tr. David Buxton (Chicago, 1960), pp. 47, 51. As Charles Picard pointed out in his review of the original French edition in *RA,* ser. 6, 21/22 (1944), 176 f., this view is untenable, if only because it is based on a misconception.

234. See text II, pp. 33 ff.

Addendum to n. 127, p. 198, above. As this volume goes to press, Elsbeth B. Dusenbery draws to my attention still another meander door—the two-leaved door decorated with rows of meanders incised on an archaic funerary stele re-used as the cover slab of a grave in the nekropolis at Efestia on the island of Lemnos. The presence of the meander on this door leading to the Underworld and the recurrence of the pattern on Lemnian cinerary urns from the eighth or seventh centuries is of the greatest interest in the context of the meanders, labyrinths, and meander-decorated doors discussed above. Reinforcing the suggestions that the meander-decorated doors of the Hieron and Temple A at Prinias were meaningful as well as ornamental and that the decoration of the main door to the Hellenistic Hieron may have been derived from its archaic forebear, these monuments add another dimension to a fascinating problem. For description and illustration of them, see Giacomo Caputo, "La stele tirrenica di Efestia," *Annuario,* 15/16 (1932/33), 279–88, and fig. 2; and Domenico Mustilli, "La necropoli tirrenica di Efestia," ibid., pp. 81 ff., 144 f., 198 f., 273, figs. 131, 173, 184 ff.

III. The Hellenistic Sculptures of the Hieron

WHEN the early Hellenistic Hieron was completed in the second century B.C., its porch was embellished with pedimental and akroterial sculptures, and the richly membered coffers of its pronaos ceiling were closed with lids carved in high and low relief. At the same time, its rear pediment was crowned with matching akroteria and decorated, it would seem, with at least one sculptured bust. It thus became the most richly adorned of all the Hellenistic Doric buildings that have come down to us.[1]

THE PRONAOS CEILING

The first of these sculptures to be lifted into place, possibly the first, too, to be executed, were the carved lids of the pronaos coffers.[2] Although none is fully preserved, fragments of the five centaurs that once pranced in the large single coffers of the pronaos ceiling are distributed between Vienna and Samothrace, in addition to the solitary fragment in lower relief in Samothrace that has been attributed to one of the smaller four-part fields.

The Vienna pieces include:

> C(V)1. Inv. No. I, 347. Kunsthistorisches Museum; on exhibition. *S,I*, pp. 12, 23, 27 f., pl. 52; *AJA*, 61 (1957), 123 ff., fig. 1; *Pedimental Sculptures*, pp. 23 f., figs. 39, 40. (Figs. 187, 204.)

Relief representing a centaur, restored by Zumbusch. The fragments combined consist of a virtually complete, though damaged, head to which part of the left shoulder and of the relief ground behind the right ear is attached; the ends of a fluttering mantle and its ground; the incomplete forepart of a right arm broken at the wrist; an irregular section of a human abdomen; a knee, part of the foreleg, and the hoof of a raised detached foreleg; part of the

---

1. All the sculptures of the Hieron were made of the same Thasian marble used to construct the building. This fact will not be repeated in the brief descrip-

tions of individual figures or fragments that occur throughout this chapter.

2. For reconstruction of the pronaos ceiling, see above, pp. 110 ff.

187. *C(V)1*

upper leg and flank, the hock and lower leg of one or more detached, bent rear legs; the hock and parts of the connecting upper and lower legs of an attached rear leg, together with part of the adjacent background; and the lower portion of a tail attached to its ground.

These fragments do not necessarily or even probably come from one and the same relief, but together they indicate the generic type of a prancing centaur moving toward the right and wearing a mantle in the form of an animal's skin that flutters behind him. The restoration is incorrect in at least two respects. Since enough remains of the left shoulder to indicate that the left arm was raised, it is clear that the head has been inclined backward too obliquely, with the result that insufficient space is left for a raised arm. More important, the plaster body of the horse is disproportionately long. When slightly contracted, the relief fits the 0.816 m. square inner field of the large coffers of the pronaos and should be attributed to one of them, as has already been reported.[3] The forehoof restored to this panel retains on its inner side part of the strut with which it was attached to its background—a device evidently characteristic of all the detached hooves (cf. *C (S) 1, 7, 8* in Samothrace, pp. 240 ff., below).

According to Conze (*S,I,* pp. 12, 23), the chief fragment used in this restored relief,

3. Karl Lehmann, "Kallistratos Meets a Centaur," *AJA,* 61 (1957), 123 ff. See above, pp. 114 f., n. 196.

238

namely, the head, was found in a position that can be identified as just west of the southwest corner of the pronaos.

C(V)2. Inv. No. 347. Storeroom of the Antikensammlung. (Fig. 188.)
Fragment of the detached bent right foreleg of a horse, broken at top and bottom. Preserved from slightly above to slightly below the knee. Generalized execution at rear.
Preserved height (as shown in fig.) 0.105 m.

C(V)3. No inv. no. Storeroom of the Antikensammlung. (Fig. 189.)
Fragment of the detached right foreleg of a horse, broken at top and bottom. Preserved from immediately below knee to below fetlock joint. Generalized execution at rear.
Preserved height (as shown in fig.) 0.09 m.

C(V)4. Inv. No. 347. Storeroom of the Antikensammlung. (Fig. 190.)
Fragment of the detached bent right rear leg of a horse, broken at top and bottom. Restored from two pieces. Upper leg, hock, and beginning of lower leg preserved. Generalized execution at rear.
Preserved height (as shown in fig.) 0.137 m.

C(V)5. No inv. no. Storeroom of the Antikensammlung. (Fig. 191.)
Fragment of the detached right rear leg of a horse, broken at top and bottom. Preserved from below hock to fetlock joint. Generalized execution and rough rasping at rear.
Preserved height (as shown in fig.) 0.098 m.

Although the specific provenance of Nos. 2–5, as of all the fragments except the head used in No. 1, is not documented, it is explicitly stated in S,I, p. 23, that they were found in the excavation of the Hieron.

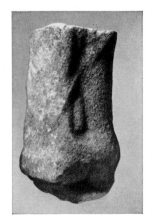

188. C(V)2   189. C(V)3   190. C(V)4   191. C(V)5

192. *C(V)6*

C(V)6. No inv. no. Storeroom of the Antikensammlung. (Fig. 192.)
Fragment of a detached right hand holding a cone-shaped object, broken at top and bottom.
Preserved across all four knuckles; lower joint of index finger and parts of those of middle
and ring fingers extant. An object held in the hand between the missing thumb and index
finger is indented with a channel (0.012 m. deep and 0.006 m. wide) and incised on its
upper surface with two parallel lines.

Preserved width across knuckles 0.058 m.; length of lower joint of index finger 0.03 m.

The fact that this fragment is preserved among the Samothracian marbles in the storeroom and that it, too, is of Thasian marble and of the same scale as the centaur's hand in
Samothrace (*C(S)9;* below, p. 243) suggests that it belonged to one of the pronaos coffers. It
differs in style too greatly from the plump, curving, little-modeled hands of the pedimental
figures to be ascribed to one of them.

Since the detached forelegs *2* and *3* slightly overlap each other anatomically (the uppermost
part of *3* repeats the lowermost portion beneath the knee of *2*), hence belonged to different
animals, and also parallel the fragments used by Zumbusch in the restored foreleg of No. *1*,
the Vienna fragments imply the existence of at least three centaurs.[4] For the detached legs,
fully executed only on the exterior, were all right legs, the inner left legs being in relief.

The fragments in Samothrace consist of:

C(S)1. 48.573. Samothrace Museum; on exhibition. (Fig. 193.)
Fragmentary detached bent right foreleg of a horse, broken at top and bottom. Restored from
two pieces. Preserved from above knee to below fetlock joint. Above missing hoof, at rear,
traces of attachment to background. Rear side summarily executed.

4. No. *4* repeats the comparable fragment used
by Zumbusch in restoring the right rear leg of No. *1.*

Theoretically it, like No. *5,* could have belonged with
either No. *2* or *3.*

Preserved height 0.145 m.; thickness 0.047 m.

Found in the cella of the Hieron, along with No. *10.*

C(S)2. 51.412. Samothrace Museum; on exhibition. (Fig. 194.)

Fragmentary detached bent right foreleg of a horse, broken at top and bottom. Preserved from above to below knee. Three creases of flesh behind knee, as on No. *1.*

Preserved height 0.092 m.

Found west of the porch ca. *3* m. south of the northern wall of the Hall of Votive Gifts.

C(S)3. 50.593. Stored in the Samothrace Museum.

Fragment of the knee of the detached right foreleg of a horse, broken above and below. Rear side summarily executed.

Preserved height 0.07 m.

Found northwest of the northwest corner of the porch of the Hieron.

C(S)4. 51.368. Samothrace Museum; on exhibition. *AJA,* 61 (1957), 123 ff., fig. *3.* (Fig. 195.)

Fragmentary relief of the bent left foreleg of a horse, broken on all sides. Preserved from above knee to sheared-off forepart of fetlock and hoof. Horizontal tooling of background, as on No. *10* (below, p. 244). Rear surface roughly picked.

Preserved height 0.24 m.; greatest thickness of block (exclusive of relief) 0.04 m.; greatest height of relief 0.02 m.

Found between the Hieron and the Hall of Votive Gifts.

194. *C(S)2*

193. *C(S)1*

195. *C(S)4*

196. *C(S)5*   197. *C(S)7*   198. *C(S)8*

C(S)5. 51.413. Samothrace Museum; on exhibition. (Fig. 196.)
Fragment of the detached right rear leg of a horse, broken above and below. Section of upper leg above joint preserved. Rear side summarily executed.

Preserved height 0.065 m.

Found in the Austrian dump west of the porch and pronaos.

C(S)6. 50.387. Stored in the Samothrace Museum.
Fragment of the detached right rear leg of a horse, broken above, below, and at the right. Portion of fragment comparable to No. *5* from upper leg above joint. Summarily executed at rear.

Preserved height 0.057 m.

Found west of the Hieron.

C(S)7. 39.558. Samothrace Museum; on exhibition. (Fig. 197.)
Detached right, probably rear, raised hoof of a horse, broken at fetlock. Lower surface with frog finished to be visible. Gouged out at rear where strut connecting it to background has broken off.

Preserved height (including fetlock) 0.07 m.; length of hoof 0.07 m.; greatest thickness of hoof 0.053 m.

Found at the southwestern corner of the Anaktoron.[5]

C(S)8. 51.708. Samothrace Museum; on exhibition. (Fig. 198.)
Detached right forehoof of a horse, broken below fetlock. Unlike No. *7*, sole not finished to be visible. Broken traces of attachment to background at rear.

Preserved height 0.06 m.; length of hoof 0.073 m.; greatest thickness of hoof 0.06 m.

Found to the southwest of the pronaos over the floor of the Hall of Votive Gifts.

5. Mistakenly referred to as 38.558 in *Hesperia,* 21 (1952), 42, n. 93, where it was suggested that this hoof might be the missing detached rear hoof of the restored centaur in Vienna (No. *1*). Comparison of a cast of 39.558 with No. *1* in Vienna has not borne out this suggestion.

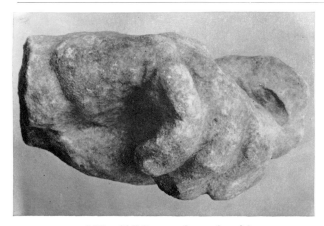

199. *C(S)9*, seen from the side   200. *C(S)9*, seen from above

201. *C(S)9*, seen from below

C(S)9. 51.293. Samothrace Museum; on exhibition. *AJA*, 61 (1957), 123 ff., fig. 2.
   (Figs. 199–201.)

Detached right hand of a male figure, broken off at wrist. Index finger unfinished at rear
and broken at tip; tips of second and third fingers broken. A roundish object was held
between the palm and curled fingers. Shallow hollow in palm ca. 0.015 m. for insertion of
this object.

   Greatest preserved length of hand 0.10 m.; width across knuckles 0.06 m.; width of
wrist 0.044 m.

   Found in the Austrian dump to the west of the porch and pronaos of the Hieron.[6]

C(S)10. 48.579. Samothrace Museum; on exhibition. (Fig. 202.)

Fragment of sculpture in low relief, broken on all sides. Background horizontally tooled like

---

   6. It has also been suggested that 51.441, a
sculptured fragment of Thasian marble found in the
Austrian dump west of the porch-pronaos, may conceivably be part of the detached upper arm (below the
armpit) of a centaur. Whether it is or not, this ill-
preserved fragment in no way affects any conclusions
to be drawn about the sculptured coffers.

202. *C(S) 10*

No. *4* (above, p. 241). Parts of two leaves, the left one grape, the right uncertain, and of an intermediate bunch of grapes preserved. Back roughly picked.

Preserved length 0.185 m.; preserved height 0.10 m.; thickness of slab (without relief) 0.028 m.; height of relief greater than 0.01 m.

Found in the cella of the Hieron south of the eastern Roman parapet, along with the fragmentary foreleg No. *1*.[7]

Again, the three detached right foreknees in Samothrace, Nos. *1–3*, indicate the existence of at least three centaurs. But Vienna fragment No. *3* could have come from the same detached foreleg as Samothrace No. *3*, and Samothrace No. *4*, the bent foreleg executed in relief, may be combined with any of the detached right forelegs, in which case the centaur to which it belonged must have reared on his hind legs. If not, it belonged to still another, fourth beast. Hence, the detached foreleg fragments in both Vienna and Samothrace prove the original existence of at least five centaurs, and theoretically could reflect either six or seven. The fact that these reliefs of rearing or prancing centaurs served as the lids of the large single coffers of the pronaos ceiling allows this point to be settled, for, as we have seen, only five such coffers can have existed (Pl. LXXXV).[8]

Since each of these mythological figures moved to the right, together they formed a unit in which four revolved endlessly above the worshiper's head, whether he entered the cella or emerged from it, while the centrally placed fifth faced only those who entered the pronaos or

7. As of the summer of 1965, Nos. *1–2, 4–5*, and *7–10* are on exhibition in Case 4 of Hall B, while Nos. *3, 6*, and 51.441 are stored in a drawer of that case. See

*Guide*², pp. 90 ff.

8. See above, pp. 110 ff., for reconstruction of the pronaos ceiling.

stood within it looking toward the great doors through which they would pass to become *epoptai* (cf. Pls. XLII, CIII). And if, as it seems, the central centaur reared in the midst of his prancing companions, he would have provided a fixed point for their revolving movement both aesthetically pleasing and capable of eliciting Kallistratos' reference to one specific centaur in the pronaos of the Hieron.[9] Finally, these powerfully-modeled high reliefs [10] alternated with four-part fields carved in low relief and decorated with a contrastingly quiet motif that provided an appropriate setting or background for their moving forms. Such is the implication of the sole preserved fragment, Samothrace No. *10,* which because of its character, technique, and provenance is best interpreted as a portion of a lid from one of the smaller, four-part fields.[11]

Ample precedent for the use of separately-worked and decorated coffer lids in the Classical and earlier Hellenistic periods lay behind their introduction into the pronaos of the Hieron when work was resumed on the building.[12] In Samothrace itself, the presence of sculptured busts in the coffered ceiling of the fourth-century Propylon of the nearby Temenos [13] provided the most obvious forerunner and, given its date in the third quarter of that century, even suggests that the original building project for the only slightly later Hieron may have included such a feature. But still closer to the specific variety of sculptured lid placed over the executed coffers of the pronaos are those from the Temple of Athena at Priene and the two great mausolea at Halikarnassos and Belevi, since they, too, are decorated with figural compositions rather than busts. Fragmentary though they are, the remnants of the separately-worked coffer lids from Halikarnassos with their representation of mythological contests (cf. fig. 93) [14] prove that this type, too, existed at least by the mid-fourth century, while

9. See above, pp. 114 f., n. 196, and *Samothrace,* Vol. 1, **128** n.

10. The detached hoof 51.708 is 0.06 m. thick. Like other comparable fragments, including those in Vienna, it was linked with the background of the lid by a strut of indeterminate length. The total height of the sculptured relief, therefore, must have been appreciably greater, doubtless to enable the figures to carry, given their lofty, ill-lit position.

11. See above, pp. 115 f., nn. 199, 200. Cf. the analogous alternation of two formal motifs in the coffered ceiling from a funerary aedicula in Berlin published by Hans Klumbach, *Tarentiner Grabkunst* (Reutlingen, 1937), no. 298, p. 49, and pl. 34.

12. Among the many known examples of separately-worked coffer lids, it will suffice to cite as samples those of the Hephaisteion (well illustrated by Herbert Koch, *Studien zum Theseustempel in Athen* [*Abh. sächs. Ak.,* Phil.-hist. Kl., 47, pt. 2 (Berlin, 1955)], fig. 50, pls. 14, 15); those conjectured for the later-fifth-century Temple of the Athenians in Delos (Fernand Courby, *Les temples d'Apollon* [*Délos,* XII], p. 139); the fourth-century examples mentioned below

in nn. 13–15; and the early Hellenistic naiskos inside the Temple of Apollo at Didyma (*Didyma,* I, p. 112, Z538/23 ff.; F545, pl. 193). Probably the Stymphalian birds carved on the ceiling of the Temple of Artemis at Stymphalos mentioned by Pausanias (8.22.7) belong to this category. The use of separately-worked coffer lids—obviously a convenience in structural procedure—must have been especially desirable when these lids were elaborately painted or carved.

13. See above, p. 115 and fig. 185. For discussion of the sculptured coffers of the Propylon and the earlier tradition of sculptured or painted busts in coffers behind this Samothracian example, see Vol. 5 of this series, forthcoming.

14. For description of these fragmentary reliefs in the British Museum, see A. H. Smith, *A Catalogue of Sculpture in the Department of Greek and Roman Antiquities, British Museum* (London, 1900), II, 121 f., nos. 1038–42. The partially restored coffer illustrated above in fig. 93 is reproduced from an address by A. S. Murray, "The Mausoleum at Halikarnassos," *Transactions of the Glasgow Archaeological Society,* n.s., 2 (1894), 296, pl. 3.

203. Fragmentary coffer lid from the Temple of Athena at Priene, No. 1165. The British Museum, London

the better preserved lids from Belevi provide a second example, whether they are dated at the end of that century or in the second century.[15] Finally, it is more than likely that the Gigantomachy carved on the coffered ceiling of the peristasis of the Temple at Priene when it was completed in the second century B.C. had been projected in the original fourth-century plan (figs. 186, 203).[16]

The vigor of these prancing centaurs is visible even in the small fragments of their

15. For illustration and discussion of these coffers, see Josef Keil, "XVIII. Vorläufiger Bericht über die Ausgrabungen in Ephesos," *JÖAI*, 29 (1935), cols. 126 ff., figs. 48, 49; idem, "XIX. Vorläufiger Bericht," ibid., 30 (1937), cols. 182 ff., figs. 59, 60. In these articles, as in his first report, "XVII. Vorläufiger Bericht," ibid., 28 (1933), cols. 28 ff., Keil advocated a mid-third-century date for the Mausoleum, primarily because of the style of a fragmentarily preserved inscription from the interior of the structure. Later ("Der Grabherr des Mausoleums von Belevi," *AnzWien*, Phil.-hist. Kl., 86 [1949], 51 ff.), he abandoned this position, accepting the late-fourth-century date proposed by Camillo Praschniker, "Die Datierung des Mausoleum von Belevi," ibid., 85 (1948), 271–93, without further comment on the few preserved letters of the inscription. In the latest edition of Keil's *Ephesos, Ein Führer durch die Ruinenstätte und ihre Geschichte* (Vienna, 1957), pp. 141 f., Fritz Eichler leaves the issue open. In the meantime, Karl Lehmann

("Kallistratos Meets a Centaur," *AJA*, 61 [1957], 124, n. 12) had favored the second-century date evidently preferred by some of Keil's associates, to judge by his own earlier discussions.

Actually, the complicated problems involved in the building history of the Mausoleum at Belevi, including the date of the original structure, cannot be solved until that extraordinarily important monument is finally published and the vital evidence afforded by its architectural members becomes available. In the meantime, the relative merits of a late-fourth- or a late-second-century date for its sculptures, the evaluation of their style as late classical or classicistic, must remain a difficult and disputed question.

16. These reliefs, previously attributed to the great altar before the temple, were convincingly identified as coffer lids by Praschniker, "Die Gigantomachie-Reliefs von Priene," *JÖAI*, 30 (1936 / 37), 45–49. See also Smith, op. cit., pp. 156 f., nos. 1165–76; H. Riemann, s.v. *Pytheos*, *RE*, XXIV, cols. 487 ff.

powerfully modeled, sinewy limbs. But it is only the head restored to the relief in Vienna (fig. 204) that allows their Hellenistic style to be defined more precisely. Clearly, it is a descendant of the mighty breed of giants carved on the Great Altar of Pergamon. Although it is looser, softer, and more pictorial in modeling than the firmly formed head of the giant opposing Moira, for example (fig. 205),[17] it nonetheless reflects a similar emphasis in its animated locks of hair and beard, its lined brows, prominent cheekbones, and parted lips. Still closer to the Vienna head is the colossal head of a centaur or satyr in the Palazzo dei Conservatori in Rome that is itself genuinely Pergamene in style (fig. 206).[18] Both heads are strikingly alike in such details as the rendering of their lined foreheads, their shaggy eyebrows hatched with linear tufts, the baggy flesh of their upper eyelids, the pattern of creases and folds at the outer corners of and beneath their eyes, their protruding cheekbones, and the shape of both their flabby cheeks and their animal's ears. In its greater force and such a feature as its windswept beard, the Palazzo dei Conservatori head is far closer to the style of the Great Altar than the less dramatic, more pathetic head in Vienna, which gives an impression of mingled timidity and injury rather than of aggressive power. Comparison of all three heads suggests that the head in Rome is contemporary with the Gigantomachy,[19] while the Samothracian centaur is somewhat later, reflecting, in its very looseness of form, a movement away from the firmer, more forceful, and dramatic Pergamene style that dominated the first half of the second century.[20] It cannot be linked with the overt neoclassicism of a Damophon; but, like the Poseidon Jameson in the Louvre (fig. 207),[21] with which it shares a similar sinuosity of beard and with which it may well be contemporary, it exemplifies one

17. Reproduced from Heinz Kähler, *Der grosse Fries von Pergamon* (Berlin, 1948), pl. 53, right.

18. Sala degli orti Lamiani, 3. The new photograph reproduced in fig. 206 shows the present condition of this head, now that the plaster restorations completing the nose and right ear mentioned by L. R. Farnell in H. Stuart Jones, *A Catalogue of the Ancient Sculptures Preserved in the Municipal Collections of Rome, The Sculptures of the Palazzo dei Conservatori* (Oxford, 1926), pp. 128 f., and visible in the illustration on pl. 47, have been removed. Unfortunately, as is apparent even in fig. 206, the head is incorrectly mounted and slopes backward obliquely.

19. The colossal head has repeatedly been associated with this phase of Pergamene work. Cf. Farnell, ibid.; A. W. Lawrence, *Later Greek Sculpture* (New York, 1927), pp. 28, 116; Gerhard Krahmer, "Hellenistische Köpfe," *GöttNachr*, Phil.-hist. Kl., n.s., 1 (1936), 228 ff. Farnell left undecided the issue of whether the head is a Hellenistic original or a Roman copy of a Pergamene work, while Lawrence considered it an Imperial copy. Krahmer's silence on this score implies that he accepted it as an original. After careful

inspection of it, I see no reason not to accept it as a Hellenistic original. It lacks any technical feature peculiar to Roman execution.

20. Both Kähler, op. cit., pp. 143 ff., and Margarete Bieber, *The Sculpture of the Hellenistic Age* (rev. edn., New York, 1961), p. 113, appear to assume that the Gigantomachy was not finished until ca. 165 B.C. But both have overlooked the excellent contribution of Diether Thimme, "The Masters of the Pergamon Gigantomachy," *AJA*, 50 (1946), 345 ff., which proves that the immense frieze could have been finished in a few years, thus making a date in the decade 190–180 B.C. not only possible but probable, given the historical circumstances with which the Altar was connected.

21. Dated by Jean Charbonneaux, "Un Poseidon hellénistique au Musée du Louvre," Foundation Piot, *Monuments et Mémoires*, 46 (1952), 33 ff., in the third quarter of the second century and considered, too, as ultimately dependent on the style of the Great Altar. The latter point is further emphasized by the same author in *Les bronzes grecs* (Paris, 1958), p. 105, where the figure appears as pl. 28, no. 3.

204. Detail of centaur relief. Kunsthistorisches Museum, Vienna

205. Detail of giant opposing Moira from the Great Altar.
The Pergamon Museum, Berlin

248

206. Head of a centaur or satyr. Palazzo dei Conservatori,
Rome

207. Detail of Poseidon Jameson. Musée
du Louvre, Paris

249

208. Detail from the frieze of the Temple of Dionysos at Teos. Depot Museum, Izmir

aspect of the aftermath of the later Pergamene style, a complex dependence upon and withdrawal from it. This very relationship, in turn, implies a date not later than the third quarter of the second century and possibly close to the mid-century for the sculptured lids of the pronaos coffers.[22]

The sparse fragments of these high reliefs yield one more clue of interest for the reconstruction and interpretation of the richly-decorated pronaos ceiling. The two partially preserved right hands, Vienna No. *6* and Samothrace No. *9,* bear traces of objects they once

22. Typologically, the monument most closely related to the Vienna centaur is the similarly fragmentary coffer lid from the Mausoleum at Belevi on which a carved centaur's head is partially preserved (Keil, "XVIII. Vorläufiger Bericht," *JÖAI,* 29 [1935], col. 127, fig. 49). Both Kähler (op. cit., p. 172, n. 57) and Karl Lehmann (*AJA,* 61 [1957], 124, n. 12) have already commented on this relationship, the former retaining the original third-century date for Belevi and assuming a similar date for the Vienna centaur, the latter preferring a date in the second half of the second century for the Belevi head, because of its "marked progress toward late-Hellenistic classicism." As I have pointed out above in n. 15, it is impossible to discuss the Mausoleum of Belevi with any objectivity until it is adequately published. Whether the Belevi centaur's head is a work of the late fourth or the late second century, it differs markedly in style from the Vienna centaur. Since it can shed no constructive light on the style and date of the pronaos coffers of the Hieron, I shall refrain from discussing it further, apart from remarking that just as Kähler's mid-third-century date for Belevi is mistaken, so his similar date for the Vienna centaur is rendered obsolete and incorrect by the building history of the Hieron. That same building history now makes it improbable that the sculptured coffer lids of the Hieron can be dated quite as early as the years following 170 B.C., as was tentatively suggested by my husband (*AJA,* 61 [1957], 123). For summary of the building history and chronology of the Hieron, see, especially, pp. 213 ff., 220 ff., above; text II, pp. 70 ff., 79 ff., 124 ff.

209. Terracotta statuette of a centaur from
Priene. Staatliche Museen, Berlin

grasped. Indeed, the former still holds part of a cone-shaped attribute, while the latter once
held something cylindrical about which his fingers curled and for which his palm was
roughly dressed (cf. figs. 199–201). A glance at the restored relief in Vienna (fig. 187) will
reinforce the suggestion that the detached right hand of each centaur doubtless held an
object. Theoretically, these unknown objects might have been branches, given the evidence
of Samothrace No. 9. But it is far more likely that they were musical instruments. Among the
reveling centaurs on the frieze from the second-century Temple of Dionysos at Teos are
several who play the cithara, the lyre, the tympanon, the krotylos, and the double flute,
including the worn figure at the right of the block illustrated in fig. 208,[23] who seemingly
holds a krotylos and whose pose is so reminiscent of the Vienna centaur's. Equally analogous
to the pronaos figures in type and possibly in date is the terracotta statuette of an ivy-crowned
centaur from Priene, who evidently once played a cithara held against the left side of his body
and struck by a plectron grasped in his right hand (fig. 209).[24] The numerous references to
musical instruments in the ancient texts alluding to Samothracian mythology and ritual

23. Izmir Depot Museum, No. 180. My interpretation of the object held in the left hand of this centaur
is based on examination of the block in May, 1953. The
other centaurs playing the instruments itemized above
on blocks 178, 188, 190, and an unnumbered block at
that time still on the site of the Temple at Teos are
better preserved and entirely legible. For the most
recent extensive discussion of this frieze, see Walter
Hahland, "Der Fries des Dionysostempel in Teos,"

JÖAI, 38 (1950), 66 ff.; for further remarks in connection with its debated date, see Francis W. Schehl, "The
Date of Hermogenes the Architect," *AJA*, 55 (1951),
152. It may be of use to add that *both* blocks mentioned
by Hahland (op. cit., p. 68) as left on the site were
still extant there in 1953, as we reported to appropriate
authorities in Ankara.

24. Found in House XIII. Now in Berlin (Staatliche Museen, No. 8628). Cf. *Priene*, pp. 345 f., fig.

that mention flutes, cymbals, castanets, tympana, the lyre, and the cithara [25] attest the role of music in the cult, as does the representation of three of these instruments on the incompletely preserved frieze of dancing maidens that adorned the Propylon and no doubt implies that ritual dances were performed in the Temenos.[26] And since it is obvious that the arms of our prancing centaurs must have been occupied in some action, it is tempting to assume that as they circled above the worshipers gathered in the pronaos they played a variety of instruments.

The frieze from Teos provides an unimpeachable document for the presence of centaurs in Dionysos' *thiasos* at the time when the porch of the Hieron was completed. Their re-

210. Misthia. Rock-cut relief

currence in the ceiling of the pronaos, together with a telltale grape leaf, implies the existence of a Bacchic element in the Sanctuary in the second century. Centuries earlier, Bacchic ingredients had penetrated the cult of the Great Mother elsewhere,[27] while the rock-cut relief in Misthia shown in fig. 210, where grapes appear as symbols of the Dioskouroi-Kabeiroi,[28]

406. Remains of a second such figure were found in House XIX. The figure illustrated above appears in Franz Winter, *Die Typen der figürlichen Terrakotten,* II (*Die antiken Terrakotten,* III, pt. 2 [Berlin and Stuttgart, 1903]), 409, no. 4.

25. See, for example, *Samothrace,* Vol. 1, **142, 214, 215, 219, 220.** In this connection note, too, François Salviat's remarks, *BCH,* 80 (1956), 144, apropos the presence of a cithara player and her suite among the initiates recorded in a second-century list.

26. See Vol. 5, forthcoming.

27. See Jane E. Harrison, *Mythology and Monuments of Ancient Athens* (London, 1890), p. 49, regarding Euripides *Bacchae* 72 ff., and the same author's *Cretes,* frg. 473. The Hellenistic terracotta relief in Leningrad discussed by Miss Harrison (pp. 47 ff.) is a

later document of the same religious phenomenon. See also the second-century parapet relief from Pergamon on which Dionysos confronts the Great Mother on one side, while Eleusinian gods appear on the other: *Pergamon,* VII, pt. 2, no. 406, pp. 317 ff., and pl. 40.

28. H. Swoboda, J. Keil, F. Knoll, *Denkmäler aus Lykaonien, Pamphylien und Isaurien* (Brünn, 1935), pp. 17 f., no. 16. The fact that the Kabeiroi are misinterpreted as the Great Gods in this discussion does not alter the significance of the monument in the present context.

In this connection, cf. also Pausanias' curious tale of a chest containing an image of Dionysos that was given to Dardanos (7.19.6).

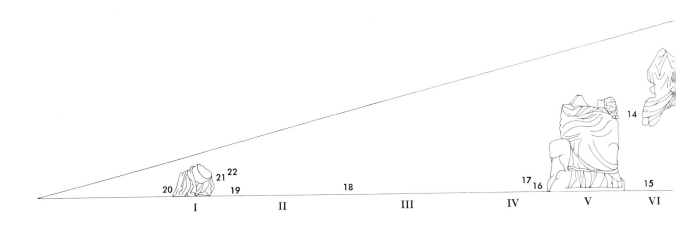

211. Diagram showing the positions of the extant fragments of the northern pedimental sculptures.
Roman numerals indicate the positions of the thirteen original figures;
arabic numbers show the location of the preserved fragments or figures

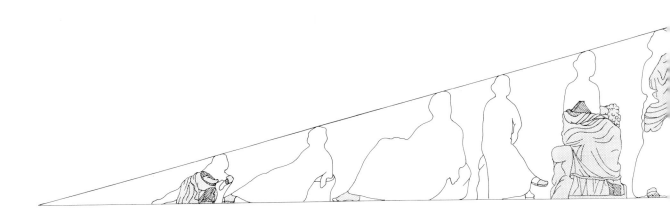

212. Reconstruction of the northern pedimental sculptures

the dedication of an exedra in the Samothrakion at Delos as a ναός to Mithradates Eupator as Dionysos,[29] and, possibly, the use of grapes as an attribute of one of the pedimental figures of the Hieron itself (fig. 233) indicate that a similar situation had developed in the Samothracian cult. Strabo could characterize those very Kabeiroi as "subject to Bacchic frenzy" and associate them with sacred rites accompanied by music.[30] Finally, the nearby Theater in the Sanctuary of the Great Gods, itself a product of the second century, must have been the scene of those literary contests commemorated by certain second-century inscriptions.[31] By this time, Dionysos had clearly become a *symbomos* of the Megaloi Theoi.[32]

In the context of this evidence, the introduction of overt Bacchic imagery into the decorative themes interwoven in the sculptures of the Hieron becomes intelligible. To the profane, the decorations of the pronaos ceiling were an obvious allusion to the Bacchic frenzy of the rites, including the public rites. To the initiate, they may have held a deeper meaning.[33] If so, they were attuned to the sculptures of the northern pediment, which, as we shall now see, were meaningful alike to the initiate and the uninitiate.

THE NORTHERN PEDIMENT

Like the fragmentary reliefs from the pronaos ceiling, the sculptures that once filled the northern pediment of the Hieron are today divided between the Kunsthistorisches Museum in Vienna and the Samothrace Museum. The better preserved figures and fragments were discovered directly before the façade in 1873, during our predecessors' first campaign. Additional fragments were recovered in 1950 in the course of our own excavation of the area immediately to the north of the porch.

Carved of the same Thasian marble employed in the fabric of the building, graduated in size, only summarily executed on their rear sides, and weathered in a fashion reflecting their function, the major pieces were immediately recognized as having fallen from the northern pediment. Their size and scale indicate the positions that they once occupied within the gable. In the following catalogue, the minor fragments attributable to these major figures have been grouped with them regardless of their present location. The twenty-two primary figures or fragments are therefore listed in an order reflecting the sequence of the

29. Fernand Chapouthier, *Le Sanctuaire des dieux de Samothrace* (*Délos*, XVI), p. 35.

30. Cf. *Samothrace*, Vol. 1, **214**.

31. Ibid., **136** n., and below, pp. 300 f. In this connection, it is interesting to recall that the Dionysiac *technitai* of Teos sent ambassadors to the Samothracian festival. See *IG*, XII (8), 163, lines 30 ff., as well as Salviat, op. cit. (above, n. 25), p. 145, and Vol. 4, pt. II, pp. 140 f.

32. Cf. his role in Eleusis as one at once intermediate between the gods and the *mystai* and among the ranks of the latter attested by the dedication to him, as Παραπαίζων, of a thymiaterion: K. Kourouniotis, «Ελευσινιακά,» *ArchDelt*, 8 (1923), 171 ff. I am indebted to my husband for this reference.

33. For amplification of this point, see pp. 298 ff.

statues within the pediment. No. *1,* the lower half of the largest of the figures, appears in the center of fig. 211, a diagram illustrating the original position of these primary fragments. It is followed first by the remaining fragments or figures from the right wing of the pediment, Nos. *2–13,* and second by Nos. *14–22* from its left wing. The subsequent items in the catalogue do not appear in this diagram, inasmuch as their nature (fragments of arms, hands, and drapery) does not allow their original position within the gable to be ascertained.

The terms "right" and "left," when applied to the movement, position, or direction of standing, seating, and reclining figures, refer to the spectator's viewpoint; when used to describe the limbs or sides of individual statues, they allude to the figure's own right or left.

NP(V) 1. Inv. No. 345. Kunsthistorisches Museum; on exhibition. *S,I,* pp. 24 ff., 44, 74, 94, pls. 39, 40; Schober, no. 4, p. 9, fig. 5, pl. 1. (Figs. 213, 214, 253, 254.)*

Lower half of a standing, draped female figure moving toward the right and wearing a himation over a crinkly chiton. Irregularly and obliquely broken from the right hip across to the upper left thigh; lacking the lowest part of the right leg and foot and the greater part of the left leg from the lower thigh downward. Two other fragments, including the upper part of the left foot shod in a soft leather shoe and a portion of the chiton immediately above it, have been fitted onto the left leg, which strides forward obliquely, escaping from the heavy folds of the mantle. The interval between the main piece and these smaller fragments, as far as it exists, has been filled with plaster.[34] Here and there, the edges or surface of the mantle are chipped. At the rear of the figure, where it was invisible and only summarily executed, the roughly picked drapery billowed out, presumably to provide additional stability (cf. fig. 214). The fact that the area between the forepart of the left leg and this windswept drapery has been partially finished with the crinkly texture of the chiton, together with the oblique position of both legs, suggests that the figure was intended to be seen somewhat more diagonally than she appears in every published photograph.[35] Traces of weathering, especially on

* References to my previous summary discussion of the northern pedimental figures in *Pedimental Sculptures* have been omitted from this chapter.

34. Cf. Schober, p. 9. This figure, like the other major fragments in Vienna, Nos. *11, 12, 14,* and *16,* was originally restored by Brestyazinsky under the direction of Zumbusch. Conze explicitly stated (*S,I,* p. 25) that pieces were not joined together unless they fitted break on break, but that in the case of No. *1* it was necessary, for the purpose of stability, to mount the figure on a cast-iron base. This base was evidently

equipped with an opening through which the lower surface of the statue's plinth could be seen. But it is no longer possible to examine the undersides of any of the figures in Vienna, so far as they are on exhibition—as a glance at the illustrations of them will make clear. Hence, these best preserved of the pedimental figures afford no information as to the manner in which the sculptures were attached to the floor of the pediment.

35. The figure cannot be photographed properly, given its present position close to a spur wall in the gallery.

213. *NP(V)1*   214. *NP(V)1*

the right thigh and in depressions of the mantle (the traces of more severe weathering on the back than on the front of both this statue and the better preserved figures *11, 12,* and *16* are the result of their long exposure to the elements lying face down on the ground after the collapse of the Hieron in the mid-sixth century A.D.).

Preserved height (without base) 0.90 m.; preserved width 0.52 m.; depth ca. 0.47 m.; height of base 0.045–0.05 m.

Found north of the façade, to the east of No. *11.*

NP(V)2. No inv. no. Storeroom of the Antikensammlung. Schober, no. 12, p. 12, fig. 13. (Fig. 215.)

Upper left arm of a female figure, preserved from the shoulder to below the biceps but broken

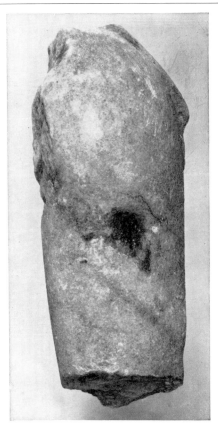

215. *NP(V)2*

at both ends. A piece of drapery adheres to the rear upper edge of the shoulder. The rear face of the arm is finished but once touched the body from which it has broken off, as the flat break at its rear indicates.

The scale of this fragment requires that it be attributed to No. *1*, the largest of the pedimental figures.

Preserved height 0.233 m.; width at bottom 0.075 m.

Specific provenance unknown; see above, p. 253.

NP(V)3. No inv. no. Storeroom of the Antikensammlung. Schober, no. 11, p. 12, fig. 12. (Figs. 216, 217.)

Fragmentary left hand, broken across the lowest joint of all four fingers and of the thumb and at the base of the hand. A piece of drapery overlaps the base of the thumb, evidently having fallen across it from the wrist. The palm has been hollowed out and retains the end of a small round dowel hole (diameter 0.05 m.) at the base of the thumb. The curving upper surface of the flat, boneless hand as it appears in fig. 216 is not weathered, whereas the drapery, the thumb, and the adjacent area of the index finger are severely pocked—an indication that the palm was held in a virtually upright position. The rear side of the hand is unfinished. Again, the scale of this hand requires that it be associated with Nos. *1* and *2* and attributed to the

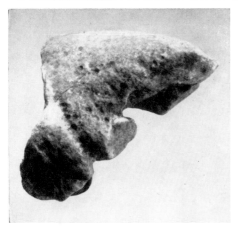

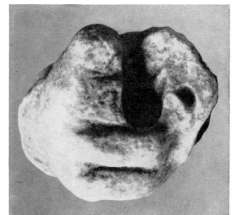

216. *NP(V)3*, seen from the side (1 : 2)   217. *NP(V)3*, seen from   218. *NP(V)4* (1 : 1)
                                                  beneath (1 : 2)

largest figure in the pediment. Schober remarked (p. 12) that our Nos. *2* and *3* (his 12 and 11) must form part of the same left arm and hand, but, mistakenly citing them (p. 14) as 10 and 11, he ascribed them to an otherwise nonexistent figure somewhat smaller than No. *1* and, without valid argument, assumed that the hand was lowered to the figure's hip and outstretched. For comment on his error in regard to the scale and position of No. *1*, see below, pp. 280 f. and n. 37.

Width across knuckles 0.075 m.; length from knuckle below little finger to wrist 0.055 m.

Specific provenance unknown; see above, p. 253.

NP(V)4. No inv. no. Storeroom of the Antikensammlung. (Fig. 218.)
Right hand broken off at the wrist. All four fingers were bent around a now missing object of curved section for which a shallow cutting ca. 0.01 m. wide was bored through the hand and narrowed to a hole 0.006 m. in diameter under the little finger. The upper two fingers are broken off at the knuckles; the lower two, together with the scarcely modeled thumb, are preserved. Conceivably, the lost attribute was metallic and pressed against or wrapped around the underpart of the hand. The lumpy undersurface of the hand cannot have been visible but must have been attached either to drapery or to a body. Therefore, the upper surface of the hand must have been held in an upright or oblique position. The tiny scale of this hand, its shape, and its pudginess, as well as the fact that the wrist appears to flare in preparation for a sudden fattening of the forearm, imply that it belonged to an infant. No trace of weathering.

Width across knuckles 0.042 m.; width at wrist 0.03 m.; length from base of little finger to wrist 0.025 m.

Specific provenance unknown; see above, p. 253.

219. *NP(V)5*, seen from the outside   220. *NP(V)5*, seen from the inside

NP(V)5. No. inv. no. Storeroom of the Antikensammlung. Schober, no. 10, pp. 11 f., fig. 11. (Figs. 219, 220.)

Left arm of a female figure. Preserved from below the shoulder to the knuckles of the hand, including part of the lowest joint of the ring finger, a stump of the forefinger, and the lowest joint of the thumb. The upper arm is wrapped in a chlamys, which drops down behind the forearm and hangs as a solid, vertical mass of drapery. The outer rear edge of the arm retains a circular dowel hole (0.0075 m. in diameter) ca. 0.016 m. from the edge, where it was evidently doweled to the torso. Particles of bronze set in stucco adhere to the dowel hole. There is no trace of lead. The entire piece is severely weathered on the upper surface and front, as well as on the bottom of the arm, doubtless from dripping water and icicles; this fact, together with the very summary execution of the drapery at the rear (cf. fig. 220), indicates that it belonged to the exposed side of a figure, hence to one standing obliquely or in profile in the right (western) half of the pediment. For the manner in which the drapery falls precludes the attribution of this arm to a seated figure, implying, on the contrary, that it belonged to a standing figure. A shallow cutting flaring from 0.005 m. at the lower part of the palm to 0.01 m. at its exit between the thumb and the forefinger reflects a lost attribute held primarily between the thumb and the first two fingers, since the ring finger was extended.

258

221. *NP(V)6*

The shallowness of this cutting, as well as the position of the arm (especially of the slightly arched wrist), suggests that the lost attribute was exceedingly light (one or more stems? part of a plant?) and passed through the hand.

The arm has been restored from two pieces, but the large piece of drapery hanging below it has been put together from a number of pieces and then attached by a modern brass dowel to the adjacent portion of the mantle, against which it fits exactly (cf. fig. 220). Schober's attribution (ibid.) of this arm to a male figure (because the scheme of the hanging cloak suggested a well-known type of Hermes) can be discarded without argument because of the blatantly feminine character of the gently rounded, curving contours of the forearm and hand. Nor could the latter possibly have held as heavy an object as a kerykeion.

Preserved height (including drapery) 0.46 m.; length of forearm from elbow to wrist 0.215 m.; length of hand from wrist to knuckles 0.06 m.; width of hand across knuckles 0.062 m.

Specific provenance unknown; see above, p. 253.

NP(V)6. No inv. no. Storeroom of the Antikensammlung. Schober, no. 8, p. 11, fig. 9. (Fig. 221.)

Lower jaw and neck of a separately worked head prepared for insertion into a torso. Irregularly broken at the top, below the lips, and through the chin, sheared off unevenly at the back, broken on its left side below the line of the chiton, and chipped below the Adam's apple. Smoothly dressed on its right side to be fitted against a marble torso. The neck muscles indicate that the head was turned slightly toward the left (its right).

The fact that some of the pedimental figures had separately worked heads is confirmed

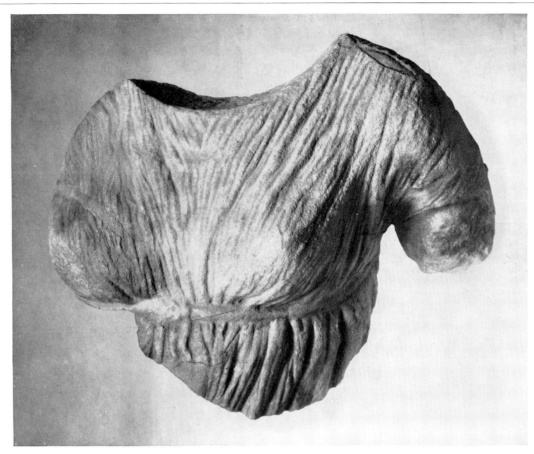

222. *NP(V)7*

by No. 7, a torso prepared to receive a similarly executed head terminating in a smoothly dressed strip below the neck. However, the two fragments do not fit together. Hence, No. 6 belonged to another figure. That this figure was also female is evident from the marked similarity of its thick, short neck to that of No. 12. Schober's interpretation (ibid.) of the fragment as the bent knee of a seated figure fits neither the appearance nor the technical features of this piece and is belied, if nothing else, by the Adam's apple and the hollow beneath it, which have no place in the anatomy of the underside of the knee.

Preserved height 0.122 m.; width of neck ca. 0.08–0.085 m.

Specific provenance unknown; see above, p. 253.

NP(V)7. Inv. No. 677. Storeroom of the Antikensammlung. *S,I,* p. 26, pl. 41, upper left; Schober, no. 5, pp. 9 f., fig. 6. (Fig. 222.)

Torso of a female figure wearing a short-sleeved chiton. The head, including the neck, was separately worked, like No. 6, and is now missing. But the curving contour of the chiton edging the neck is fully preserved, and the surface behind it is finely tooled to receive that member. The right shoulder and arm are also missing, having broken off, while the left arm,

260

pulled decidedly backward, is preserved to an irregular break in the bare upper arm below the short sleeve. A narrow girdle tied immediately below the breasts and knotted between them separates the upper torso from the stomach. Beneath it, on the figure's left side, the torso is irregularly broken, as it is at the back. But under the line of the girdle below the right breast it is smoothly dressed, as is the right side of the breast, indicating that another piece was fitted onto the figure here and that the statue, thus, was composed of several pieces. The preserved torso has been put together from five fragments. Five buttons separated by four openings revealing the flesh of the shoulder close the fine, crinkly chiton. The torso lacks any trace of weathering.

Preserved height 0.27 m.; width from nipple to nipple 0.165 m.

Found along with other fragments of the pedimental sculptures north of the façade (cf. *S,I*, loc. cit.).

An unnumbered fragment of the crinkly material of this chiton (0.115 m. long) preserved among the sculptures from the Hieron in the same storeroom actually fits onto the upper edge of the right shoulder. It slightly raises the neckline of the chiton on that side of the figure and is of value in confirming the oblique position of the torso and the fact that the right shoulder was held to the fore of the left.

Three additional fragments of the same crinkly material found in the debris of building material and sculpture on the surface close to the façade appear to belong to this same figure and are stored in the Samothrace Museum: 51.132, a section of the lower edge of the skirt of the chiton 0.09 m. wide and 0.05 m. high; 53.525, a fragment of drapery ca. 0.105 m. wide; and 53.590, a splinter 0.077 m. high, from the part of the torso above the girdle, a portion of which is preserved.

NP(V)8. No inv. no. Storeroom of the Antikensammlung. *S,I*, p. 26, pl. 41, lower left; Schober, no. 6, p. 10, fig. 7. (Fig. 223.)

Left foot of a female figure wearing a sandal having the same contour as the foot and indented between the first two toes. Apart from the toes, the foot is concealed by the lower edge of the skirt of a crinkly chiton, which emerges beneath the lower edge of a mantle and dragged on the floor of the pediment, level with the sole of the sandal. The dressing of the sole indicates that the foot was not finished to be seen from below but rested flat on the ground. The piece is fully preserved, having been separately worked and attached to the figure to which it belonged by a circular dowel (hole 0.018 m. in diameter in the smoothly-dressed rear surface), a technique also found on Nos. *16*, *17*, and *19*. The chiton and toes are deeply pocked and strongly weathered.

As Schober recognized (ibid.), Nos. *7* and *8* belonged to the same figure. For further

223. *NP(V)8*   224. *NP(S)9*, seen from above

225. *NP(S)9*, seen from the outside   226. *NP(S)9*, seen from the inside

statements regarding its character and position, see No. *9*. Schober did not recognize that the "plinth" on which the foot seemed to him to rest is the sole of the sandal; hence, his description is faulty and confusing. But the fact that the edge of the chiton covers all but the toes and that he could not know the then unexcavated mate to this foot, No. *9*, on which the sandal straps are plainly indicated, accounts for this error.

Length 0.13 m.; height 0.10 m.; width of foot behind toes 0.07 m.; preserved length of big toe 0.035 m.; sole 0.02 m. high at left and front, rising to 0.026 m. at instep.

Same provenance as No. *7*.

NP(S)9. 49.613. Samothrace Museum; on exhibition. *Hesperia*, 20 (1951), 24, fig. 13 e; *Guide*, pp. 66, 87; *Guide²*, pp. 67, 90. (Figs. 224–226.)
Fragmentary right foot of a female figure wearing a notched sandal, two straps of which are

visible at the base of the toes beneath the lower edge of the skirt of a crinkly chiton that covers the arch of the foot and falls down below the heel of the sandal on both sides of the foot. The bottom of the sole is roughly picked, and its surface, combined with the evidence of the trailing drapery, indicates that the heel was slightly raised from the ground and that the foot belonged to a seated figure. The fragment is irregularly broken through the heel. The toes are slightly weathered.

As was recognized in *Hesperia,* loc. cit., this foot is the counterpart in scale, type, and style to No. *8* and, like it, comes from the same figure as No. *7.* The total evidence afforded by these three fragments indicates that the figure to which they belonged turned toward the center of the pediment, sitting slightly obliquely in the right or western side of it; that she wore a mantle over her chiton and the lower part of her body; and that she sat with her right foot drawn slightly back, resting on the toes, with her left foot extended forward, and leaned on her left elbow or hand. The greater weathering of the extended left foot, as well as the absence of weathering on the torso—easily understandable if the left leg projected beyond the more protected torso—confirms this reconstruction. Schober's tentative suggestion (p. 15) that Nos. *7* and *8* belonged to a reclining figure, as Zumbusch had originally proposed (*S,I,* p. 26), must therefore be discarded.

Preserved length 0.115 m.; greatest preserved height ca. 0.07 m.; width of foot behind toes 0.07 m.; width of first three toes at their base 0.045–0.05 m.; length of big toe 0.035 m.; height of sole 0.015–0.02 m.; width of toe of sandal beneath first two toes 0.036 m.

Found on the surface southwest of the Arsinoeion in the vicinity of a late antique lime-kiln.

227. *NP(S)10*

NP(S)10. 50.516. Stored in the Samothrace Museum. (Fig. 227.)

Nude bent right arm of a leaning figure, preserved from slightly above to slightly below the elbow, along with an irregularly broken piece of the seemingly rocky terrain or support on which it rests. The back of the upper arm (the left edge in fig. 227) and nearly a third of the outer face are only roughly dressed and hence were invisible. The figure must have been viewed from an oblique position. Since Nos. *11* and *12* retain the bent right elbows on which they recline and their counterparts in the opposite wing of the pediment must have leaned on their left arms, this fragment belonged to a seated figure. Its smoothness and lack of muscularity imply that that figure was female. For further reference to this fragment, see below, p. 283.

Width across elbow 0.085 m.

Found at the northeast corner of the Hieron.

NP(V)11. Inv. No. 343. Kunsthistorisches Museum; on exhibition. *S,I*, pp. 9, 24 ff., 74, pl. 36; Schober, no. 2, p. 8, fig. 3. (Figs. 228, 255.)

Reclining male figure leaning on his right arm, crossing his left leg over his bent right, and stretching both legs toward his left (i.e., toward the right, western corner of the pediment). His right hand clasps the very generalized rocky support on which he leans, while the left arm rests on the left thigh, the hand having held a now missing attribute. His mantle falls from beneath his right elbow in a gentle curve; ascends across the lower abdomen, leaving the upper part of the figure undraped; passes under the left elbow; and falls forward over the left forearm and thigh onto the right thigh, presumably having been wrapped entirely around both legs. The figure lacks the head and most of the neck; portions of the right forearm, wrist, and hand; the index and parts of the next two fingers of the left hand; the attribute once grasped in this hand; and the lower portions of both legs, the right from below the knee, the left from below the mid-shin, the knee itself having been sheared off. The rear side of the left arm and the adjacent areas of the back of the figure are also sheared off, and the edge of certain folds of the mantle—for example, below the abdomen and over the left thigh—are chipped and worn. The back is not fully finished but roughly picked in the fashion of a building block. The object once held in the left hand under the thumb and forefingers must have been light (of metal?), since it has left no trace on the finished folds of the himation.

A rectangular hole 0.053 m. wide × 0.043 m. high is cut in the once invisible lateral face of the rock 0.085 m. above its lower surface. Presumably, it provided a kind of pry hole for use in maneuvering the figure into position. (Schober, pp. 8 f., 16, interpreted this and the analogous cuttings on Nos. *12* and *16* as clamp holes, but they are not well placed for this purpose.) If a second such hole existed on the missing right end of the statue, they could

264

228. *NP(V)11*

conceivably have served, too, in lifting the figure into position. If the extant cutting served as a pry hole, it implies that the figures in the western half of the pediment were set from the corner inward toward the center; possibly those in the eastern half were similarly placed from the corner inward, and the central figure was the last to be set in position and inserted between the two wings. The preserved figure has been restored primarily from three pieces, the break below the right shoulder being filled with plaster. The lower part of the abdomen and the projecting folds of the mantle are slightly weathered.

Preserved length 0.875 m.; preserved height 0.48 m.; depth 0.35 m.; height of right arm from shoulder to elbow 0.25 m.; length from elbow to wrist 0.21–0.22 m.; width from nipple to nipple 0.185 m.; length of right leg from hip to knee 0.36 m.

Found north of the façade to the east of No. *12*.

NP(V)12. Inv. No. 342. Kunsthistorisches Museum; on exhibition. *S,I,* pp. 10 f., 24 ff., pl. 35; Schober, no. 1, pp. 7 f., fig. 2. (Figs. 229, 257.)

Reclining female figure turning sharply to the left and leaning on her right arm on a damaged, rock-like support covered by her own drapery. Her legs stretch to the right, her right leg passing backward beneath her left. Her left arm, adorned with an armlet in the form of a snake, the head and tail of which compose two of its three twists, lies curled over her left thigh and held a now missing attribute. Her mantle descended over the support, rising across the lower abdomen to cover both legs and leave the figure otherwise undraped. The torso and

229. *NP(V)12*

head twist strongly, allowing the backward tilted head to look toward the center of the pediment. The hair, parted in the center and clasped by a simple fillet, falls in loose tresses on each side of the head but especially over the left shoulder. The large, wide eyes are cast upward and greatly emphasized by the narrowness of the mouth. The back of the figure from head to legs retains rasp-like strokes of the chisel and has been left unfinished. The right forearm is irregularly broken and lacks the wrist and hand; the left, although broken at about the same point, preserves traces of the curving wrist, the outline of the hand, and the little finger, but the remaining fingers and the larger part of the thumb have broken off. The right leg is preserved almost to the ankle, the left to the mid-shin. The weathered face is slightly chipped on the left cheek and chin. The drapery over the support has been obliquely sheared off. In its present state, the figure seems to have been restored primarily from five pieces.

Conze (*S,I*, p. 25) described a rhyton terminating in a calf's head with a perforated outlet, together with a second fragment of the upper edge of the horn found in the debris at the north of the building, which he reports as fitting a broken surface on the figure. His fig. 10 suggests the original form of the vessel. All trace of this object had already vanished by

266

Schober's time and, although it is apparent that the hand has been worked for something to fit against it below the thumb joint, no trace of contact with any object is preserved either on the shoulder or the drapery. Conceivably, it curved upward toward the spectator's right. In any case, this lost attribute must be accepted as a documented part of the figure and considered in its interpretation.

Like No. *11*, this statue has been equipped with a rectangular cutting 0.043 m. wide, more than 0.03 m. deep (it is broken), and 0.07 m. above the lower surface of its left lateral face. Both holes certainly served the same purpose, probably, as suggested above, as pry holes.

The weathering of the figure (on the abdomen and forepart of the drapery), as well as the finished execution of the long tresses at the right side of her head (the spectator's left), suggests that the statue was intended to be seen obliquely, its face shown in a three-quarter view, its bent legs receding into the field of the pediment, rather than being parallel with its front plane.

Greatest height 0.58 m.; preserved length 0.83 m.; depth 0.31 m.; height of right arm from shoulder to elbow 0.22 m.; width from nipple to nipple 0.18 m.; length of left leg from hip to knee ca. 0.39 m.; height of face from brow to chin ca. 0.12 m.; width at cheekbones ca. 0.09 m.

Found north of the façade, west of No. *11*, and closest to the western corner of all the figures discovered by the Austrians.

NP(V)13. No inv. no. Storeroom of the Antikensammlung. *S,I*, p. 23. (Fig. 230.) Right arm clad in a sleeve. Preserved from above the elbow to the end of the sleeve—that is, to or slightly above the wrist. Upper and outer surfaces fully executed, but rear and inside of elbow unfinished. Trace of attachment on undersurface at mid-forearm. No trace of weathering.

230. *NP(V)13*

The scale and pudgy proportions of this arm indicate that it belonged to a child. It appears to be the fragment mentioned by Conze (*S,I,* ibid.) as "ein mit einem Aermel, wie barbarisch, bekleideter Arm" and attributed to the hypothetical large relief in which he proposed to include both the restored centaur, No. *1,* and other fragments that we now know come from the sculptured lids of the large pronaos coffers, each of which was decorated with the figure of a single centaur (above, pp. 237 ff.). The fact remains that this arm was found north of the façade among sculptured fragments undeniably belonging to the porch. Considering both its provenance and the fact that we now know that each corner of the pediment was occupied by a figure of precisely this scale, it is evident that this fragment must be attributed to the pediment. For further discussion of this point, see below, pp. 284 f.

Preserved length from elbow to end of sleeve 0.105 m.; measurement of wrist 0.043 × 0.03 m.

Found north of the façade among sculptured fragments belonging to the porch.

NP(V)14. Inv. No. 696. Storeroom of the Antikensammlung. *S,I,* p. 26, pl. 41, right; Schober, pp. 17 ff., fig. 16. (Fig. 231.)

Standing draped female figure wearing a sleeveless chiton and a himation which falls over her left shoulder and presumably passed behind and between her upper arm and hip, whence it curves toward her right thigh and covered her legs. The figure stands with her weight on her left leg, the right being relaxed. Her left arm, bent back obliquely, probably held an attribute attached to or moored in the dowel hole (0.027 m. square) located at the back of the shoulder just below (0.01 m.) its upper surface. A second circular hole (ca. 0.04 m. in diameter) retaining lead appears on the back of the figure, at a point behind the area between the breasts and at the top of the chiton, reflecting the original attachment of another piece. The entire back is irregularly broken and sheared off. In its present state, the figure, which has been reassembled from five pieces, consists primarily of the left half of the torso from the base of the neck downward, the upper part of the left arm, and an oblique section of the abdomen and thighs running from the left hip to the right thigh. An irregular line defines its broken contour from the left side of the neck, through the right breast, down the abdomen to the right thigh, and upward to the left. Originally, still another fragment, including a portion of the right side of the neck and running down below the right breast, was preserved and fitted against the present irregular contour, as the illustration in *S,I,* pl. 41, makes clear. Evidently it became loose and has either disappeared or been misplaced. The left arm is irregularly broken above the elbow. Thus the head, the right part of the torso (including the arm), the lower left arm, and the larger part of both legs are missing. The folds of the mantle falling over the left hip are chipped. Plaster is visible in the joints of the reconstructed pieces.

Schober (loc. cit.) interpreted this figure as one of the northern akroteria. It is unneces-

268

231. *NP(V)14*

sary to refute his argument in detail because of the discovery, in the meantime, not only of the original Hellenistic figural akroterion from the southwest corner of the building (cf. pp. 364 ff., below), but also of sufficient fragments of the northern lateral akroteria to prove that they were identical in every typological respect with the scheme and drapery of the rear akroteria (cf. below, pp. 372 ff., *NLA 1–8*). Hence the present figure, which differs significantly from them, must be eliminated from this category and, given its provenance, scale, and style, included among the pedimental sculptures, as Conze (*S,1*, p. 26) originally proposed.

Greatest preserved height 0.525 m.; height from left shoulder to hip ca. 0.20 m.; width from center of chest to left nipple ca. 0.085 m.

Found along with other fragments of the pedimental sculptures north of the façade (cf. ibid.).

232. *NP(S)15*

NP(S)15. 50.515. Stored in the Samothrace Museum. (Fig. 232.)
Right foot of a female figure wearing an indented sandal. Only the slender toes emerge beneath the lower edge of a skirt, presumably a chiton. Beneath the foot, part of the curving contour of the base on which it stood is preserved, including its flat, roughly picked undersurface. The fragment is irregularly and obliquely broken at the top, across the arch, and at both sides. It is worn and weathered. It evidently belonged to a figure standing with her weight on her left leg, the right being relaxed and resting lightly on the ball of the foot.

Greatest preserved height 0.085 m.; width of obliquely placed toes 0.10 m.; height of sole ca. 0.013 m.; height of base below sandal 0.02 m.

Found just northeast of the northeast corner of the façade.

NP(V)16. Inv. No. 344. Kunsthistorisches Museum; on exhibition. *S,I*, pp. 10, 24 ff., 74, pls. 37, 38; Schober, no. 3, pp. 8 f., fig. 4. (Figs. 233, 256.)
Lower half of a female figure clad in chiton and himation, sitting toward the right on a rocky support that continues as a low ledge under her feet. Her right leg is drawn diagonally back, causing the foot to be completely concealed behind the heavy folds of the chiton; her left leg is crossed before it. Her right forearm, enveloped in the mantle, lies tightly across the abdomen, the hand seemingly passing beneath the left forearm, which, turned upward, allows a mighty cluster of grapes to rest partly on the palm, partly on the left knee. Their stem lies across the open palm. The head and torso are lacking, except for a splinter at the back, as is the upper surface of the right upper arm, the entire left upper arm, and the separately worked forepart of the left foot. The lower edge of the mantle within which the left arm, too, was largely wrapped is partially preserved above the bare part of the lower arm. The extant figure consists of one unbroken piece, apart from the left hand and grapes which could be

270

233. *NP(V)16*

refitted on the figure, owing to the traces of their breaks (cf. Conze, *S,I,* loc. cit.). The left foot retains its anathyrosis, dowel hole, and lead for the forepart originally doweled to it (cf. Nos. *8, 17, 19*). The entire rear side of the figure is roughly picked. Like Nos. *11* and *12*, this statue is equipped with a pry hole (0.038 m. square) on the left side of the rocky seat, close to its upper surface (again misinterpreted by Schober, pp. 8 f., 16, as a clamp hole). Its position 0.395 m. above the bottom of the seat eliminates any thought that it could have served as a clamp hole, so ungainly and visible would such an attachment have been. Behind the left foot, there appear to be broken remnants of another such hole ca. 0.11 m. above the bottom of the figure. The oblique folds over the right shin have been chipped. The right thigh, too, is pocked and weathered, especially in the deep folds of the drapery toward the buttock, as are the ridges of drapery over the lap.

Preserved height 0.78 m.; width 0.63 m.; depth 0.375 m.; height of ledge beneath legs 0.03–0.04 m.; length of right arm from elbow to wrist 0.18 m.; length of right thigh from buttocks to knee ca. 0.41 m.

Found north of the façade, to the east of No. *1*.

234. *NP(S)17,* seen from above

235. *NP(S)17,* seen from the side

236. *NP(S)17,* seen from below

NP(S)17. 53.515. Samothrace Museum; on exhibition. *Guide,* pp. 66, 87; *Guide²,*
pp. 67, 90. (Figs. 234–236.)

Fragmentary right foot of a female figure wearing a notched sandal with a high, profiled sole.
The first three toes and part of the fourth are preserved, together with a portion of the foot
behind them and the beginning of the sandal strap between the first two toes. In addition
to its present obliquely-broken rear surface, a broken dowel hole 0.004 m. in diameter in the
lower center of its rear side indicates that this fragment was a separately worked forepart of
a foot prepared for attachment to its figure in the technique also used on Nos. *8, 16,* and *19.*
The lower surface of the sole (fig. 236), unlike those of the other sandals preserved from the
pediment, has been smoothly dressed to be visible, an indication that it belonged to a seated
figure whose right leg was crossed over her left. Furthermore, it was plainly made to be seen
obliquely from its right; hence, it must have belonged to a figure seated in the left, eastern
wing of the pediment.

Preserved length 0.065 m.; width of three preserved toes at their base 0.04 m.; length
of big toe 0.037 m.; height of sole 0.02 m.; width of toe of sandal beneath first two toes
0.026 m.

Found east of the northeastern corner of the façade.

237. *NP(V)18*, seen from the inside

NP(V)18. No inv. no. Storeroom of the Antikensammlung. Schober, no. 7, pp. 10 f., fig. 8. (Fig. 237.)

Right foot preserved from the ankle downward on the instep side; of the toes, only the lower joint of the big toe is preserved. Outer and top surfaces sheared off. Only the left edge of the sole is entirely finished, the rear right side remaining less fully executed. Strongly weathered, especially on the instep and heel. Both facts indicate that the upper surface, left side, and left part of the sole of the foot were exposed and visible; that is, that it belonged to a figure reclining with its legs toward the spectator's left in the left, eastern wing of the pediment. The less finished character of the rear side of the heel is easily explained if, like the reclining figures in the western wing, the figure lay with one leg crossed over the other—in this case, naturally, the right over the left, in logical reversal of the western scheme. Schober, too (ibid.), drew the same conclusion.

Preserved length 0.186 m.; height at metatarsal arch ca. 0.063 m.; width from center of anklebone back to heel 0.06 m.

Specific provenance unknown; see above, p. 253.

NP(V)19. No inv. no. Storeroom of the Antikensammlung. Schober, no. 9, p. 11, fig. 10. (Figs. 238, 239.)

Rear half of a right foot wearing a sandal of singular type leaving the heel and part of the forefoot exposed, while a low openwork shank, edged by a strap that passes backward over the heel and forward toward the toes, rises from the sole below the anklebone. Preserved from slightly above the ankle to the middle of the foot, the upper edge having an irregular break, the forward one smoothly dressed and equipped with a dowel hole 0.015 m. in diameter for attachment of the separately worked, now lost, forepart of the foot (cf. Nos. 8, 16, 17). The bottom of the sole, although not finished for visibility, has an oblique surface; hence, it cannot have belonged to a standing figure. Again, like No. 18, it is best understood as the right foot of a reclining figure which stretched its legs toward the spectator's left and lay with the right leg crossed over the left. Both the slight obliquity of the foot lying

238. *NP(V)19*, seen from the outside

239. *NP(V)19*, seen from the inside

tilted on its right side and its almost equal weathering on all sides would thus be intelligible. For further comment on the position of the figure to which this foot belonged, see below, p. 281.

Length 0.11 m.; height from bottom of sole to center of anklebone ca. 0.072 m.; width of ankle at this point ca. 0.085 m.; width from center of anklebone back to heel 0.045–0.05 m.; height of sole on right side 0.016 m.

Specific provenance unknown; see above, p. 253.

NP(S)20. 49.491. Samothrace Museum; on exhibition. *Hesperia,* 20 (1951), 23 f., pl. 14 a; *Guide,* pp. 66, 90; *Guide²,* pp. 67, 94. (Figs. 240, 241.)

Fragment of a reclining female figure, preserved from above the navel to the mid-thighs and draped with a mantle that falls over and totally conceals the extant portion of the right thigh and is pulled across the buttocks to emerge behind the stump of the badly shattered left thigh. Hence, the head, torso, arms, and lower legs are lacking. Nevertheless, it is apparent that the figure knelt on her left knee, extending or bending her right leg toward the spectator's left and, judging by the slight twist of the abdomen, looked toward her left. The lower edge of the mantle falling over the right thigh, although chipped, retains its original contour, but behind the left thigh it is broken. The base on which the figure reclines (average height 0.065 m.) is now visible only from the left side (cf. fig. 241). There is no trace of a dowel hole on the bottom of this portion of the original figure. The back of the body is not fully finished, and the invisible rear portions of the drapery are only very roughly picked. Scarcely weathered except on the lower front edges of the drapery.

Preserved height 0.25 m.; preserved length 0.307 m.; depth 0.23 m.; width of waist 0.155 m.; depth of waist 0.115 m.

Found southwest of the Arsinoeion close to an antique limekiln.

240. *NP(S)20*

241. *NP(S)20*, seen from the side

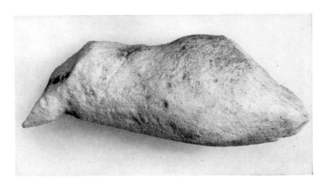

242. *NP(S)21*

NP(S)21. 48.610. Stored in the Samothrace Museum. (Fig. 242.)
Right forearm of a child, preserved from a diagonal break just above the elbow to the wrist and including a portion of the base of the hand. The marble is white and calcinated, whether from fire or moisture. The proportions of this arm, including the taper of the wrist and flare of the hand, as well as its plump surface and modeling, indicate that it belonged to a child. Given its scale, it must be attributed to the figure to which No. *20* belonged, thus explaining the pudgy, soft forms of its abdomen. For further consideration of this point, see below, p. 285.

Preserved length (including portion of hand) 0.15 m.; preserved length from wrist to elbow 0.12 m.

Found in the northwestern part of the cella of the Hieron.

NP(S)22. *53.523.* Stored in the Samothrace Museum. (Fig. 243.)
Fragment of a left arm, preserving the lowest portion of the upper arm above the elbow and the beginning of the lower arm. Irregularly broken at top and bottom. The scale of this fragment suggests that it, too, may have belonged to the reclining female child to which Nos. *19* and *20* can surely be attributed. If so, that figure turning toward her left—that is, toward the spectator's right—certainly leaned on her bent left arm, resting it on some kind of support. Such a reconstruction of the figure is, in any case, almost obligatory, given the precedent of Nos. *11* and *12.* For further comment on the position of this figure, see below, p. 285.

Greatest preserved height above elbow ca. 0.05 m.; width of arm 0.055 m.

Found in the debris of the building east of the northeast corner of the façade.

NP(S)23. *51.220.* Stored in the Samothrace Museum. (Figs. 244, 245.)
Fragmentary right hand of a female figure, preserved from above the wrist through the irregularly-broken lowest joints of the fingers and thumb. The ring finger was slightly bent or raised. The palm shows oblique scratches below the fingers and two circular depressions, one at the juncture of the thumb and the palm, the other farther down and less well preserved on its lowest joint. All attest the presence of a lost, lightly held attribute. Slightly weathered between the fingers and on the lowest joint of the thumb. The fleshy, boneless modeling of this hand justifies its attribution to one of the numerous female figures of the pediment.

Greatest preserved length 0.065 m.; width across knuckles 0.065 m.

Found northwest of the northwest corner of the Hieron.

NP(S)24. *50.612.* Stored in the Samothrace Museum. (Fig. 246.)
Fragmentary right hand of a female figure, preserved from above the knuckles through the irregularly-broken lowest joints of three fingers and the base of the little finger. The thumb is lacking. The sloping position of the fingers suggests that they were partially extended. Its marked similarity in form, execution, and scale to No. *23* makes it highly probable that this plump hand belonged to one of the female figures of the pediment.

Greatest preserved length 0.056 m.; width across knuckles ca. 0.068 m.

Recovered from a dump of excavated earth northwest of the Temenos. Evidently, this battered fragment was accidentally carried off from the excavation north of the façade but immediately thereafter retrieved.

NP(S)25. *55.182.* Stored in the Samothrace Museum. (Figs. 247, 248.)
Fragmentary left hand, preserved from the wrist to the base of the fingers and retaining the lower half of the thumb. The chipped surface of the palm shows no trace of an attribute.

243. *NP(S)22*

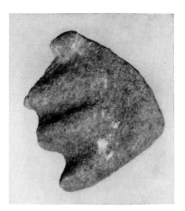

244. *NP(S)23*, seen from below   245. *NP(S)23*, seen from above   246. *NP(S)24*, seen from above

247. *NP(S)25*, seen from above   248. *NP(S)25*, seen from below

Again, the style of this rounded, fleshy hand, which is similar to but slightly smaller in scale than Nos. *23* and *24*, suggests that it should be attributed to the pedimental sculptures, in spite of the uncertainty of its provenance.

Preserved length from knuckle to wrist 0.065 m.; width across knuckles 0.058 m.

Provenance unknown.

NP(S)26. 50.47. Stored in the Samothrace Museum. (Fig. 249.)
Unidentified object of Thasian marble, broken below and having a backward curving contour, an oval section, and a blunt tip. Its rear surface (at the left in fig. 249) is arris-like, formed by the meeting of the sides, and from 0.08 m. below the tip, downward, it is less smoothly dressed than elsewhere. Its face (the right edge in fig. 249) bears a shallow indentation in the shape of an arc ca. 0.068 m. below the tip. Given its provenance, it is conceivable, but by no means certain, that this enigmatic fragment formed part of an inanimate object or attribute in the pediment.

A second, related fragment, smaller in scale but similar in section, exists among the unnumbered marble fragments from Samothrace in the storeroom of the Antikensammlung.

Preserved length 0.135 m.; width at tip ca. 0.03 m.

Found on the surface north of the façade of the Hieron.

NP(V)27. No inv. no. Storeroom of the Antikensammlung. Schober, p. 19, fig. 18.
(Fig. 250.)
Fragment of hanging drapery, broken above and below and restored from several pieces. Schober attributed it to one of the akroteria, because of its supposed analogy to a portion of drapery on the Vienna Victory (text II, pp. 113 ff.). But that statue, as we now know, is a Roman replacement of one of the Hellenistic Victories, while this fragment is undoubtedly Hellenistic, as Schober correctly estimated (cf. its relationship to the drapery of No. 5). Therefore, since it offers no parallel in scheme to any motif of the drapery of the fully pre-

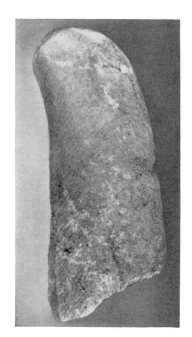

249. *NP(S)26*

250. *NP(V)27*

served Hellenistic akroterion (figs. 317, 319, 335), it is reasonable to assume that this fragment formed part of the drapery of one of the pedimental figures.

Preserved height 0.28 m.; greatest width 0.11 m.

Specific provenance unknown.

A number of small fragments or splinters of drapery, as well as a few sections of arms, that very likely come from the pedimental sculptures are preserved in the storerooms of both the Vienna and Samothrace collections. Since they cast no light on these sculptures, because of their exceedingly fragmentary state, and in no case can be fitted onto or associated with any of the better preserved fragments or figures illustrated in the catalogue, it is needless to describe them in detail or to reproduce them.

The fragments stored in Samothrace were all found north of the façade of the Hieron, especially in the vicinity of the two corners or in the southern part of the adjacent Temenos. They differ in style so markedly from fragments belonging to the figural akroteria as to be easily separable from them. The following items are fragments of drapery: 50.231, 50.434, 50.458, 50.465 A, 50.466, 50.475 A, 50.476, 50.477, 50.510, 50.529 A, B, D, G, 50.550 A–L, 50.564, 51.123, 51.124, 51.133, 51.216, 51.217, 53.524, 53.526 A, 53.542, 53.545,

279

53.597, and, conceivably, 50.50 and 51.207. 51.417 from the Austrian dump near the porch surely belongs in this category, too, while 50.578, 51.463, and 52.118 may belong. The two fragments of arms are 51.212 (the sheared-off surface of an upper arm with armlet? preserved height 0.082 m.) and 49.684 (the base of a shoulder? preserved width ca. 0.09 m.), the latter found at the center of the western foundation.

The fragments in Vienna, for the most part also of drapery, cannot be specified, since they have never been individually accessioned. Yet, like the items singled out in the catalogue, they form part of the material traditionally and indubitably brought back from Samothrace after the two campaigns of the seventies. But their precise provenance is unknown, and, as Conze observed (*S,I*, pp. 26, 28), the sculptures found north of the building included both fragments of the pedimental figures and remnants of miscellaneous monuments, an observation equally applicable to our own experience. In addition to the approximately seven fragments of drapery that conceivably come from the pediment, there is an eighth, a knobby piece probably belonging to a rocky base (preserved length 0.155 m.; preserved height 0.072 m.; greatest preserved width 0.145 m.). Schober's No. 13 (pp. 12 f., fig. 14), a portion of a forearm, should be included in this category of unrevealing, probable, but not provable fragments.

The provenance of these sculptures, together with the incomplete execution of their rear sides, allows them to be attributed to the northern pediment of the Hieron with absolute certainty. The varying sizes of the larger, better preserved pieces and of the smaller, often highly revealing fragments that can be ascribed to them; the traces of weathering left by centuries of exposure to the harsh Samothracian winters; and the telltale fashion in which individual pieces, both large and small, reflect the specific positions that the statues once occupied and the angles from which they were intended to be seen, hence for which they were executed—all these considerations permit them to be placed within the triangular field of the pediment with a high degree of accuracy. The physical reconstruction of the pedimental sculptures of the façade, in turn, provides the means of interpreting them.

The field into which these figures were introduced was 1.47 m. high at the center of the gable, 11.72 m. wide, and 0.47 m. deep, for it will be recalled that the pediment was provided with a floor ca. 0.05 m. high, which was doweled to the horizontal geison and served as a low plinth on which the sculptures were set.[36] They occupied the entire available space, in so far as height and width are concerned, but only rarely required its full depth. Obviously, the known or restored height of the statues is the most crucial of these dimen-

36. See above. pp. 106 f.

sions, indicating, as it does, the precise point at which a given figure may be fitted under the sloping raking geison. And as a result of the fixed positions to which certain of the better preserved figures must be assigned, it is possible to determine the areas left available for other, more fragmentary figures.

When restored to an appropriate height, No. *1*, the largest in scale of the pedimental sculptures, can occupy only one position: the center of the composition (VII in fig. 211), as Hauser long ago realized (see fig. 7, p. 10).[37] As the sole figure to which the fragmentary upper left arm and hand, Nos. *2* and *3*, can be ascribed because of their scale, it proves to have been a mighty female figure clad in chiton and himation striding obliquely to the right, her bent left arm held close to the body, her left hand occupied in carrying, supporting, or bracing an object that was doweled to the upright palm.[38] The well preserved reclining figures, Nos. *11* and *12*, are equally easily assigned to positions XI and XII in fig. 211, as has, again, long been evident.[39] Even if the specific provenance of these statues were not documented, the larger size of the male figure is immediately apparent to the spectator's eye, attesting a position somewhat more removed from the corner. Both of these half-draped figures, wrapped in their mantles, stretch their crossed legs toward the right, western corner of the pediment and, leaning on their right arms, turn backward to look toward the center of the field. No. *12*, at least, as her face reveals, reclined obliquely rather than in full profile.

Nos. *11* and *12* at positions XI and XII imply the original existence of counterparts in the left wing of the pediment at II and III. Only a single fragment of each of these balancing figures is preserved: the two right feet, Nos. *18* and *19*. But incomplete though they are, each of these feet can have belonged only to a reclining figure stretching its legs toward the spectator's left, the right crossed over the left (that is, in exact reversal of Nos. *11* and *12*), as is proved by the manner in which they have been executed, the degree to which they have been finished, and their weathering. The slightly larger size of the bare foot, No. *18*, is in accord with a position at III to the right of the sandaled figure at II.[40]

---

37. *S,I*, p. 74, pl. 42. He estimated its original height between 1.40 m. and 1.50 m. Schober (pp. 13 ff. and fig. 15), working with an incorrect figure probably scaled from Hauser's plates, assumed the greatest available height at the center of the pediment to have been 1.60 m. But less in consideration of scale than because of his hypothesis regarding the thematic appropriateness of four figures at the center of this composition, he pushed statue No. *1* into the equivalent of our position VI, thereby forcing himself to invent a counterpart at VIII for which he candidly admitted there was not the slightest trace of evidence. But No. *1* is simply too tall to be fitted into the pediment at this point. For further discussion of the issue, see below, pp. 286 ff.

38. Since the detailed evidence in regard to dimensions, degree of execution, weathering, provenance, and any other factual observations pertinent to the physical interpretation and reconstruction of the individual figures and fragments has been fully stated in the catalogue, it will not be repeated in the following pages. When in doubt about a given point or detail, the reader must refer to appropriate entries in the catalogue.

39. Cf. *S,I*, pl. 42, and Schober, p. 13 and fig. 15.

40. By attributing our No. *18* (his No. 7) to the

Hauser and Schober have again been correct in placing the seated female figure wrapped in her mantle and holding a bunch of grapes in her left hand, No. *16*, to the left of No. *1* and in allowing for an interval between the two sufficient to accommodate an intermediate figure.[41] Sitting slightly obliquely on a rocky support at position V (fig. 211), her left leg stretched forward, her right drawn back, she, too, looked directly toward the center of the pediment. Specific provenance, execution, and especially size require that she be located there rather than in positions IV or VI. This position, in turn, dictates the location of the seated female figure to which, as we have seen, the sandaled right foot, No. *17*, belonged. For since the character of its modeling and execution indicates that it comes from a figure seated in the left wing of the pediment with her right leg crossed over her left in a fashion that made it desirable to fully execute the visible sole of the sandal (a technical feature reserved for such a position, to judge by the extant feet), this figure must have occupied position IV, the only space remaining for a seated figure. The fact that No. *16* conceals her right foot within her drapery prevents comparison of the relative size of these members; but, fortunately, the comparable foot of her counterpart at position IX was exposed, is preserved, and affords welcome confirmation of the correctness of assuming that a second figure, slightly smaller in scale than No. *16*, once sat at IV. For the sandaled right foot of the statue at IX is markedly larger than No. *17*, the sole fragment preserved of the seated female who once occupied position IV.

Even were there no trace of the statues that once served as counterparts in the right wing of the pediment to the two seated female figures at positions IV and V, it would be obvious that they must once have existed. But sufficient remains of the statue seated at IX (fig. 211) to establish that, once again, it represented a female figure wearing chiton and mantle, sitting with her right foot drawn slightly back, resting on its toes, and her left foot extended forward.

---

reclining figure at our position II, Schober, p. 15, may seem to have implied that it is smaller than No. *19* (his No. 9), which he attributed to a seated figure in the western half of the pediment. Actually, he did not comment on their relative sizes, since, coupling No. *19* with the so-called "bent knee" (his No. 8, our No. *6*), which we have seen is not a knee but the lower part of the face and neck of a female figure, he was forced to attribute it to a seated figure. Direct comparison of the relative sizes of the two feet does not occur in his discussion, doubtless because he did not recognize that the peculiar features of No. *19* require that it be attributed to a reclining figure. But he did realize that it must have belonged to a right leg crossed over a left and that it could not have supported the weight of the figure. Had he not been misled by his interpretation of the so-

called "knee," he might have placed both Nos. *18* and *19* correctly.

Before full investigation of the pedimental fragments in Samothrace and Vienna had taken place, Schober's incorrect attribution of No. *18* to a figure close to the eastern corner was repeated in *Hesperia*, 20 (1951), 24, n. 87, where it was further speculated that it might belong to the actual corner figure, No. *20*, which it is now clear is quite impossible.

41. Cf. *S,I*, pl. 42, and Schober, p. 16, fig. 15. The fact that Schober put our No. *16* (his No. 3) in a position more akin to our IV than to V, as a result of his incorrect placing of No. *1* (his No. 4), does not alter the relative positions he assigned to Nos. *16* and *1*. See above, n. 37.

Not only can the torso, No. *7*, to which the left and right feet (Nos. *8* and *9*) have long been correctly attributed,[42] be ascribed to position IX with certainty, because of its scale, execution, and the revealing implications of its feet, but also, as a result of the relative sizes of Nos. *9* and *17*, the placing of the latter at IV is confirmed. Like her counterpart at V, the female figure at IX sat somewhat obliquely and looked toward the center of the composition. Otherwise, they were differentiated in costume and posture, as figures IV and V were varied in position, to create variety within the basically strict symmetry of the pedimental field.[43] Unfortunately, no such precise comment can be made about the virtually unknown figure which, logic demands, must have sat at X. It is possible that No. *10*, the bent right arm of a female figure seemingly coming from the right half of the pediment and made to be seen obliquely, is the sole preserved fragment of that figure, but in its present state it does not allow absolute certainty on this score. Conceivably, it could have belonged to IX. If it did belong to the figure seated at X, it would bear witness to still another female figure.

As Hauser and Schober recognized in their differing ways, an interval must be predicated between Nos. *1* and *16*, a space sufficient for and demanding a standing figure.[44] And, although neither Conze nor Schober realized it, a considerable portion of this statue, No. *14*, is preserved.[45] It represents a female figure wearing a sleeveless chiton and mantle, standing with her weight on her left leg, and holding her bent left arm drawn slightly backward. In itself, this figure could be placed at position VIII, as well as at VI; but the existence of No. *5*, a fragment of a second standing figure which, because of its drapery, execution, and weathering, must be assigned to position VIII (the only other place high enough to receive such a figure), implies that No. *14* did stand at VI. Owing to her stance, it is possible to attribute to her a second fragment, No. *15*, the right sandaled foot of a female figure standing with her weight on her left leg, her right foot poised on its toes. The scale of this foot, which is slightly larger than No. *9*, confirms its attribution to a standing figure, as the character of its drapery is sufficiently clear, in spite of weathering, to prove that it could not have belonged to No. *1*, whose right leg was also relaxed.

42. Schober, p. 16, recognized that Nos. *7* and *8* (his Nos. 5, 6) belonged to the same statue, and in *Hesperia*, 20 (1951), 24 and n. 88, the newly discovered fragment No. *9* was immediately linked to them.

43. Schober, p. 15, following Conze and Zumbusch, *S,I*, p. 26, attributed No. *7* (his No. 5) to a reclining figure and placed it in the eastern half of the pediment as a counterpart to No. *11* (his No. 2). Strangely enough, neither Conze nor Zumbusch recognized that the left foot in Vienna, No. *8*, must be attributed to the same statue as the torso, No. *7*. Schober, who had recognized this fact, evidently remained under the spell of their suggestion.

44. Cf. *S,I*, pl. 42; Schober, p. 16, fig. 15; and above, n. 41.

45. Conze (*S,I*, p. 26) unhesitatingly included this figure among the pedimental sculptures without proposing a specific location for it. But Schober (pp. 17 f.) mistakenly interpreted it as one of the two northern lateral akroteria. It is needless to repeat or refute his argument, since it collapses owing to the discovery, in the meantime, not only of the single well-preserved Hellenistic figural akroterion from the Hieron (*SLA 1*, below, pp. 364 ff.), the statue once standing above its southwestern corner, but also of sufficient fragments of her northern counterparts (cf. *NLA 1–6*, pp. 372 ff.)

Not only do the execution and weathering of No. *5,* the bent left arm of a female figure facing toward the spectator's left, indicate that the statue to which it belonged occupied a place in the right, western half of the pediment, but, in addition, the manner in which the cloak wrapped around this arm falls downward in rigid, vertical folds behind the forearm can hardly be explained save as a feature of a standing figure.[46] Nor would its size be appropriate for the figure seated at X, the only other vacant position to which the fragment could conceivably be assigned. Similarly, No. *6,* the lower part of the face and neck of a female figure looking toward her right and prepared for insertion into a torso, can have belonged only to the figure at VIII or X, since it does not fit the similarly executed torso, No. *7.*[47] The absence of comparable pieces with which to contrast this fragment in size precludes the possibility of assigning it to either position with total assurance. Fortunately, the fact that the figure at VIII was unquestionably female and the one at X very probably so renders this uncertainty of little consequence. In fig. 211, No. *6* has been arbitrarily assigned to the figure at VIII.

Two spaces, and two only, remain unoccupied in fig. 211—I and XIII. Schober was content to leave them empty.[48] But quite apart from the unsatisfactory appearance of empty corners in an otherwise so densely filled composition, the discovery of No. *20,* the largest and best preserved of the recently excavated fragments, proves that they were, of course, occupied. For provenance,[49] execution, style, and, most important, scale indicate that this damaged but still entirely recognizable statue of a little girl was the easternmost figure of the pediment. Kneeling on her left leg and stretching her right into the corner at position I, she,

to prove beyond any doubt that they were identical in type with those of the south, which differ radically (for example, in costume) from No. *14.*

46. Schober, too (pp. 11 f., 13 ff.), attributed this fragment to a standing figure in the right wing of the pediment; but, as pointed out above (p. 259), he mistakenly interpreted it as a male arm, as a result of his desire to see in it evidence for a statue of Hermes. See below, p. 287, for further comment on this illusion, which became the point of departure for his reconstruction and interpretation of the pedimental sculptures.

47. For correction of Schober's misinterpretation of this fragment (his No. 8) as the bent right knee of a seated male figure (pp. 11, 15) placed in the western half of the pediment as a foil to our No. *16,* see above, pp. 260 and 281 f., n. 40.

48. Cf. p. 13, and fig. 15, p. 16. The fact that no figures appear in *S,I,* pl. 42, simply reflects the admitted incompleteness of Hauser's "restoration" in

which even fragments explicitly attributed to the pediment, like our No. *14,* do not figure. Schober's view, however, was a considered opinion.

49. Although this fragmentary statue was not found directly below or in front of the pediments, like the majority of the pedimental figures or fragments, but recovered from the periphery of an antique lime-kiln somewhat to the north of the Hieron, it will be recalled that it is not the only *preserved* fragment of the pedimental sculptures to have met this fate or been discovered at this very point. No. *9,* the right foot of the statue seated at position IX, had also found its way into a heap of marble fragments carried off and assembled for burning at this kiln, while the other preserved remnants of the same statue, Nos. *7* and *8,* were not taken, hence remained close to the façade, implying that the figure had smashed in falling to the ground. Obviously, it was the smaller, more easily portable fragments that were carried to this strategically placed kiln located in the midst of the major

too, evidently turned her childish body to look toward the center of the field. Judging by the implications of No. 22 which, given its scale, can be attributed only to this figure, she leaned on her bent left arm, resting it on some now-lost support. The position of her right arm must remain unknown, in spite of the fact that its chubby forearm and the beginning of its childish hand are preserved in No. 21, which again, because of scale and type, can be ascribed to no other statue in the pediment.

Once the presence of a figure, more especially of a child, has been ascertained at position I, it is obvious that she had a counterpart at XIII. And among the fragments of unimpeachable provenance taken to Vienna by our predecessors, one, No. 13, can now be identified as the sole remnant of that figure.[50] It is the bent right forearm of a pudgy child wearing a sleeved garment, a fragment identical in scale with No. 21 which surely comes from what was once the westernmost figure of the pediment.[51] Like its counterpart, this statue, whether male or female, leaned on one arm and presumably was disposed in a similar half-reclining position.

Only one significant and telltale fragment of the pedimental sculptures remains unplaced: No. 4, the tiny right hand of a child or infant.[52] Since it is too small to be connected with either child at I or XIII (both of whose right wrists afford a reliable check), it must have belonged to an infant, in fact to an infant that was carried, if for no other reason than that the width of the pedimental field is entirely occupied by figures I–XIII and incapable of receiving even the smallest additional statue. The most plausible figure with which to

marble buildings of the Sanctuary. How many other fragments of the pedimental sculptures were actually destroyed in this appalling and traditional manner, one can only speculate. In any case, even without the analogy of No. 9, it would be clear that No. 20 was the easternmost figure of the pediment on the basis of the internal evidence of technique, execution, scale, and style, for no other Hellenistic building in the Sanctuary—indeed, no other building upright there in late antiquity—had pedimental sculptures.

50. It is not surprising that Schober overlooked this fragment. Before the discovery of No. 20, no one would necessarily have thought of attributing an arm of this size—or of the size of No. 21—to the pedimental sculptures. With the discovery of Nos. 20 and 21, the relationship became obvious.

51. See p. 114, n. 195, above, for comment on Conze's incorrect attribution of this fragment to a hypothetical (nonexistent) figural relief. A fortunate by-product of this misinterpretation is the fact that the provenance of this piece is much more definite than

that of many other Samothracian fragments in Vienna. For its having been found with what we now know were parts of the centaurs carved on the lids of the pronaos coffers proves that it was discovered among the debris of the porch. See also S,I, p. 23.

52. The female hands, Nos. 23–25, cannot be precisely placed or attributed. Because of their fragmentary condition, they cannot be assigned with certainty to one side of the pediment rather than to the other, or to seated rather than to standing figures. They cannot have belonged to statues I, VII, or XIII, because of their scale, or to V, or XII, because of the preservation of the hands of these statues, or, in all likelihood, to II, III, or XI; and it would be unwise and unproductive to press them into any of the remaining available positions.

I have refrained from restoring specific attributes to the figures in fig. 212. But, as the catalogue entries above indicate, the traces of lost attributes present on the extant figures and fragments, including hands, suggest that the figures were provided with appropriate attributes.

associate this infant is No. *1,* the central figure of the composition occupying position VII.[53] Furthermore, it will be recalled that the left hand of this statue, No. *3,* bears unmistakable traces of having supported or braced an object doweled to it. If this striding female figure bore a child on her bent left arm and its small body was partly braced by her left hand and doweled to it, these technical features would be both necessary and intelligible. The mantle falling behind her left shoulder and visible across her wrist could then be explained as caught up and draped beneath the child in a fashion both convincing and conventional. Hence, theoretical probability confirmed by tangible physical characteristics demands that the infant to which this little hand belonged be reconstructed as borne by the central figure of the pediment. That the scale of both adult and infant was life-size is welcome confirmation of the correctness of this conclusion. But the exact appearance and posture of this infant, as well as the very attribute once grasped in its tightly clasped fist, must remain hypothetical. Even its sex, like that of the child at XIII, must for the moment be uncertain.[54]

Examination of the pedimental fragments of the Hieron, large as well as small, long known or recently discovered, establishes the fact that its northern tympanum was occupied by thirteen statues (figs. 211, 212). At the center, a life-size female figure moved toward the right, carrying an infant on her left arm. On each side, she was flanked by three standing or seated figures of which five certainly, six probably, were female. This central group of sitting and standing female figures was framed, in turn, by a pair of reclining figures, the pair at the right including one male and one female, that at the left conceivably, but by no means certainly, similar in scheme. Finally, the composition was closed by two semi-reclining children, one in each corner. To a degree undreamed of in Conze's day, the empty areas in Hauser's restored gable have been entirely filled as a result of re-exploration of the site and re-examination of the original finds.[55]

---

53. It is evident that the figure to which No. *4* belonged cannot be linked with the partially preserved statues I, V, XI–XIII or, very likely, with the counterparts to XI–XII at II–III. Were it to be associated either with one of the smaller seated figures at IV and X or one of the standing figures at VI and VIII, it would probably imply the existence of still another child in the arms or lap of the counterpart to any of these figures. Apart from the fact, in itself inconclusive, that no trace of such a fourth child is extant, interpretation of the preserved pedimental sculptures will make clear that whereas the presence of three children in the pediment is both provable and in full accord with the testimony of Samothracian legend, the existence of a fourth child could in no way be rendered plausible or explained by any of the extensive literary sources referring to the island, its cult, and its legend.

54. Again, it is natural that Schober overlooked this piece among the Samothracian fragments stored in the Antikensammlung. Before unequivocal proof existed that two of the three children of Samothracian legend were represented in the pediment, the small scale of this hand would understandably have seemed to preclude its attribution to the pedimental sculptures.

55. Thus, the present reconstruction supplements but does not contradict Hauser's plate (*S,I,* pl. 42). On the contrary, it does contradict Schober's reconstruction (p. 16, fig. 15) in almost every respect. Since his specific errors of allocation or interpretation of the Vienna figures and fragments have been pointed out above in the catalogue of pedimental sculptures and in the subsequent discussion of their reconstruction and position within the northern gable, it is needless to repeat them in detail. It will suffice to point

Apart from remarking on what he regarded as the Bacchic implications of the grapes held by the seated female at V and of the rhyton held by the reclining figure at XII, whom he thought of as Cabiric nymphs,[56] and suggesting that the mighty figure in the center of the field represented Demeter searching for Persephone,[57] Conze refrained from any attempt to reconstruct the theme of the pedimental sculptures as a whole, in view of their incomplete preservation. But Schober, for the first time taking into consideration the lesser fragments in Vienna, expanded Conze's suggestion that Demeter occupied the primary position in the gable. Misinterpreting the female arm, No. *5*, as male [58] and inferring from its mantle that

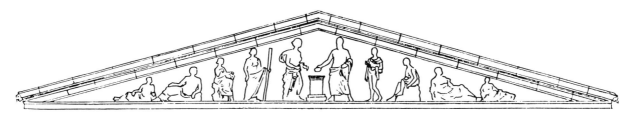

251. Reconstruction of the northern pediment by A. Schober

it must have belonged to a well-known statuary type of Hermes, he drew the far-reaching conclusion that the center of the pediment ought to have contained four figures representing the Μεγάλοι Θεοί and Hermes Kadmilos.[59] By placing No. *1* off center in a position for which she is too tall, by introducing a nonexistent "charakteristisches mystisches Objekt des Kabirenkults" or altar between Demeter and an admittedly entirely hypothetical, antithetical Hades, and by creating a figure of Persephone from fragments Nos. *2* and *3* (which scale demands be attributed to his "Demeter") to juxtapose to his female "Hermes," he fulfilled the requirements of his ill-conceived theory. No attempt was made to interpret the remaining six figures in his restored sketch (fig. 251).[60]

As has been repeatedly demonstrated, eight of the ten figures in this reconstruction (all but the two well-preserved reclining figures at the right) reflect a succession of blunders.[61]

out that his composition, made up of five figures on each side of a centrally placed (nonexistent) altar, forces figures into positions for which they are actually too tall (his figures 3–8, as far as they exist, 6 being admittedly hypothetical, 4 and 8 the result of incorrect interpretation and allocation of fragments); includes figures composed of misinterpreted, mislocated fragments (his figures 1, 2, 4, 7, 8); omits fragments in Vienna that must be included but were easy to overlook before the discovery of the newly excavated pieces in Samothrace; and reflects his unfortunate confusion and overlapping of what should be the *successive* problems of physical reconstruction and interpretation. For further comment on Schober's faulty

method and erroneous conclusions, see pp. 287 f. Given the combination of errors and the unavoidable omission of essential fragments underlying this, the only other reconstruction of the northern pediment of the Hieron thus far attempted, it is unnecessary to repeat and summarize the bases for its formal arrangements or to refute them at greater length.

56. *S,I*, pp. 26 f.
57. Ibid., pp. 43 f.; *S,II*, p. 26.
58. Schober, pp. 11 f.
59. Ibid., pp. 13 ff.
60. Ibid., p. 16, fig. 15.
61. Above, pp. 256 ff., Nos. *3, 5, 6, 9, 14;* nn. 40, 41, 43, 45–48, 50, 54, and, especially, 55.

They range from placing the larger figures in positions within the gable for which they are too big, to incorrect interpretation, hence, subsequent misallocation of the smaller fragments to figural types to which they cannot belong and which, in turn, are either faulty or without basis. The "bent knee" that is the sole basis for the seated figure in the right wing of Schober's reconstruction but is actually the lower jaw and neck of a female figure (No. 6) will suffice to illustrate this point. These multiple mistakes would in themselves invalidate the physical reconstruction of the pedimental sculptures on which Schober's interpretation purports to rest. But there remains, in addition, the illuminating evidence yielded both by the fragments subsequently excavated in Samothrace and by those previously excavated but hitherto overlooked in the Vienna storeroom. Thus it is needless to linger further over this ill-founded and now outmoded interpretation.

Two striking facts emerge from the reconstruction of the pediment described above and illustrated in figs. 211, 212: namely, that three children appeared among its cast of characters and that eight, probably nine, of the remaining figures were female. These objective facts afford the prime clues for the interpretation of the pedimental sculptures.

In the context of Samothracian legend, the three children are immediately identifiable. They must be Dardanos, Aëtion, and Harmonia, the familiar offspring of Zeus and Elektra.[62] The precious, recently recovered fragment of a female child occupying the left corner of the gable (fig. 240) can only be Harmonia. She was balanced in the right corner, as we have seen, by the figure of a child of identical scale wearing a sleeved garment (fig. 230). This telltale element of clothing, implying the presence of a figure clad in the Phrygian costume used to depict Trojans, bespeaks the original presence of her brother Dardanos, alluding to his future role as the founder of Dardania and the transmitter to the Trojans of the Samothracian mysteries.[63] By this iconographic device, Dardanos could be rendered easily identifiable and distinguished from his brother, Aëtion, whose role in the Samothracian Sanctuary was of even greater significance. For it was Aëtion "who founded the secret and mystic rites of the Samothracians," [64] who was "reputed to have been the first to celebrate the mysteries performed in Samothrace to Rhea," [65] and who, in the words of Diodorus, was instructed by Zeus himself "in the initiatory rite of the mysteries, which had existed on the island since ancient times but was at that time, so to speak, put into his hands; . . . And Iasion [Aëtion] is reputed to have been the first to initiate strangers into them [the mysteries]

62. See Diodorus Siculus 5.48.3; Nonnus *Dionysiaca* 3.180 ff.; Scholia Laurentina to Apollonius Rhodius *Argonautica* 1.916; Scholia Parisina to Apollonius Rhodius *Argonautica,* 1.915–16; Scholia to Euripides *Phoenissae* 7 (*Samothrace,* Vol. 1, **32, 68, 70, 70a, 75**).

63. Strabo 7, frg. 49 (331c) (Vol. 1, **60**): ". . . Dardanus set out from Samothrace and went and settled at the foot of Mt. Ida, calling his city Dar-

dania, and taught the Trojans the Samothracian mysteries." See also ibid., **145, 182**, lines 1–3, **183, 184, 188, 189.**

64. Clemens Alexandrinus *Protrepticus* 2.13.3 (Vol. 1, **145**).

65. Scholia to Clemens Alexandrinus *Protrepticus* 2.13.3 (Vol. 1, **146**).

and by this means to bring the initiatory rite to high esteem." [66] Once two of the three legendary Samothracian children have been identified as Harmonia and Dardanos, it becomes obvious that the infant carried by the central figure of the pediment must have been Aëtion [67] and that the birth or, rather, the infancy of the hero-founder of the Samothracian mysteries constituted the main theme of the pedimental sculptures.

The passages in ancient literature alluding to Samothrace and its cult which allow these so fragmentarily preserved traces of three children to be identified with reasonable certainty include one that appears to provide the key to establishing the identity of four of the seven female figures occupying the center of the field: Nonnus' description of Elektra's children. Here Dardanos is depicted as nursed by Dike and nurtured by the Seasons.

This Dardanos, Emathion's [Aëtion's] brother, was one whom the bed of Zeus had begotten, whom Justice nursed and cared for at the time when the Seasons ran to the mansion of Queen Elektra, bearing the scepter of Zeus, and the robe of Time, and the staff of Olympos, to prophesy the indissoluble dominion of the Ausonian race. The Seasons brought up the baby. . . .[68]

In the context of Nonnus' description, it is Dardanos who dominates the stage, the elder brother to whom "the reins of sovereignty" had once belonged but who has "left his native soil, and migrated to the soil of the continent opposite," there to found the fortified city bearing his name. Emathion-Aëtion, inheritor of the "scepter of the Kabeiroi," thus clearly the younger of the two, here plays a lesser role. But in the context of the pedimental sculptures of the Hieron, where this younger child occupies the central position in the field and where he is celebrated as founder of the mysterious rites that reached their solemn culmination in that very building, his is the primary role. And if, following Nonnus' clue, we investigate the possibility that three of the six female figures flanking the mighty striding figure bearing Aëtion on her arm represent the Seasons, we are well rewarded.

For in both literature and art, the Horai appear as the nurturers of divine and heroic children, fulfilling their time-honored function as presiders over the flourishing of life in all its forms. In the venerable hymn to Hera quoted by Pausanias,[69] the goddess is described as having been reared by the Horai, as Hermes, too, is depicted in the *Imagines* of Philostra-

---

66. 5.48.4 (Vol. 1, **142**, lines 1–7).

67. I have used the form Aëtion in preference to the equivalents Iasion or Eëtion more commonly found in the sources, because it occurs in an inscription approximately contemporary with the pedimental sculptures that honors one Herodes of Priene for poems about Dardanos, Aëtion, and Harmonia. (See Vol. 1, pp. 57 f., **136** n.; *IG*, XII (8), p. 38, *ad a.* 150; and text II of this volume, p. 30, n. 135.) It thus seems to have been a form current in the second century B.C.

68. *Dionysiaca* 3.195 ff. (Vol. 1, **68**, lines 195–99). Cf. the related motif on a relief in the Temple to the Great Goddesses at Megalopolis, where the infant Zeus was carried by the nymph Neda in the presence of other nymphs: Pausanias 8.31.3–4.

69. 2.13.3. Again according to Nonnus (9.11 ff.), "the childbed Seasons" were the first to greet the infant Dionysos when he had been delivered from Zeus' thigh—i.e., they were present at this divine birth even though, in this instance, they did not serve as the child's nurses.

tus [70] as cared for by the Seasons at his birth. Still more analogous is their performance of this function on behalf of Aristaios, the hero-founder of Kyrene who, like Aëtion, was ultimately divinized.[71] Pindar gave graphic expression to this concept, reflecting a primary activity of these nameless goddesses long before they became the individualized Seasons,[72] when he caused Cheiron to prophesy that Aristaios' mother would bear a son "whom glorious Hermes shall take from his mother's womb and bear away to the enthroned Horai and to Gaia; and they shall place the babe upon their laps and drop water and ambrosia on his lips."[73]

Philostratus' description of a painting showing the birth of Hermes on the very crest of Olympos implies the original existence of this iconographic type in art as well as literature:

There the Horae care for Hermes at his birth. The painter has depicted these also, each according to her time, and they wrap him in swaddling clothes, sprinkling over him the most beautiful flowers, that he may have swaddling clothes not without distinction.[74]

But among the rare representations of the Horai in Greek art that are preserved, no certain illustration of such a scene exists. Nevertheless, in spite of their scantiness, the extant monuments on which the Horai appear establish the fact that they were shown as draped figures, both seated and standing (cf. fig. 252).[75]

Throughout the Archaic age and well into the Classical period, these golden-filleted daughters of Zeus were thought of as three in number.[76] Collectively the givers of all good

70. 1.26.2. Cf. below, n. 128.

71. See Franz Studniczka, *Kyrene* (Leipzig, 1890), pp. 21, 40 f., 133, and passim regarding Aristaios.

72. For the Seasons, in general, see the extensive material collected by George M. A. Hanfmann, *The Season Sarcophagus in Dumbarton Oaks* (Cambridge, 1951).

73. *Pythian Odes* 9.59 ff. (ed. Sir John Sandys, Loeb edn., p. 279):

τόθι παῖδα τέξεται, ὃν κλυτὸς Ἑρμᾶς

εὐθρόνοις Ὥραισι καὶ Γαίᾳ

ἀνελὼν φίλας ὑπὸ ματέρος οἴσει.

ταὶ δ' ἐπιγουνίδιον κατθηκάμεναι βρέφος αὐταῖς,

νέκταρ ἐν χείλεσσι καὶ ἀμβροσίαν στάξοισι. . . .

74. *Imagines* 1.26.2 (tr. Arthur Fairbanks, Loeb edn., p. 101). Hanfmann (op. cit., I, 80) assumes that the Horai are present in a scene depicting the birth of Athena on a fragmentary black-figured skyphos from the Akropolis. Conceivably they are, but the fact that the relevant figures lack an inscription makes this point uncertain. Cf. Botho Graef and Ernst Langlotz, *Die antiken Vasen von der Akropolis zu Athen* (Berlin, 1925), I, 66, no. 597 a, b, pl. 24.

The so-called cup cited by A. Rapp, s.v. *Horai*, in Roscher, I, pt. 2, col. 2739, as showing Dionysos received after his birth by a Hora rather than the customary nymphs, is actually an Etruscan mirror. E. Gerhard (*Etruskische Spiegel*, I [Berlin, 1841], pl. 82; III [1863], 84 ff.) rightly considered this earlier interpretation of the scene still followed by Rapp as dubious.

It may be worth remarking, apropos of Etruscan mirrors, that Gerhard's thesis, "Die Geburt der Kabiren," *Abh. Preuss. Ak.*, 1862, pp. 401 ff., that certain mirrors showing the birth of three children allude to Samothrace and the Kabeiroi is unlikely, given the context of divinities occurring with them. More probably, these scenes reflect a local Etruscan myth.

75. In fig. 252, a detail from a red-figured Apulian amphora from Ruvo now in the Hermitage, the two Horai are identified by an accompanying inscription. One of these figures is mistakenly described as dancing by Hanfmann, op. cit., II, 136, no. 10.

76. For documentation of the following general remarks regarding the Horai, see Rapp, loc. cit., cols. 2716 ff.; P. Stengel, s.v. *Horai, RE*, VIII, cols. 2300 ff.; Roger Hinks, *Myth and Allegory in Ancient Art* (Stud-

252. Detail of a red-figured Apulian amphora from
Ruvo. The Hermitage, Leningrad

gifts, their attributes are flowers, stalks of grain, and fruit. Although this original concept
of a triad of essentially undifferentiated figures reflecting a tripartite division of the year
was altered in the course of the later Classical period and correlated with a four-season year
marked by solstices and equinoxes,[77] the traditional view of these goddesses as members of
an indivisible group of three did not wholly disappear. It recurs repeatedly in Hellenistic
and Roman literature, in one form or another, from Theocritus to the very passage in
Nonnus quoted above.[78] And, since the Horai are commonly associated with other female
triads like the Graces and the Fates, a point to which we shall return, it seems reasonable
to assume that three rather than four of the six draped female figures flanking the central
figure represent the Horai. The fact that the seated figure in position V holds a mighty

ies of the Warburg Institute, VI [London, 1939]), pp.
43 ff.; and, especially, Hanfmann, op. cit., I, 78 ff.

77. Hanfmann, ibid., I, 88 ff., 104; Hinks, loc.
cit.

78. For example, Theocritus 15.103 ff. (where
they are actually numberless, i.e., pre-Hesiodic or
Homeric); Diodorus Siculus 1.26.5; and other writers
cited by Stengel, loc. cit., col. 2304, and Hanfmann,
op. cit., I, 105 ff., 117.

cluster of grapes not only fits this proposal but implies, too, that it is the group to the left of the center, comprising figures IV–VI, that represented the Horai.⁷⁹ Indeed, this triad of draped female figures, two of whom sit, while one stands, and which includes a figure characterized by a bunch of grapes, fits the formal requirements of representations of the Horai as well as their presence in this pediment suits its content and accords with their traditional role as beneficent nurses of divine and heroic children.

Nonnus' Horai are three, as his reference to the gifts they bear to the newborn child makes clear,⁸⁰ and that child is carried to them by Dike. According to the venerable tradition stemming from Hesiod and Pindar, Dike was herself one of the triad of Horai, the daughters of Zeus and Themis.⁸¹ But another genealogy, reflected in Cornutus, describes Zeus as the father of Dike *and* of the Charites *and* of the Horai.⁸² So, too, the names employed for the Horai in Attica—Thallo, Auxo, and Karpo, names obviously alluding to specific periods of the year—attest the existence of another tradition, according to which Dike was differentiated from the Horai. This less common tradition was evidently followed by Nonnus and his learned Hellenistic sources.⁸³ In any case, the very existence of this tradition, coupled with Nonnus' description of a specifically Samothracian scene, would in itself make it tempting to interpret the central figure of the pediment as Dike. But still another factor, the emphasis on Dike in the Samothracian mysteries reported by Diodorus (in the very discussion in which there occurs the previously quoted explanation of Aëtion's role as first to initiate strangers into the mysteries), heightens the plausibility of interpreting this figure as a personification of Dike.

The claim is also made that men who have taken part in the mysteries become both more pious and more just [δικαιοτέρους] and better in every respect than they were before. And this is the reason, we are told, why the most famous both of the ancient heroes and of the demigods were eagerly desirous of taking part in the initiatory rite. . . .⁸⁴

79. No. *14,* the standing figure at position VI, also held an attribute moored in the dowel hole at the back of her left shoulder. A sheaf of grain, a bunch of pomegranates, or some other variety of tall plant held in her bent left arm could easily require such doweling, especially when attached to a figure standing in the exposed, windswept northern pediment of the building. Nos. *23* and *25,* female hands that I have not ventured to attribute to one or another of the incomplete figures, also bear traces of having held attributes.

80. Hanfmann (op. cit., I, 148 f.) has evidently overlooked this implication of Nonnus' passage in stating that his Horai are the four Seasons—i.e., that they always reflect the later, solar concept.

81. *Theogony* 900 ff.; *Olympic Odes* 13.6 ff. Cf. other passages cited by Hanfmann, op. cit., I, 84 ff.

82. *Theologiae Graecae Compendium,* ed. Lang (Leipzig, 1881), p. 9, chap. 9, lines 20 ff.: οὕτω δ᾽

ἐρρήθη καὶ τῆς Δίκης πατὴρ εἶναι . . . καὶ τῶν Χαρίτων . . . καὶ τῶν Ὡρῶν. Both traditions occur in this compendium. Cf., for example, the more traditional one, p. 57, chap. 29, lines 7–8.

83. For reference to Nonnus' sources, see below, p. 301, n. 122.

84. 5.49.6 (*Samothrace,* Vol. 1, **142,** lines 41–47): γίνεσθαι δέ φασι καὶ εὐσεβεστέρους καὶ δικαιοτέρους καὶ κατὰ πᾶν βελτίονας ἑαυτῶν τοὺς τῶν μυστηρίων κοινωνήσαντας. διὸ καὶ τῶν ἀρχαίων ἡρώων τε καὶ ἡμιθέων τοὺς ἐπιφανεστάτους πεφιλοτιμῆσθαι μεταλαβεῖν τῆς τελετῆς.

Julian's allusion to "the souls of those who have lived most righteously and justly" as mounting upward toward divinity is of interest in connection with this emphasis on piety and justice in the Samothracian mysteries: *Orationes* 4.136A (ed. W. C. Wright, Loeb edn., I, 399).

What more appropriate concept in an age given to associating abstract personifications with the mysteries [85] than that the hero-founder of the rites celebrated within the Hieron, rites which left the initiate more pious and more just, should be attended at his birth by Justice herself? [86]

There remains the alternate possibility that, following the Hesiodic tradition, the Horai to whom the infant Aëtion was carried were Eunomia, Dike, and Eirene. If so, another personification, for example, Themis or Eusebeia, embodiment of that moral quality so persistently stressed in the catalogues of Samothracian *mystai*,[87] may have borne him. But, given the likelihood, as we shall see, that the theme of the pedimental sculptures reflects a literary tradition popular in Samothrace and that that tradition was known to Nonnus, whether directly or indirectly,[88] it is more probable that the central figure of the pediment represented Dike and that the seated figure characterized by a bunch of grapes may not inaccurately be called Karpo, the season of fruitfulness.

Similarly, the triad of female figures that once balanced the Horai in the right wing of the pediment lend themselves to either of two explanations. They may be either the Charites or the Moirai, both traditionally linked with the Horai.[89] If the central figure is interpreted as Themis and the group to her left as Eunomia, Dike, and Eirene, it is doubtless reasonable, continuing to follow the Hesiodic tradition and the specific text of the *Theogony*,[90] to assume that the group to the right represented the Fates: Klotho, Lachesis, and Atropos. And, to be sure, the Horai and the Moirai appeared above Zeus' head on his chryselephantine image at Megara, as well as on the Amyklean throne.[91] But the Horai and the Graces seem to have been coupled on monuments even more frequently, to judge by literary allusion. They occurred as groups on each side of Zeus' head on the throne of Phidias' cult image at Olympia, on the crown of Polykleitos' Hera of Argos, before the Temple of Athena Polias in Erythrai and, reduced to pairs, as supports of the Amyklean

---

It was Dike, it is also worth noting, who opened the gates of knowledge to Parmenides. See Hermann Diels, *Parmenides* (Berlin, 1897), frg. 1, 11 ff., and the comments of C. M. Bowra, "The Proem of Parmenides," *Classical Philology*, 32 (1937), 107 ff., including his reference to Parmenides' use of religious phraseology. (I am indebted to my husband for knowledge of this passage.)

85. Cf., for example, Eudaimonia and Arete in connection with the cult of Agdistis in Philadelphia (*Syll*[4], 985); the altars to Homonoia, Telete, Arete, Sophrosyne, etc., in the Sanctuary of Demeter at Pergamon (*AM*, 35 [1910], 457 ff.).

86. Presumably the Horai and Dike, again differentiated from each other, were present at the birth of still another divine child: see Jane E. Harrison, *Themis* (2d edn., Cambridge, 1927), pp. 5 ff., regard-

ing the Hymn of the Kouretes found at Palaiokastro in the precinct of Diktaean Zeus.

87. For the formula μύσται εὐσεβεῖς commonly used in these catalogues, see Vol. 2, pt. I, p. 150, Index 1 E e, s.v. μύστης. In the Orphic passage cited by Martin P. Nilsson, *The Dionysiac Mysteries of the Hellenistic and Roman Age* (Skrifter Utgivna av Svenska Institutet i Athen, 8°, V [Lund, 1957]), p. 124, Dike appears as the daughter of Nomos and Eusebeia.

88. Below, pp. 300 f.

89. See Rapp, loc. cit., cols. 2716 f.

90. Lines 900 ff., where the Fates are named immediately after the Horai. A statue of Themis stood next to the seated Horai in the Temple of Hera at Olympia: Pausanias 5.17.1.

91. Megara: Pausanias 1.40.4; the Amyklean throne: idem, 3.19.4.

throne.[92] Hence, it may be wiser to think of the three figures juxtaposed to the Horai in the right wing of the pediment as the Charites. Grouped in the center of the gable, yet, following tradition, divided into canonical triads, these beneficent forces formed a plastic unit into which the infant Aëtion was borne by a figure moving obliquely forward from the center of the field. For, to a degree that only one old photograph suggests (fig. 253), his nurse moves forward into the total group rather than to one side, as the majority of views erroneously imply.

Whichever of these alternative solutions is the correct one, whether Dike, Themis, or Eusebeia held the infant Aëtion or the Graces rather than the Fates were present at his birth, the essential point remains that, owing to the testimony of ancient authors writing about Samothrace, there can be little doubt that the heroic child destined to establish the Samothracian mysteries was shown in the center of the pediment being carried to the Horai to be nurtured and that his celebrated brother and sister, Dardanos and Harmonia, occupied its corners. Before considering the appropriateness of this theme or the special requirements that must have dictated its selection or its possible literary source, let us try to identify the four remaining figures of the pediment.

They consist of two antithetical pairs of reclining figures placed in positions II–III and XI–XII (fig. 211). Those at the right, the best preserved of the pedimental sculptures, lean on generalized rocky supports and turn to regard the event taking place in the center of the gable (figs. 228, 229). They provoke the obvious thought that some form of natural personification alluding to the actual locale in which the Nurturing of Aëtion took place would be both logical and conventional. Equally obvious to anyone familiar with Samothrace is the immediate suspicion that the most likely feature of its grandiose landscape to be singled out would be the great mountain known today as Phengari, Mountain of the Moon, but, in antiquity, sometimes called Mount Saoce.[93] The female character of this

92. Olympia: idem, 5.11.7; Argos: idem, 2.17.4; Erythrai: idem, 7.5.9; the Amyklean throne: loc. cit. Among the literary passages in which these triads are coupled, note, especially, the charming lines in the Homeric Hymns (Hymn to Pythian Apollo 194 ff.), where the rich-tressed Graces and the εὔφρονες Ὥραι dance with Harmonia, Hebe, and Aphrodite.

Theoretically, the triad of female figures in the right wing of the pediment could represent nymphs, especially given the existence of a cult of three nymphs in Thrace (see V. Dobrusky, "Inscriptions et monuments figurés de la Thrace," BCH, 21 [1897], 119–40) and their well-known role as the nurses of such divine children as Zeus and Hermes. But the fact that we have to reckon with two triads, rather than one, and that both the Moirai and the Charites are so frequently

associated with the Horai makes the presence of either of the latter groups more plausible than that of the nymphs. It should be noted that the three Cabiric nymphs mentioned by Strabo 10.3.21 (473c) (Samothrace, Vol. 1, 163, lines 20 ff.), together with the three Kabeiroi, the children of Kabeiro and Hephaistos, figured in the Lemnian, not the Samothracian, cult.

93. Scholia Townleiana to Iliad N 12 (Vol. 1, 18); Scholia (A) to Iliad N 12 (Vol. 1, 46). Pliny Naturalis historia 4.12.73 (Vol. 1, 7) uses the form "Mount Saocis." It was my husband's suggestion that the Latin text be emended to read Saoca instead of Saoce—i.e., that the original Greek form Σαώκη has been mistakenly transliterated, either by Pliny or as the result of a corrupt text.

253. Fragmentary striding female figure (VII.1). Kunsthistorisches Museum, Vienna

name, together with one antique description referring to the peak called by Nonnus "flowery
Saoce," [94] yields support for this suggestion.

They call the streams [flowing] from lofty places "collectors," thanks to the overlying terrain, where
the so-called Saoces lies at hand and has, not far from the peak, rough and ravine-like places able
to receive most of the rainwaters.[95]

According to Conze, a fragmentary rhyton terminating in a calf's head was found
with the pedimental sculptures and fitted a broken surface on this figure. Although this
object had already been lost by Schober's time, it is evident that the figure's left hand has

94. *Dionysiaca* 13.397 (Vol. 1, **69**).
95. *Geoponica* 2.6.10. Cf. Vol. 1, under **18**.

been prepared for an attribute to be fitted against it below the thumb joint, and there is no reason, therefore, to doubt Conze's statement. A rhyton, alluding to the streams collecting on its slopes, would be an entirely appropriate attribute for a personification of Mount Saoce.[96]

If there is reason to interpret this reclining female figure as Mount Saoce, no mighty river or other feature of the Samothracian landscape exists to aid us in identifying the reclining male next to her (figs. 228, 255). Nor does any other natural feature of the island seem to have impressed ancient commentators, who mention only its rugged mountain rising from the sea and towering over the North Aegean. But one other logical member of the *dramatis personae* of the pediment is repeatedly mentioned: Saon, eponymous hero of Samothrace. According to Diodorus, after the great flood,

one of the inhabitants of the island, a certain Saon, who was a son, some say, of Zeus and a nymph, but, according to others, of Hermes and Rhene, gathered into one body the peoples who were dwelling in scattered habitations and established laws for them; and he was given the name Saon after the island, but the multitude of the people he distributed among five tribes which he named after his sons.[97]

It is worth remarking, in connection with the cast of Samothracian characters selected to appear in the pediment, that in the very next sentence Diodorus continues:

And while the Samothracians were living under a government of this kind, they say that there were born in that land to Zeus and Elektra, who was one of the Atlantids, Dardanos and Iasion [Aëtion] and Harmonia.

Given the primary theme of the pedimental sculptures and its emphasis on heroic figures responsible for the installation of the rites in Samothrace and the mission of establishing them in the Troad, no more appropriate figure could have been included among these founders of rites, institutions, and a city than Saon, establisher of laws and organizer

---

96. It is interesting to note that the rhyton occurs as an attribute within the Cabiric circle. Among the coin types of Thessalonike from the Augustan to the Gallienic periods, there is one bearing on its reverse a standing Kabeir equipped with two attributes—a hammer and a rhyton having a shape similar to that recorded by Conze. Cf. Hugo Gaebler, *Die antiken Münzen von Makedonia und Paionia* (Theodor Wiegand, *Die antiken Münzen Nord-Griechenlands*, III [Berlin, 1935]), pp. 123 f. and pl. 23, nos. 25–27. For ritual use of rhyta, cf. M. Rostovtzeff, *Iranians and Greeks in South Russia* (Oxford, 1922), p. 105 and pl. 23, no. 2; and E. von Stern, "Die politische und sociale Structur der Griechencolonien am Nordufer des Schwarzmeergebietes," *Hermes*, 50 (1915), 221.

The lost Samothracian rhyton is grouped with similar vessels, both actual examples of silver or bronze and representations of such objects in sculpture and painting, in Ernst Buschor's article, "Das Krokodil des Sotades," *Münchner Jahrbuch der bildenden Kunst*, 11 (1919/20), 29.

97. 5.48.1 (Vol. 1, 32, lines 40 ff.). For the variant form "Samon," see Dionysius of Halikarnassos *Antiquitates Romanae* 1.61.3 (Vol. 1, 59, lines 9–13: "They called the island Samothrace, a name compounded of the name of a man and the name of a place. For it belongs to Thrace and its first settler was Samon, the son of Hermes and a nymph of Cyllene, named Rhene." The tradition of a place-name, Saos or Saon, employed for the mountain or the island as a whole occurs in certain other sources: Vol. 1, **16, 22, 37, 53, 53a, 157, 226a**, lines 10 f. Cf. also the explanation given by Eustathius, ibid., **39**, and Hemberg's suggestion (pp. 119 f.) that the Samothracian priestly title "Sai" derives from the name of the island's first heroic inhabitant.

of the political life of the island. Probably he was bearded, and he evidently held some revealing attribute in his left hand. But its nature must remain uncertain.

If the reclining figures in Vienna can be plausibly interpreted as Saon and Mount Saoce, their counterparts in the left wing of the gable are far more elusive. The only clues to their identity, the two right feet, Nos. *18* and *19* (figs. 237–239), belonged to reclining figures who stretched their legs toward the spectator's left. In predictable reversal of the position adopted by the balancing figures at XI–XII, they crossed their right legs over their left.

One wonders, again, whether either of these recumbent figures can have alluded to some natural or geographical feature characteristic of Samothrace. As we have seen, there is no evidence that any feature of the local landscape, apart from its majestic mountain, was singled out for comment in antiquity. But the very fact that the seat of the cult was an island and that the voyagers who came to Samothrace to be initiated into its mysterious and saving rites believed that they gained protection at sea [98] might well have suggested the appropriateness of some allusion to its insular character. Among the divinities regularly represented as barefoot and reclining, one, Okeanos, not only fits the formal requirements of the pediment but also seems to have been especially and understandably associated with islands. Father of all rivers, brooks, and streams, together with his spouse Tethys the primordial source of life, he is shown as a bearded, half-nude figure leaning on a sea monster or vessel and holding one or more of a variety of attributes, including a cornucopia, reeds, or a rudder.[99] It is unto Okeanos and Titan Tethys that the islands gather, led by Delos, to paraphrase Callimachus' words.[100] What is more, Okeanos is also associated with the Seasons by Nonnus [101] (as he so often appears with them on Season sarcophagi [102]), and Plutarch refers to Tethys as "the kindly nurse and provider of all things." [103] Hence, the presence of these two figures in the pediment would both intensify and amplify its emphasis on the benign nurturing of life and, in addition, introduce into the setting of the main action a specific reference to the geographical locale of the Sanctuary, to the nature of Samothrace as an island.

Obviously, the suggestion that Okeanos and Tethys figured in the pediment and that

98. Cf., for example, Vol. 1, **174, 174***a***, 179, 226***a*, **227, 229, 229***b***, 229***c***, 229***g***, 229***h***, 230, 233.**

99. Regarding Okeanos, see s.v. *Okeanos* ('Ὠκεανός), Roscher, III, pt. 1, cols. 809 ff., and *RE*, XVII, cols. 2308 ff.; regarding Tethys, see s.v. *Tethys* (Τηθύς), Roscher, V, cols. 394 ff. Their children, too, the life-giving rivers, streams, and brooks, were known as κουροτρόφοι.

100. Hymn IV, lines 16 ff., regarding Delos:
ἀλλά οἱ οὐ νεμεσητὸν ἐνὶ πρώτῃσι λέγεσθαι,
ὁππότ' ἐς Ὠκεανόν τε καὶ ἐς Τιτηνίδα Τηθὺν

νῆσοι ἀολλίζονται, ἀεὶ δ' ἔξαρχος ὁδεύει.
It is interesting to note that this poem is dated in the year 271 B.C. See A. W. Mair's introduction to *Callimachus and Lycophron*, Loeb edn., p. 29.

101. *Dionysiaca* 12, passim.

102. See Hanfmann, op. cit. (above, n. 72), passim.

103. *De Iside et Osiride* (*Moralia* 364D): τὸν γὰρ Ὠκεανὸν Ὄσιριν εἶναι, τὴν δὲ Τηθὺν Ἶσιν, ὡς τιθηνουμένην πάντα καὶ συνεκτρέφουσαν. (Ed. F. C. Babbitt, Loeb edn., V, 82–83.) Cf. also *Iliad* Ξ 200 ff., 301 ff.; Plato *Cratylus* 402B–C.

the two right feet in Vienna, one bare, the other sandaled, are to be interpreted as the sole reflections of this particular pair of reclining divinities is at best hypothetical. But both their normal iconographic type and their widely attested functions make them the most suitable candidates for the lost figures that once occupied positions II and III.[104]

To recapitulate: thanks to the testimony of ancient writers, for the most part writers referring specifically to Samothrace and its cult, it is possible to interpret the so fragmentarily preserved sculptures from the northern pediment of the Hieron. Its primary theme was the Nurturing of Aëtion. The infant destined to establish the Samothracian mysteries appeared in the center of the pediment in the arms of a mighty striding figure, probably Dike, who bore him to the Horai, attended by the Charites or Moirai, to be reared. His elder brother and sister [105] reclined in the corners of the gable: Dardanos, who later carried the rites to Troy, and Harmonia, whose marriage to Kadmos was celebrated in the annual festival.[106] Between these prime characters in the Samothracian legend lay two pairs of reclining figures: to the right, Saon, eponymous hero of the islanders, and Mount Saoce, personification of the grandiose mountain that dominated their land; to the left, two counterparts, possibly Okeanos and Tethys, life-giving forces associated with islands. All four turned to regard this auspicious moment in Aëtion's life, as did their neighbors, Harmonia and Dardanos.

The choice of this theme and the selection of these accessory figures doubtless reflects the special problem posed by the use of meaningful decoration on the exterior of the Hieron. On the one hand, the Sanctuary was accessible to all visitors, initiated and uninitiated alike; on the other, this building in which the *epopteia* took place could be entered only by

104. Carl Robert, *Archaeologische Hermeneutik* (Berlin, 1919), p. 347, has suggested that the seated female figure behind and next to Okeanos on the well-known sarcophagus in the Villa Medici, representing the Judgment of Paris, is Tethys. If he was correct, her presence adjacent to rather than opposite Okeanos on this monument is of interest not only because of its analogy to the coupling of these figures proposed above, but also because this position evidently differentiates Tethys from Tellus, who here, as elsewhere on Roman sarcophagi, is juxtaposed to Okeanos. See, for example, Hanfmann, op. cit., I, 38, 257; II, 18, n. 49, and 102, n. 131. It may be worth noting that there are monuments on which Okeanos appears in the context of the newly-born or childish Apollo and Artemis: O. Brendel, "The Corbridge Lanx," *JRS*, 31 (1941), 120 ff.

It should be remarked that the fact that the male figure in position XI leans on a rocky support, rather than on any of the supports alluding to or representing the element of water regularly employed for Okeanos, eliminates the possibility that that statue could have represented a marine divinity.

105. That Nonnus' characterization of Dardanos and Aëtion (*Dionysiaca* 3.180 ff.; Vol. 1, 68), implying, as it does, that Aëtion was the younger, was not simply the product of poetic license but was rooted in earlier tradition is established by the reflection of this same tradition in the pedimental sculptures. Various traditions existed, and it is interesting to note that Nonnus evidently tried hard to reconcile them. In presenting Harmonia as the child of Aphrodite and Ares, brought up by Elektra as foster-mother, along with her younger child Emathion-Aëtion (3.373 ff.), he was clearly attempting to reconcile the divergent traditions that made Harmonia either the daughter of Aphrodite and Ares or, like Dardanos and Aëtion, a child of Zeus and Elektra. Of course, it is conceivable that there was earlier precedent for this solution. And, in the present instance, it is likely that the presentation of Dardanos and Aëtion as brothers rather than twins in both the pediment and Nonnus' poem reflects the derivation of this motif from a common source. Cf. below, pp. 300 f.

106. Scholia to Euripides *Phoenissae* 7 (Vol. 1, 75). See also *Guide*², pp. 24 ff.; text II, p. 40, n. 183.

epoptai or by those who, having already become *mystai* and passed the rite of confession preliminary to the *epopteia,* were to be admitted to that higher degree.[107] No overt allusion to the mysterious content of the rites performed in either the Anaktoron or the Hieron was permissible, as the literary sources referring to the Samothracian cult repeatedly attest. Where Herodotus pointedly stops short of any revealing remark, Diodorus explicitly states:

Now the details of the initiation are guarded among the matters not to be divulged, and are communicated to the initiated alone;

and

it is not lawful . . . for any but the initiated to hear about the mysteries.[108]

Hence, the meaningful subject matter that could be depicted in a permanently and publicly visible part of the Sanctuary was severely restricted.

But, as the very coexistence in the Sanctuary of a public annual festival and of rites limited to initiates reflects,[109] and as the constant differentiation in the literary sources between Samothracian legends known to all and the crucial content of the mysteries indicates, two categories or two levels of experience and reference existed. Obviously, the thematic material of the pedimental sculptures of the Hieron could be drawn only from aspects of the cult that were public knowledge. And what would be more appropriate decoration for the *epopteion* than a scene emphasizing the birth and nurturing of the heroic founder of the very rites taking place within it and alluding, in addition, not only to the transplanting of those rites beyond Samothrace by his brother and the role of his sister in the annual festival, but also to another ancestral figure, the island's eponymous hero? [110] This cast of characters, all of the utmost significance in the history of the Sanctuary, performed publicly-viewed parts on the Samothracian stage. At once meaningful and unrevealing, they and their actions provided the ideal content for a scene to be viewed by both initiate and uninitiate. It is altogether possible that that scene held a deeper meaning to the former than to the latter, that to the initiate these figures conveyed a still more profound content. The presence of a

107. See text II, pp. 17 ff.

108. 5.49.5 and 5.48.4 (Vol. 1, **142**, lines 36 ff., 4 f., respectively).

109. See *Guide²*, pp. 21–35, for a general statement on the Samothracian religion.

110. In emphasizing the appropriateness of this scene, given the special requirements of the Hieron, I do not overlook the obvious fact that behind the choice of such a subject there lay, too, the classical tradition of representing divine or heroic births in pedimental sculptures and on the bases of cult images. Indeed, a related solution has been proposed for the pediment of the Argive Heraion, in which the Birth of Zeus was

represented: see Etienne Lapalus, *Le fronton sculpté en Grèce des origines à la fin du IVᵉ siècle* (Bibliothèque des Écoles françaises d'Athènes et de Rome, 165 [Paris, 1947]), pp. 195 ff., 430, for a summary of earlier discussions of and bibliography on this topic. For the appearance of such scenes on the bases of cult images, see Semni Papaspyridi-Karusu, "Alkamenes und das Hephaisteion," *AM,* 69/70 (1954/55), 80 ff. H. Herter, "Das Kind im Zeitalter des Hellenismus," *Bonner Jahrbücher,* 132 (1927), 250 ff., ignores or underestimates this tradition in his thesis that the child as such—his birth, nurturing, and behavior—does not appear and is not of interest in poetry and art until the Hellenistic age.

crucial figure evidently alluding to justice or piety, those qualities characteristic of the initiate, may point in that direction. If so, we cannot fathom that deeper content.[111]

Finally, it should be remarked that it is conceivable, but by no means certain or necessary, that the pedimental sculptures contained a faint Bacchic allusion. The grapes held by the seated Hora (fig. 233) are satisfactorily explained as a normal seasonal attribute. But the fact remains that grapes occurred in the overtly Bacchic context of the sculptures of the pronaos ceiling.[112] For obvious reasons, Dionysos and the Horai, or one specific Hora, shared this attribute. Yet the presence of an altar to the god in the sanctuary of the Horai in Athens [113] and the legend that Hephaistos gave an image of Dionysos to Dardanos,[114] in conjunction with the previously cited evidence of Dionysos' having become a *symbomos* of the Great Gods by the second century [115] and of the Bacchic imagery in the pronaos, suggest that the seated Hora in the pediment may have provided a dual allusion, a subtle link in content between pediment and ceiling.[116]

The degree to which the incompletely preserved passages in ancient literature referring to Samothrace, its cult, and its legends have shed light on the meaning of the fragmentary pedimental sculptures of the Hieron raises a last interesting question. Is it possible that certain later writers—for example, Nonnus—drew on a lost literary work that provided the basic program for these sculptures? According to the late Roman rhetorician Menander of Laodikeia, genealogic hymns constituted a specific category of ancient literature.

But since this literary form is found among the ancients, and some ere this have sung of the birth of Dionysos and others of the birth of Apollo, and Alcaeus of that of Hephaestos also and again of that of Hermes, I have made it a separate class. . . . The form is useful only to the poet, never to

111. For this question of stories having a double content, one commonly divulged, the other revealed only in the mystery rites, see Odo Casel, *De philosophorum graecorum silentio mystico* (*RVV*, XVI, pt. 2 [Giessen, 1919]), 8, 15 f.; and for the dual aspect of public ceremonies and initiation in the cult of Magna Mater, see Henri Graillot, *Le culte de Cybèle* (Bibliothèque des Écoles françaises d'Athènes et de Rome, 107 [Paris, 1912]), pp. 174 ff. (I owe these references to my husband.) See also the brief remarks of Salviat, op. cit. (above, n. 25), p. 143.

112. Above, pp. 252 f.

113. Athenaeus *Deipnosophistae* 2.38c. The fact that this altar is reported to have been a gift of Amphiktyon implies that the tradition linking the Horai with Dionysos was a venerable one. Cf. also the previously cited passage in Nonnus (above, n. 69).

114. Pausanias 7.19.6.

115. Above, pp. 252 f.

116. Chapouthier, pp. 236 f., apropos of this

figure and the rhyton once held by the statue interpreted here as Mt. Saoce, puzzled over the implications of grapes and wine in the Samothracian context. But I am totally at a loss to understand how Charles Picard (in a review of B. Hemberg, *Die Kabiren,* in *Revue de l'histoire des religions,* 141/42 [1952], 222) could remark: "au fronton Nord du Nouveau-Temple, on a rencontré le dionysiaque à la place triomphale, *avec le dieu et tout son cortège des fervants de la grappe et du pressoir.*" (Italics mine.) This statement, together with his additional reference to the pediments as "dionysiaque" (*Manuel d'archéologie grecque* [Paris, 1935], I, 325, n. 4), and the equally fanciful remarks of Fernand Robert, *Thymélè* (Bibliothèque des Écoles françaises d'Athènes et de Rome, 147 [Paris, 1939]), p. 256, and in a review of Hemberg, *Die Kabiren,* in *RA,* 45 (1955), 89, regarding "le jeune dieu identifié de Dionysos" (!) in Samothracian legend require no refutation.

the prose writer; for the one deals with the midwifery of the Graces and the nursing of the Seasons and the like, whereas the other will of necessity express himself as briefly as possible.[117]

This statement is of interest not only because it offers additional confirmation of the standard function of the Seasons and the Graces illustrated in the pediment of the Hieron, but also because it suggests that the poems written by Herodes of Priene about Dardanos, Aëtion, Kadmos, and Harmonia [118] may have belonged to that category of literature. And if we recall that an inscription found in Priene records that the people of Samothrace awarded honors to Herodes for these poems in the very century in which the porch of the Hieron was completed,[119] it is tempting to consider that one may have been derived from the other. The more likely alternative, in this case, is that the lost poems provided the program of the pediment.[120] Again, if a lost poem, whether by Herodes or another, provided the program of the pediment and later served as one of the sources for Nonnus' information about Samothrace, the fact that the basic motif of the pediment recurs in his narrative would be entirely understandable.[121] Some such source he must have had. And it is on precisely such learned Hellenistic poems that he is known to have drawn.[122]

So much and no more can be deduced about the content of the pedimental sculptures.

Although only one previous attempt has been made to interpret the pedimental sculptures of the Hieron in the ninety years since their discovery, they have figured repeatedly, if

117. Περὶ ἐπιδεικτικῶν 7 (*Rhetores Graeci*, ed. L. Spengel [Leipzig, 1856], III, 340). The translation quoted above is that of J. M. Edmonds, *Lyra Graeca*, Loeb edn., I, 323.

118. Cf. *Samothrace*, Vol. 1, pp. 57 f., **136** n.

119. See F. Frhr. Hiller von Gaertringen, *Inschriften von Priene* (Berlin, 1906), nos. 68–70, pp. 66 f.; *FGrHist*, 548 F 6; *IG*, XII (8), p. 38, *ad a.* 150; and especially Salviat, op. cit., pp. 142–45, and L. Robert's review of Vol. 2, pt. i, in *Gnomon*, 35 (1963), 59 f., for discussion of and bibliography on this decree.

120. Retention of the archaic-classical concept of the three Horai at a time when they had generally been replaced in art by the four Seasons would be easily accounted for by such dependence, since, as has been remarked above (p. 292), that original concept lingered on in literature.

For speculation on the implications of these interrelationships with regard to the building history of the Hieron, see text ii, pp. 77 f.

121. Otherwise, one must assume that Nonnus' familiarity with Samothracian motifs was partially the result of personal knowledge of the Sanctuary, as Hemberg (p. 117) hesitantly suggested. Although any visit that he could have paid it would presumably have

taken place after the official cessation of the cult, the earthquake which caused the collapse of its buildings did not take place until long after his lifetime, quite apart from the fact that its traditions, forms, and practices doubtless remained common knowledge for a long time.

122. See the discussions of Nonnus, his sources, and his reliability by Rudolf Keydell, *RE*, XVII, s.v. *Nonnos*, cols. 904 ff., and Otto Eissfeldt, *Ras Schamra und Sanchunjaton* (*Beiträge zur Religionsgeschichte des Altertums*, 4 [Halle/Saale, 1939]), pp. 128 ff.

Apropos of Samothracian literary sources of value for the interpretation of the pediment, the recurrence of several of its motifs in the coherent section of Diodorus' account of Samothracian cult and myth should not be overlooked. Not only do the primary figures Dardanos, Aëtion, and Harmonia appear in it, but also Saon, all four being described and their roles defined. In addition, there is his clear statement regarding the character of the mysteries and their secrecy. Obviously Diodorus' knowledge about Samothrace was of the best, as his remarks about its native language—now confirmed in Vol. 2, pt. ii—would in themselves indicate. Cf. Salviat's suggestion, op. cit., p. 142, n. 5, that Diodorus drew on "la poésie agonistique de Samothrace."

briefly, in general discussions of Hellenistic sculpture and Hellenistic style.[123] With the exception of Schober,[124] whose mistakenly arrived-at but essentially correct mid-second-century date found but one solitary supporter before ourselves, every writer alluding to these sculptures has dated them at some point in the third century B.C.[125] Ultimately, this date was derived from Conze's original suggestion that the "New Temple" must have been built in the same general phase of Samothracian history as the Arsinoeion and the Ptolemaion.[126] Its widespread acceptance and retention are ironic, given the fact that throughout the third century no pediment existed within which to place these sculptures, since, as we have seen, the building remained incomplete and façadeless for more than a century and a half, once work on it was interrupted late in the fourth century.[127] Before thorough investigation of their architectural milieu, these fragmentary sculptures were understandably difficult to date. Their incompleteness still makes it futile to consider them from the standpoint of iconographic type,[128] but it is not so great as to prevent us from making certain technical and stylistic observations about them. Further consideration of their date is best postponed until they have been examined from this standpoint.

Viewed as a whole, the pedimental composition appears to have been classicistic in

123. The four figures included in Hauser's restoration of the façade, *S,I*, pl. 42, appear in S. Reinach, *Répertoire de la statuaire grecque et romaine*, II, pt. 2 (Paris, 1898), 515, nos. 4, 5, 7 (our Nos. *12, 11, 16*, respectively); and VI (Paris, 1930), 132, nos. 6, 7 (our No. *1*).

124. For further reference to the bases of Schober's date, see above, pp. 16 f. and nn. 42, 43. His view was accepted by Ernst Pfuhl, "Spätionische Plastik," *JDAI*, 50 (1935), 38, n. 1. We have reported the second-century date of the porch and its sculptures since 1950: cf. *Hesperia*, 19 (1950), 5; ibid., 20 (1951), 23, n. 85; *Guide*, pp. 61, 78, 87; *Guide*², pp. 61, 81, 90 f.

125. In the first decades of the third century: Martin Schede, "Zu Philiskos, Archelaos und den Musen," *RM*, 35 (1920), 82; Franz Studniczka, "Imagines illustrium," *JDAI*, 38/39 (1923/24), 123, and "Artemis und Iphigenia," *Abh. sächs. Ak.*, Phil.-hist. Kl., 37 (1925), no. 5, p. 82; A. Rumpf, "Classical and Post-Classical Greek Painting," *JHS*, 67 (1947), 16.

Mid-third century: W. Zschietzschmann, *Die hellenistische und römische Kunst* (*Die antike Kunst*, II, pt. 2 [Potsdam, 1939]), p. 37; Gerhard Kleiner, *Tanagrafiguren* (*JDAI*, Suppl. 15 [Berlin, 1942]), pp. 153 ff.; Kähler, op. cit. (above, n. 17), pp. 73 f., 103, 178, n. 58; Georg Lippold, *Die griechische Plastik* (*Handbuch der Archäologie*, III, pt. 1 [Munich, 1950]), p. 318 and pl. 153, figs. 2, 4; Peter Hommel, *Studien zu den römischen Figurengiebeln der Kaiserzeit* (Berlin, 1954), p. 30 and n. 277; Tobias Dohrn, "Gefaltete und verschränkte Hände," *JDAI*, 70 (1955), 62.

First half of the third century: Lawrence, op. cit. (above, n. 19), p. 106.

Third century: Fritz Eichler, *Führer durch die Antikensammlung* (Vienna, 1926), p. 28; Rudolf Horn, "Stehende weibliche Gewandstatuen in der hellenistischen Plastik" (*RM*, Suppl. 2 [Munich, 1931]), pp. 5 f., 47; by implication, A. S. Murray in his review of *S,I* in *The Academy*, 9 (1876), 269; and Georges Perrot in his review of the same volume, *Journal des savants*, 1877, p. 375.

126. *S,I*, pp. 24, 26; especially, *S,II*, pp. 25, 112.

127. For discussion of the building periods and history of the Hieron, see above, pp. 84 ff.; text II, pp. 70 ff., 79 ff., 124 ff.

128. It is needless, too, to cite obvious examples of the earlier classical groups composed of an adult female figure carrying an infant or of half-draped reclining figures. But for monuments representing the related theme of Hermes taking the infant Dionysos to a nymph or nymphs to be nurtured, see George M. A. Hanfmann, "Notes on the Mosaics from Antioch," *AJA*, 43 (1939), 229 ff.; Doro Levi, *Antioch Pavement Mosaics* (Princeton, 1947), I, 286 ff. In *The Season Sarcophagus in Dumbarton Oaks* (n. 72, above), I, 113, Hanfmann suggested that Philostratus' description of the birth of Hermes (above, p. 290) might have been derived from a Hellenistic painting similar in type to this late antique mosaic. In the same context, he remarked, very properly as we now see: "There may have been other Hellenistic works of art, lost to us, which portrayed the Horae in traditional mythological scenes."

its emphasis on balance and symmetry. An orderly sequence of figures, each occupying the total space allotted to it and in no case overlapping another, was distributed throughout the gable. The right and left wings of the pediment seem to have been composed of literally antithetical counterparts at positions II–III and XI–XII—to judge by the evidence of Nos. *18* and *19*—and pairs of adjacent figures to have echoed each other in posture. Whether seated, standing, or reclining, all figures either leaned on one arm or held one in a bent, angular position, as all appear to have turned their gaze toward the center of the field. But this very action and the turning or twisting of the body attendant upon it animated the composition. Together with the recurrent obliquity of position characteristic of individual figures, the slight nuances differentiating arms and legs in their essentially antithetical positions, their varied combinations of clothing and fabric, and the presence of both draped and half-draped figures, it resulted in a composition marked by considerable, if subtle, variety and by undulating movement.[129]

Although certain stylistic features recur throughout the pediment—for example, boneless hands having gently curved backs—the preserved fragments differ from each other sufficiently in style and execution to indicate that the thirteen original figures were carved by at least six, more probably seven, sculptors.

Chief among them, in all likelihood, was the master who executed the mighty figure in the center of the pediment (figs. 213, 214, 254). The heavy himation worn over her crinkly chiton is boldly carved, its few quiet areas set off by the strong heavy contours of curved or looped ridges and deep, shadow-filled hollows. Its large, powerful forms contrast with the narrow, animated crinkles of the chiton which seems to stream over her body in rivulets that collect into projecting windswept billows. Yet in spite of their complexity of texture, pattern, and modeling, these heavy draperies in no way impair our sense of the underlying structure and movement of the figure. Vigorous rather than delicate, it is the most dynamic of the preserved figures even in its present incomplete state. No other statue from the pediment can be ascribed to the hand of the leading master who carved this figure, as no other stands on a plinth-like base like hers.[130]

It is equally obvious that the two reclining figures at positions XI and XII (figs. 228,

129. Unfortunately, all the larger, better preserved figures are mounted and exhibited (hence, must be photographed) as though they had sat, reclined, or moved parallel to the plane of both the tympanum wall and the horizontal geison. This was decidedly not the case, as investigation of their weathering and the angles from which they were intended to be seen—i.e., for which they were completely executed—makes clear.

Kähler, op. cit. (n. 17, above), p. 74, was quite correct in emphasizing that the pedimental figures were forced to participate in a general event through the turning of their heads.

130. Unfortunately, there is no record as to whether the main figures exhibited in Vienna had dowel holes on their undersurfaces or not, and these undersurfaces are today virtually inaccessible. The incompletely preserved corner figure in Samothrace lacks any dowel hole but conceivably had one. Thus, since the low course that served as the floor of the pediment is no longer extant (see above, pp. 106 f.), it is not possible to make any specific statement regarding the fashion in which the pedimental sculptures were attached to this lost floor.

254. Fragmentary striding female figure (VII.1). Kunsthistorisches Museum, Vienna

255. Reclining male figure (XI.11). Kunsthistorisches Museum, Vienna

229, 255, 257) are the work of one master. In spite of their difference in sex, both are characterized by firm, relatively youthful flesh beneath which the underlying bony structure is visible; both are encased in broadly executed mantles marked by low, blunt ridges, shallow hollows, and a similar and more extensive use of the *Liegefalten* sparingly present on the central figure. They are alike to the extent of having identically-shaped, deeply-hollowed oval navels. The sculptor who executed them does not appear to have produced additional figures for the pediment.

On the contrary, the three largest and best preserved of the remaining fragments in Vienna must each be ascribed to an additional sculptor. A glance at the seated figure at position V (figs. 233, 256), her neighbor standing at VI (fig. 231), and the figure seated at IX (fig. 222) will reveal that they are not only unrelated to each other in the fashion in which their draperies have been executed, but that they are also unlike any of the three previously described figures. Neither the enveloping strands of regularly reiterated, sagging folds of heavy, rounded section on the first, nor the relatively flat but deeply slashed folds of the second, nor the firmly modeled vital forms of the third recur among them, although individual features—the presence of *Liegefalten* on the standing figure or the use of a chiton related in type but not in execution to that of the central figure—are repeated.

Finally, the child in Samothrace from the left corner of the gable (fig. 240) is the work of still another hand. Her firmly rounded abdomen is not unrelated in form to those of

305

256. Fragmentary seated draped figure (V.16). Kunsthistorisches Museum, Vienna

the reclining figures at positions XI and XII, but her fluttering, windswept drapery animated by deeply-cut baroque folds is totally unlike their flat, lamely executed mantles. The only figure to which it bears the slightest resemblance in this respect is the central one. But the resemblance is only general, springing from the vigor and movement common to both. The drapery falling over this childish body is looser and freer in movement, still more varied and complex in its contrasting folds and surfaces, than that of the striding figure. And like all the other statues from the pediment, this one lacks the sharply defined base on which the central figure stands. Clearly, it is the work of another and sixth master.

Theoretically, these six masters could have executed all thirteen of the original figures. But if we follow the clue afforded by the fact that the reclining figures in the right wing were the work of one sculptor of whom there are no certain traces elsewhere in the pediment, and take into consideration the scanty evidence yielded by the smaller fragments, it seems likely that there was a seventh master and that six of the seven carved two figures apiece, while the seventh—the sculptor responsible for the largest of the statues—produced only one. Inasmuch as that largest statue was actually a group composed of two figures, such a division of work would not be unreasonable.

To turn to details, the chlamys hanging from the arm of the figure standing to the right of the central figure (No. 5: figs. 219, 220) is sufficiently similar in character to the drapery of her counterpart to the left (No. 14: fig. 231) to suggest that this pair of standing figures was the work of one sculptor. His folds are heavy, rigid, and lifeless, marked by the use of regularly slashed hollows. If one master produced these figures and another the pair reclining to the right, and, as we have seen, one of the two intervening figures was executed by a third (figs. 222–226), it is logical to assume that both of the seated figures at positions IX and X were assigned to the same master. Furthermore, this third master not only did not execute the figures at positions I, V, and VI in the opposite wing of the pediment, but also did not produce the seated figure at IV. For although only a tiny fragment of this figure remains (No. *17:* figs. 234–236), it may be compared with the exactly analogous right foot of his figure at position IX (No. *9:* figs. 224–226). Despite their general similarity in style, these feet reflect a different eye and emphasis. The toes of No. *17*—slender, evenly spaced one from another, and slightly upturned at the tip—show an emphasis on joints, on the bony structure of the foot. Those of No. *9*, on the contrary, emphasize the fleshy surfaces and are grouped into two units, the big toe widely separated from the four others combined and set apart from it, even though the sandals worn by both these figures are notched. In all probability, the seated figure at position IV to which the separately-worked right foot No. *17* was doweled was the work of the sculptor who carved the adjacent figure at V, which is also characterized by this technical feature. And although there is no evidence that the master responsible for the reclining figures at positions XI–XII did not execute their almost wholly lost counterparts at II–III, it seems unlikely that one master— by no means the best—would have been assigned the making of four figures, when all the others appear to have made either one or two. This pair was doubtless the work of a seventh master, of whom almost no tangible trace remains. Finally, in view of all these considerations, it is plausible to assume that the only other unaccounted-for figure, the child at XIII, was made by the master who carved his counterpart at I.

To repeat: examination of the preserved sculptures of the pediment indicates that its thirteen figures were carved by at least six, more probably seven, sculptors. Six of the seven appear to have been assigned a pair of similar figures: one produced the two standing figures; two others, the two groups of seated figures; another two, the two groups of reclining figures; and the last of the six, the pair of semi-reclining children. The seventh, sculptor of the central group, may well have been the leading master, the artist responsible for the over-all design of the pediment. In any case, whoever provided this design, it was executed by sculptors of widely varied personal style and skill, some decidedly inferior to others.

If the organization of work proposed here is correct—and it would be an exceedingly reasonable and efficient one—its chief implication is of considerable interest, namely, that the pedimental sculptures of the Hieron were executed within a remarkably short time, probably within a year.[131]

131. At Epidauros, where the execution of the sculptures for each pediment of the Temple of Askle- pios took about two years, only three masters were engaged on a given pediment. As the building inscrip-

257. Reclining female figure (XII.12). Kunsthistorisches Museum, Vienna

One technical feature of these sculptures deserves brief comment: the practice of carving certain members of the body separately and doweling or inserting them into surfaces especially prepared to receive them. It will be recalled that the forepart of one foot was separately worked and attached to the figures in positions II, IV, and V; that the head and neck of both figures at VIII and IX were similarly a separate unit; and that even a portion of the lower body of the latter figure was carved independently. This technique seems to have been particularly commonly employed by Pergamene sculptors, although it was evidently not limited to them.[132] Its use by artisans working both in Samothrace and in Pergamon, coupled with the previously remarked dependence of the pronaos coffer-reliefs on Pergamene tradition,[133] provokes the thought that the pedimental sculptures of the Hieron

tions indicate, a single figure required four months' work (see Johann Friedrich Crome, *Die Skulpturen des Asklepiostempel von Epidauros* [Berlin, 1951], pp. 14 f.). At the same rate, the more than twice as many sculptors at work on the pedimental figures of the Hieron could thus have completed their task in less than a year.

132. Among the Pergamene examples having separately worked heads, feet, and limbs, cf. *Pergamon*, VII, pt. 1, no. 25, pp. 46 f.; no. 45, pp. 69 ff., pl. 12; no. 47, pp. 76 ff., pls. 14, 15; no. 48, pp. 80 f., pl. 16; no. 49, pp. 81 f., pl. 17; no. 54, pp. 88 f., pl. 21; no. 57, pp. 90 ff.; nos. 60–62, pp. 92 ff., pl. 22; no. 69, pp. 100 ff., pl. 23; no. 78, pp. 107 f.; no. 89, pp. 115 f. and Beiblatt 14; no. 116, pp. 133 f., pl. 27; no. 122, pp. 137 f., pl. 29; see also ibid., pt. 2, no. 209, pp. 197 f.; no. 211, pp. 199 f.

For two non-Pergamene examples, cf. Horn, op. cit. (n. 125, above), pl. 29, fig. 1 (a fragmentary statue from Delos), and A. Maiuri, *Clara Rhodos*, II, pt. 1, no. 8, fig. 11.

133. Above, pp. 247 ff.

258. Detail from the Telephos frieze. The Pergamon Museum, Berlin

259. Fragmentary marble group. The Walters Art Gallery, Baltimore

may be linked with that same stylistic tradition. Indeed, such a suggestion has already been advanced in connection with both the central figure and the reclining figures at positions XI and XII.[134]

Although the majority of comparisons hitherto made between these statues and Pergamene figures reflect, at best, a generally analogous point of view on the part of their sculptors, one is striking and convincing: Schober's comparison of the head of our reclining female figure (No. *12:* figs. 229, 257) with a head from the Telephos frieze (fig. 258).[135]

134. Schober, pp. 21 f., followed by Pfuhl, loc. cit. (n. 124, above). But for the opposite point of view, cf. Horn, p. 98; Kleiner, p. 153; and Kähler, pp. 83 ff. (op. cit., n. 125, above).

Studniczka's emphasis on the similarity of the central figure of the pediment and the Victory of Samothrace, op. cit. (n. 125, above), pp. 120, 123, an emphasis doubtless reflecting the dynamic quality characteristic of both statues, was rightly criticized by Horn, loc. cit., and Kleiner, pp. 153 f. However, their counter comparison of this statue with the Kommodia of Thasos (pp. 24; 150, 153, respectively) is still less tenable.

Presumably, it was a comparison with this same statue, too, that motivated Rumpf, followed by Dohrn, (loc. cit., above, n. 125), in his proposal of a third-century date for the originals of the Dioskourides mosaics, a date now invalid on the basis of this comparison, whatever its merits otherwise may be.

135. *Pergamon,* III, pt. 2, pl. 36, fig. 8 (here fig. 258), cited by Schober on p. 22. Kleiner, in his discussion of the Samothracian figure (op. cit., p. 155), overlooked this telling comparison that conflicts with the incorrect date to which he clung for the pedimental sculptures.

In spite of their difference in sex, they are alike in their facial proportions, their broad, short faces, fleshy cheeks, wide, double-outlined eyes, and narrow mouths. Both are superficially carved; both show a similar sketchiness in the design and execution of the hair. Their similarity becomes even more apparent when they are compared with another, generally contemporary, sculpture in Baltimore: a fragmentary marble group of a young man bearing a child on one shoulder (fig. 259).[136] Closely related to the Samothracian and Pergamene heads in facial proportions, in the relative size of its features, and in the treatment of the eyes, this male head is, nevertheless, firmer in form and more vigorous in execution, thereby underlining the very intimacy of the relationship between the Samothracian and the Pergamene heads.[137]

The only other tangible stylistic connections between the so fragmentarily preserved pedimental statues and an at least approximately dated monument of certain provenance lead to Lagina.[138] The doughy folds separated by deep, simply carved channels, in which strong shadows collect, that characterize the chiton emerging beneath the mantle of the seated figure at position V (fig. 233) recur on the frieze of the Hekateion (fig. 260),[139] as

136. In the Walters Art Gallery: No. 23.69. According to Dorothy K. Hill, with whose kind permission this statuette is reproduced here, its provenance is unknown. Bieber, op. cit. (above, n. 20), pp. 139 f. and fig. 571, has interpreted it as a satyr carrying the child Dionysos. As far as I can see, the ears of the adult figure are invisible; hence, the identity of the figures is by no means clear. It may be worth remarking that the elder head has certain features in common with the head interpreted as Mithradates the Great by Jean Charbonneaux, "La Vénus de Milo et Mithridate le grand," *La revue des arts*, 1 (1951), 12 ff., especially fig. 8. Making allowance for the latter's character and special features as a portrait, it reflects an emphasis on the wide, smooth areas of the broad-cheeked face similar to that of the Baltimore head and is further related to it in the shape of the forehead and brows and the rather shallow treatment of the eyes. Charbonneaux dates this portrait at the end of the second century B.C.

137. Still closer to our reclining figure, especially in the sharp turn of the head and the form of the neck and breasts, is a "Nereid" published by Reinhard Lullies, *Eine Sammlung griechischer Kleinkunst* (Munich, [1955]), p. 83, no. 266. The author considers that this fragmentary marble figure belonged to a group and is an early Imperial work dependent upon a Hellenistic prototype. If so, that prototype can hardly have been other than the Samothracian figure to which it is so strikingly similar. And, again, if so, it would be the

solitary later reflection of the pedimental sculptures of the Hieron. Although I have not had an opportunity to examine this smaller figure at first hand and therefore, knowing it only from this publication and photographs with which Dr. Lullies very kindly provided me, am loath to take a definite stand in regard to its authenticity, I am puzzled by a number of technical features, in addition to the similarities already observed. Among them are the recurrence of similar breaks in the face and the character of a curious pendant lock dangling at the edge of the left cheek, quite apart from the admittedly modern undersurface of the incompletely preserved torso. In all fairness, I should add that Dr. Lullies does not share my skepticism but writes: "Die Nereide ist jedenfalls nicht eine Kopie oder Umbildung der Giebelfigur von Samothrake, geht aber möglicherweise auf ein griechisches Vorbild aus derselben Zeit zurück. Sie ist ohne Zweifel antik, also nicht etwa eine moderne Fälschung nach der Giebelfigur aus Samothrake."

138. Dated by Schober, in the most extensive discussion of the frieze yet attempted, *Der Fries des Hekateions von Lagina* (*Istanbuler Forschungen*, II [Baden bei Wien, 1933]), p. 26, in the last quarter of the second century B.C. For further reference to the date of these sculptures, see below, pp. 381 ff.

139. *Lagina*, no. 212, pp. 29 ff., fig. 7 on pl. 4. Again, Kleiner's comments on the significance of the drapery of the Samothracian figure (op. cit., pp. 154 f.), based as they are on faulty chronology, must

260. Detail of the frieze of the Hekateion at Lagina. Archaeological Museums of Istanbul

do the strongly contrasting ridges set off from smooth areas of adjacent drapery typical of Saon's mantle (cf. figs. 255, 261).[140]

The stylistic connections of these sculptures with the Telephos frieze, on the one hand, and with Lagina, on the other, are not without significance, scant, hence inconclusive, as

be discarded. Studniczka's comparison of the drapery of this statue with that of the Citharist from Boscoreale (op. cit., p. 122 [above, n. 125]) simply reflects the Hellenistic tradition behind that Roman painting (cf. my *Roman Wall Paintings from Boscoreale in the Metropolitan Museum of Art* [Cambridge, 1953], pp. 135 ff.).

140. Schober, *Lagina,* no. 221, p. 38, fig. 2, pls. 14, 15. Lippold, op. cit. (n. 125, above), p. 326, compared a marble statuette of the Nile in Stuttgart (his pl. 115, no. 3) with this Samothracian reclining figure and, evidently on the basis of this comparison and his retention of the widely accepted, incorrect third-century date for our pedimental sculptures, dated it between 280 and 230 B.C. and considered it the prototype of the later representations of the Nile. Despite their obvious similarity in position, I do not find the two figures sufficiently close in modeling or, more

especially, in style of drapery, to agree with his conclusion that the Samothracian sculptures are, therefore, to be linked with the art of Alexandria. Carl Watzinger, *Die griechische-ägyptische Sammlung Ernst von Sieglin,* I B, *Malerei und Plastik (Expedition Ernst von Sieglin,* II [Leipzig, 1927]), no. 98, pp. 111 ff. (fig. 42, pl. 43), evidently considered the Stuttgart statuette Roman in execution, if close to the Hellenistic prototype of the famous river god; and, more recently, Eugen Thiemann, *Hellenistische Vatergottheiten* (Münster Westf., 1959), pp. 126, 142, has labeled it Julio-Claudian.

Lippold's further tentative suggestion (op. cit., p. 318) that the frieze of dancing maidens which we now know belonged to the Propylon of the Temenos (see *Guide²,* pp. 58 f.) might also have belonged to the "New Temple" was, of course, wholly unfounded.

311

261. Detail of the frieze of the Hekateion at Lagina. Archaeological Museums of Istanbul

they may seem to be. They appear to reflect the physical and chronological position of the pedimental sculptures between the carved coffer lids of the pronaos and the akroteria. The former, of necessity the first of the sculptures of the porch to be put in place (thus, presumably the first to be executed), prove to have been dependent stylistically upon the earlier Gigantomachy of the Great Altar; the latter, the loftiest and presumably the last of the sculptures of the Hieron to be lifted into position, exhibit equally marked relations with the frieze of the Hekateion, as we shall see.[141] The fact that the only tangible connections between the pedimental figures and other Hellenistic sculptures again point to both the Great Altar and Lagina, monuments in themselves radically divergent in stylistic character, implies for them an intermediate position in time as well as space. It implies, too, that they were the product of local sculptors whose style was partially formed by earlier Pergamene tradition yet did not lack a certain affinity with contemporary Carian work—i.e., in both instances, with artistic currents of the eastern Aegean. The fragmentary preservation of these figures makes it unwise to press these implications further. But if the pedimental sculptures of the Hieron are, indeed, the work of local sculptors, the difficulty of dating and placing them before the chronology of their architectural milieu had been firmly es-

141. Below, pp. 381 ff.

tablished or their true akroterial companions had been discovered is all the more under-standable.[142]

For however tenuous their stylistic affiliations, their date, broadly speaking, is certain. Like the other sculptures of the porch, they cannot have been executed before the second half of the second century B.C. This date results from the fact that the upper courses of the foundation and the entire superstructure of the porch were not constructed before that time and that the building, consequently, remained façadeless for the better part of two centuries. Whether the original fourth-century building plan called for pedimental sculptures, akroteria, and richly adorned coffers, we shall never know. But within the limits of a half-century, the date of their actual execution is attested by ample archaeological evidence.[143]

Although this evidence affords a general date for the sculptures of the porch, it does not in itself allow them to be more precisely dated within the second half of the second century. The stylistic testimony seems to imply that the pedimental sculptures were pro-duced during the third quarter of the century; for, even if they were wholly devoid of sty-listic affiliations themselves, structural procedure would suggest that they be dated between the coffer reliefs and the akroteria. And since the former are unlikely to have been executed much later than the mid-century, in view of their dependence on the style of the Gigan-tomachy of the Great Altar, and the latter have analogies with the frieze at Lagina, which is normally dated toward the end of the century but quite possibly was produced somewhat earlier,[144] it is probable that the pedimental sculptures are works of the third quarter of the second century B.C. The likelihood that they were executed within a year or less lends additional credibility to this thought. While at the moment this possibility must remain a matter of speculation, the more general placing of these sculptures in the second half of the century may no longer be questioned, resting, as it does, on the solid foundation of structural, ceramic, and archaeological evidence.[145]

---

142. For specific reference to the singular fact that the stylistic differences between the pedimental sculptures and the Roman akroteria in Vienna have without exception gone unremarked before the recent discovery of their Hellenistic prototypes, see text II, pp. 109 f., 122 f.

143. The varied evidence on which this state-ment rests is presented above, pp. 246 ff.; below, pp. 381 ff. See also text II, pp. 77 f., for the fact that the very subject of the pedimental sculptures reflects offi-cial Samothracian literary taste in the second half of the second century B.C.

144. See below, pp. 381 ff.

145. One item of clothing that recurs among the pedimental figures, namely, their sandals with soles incurved or notched between the first two toes (cf. Nos. 8, 9, 15, 17), has been claimed as specifically Hel-lenistic and particularly popular in the second century by Mary Wallace, "Sutor supra crepidam," AJA, 44 (1940), 215 ff. This chronological claim has been cogently refuted by Margarete Bieber, "Ne supra crepidam sutor indicaret," ibid., 45 (1941), 62 f. The fact remains that this type of sandal was evidently especially popular in the Hellenistic period, as its oc-currence on many statues, including the following random examples, attests: Pergamon, VII, pt. 1, nos. 51–54, 62, 76, 88, 115; pt. 2, no. 209; Clara Rhodos, V, pt. 2, pls. 9, 12, 14, figs. 21, 26; Magnesia, figs. 188, 197; Kleiner, op. cit. (above, n. 125), pl. 52 a, b; Margarete Bieber, Griechische Kleidung (Berlin and

262. Pedimental statue from the Temple of Dionysos at Teos. Depot Museum, Izmir

263. Pedimental statue from the Temple of Dionysos at Teos. Depot Museum, Izmir

264. Detail of the frieze of the Temple of Dionysos at Teos. Depot Museum, Izmir

Apart from their interest as documents of the cult of the Great Gods in Samothrace, the pedimental sculptures of the Hieron are of prime importance simply as pedimental sculptures. However they have been dated in the past, they have been regarded not only as the latest but also as the only example of this most characteristic and conspicuous category of Greek art after the fourth century.[146] Actually, they are not unique. At least one other certain example of this typical manifestation of the Classical Revival of the mid-second century B.C. exists—a pedimental figure from the Temple of Dionysos at Teos (figs. 262, 263).[147] Curiously enough, considering the fame of this temple by Hermogenes and the repeated discussion of its sculptured frieze,[148] the fact that it was also embellished with

Leipzig, 1928), pls. 27, no. 2; 64, no. 1; W. Amelung, *Die Skulpturen des vaticanischen Museums,* I (Berlin, 1903), no. 176, pl. 44.

I have not been able to find an exact parallel for the variety of sandal partially preserved on No. *19.*

146. See, for example, Lapalus, op. cit. (n. 110, above), pp. 16, 30; Kähler, pp. 73 f., 103; Kleiner, p. 155. The latter's contention that the disappearance of pedimental sculpture after the fourth century constitutes an argument for dating the sculptures of the Hieron in the third century rather than the second (as Schober had proposed), i.e., by implication that survival of a form, after a considerable interval, is in itself more plausible than revival, was, of course, untenable even before the objective criteria by means of which the pedimental sculptures can now be dated were known.

But the omission of any reference either to the

sculptures of the Hieron or to the general problem of the disappearance of certain varieties of figural architectural sculpture after the early third century and their reappearance in the second century in recent handbooks on Greek sculpture (e.g., Gisela M. A. Richter, *The Sculpture and Sculptors of the Greeks,* 2d revised edn., New Haven, 1950) or, worse, on Hellenistic sculpture (e.g., Margarete Bieber, *The Sculpture of the Hellenistic Age,* rev. edn., New York, 1961) is even more astonishing.

147. I am indebted to Ahmet Dönmez for his great kindness both in providing me with the photographs reproduced above of this statue found at Teos and now in the Izmir Depot Museum (Inv. No. 99) and for checking on my queries regarding its provenance.

148. Recently extensively discussed, for example, by Walter Hahland, *JÖAI,* 38 (1950), 66 ff.

265. Seated figure from Athens. National Archaeological Museum, Athens

pedimental sculptures has escaped the attention of recent students of Greek sculpture. But this statue of a bearded, reclining male figure, long recorded by Reinach,[149] can only have come from one of the two pediments of that building, given its provenance, its indubitable character as a pedimental statue, and its style. It is precisely comparable both in drapery style and in the rendering of the torso to such a figure as the one toward the end of slab No. 175 from the frieze of that temple (fig. 264). Thus, like the Doric Hieron in Samothrace, the Ionic Temple of Dionysos in Teos was adorned with both pedimental sculptures and floral akroteria, in addition to its extensive figural frieze.[150] Doubtless they were not

149. Op. cit. (n. 123, above), IV, 28, no. 2, where it is described as: "Figure d'un fronton (?) dessinée par moi en 1880 à Téos; cf. *Rép. des reliefs*, t. I, p. 421 [i.e., the preamble to the drawings of the frieze]."

150. For reference to and illustration of Pullan's unpublished sketch of this fragmentary floral akroterion, see below, p. 363.

the only buildings for which the use of this venerable and typical feature of classical architectural sculpture was revived in the second century. Indeed, it is tempting to think that the seated figure illustrated in fig. 265 may also be interpreted as a pedimental statue—in this case, from a small Athenian monument of the later second century.[151] Be that as it may, the very fact that two conspicuous buildings, one Doric, the other Ionic, were equipped with pedimental sculpture, seemingly for the first time in nearly two centuries, indicates that this most natural and obvious feature of the Classical Revival was not peculiar to the Hieron, but that its appearance in Samothrace reflects a more widespread contemporary fashion, a fashion involving the revival of key elements of classical architectural design, as well as of those prime features of the classical tradition—figural friezes and pedimental sculptures.[152]

151. National Archaeological Museum, No. 3257. This marble figure (ca. 0.365 m. high), described by Oscar Broneer, "Excavations on the North Slope of the Akropolis," *Hesperia,* 4 (1935), 146 f., as "found at the Varvakeion on Athena Street" and interpreted as Aphrodite attended by Eros and a representation of their shrine on the north slope of the Akropolis, was originally called to my attention by my husband. When we examined it briefly in the National Museum in Athens, thanks to the courtesy of Semni Karousou, we were struck by several features easily explained if this figure, seated over a rocky cave and against a rocky background, had once formed part of the decoration of a pediment: its base (0.022 m. high) is prepared for insertion; a small vertical dowel hole (0.02 m. high × 0.018 wide × 0.015 deep) on the roughly picked back of the monument evidently served to attach it to a background. Cf. the similar dowel hole on the back of the rocky seat of the seated figure from Eleusis (National Museum, No. 201), referred to below. The date mentioned above is suggested solely because of the stylistic analogies between this figure and the Hellenistic akroterion of the Hieron. For further reference to this point, see below, n. 233.

152. For reference to the main architectural aspects and exemplars of this revival, see above, pp. 221 ff.

I wonder whether the Hellenistic date originally proposed by Treu for the pedimental figure recently republished by W. Fuchs, "Dionysos aus dem Metroon-Giebel?" *AM,* 71 (1956), 66 ff., did not point in the right general direction. Whether the figure is post-classical (i.e., early fourth century), as Fuchs believes, or classicistic is difficult to determine. Certain analogies in figure and drapery between this youth and "Saon" lead me to wonder whether the latter alternative is not possible. Unfortunately, I have not seen the statue itself nor do I venture to consider whether a second-century pediment could be fitted into the building history of Olympia.

Until recently, the date of the small replicas in Eleusis and Athens of certain figures from the west pediment of the Parthenon has seemed uncertain (cf., especially, Rhys Carpenter, "New Material for the West Pediment of the Parthenon," *Hesperia,* 1 [1932], 11 ff., 23 ff., and the additional material or remarks published earlier by D. Philios, *ArchEph,* 1890, cols. 218–21, pls. 12, 13; Maximilian Mayer, ibid., 1893, cols. 191–99; Noack, p. 87; K. Kourouniotis, *Eleusis, A Guide to the Excavations and the Museum* [Athens, 1936], p. 86; W.-H. Schuchhardt, "Die Eleusinischen Kopien nach Parthenonskulpturen," *Festschrift Kurt Bauch* [Munich and Berlin, 1957], pp. 21–28). But the latest re-examination of the building to which they are attributed appears to confirm a date in the second century A.D.: see J. N. Travlos, Χρονικά, *ArchDelt,* 16 (1960), 56–60.

See above, pp. 221 ff., for further reference to the Classical Revival of the second century.

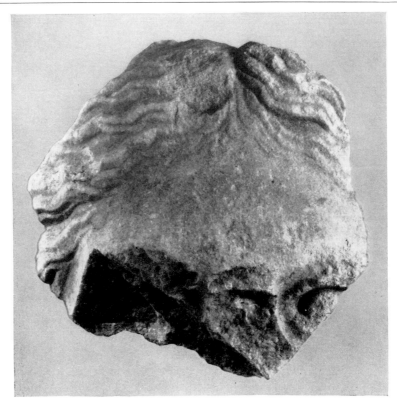

266. *SP(V)1*

THE SOUTHERN PEDIMENT

Among the additional sculptures that must be ascribed to the fabric of the Hieron are ten fragments: four found in the nineteenth century by our predecessors, hence in Vienna; and six recovered in the course of our own excavations, thus stored in the Museum in Samothrace.[153] All ten are carved of the Thasian marble used throughout the building both for its structure and for its decoration.[154]

The pieces in Vienna include:

SP(V)1. No inv. no. Storeroom of the Antikensammlung. (Fig. 266.)
Fragment of a colossal female head. The brow, part of the skull, with the hair parted in the center of the head and drawn over its sides in loose strands, and slightly more than half of the left eye are preserved. Traces of the nose are apparent. The fragment is broken on all edges of its visible periphery and sheared off at the back. Seen from the side, it is

153. It is conceivable that still another fragment stored in the Museum in Samothrace should be ascribed to this group: 52.171. Found on the surface south of the Altar Court. Broken on all sides, but retaining a portion of two folds of drapery sufficiently

unlike that of the akroterial figures to preclude associating it with them.

154. Two of the fragments now in Samothrace were mistakenly described in *Hesperia,* 20 (1951), 24, as carved of Rhodian marble.

singularly flat, giving the impression of a relief: its greatest preserved thickness is ca. 0.075 m.

Preserved height ca. 0.22 m.; preserved width ca. 0.245 m.; height of brow from part of hair to top of nose 0.11 m.; greatest width of widest lock of hair (lowest on spectator's left) 0.04 m., subdivided into two strands, each 0.02 m.

Found toward the southern end of the Hieron above the eastern foundation.[155]

SP(V)2. No inv. no. Storeroom of the Antikensammlung. (Fig. 267.)
Fragment of drapery. Broken on all but one edge and at back. The unbroken surface is oblique and picked but not dressed to be visible. Part of a broken dowel hole on rear (original preserved width 0.021 m.; present incomplete length 0.049 m.). Folds of drapery, seemingly radiating from a center, carved in very shallow relief.

Preserved height ca. 0.17 m.

SP(V)3. No inv. no. Storeroom of the Antikensammlung. (Fig. 268.)
Fragment of drapery. Entire periphery broken; sheared off at back. Gently curving in section; right edge rasped and not intended to be seen. Folds of drapery similar in effect to those of No. 2.

Preserved height ca. 0.29 m.; preserved width ca. 0.24 m.

SP(V)4. No inv. no. Storeroom of the Antikensammlung. (Fig. 269.)
Fragment of drapery? Entire periphery and back broken. Curved in section. A portion of the surface is conceivably unfinished.

Preserved dimensions ca. 0.27 × 0.245 m.

The fragments in Samothrace consist of:

SP(S)1. 49.496 A. Stored in the Samothrace Museum. (Fig. 270.)
Fragment of a colossal bust? Broken at the top and on both sides and sheared off at the back; bottom smoothly dressed, evidently to serve as resting surface. What appear to be locks of hair fall obliquely toward the left over drapery carved in lower relief. Greatest width of locks 0.04 m.; subdivided into strands each 0.015–0.02 m. wide.

Preserved height ca. 0.155 m.; preserved length 0.28 m.

Found between the Hieron and the Altar Court in an area 6–9 m. north of the southwest corner of the Hieron.

---

155. *S,I,* p. 12; cf. also p. 28.

267. *SP(V)2*

268. *SP(V)3*

269. *SP(V)4*

SP(S)2. 49.496 B. Stored in the Samothrace Museum. (Fig. 271.)
Fragment carved with two locks of hair, each ca. 0.03 m. wide, rising from a smooth background. Splintered on all sides.

Preserved length 0.19 m.

Found with 49.496 A.

270. *SP(S)1*

271. *SP(S)2*

272. *SP(S)3*

SP(S)3. 49.82. Stored in the Samothrace Museum. (Fig. 272.)
Fragment carved with a lock of hair, 0.115 m. wide, rising from a smooth background. Splintered on all sides.

Preserved length ca. 0.17 m.

Found in the center of the apse.

SP(S)4. 49.1023. Stored in the Samothrace Museum. (Fig. 273.)
Fragment of drapery. Broken on all edges save for oblique strip on upper left margin, ca. 0.05 m. wide, that has been roughly picked. On rear, broken dowel hole (original preserved width 0.22 m.). The curving surface of this fragment is carved in very low relief with what appear to be folds radiating from a boss.

Preserved width 0.18 m.; preserved height 0.14 m.

Found in the southern part of the Hieron.

SP(S)5. 57.833. Stored in the Samothrace Museum. (Fig. 274.)
Fragment of drapery. Broken on all edges except for oblique dressed strip on left side ca.

321

273. *SP(S)4*

274. *SP(S)5*

275. *SP(S)6*

0.05 m. wide. Back roughly picked or ridged. Curving surface carved in very low relief with what appear to be folds radiating from a lost center. Broken dowel hole on lower surface.

Preserved height ca. 0.135 m.

Found in the river bed south of the Hieron.

SP(S)6. 52.175. Stored in the Samothrace Museum. (Fig. 275.)

Fragment of drapery? Broken on all sides but one (right in fig.) and split at the back.

322

Preserved side roughly picked and not to be seen. On back, broken cutting 0.04 m. wide at preserved end; cutting tapers and narrows toward that end, like a lewis hole, but too little is preserved for certain identification. Curved surface carved with oblique curving lines between two of which a circular cutting is incised.

Preserved height on picked side 0.14 m.; preserved width 0.18 m.

Found 2–3 m. south of the southeastern corner of the Altar Court.

In the seven instances where the provenance of these fragments is known, they were found at the very southern end of the building—in the majority of cases, just outside it. The three fragments for which no specific provenance is recorded but which are stored among the marbles from Samothrace in the Antikensammlung, *SP(V)2–4*, are so obviously related to *SP(S)4–6* in Samothrace as to require that they be attributed to the same fragmentary group of sculptures.

This group includes fragments of two varieties: portions of a female head and of hair of colossal scale (*SP(V)1* and *SP(S)1–3*); and remnants of what appear to have been draped busts prepared for insertion into a frame or background to which they were also doweled (*SP(V)2–4* and *SP(S)4–6*).[156] Still another fragment should be considered with the extant pieces: part of a colossal hand found with the head in Vienna but no longer preserved.[157]

We have already seen that the horizontal geison of the rear pediment of the Hieron bears traces of having supported an object or objects doweled to it after its original construction.[158] The most reasonable explanation of both this technical feature and the presence and provenance of the fragmentary sculptures now under discussion is that the latter formed part of the decoration of the rear pediment. And if, as we may assume, the decorating of that pediment constituted part of the program according to which the building was completed and adorned in the second century B.C., the sculptures made for it would have been *added to* an earlier pediment, unlike the free-standing sculptures of the northern gable, which were placed in a pediment built in their own period expressly to receive them. For it is unthinkable that the rear pediment of a building that remained so long incomplete and façadeless would have been embellished with sculpture during the original building period.

The use of relief sculpture—in fact, of busts—for the decoration of pediments is not without parallel in the very period in which the Hieron was completed.[159] The tympanum of the mid-second-century Doric Temple of Isis in Serapeion A in Delos was adorned with a

156. The similarity in size of the dowel holes on the rear of *SP(V)2* and *SP(S)4* is worthy of remark.

157. *S,I*, pp. 12, 28. In his review of *S,I* in *The Academy*, 9 (1876), 259, A. S. Murray appears to have interpreted the fragments found by our predecessors as remnants of a group of statues that once stood in-

side the building, near the apse.

158. See above, p. 76.

159. See Peter Hommel, "Giebel und Himmel," *Istanbuler Mitteilungen*, 7 (1956), especially pp. 22 ff., for discussion of the varied types of monuments on which *imagines clipeatae* appear in both Hellenistic and Roman art.

276. Delos, Serapeion A. View of the Temple of Isis

bust, presumably of a divinity (fig. 276).[160] The pediment of the probably slightly earlier Gymnasium Temple in Pergamon was also prepared to receive such an image, although in this respect, as in others, it remained unfinished.[161] At the end of the century, the pediment of the exedra dedicated to Mithradates Eupator in the Samothrakion in Delos was decorated with a bust of the king (fig. 277).[162] In this ναός, where Mithradates was honored as Diony-sos, a divine or divinized being again appeared in the center of the field. Even closer in type

160. Pierre Roussel, *Les cultes égyptiens à Délos* (Nancy, 1916), pp. 56–62, 127 f.; N. M. Kontoleon, Ὁδηγὸς τῆς Δήλου (Athens, 1950), pp. 123 f.; Hommel, op. cit., p. 26. The head of the bust (assumed to have represented Helios) was originally doweled to the tondo but is now missing.

161. *Pergamon*, VI, p. 76, pl. 27, fig. 12.

162. Fernand Chapouthier, *Le Sanctuaire des dieux de Samothrace* (*Délos*, XVI), pp. 13–42, fig. 56 (here fig. 277). For revision of this preliminary reconstruction of the building, see Sven Risom, " 'Le monument de Mithridate' à Délos," *ActaA*, 19 (1948), 204 ff., especially pl. 1. Cf. also Walter H. Gross, "Die Mithradates-Kapelle auf Delos," *Antike und*

Abendland, 4 (1954), 105–17, and Hommel, op. cit., p. 27. Here, too, the face, carved as a separate piece, is missing. For the appearance of this motif in the pediment of a sarcophagus or of terracottas in the shape of a temple façade, cf., for example, Gerhard Kleiner, "Hellenistische Sarkophage in Kleinasien," *Istanbuler Mitteilungen*, 7 (1956), 8; Alda Levi, *Le terracotte figurate del Museo Nazionale di Napoli* (Florence, 1926), no. 773, pp. 173 f., and fig. 134; and Hetty Goldman et al., *Excavations at Gözlu Kule, Tarsus*, I (Princeton, 1950), no. 530, pp. 373 f., pls. 250, 251. For still later examples of *imagines clipeatae* in pediments, see Hommel, op. cit., pp. 27 ff.

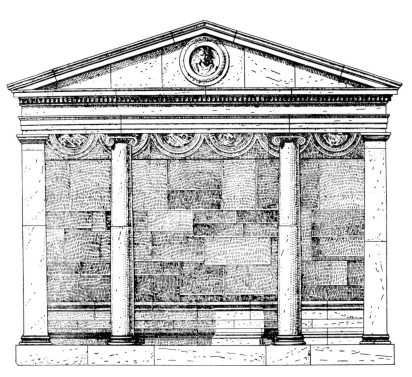

277. Delos, Samothrakion. Restored façade of the Monument of Mithradates Eupator

to the colossal female bust from the Hieron is the image of the Great Mother or Demeter represented in the pediment of an Ionic naiskos on an earlier second-century grave stele from Kertsch (fig. 278).[163] For she, too, emerges from the floor of the pediment as a bust or protome, rather than being inscribed within a tondo.

Given the exceedingly fragmentary character of the Samothracian sculptures, it would be rash to attempt a precise definition of their original appearance. Hence, they have not been represented in the restored rear elevation of the building (Pl. CIX). Nor can the number or identity of these busts be established with certainty. But their very existence lends new interest to a suggestion made long ago that one of the reliefs from the Monument of the Haterii represents the Great Gods (fig. 279).[164] The four divinities shown on it are plausibly inter-

163. G. von Kieseritzky and Carl Watzinger, *Griechische Grabreliefs aus Südrussland* (Berlin, 1909), no. 407, p. 71, and pl. 28. Dated at the beginning of the second century B.C. Here interpreted as Demeter (because of the ear of corn held in the left hand) but referred to by H. Bulle, "Eine Jagddenkmal des Kaisers Hadrians," *JDAI*, 34 (1919), 163 f., and Hommel, op. cit., p. 27, no. 1, as a city goddess (doubtless because of her mural crown).

For a curious protome of Demeter from Eleusis, cf. Otto Rubensohn, "Das Weihehaus von Eleusis und sein Allerheiligstes," *JDAI*, 70 (1955), 40 ff. It is needless, in the present context, to cite examples of the representation of female divinities in bust form, especially in Magna Graecia. But Pausanias' reference (4.16.5) to a bust-length cult image of Demeter Thesmophoros in her sanctuary at Thebes is not without interest. I am indebted to my husband for knowledge of this passage.

164. In making this proposal, R. Pettazzoni, "Una rappresentazione romana dei Kabiri di Samotracia," *Ausonia*, 3 (1908), 79–90, also suggested that

278. Grave stele from Kertsch

preted as Hermes, Persephone, Hades, and Demeter, or, in Samothracian terms, Kadmilos, Axiokersa, Axiokersos, and Axieros. Like the Samothracian images, they appear as draped busts. Both goddesses wear their hair in the same fashion as the best preserved of the Samothracian fragments $(SP(S)1)$; their hands are prominent, recalling the lost colossal hand found with that fragment.[165] If the Lateran relief is, in fact, a later reflection of the largely vanished sculptures once visible in the rear pediment of the Hieron, it implies that they were

one of the Haterii was a Samothracian initiate. Pettazzoni's interpretation of the Lateran relief was accepted by Schober, p. 14.

165. The character of that lost hand is, of course, uncertain. Theoretically, it need not have held an attribute but could have been raised in a gesture like that of the left hand of the bust of Demeter or Kore

painted on the vault of a well-known tomb at Bolshaja-Blisnitza: M. Rostovtzeff, *Ancient Decorative Painting in South Russia* (in Russian; St. Petersburg, 1913), pls. 7 (fig. 2), 8. For discussion of this important monument, see Karl Lehmann, "The Dome of Heaven," *The Art Bulletin*, 27 (1945), 4.

279. Relief from the Monument of the Haterii. The Lateran Museum, Rome

four, however unsatisfactory that number may seem for the decoration of a triangular field. The fragments themselves imply the existence of more than one bust—indeed, quite possibly, of more than one female figure. The discovery of a terracotta bust representing a bearded male divinity in a fill containing objects belonging to the Hieron increases the likelihood that at least one of the busts was male. For it is best interpreted as Axiokersos and is itself plainly a reflection of a monumental prototype dating from the second century B.C. (Cat. 177).[166] Hence, it is likely that the colossal busts added to the rear pediment when the building was completed in the second half of that century were images of the Megaloi Theoi. If so, the sculptural decoration of the rear pediment was again meaningful, displaying to initiate and uninitiate alike the powerful divinities whose mysterious and saving rites drew worshipers to the Sanctuary from far and near.

Only one of these fragmentary sculptures is sufficiently preserved to allow even a single stylistic comment: the head in Vienna $(SP(V)1)$, which invites comparison with the Aphrodite of Melos (fig. 280). On both heads, the wavy locks of hair are separated from each other by narrow, shadow-filled crevices and subdivided into two lesser strands; on both, the centrally parted hair frames a similarly shaped brow. The locks of the Samothracian frag-

166. See text II, pp. 256 ff., for discussion of this piece, which seems to be a votive terracotta. The early Imperial fill in which it was found near the southeast corner of the Hieron contained both fragments from the building itself (e.g., of the original akroteria and door studs) and quantities of vessels used in the Sanctuary. See below, pp. 329 ff., and text II, pp. 191 ff., 245, for representative examples of these finds.

It should be remarked that one fragment of a draped bust in Samothrace, $SP(S)6$, is so inferior to the others in execution as to suggest that it was one of the Roman replacements of the original second-century sculptures placed on the building in the early Imperial age. The very fact that this fragment differs from the others implies the existence of more than one bust.

For references to these repairs, see above, p. 28, and text II, pp. 79 ff., 191 ff.

280. Detail of Aphrodite from Melos. Musée du Louvre, Paris

ment are somewhat softer and looser in execution, in accord with its slightly earlier date. But it is sufficiently analogous in style to the celebrated statue in the Louvre, which has recently been convincingly dated between 120 and 90 B.C.,[167] to confirm the plausible assumption that the sculptures added to the rear pediment of the Hieron were executed in the second half of the second century B.C. as part of the elaborate program whereby the building was completed and embellished at that time.[168]

167. Jean Charbonneaux, "La Vénus de Milo et Mithridate le grand," *La revue des arts*, 1 (1951), 8 ff., and, still, more recently, *La Vénus de Milo (Opus Nobile*, 6 [1958]), especially pp. 13 ff. This date has also been accepted by Gerhard Kleiner, "Bildnis und Gestalt des Mithradates," *JDAI*, 68 (1953), 84, n. 5. The Aphrodite of Melos constitutes another example of the technique of assembling a statue from several pieces employed in executing both the pedimental and akroterial figures of the Hieron.

168. Although the earlier discovery of both Vienna fragment No. *1* and the lost fragment of a colossal hand were recalled in *Hesperia*, 20 (1951), 24, n. 89, when recovery of the Samothracian fragments *1, 2,* and *4* was reported (pp. 24 f.), the function of these pieces was not yet clear, nor had the architectural evidence in support of their attribution to the rear pediment become apparent; hence the uncertainty reflected in this preliminary report and the incorrect statement in the *Guide,* p. 63 (repeated in *Guide²,* p. 65), that only the front pediment contained sculptures. Renewed examination of all the sculptures from the Hieron in 1959, in both Samothrace and Vienna, yielded the results presented here.

281. Diagram of the restored Hellenistic central akroterion,
showing the location of the preserved fragments

THE ORIGINAL AKROTERIA

Both the northern and southern pediments of the Hieron were crowned with akroteria. An exuberant floral akroterion rose over the center of each gable, while a slender figure of Victory stood above each corner and poured a libation into the patera held in her outstretched hand (Pls. CVIII, CIX). Although the northern akroteria remained in place until the final destruction of the building in late antiquity, the original southern akroteria were replaced by Roman counterparts as the result of damage sustained by the structure, presumably in an earthquake.[169] The extensive remains of these Roman replacements, now in Vienna, were obviously recovered by our nineteenth-century predecessors in fallen position at the rear of the building; [170] but the original akroteria were excavated below the latest antique ground level and appear to have been intentionally buried in the vicinity of the pediment over which they had once presided.[171] For this reason, they are far more extensively preserved than their counterparts at the north, whose sparse remains, though sufficient to attest the existence and date of the façade akroteria, imply that—like the pedimental figures beneath them—they crashed to the ground, splintered, and very likely were largely dragged off to the nearby antique limekiln from whose periphery the little figure of Harmonia was rescued.[172]

The Central Floral Akroteria
(Pls. CXI–CXIV; Figs. 281–316)

Among the fragments of the original central akroterion of the rear, southern pediment of the Hieron, sixty-one are sufficiently well preserved to merit publication.[173] The largest, *SCA 1*, was discovered 1.0 m. east and 0.75 m. north of the southeastern corner of the building at the level of the euthynteria. The majority of the other fragments listed below were either clustered in the vicinity of this piece or excavated slightly farther to the southeast, near the terrace wall to the rear of the building. The latter, as well as sporadic fragments recovered south of the Hieron, between it and the terrace wall, were found incorporated in a fill brought into this

169. For further reference to this damage, see text II, pp. 79 ff.

170. For discussion of these sculptures, see text II, pp. 83 ff.

171. See below and p. 368, for the precise provenance of the main fragments, as well as *Hesperia*, 20 (1951), 25 f., and *Archaeology*, 7 (1954), 93, for reports on their discovery.

172. Above, pp. 274 f.

173. The additional, literally shapeless marble fragments and splinters recovered with these pieces were preserved in the hope that they might fit the rear sides of broken pieces or prove of some other value in connection with their reconstruction and interpretation. They are stored in Hall A of the Museum in Samothrace in drawers of the case where a selection of the better preserved fragments is exhibited. To itemize them here would be meaningless. Certain other fragments, although sufficiently preserved to be recognizable as splinters from this akroterion, are so weathered as to preclude identification. They, too, are stored in the same case and have been eliminated from the summary catalogue. A glance at Pl. CXI will indicate that there is ample space in the reconstruction to absorb the sheer physical bulk of innumerable additional fragments of marble.

282. *SCA 1*

area when the building was repaired. In view of the uniformity of their provenance, the specific location of the individual fragments itemized in the summary catalogue has not been included in the brief characterization of each piece.

The sixty-one intelligible fragments of the original southern central akroterion catalogued below are listed in the order of their appearance in the diagram, fig. 281, where they follow a movement leading from lower left to the summit of the double palmette, descend along the right, and rise again into the center of the field. Each fragment is portrayed, unnumbered, in the reconstruction drawing on Pl. CXI. Wherever two joining fragments have been restored without any interval of plaster, they are classified under one number (for example, *SCA 13, 19, 22, 24, 36*).[174]

> *SCA 1.* 53.651. *Archaeology*, 7 (1954), 91, 93; *Guide*, p. 78, fig. 39; *Guide²*, p. 81,
> fig. 42; *BCH*, 78 (1954), 144, fig. 40; *Pedimental Sculptures*, pp. 24 ff.,
> fig. 56. (See figs. 281, 282, showing fragment after the addition of *SCA 2,
> 3, 5–7.*)

174. The fact that many of these sixty-one fragments do not bear an individual accession number reflects the extreme corrosion of their weathered, waterworn, sugary surfaces which will not accept or retain such numbers without damage. It should be emphasized, therefore, that such pieces have at all times been kept with the numberable fragments in whose context they were found.

Nos. *11, 19, 22, 27, 32, 36, 45, 50, 55, 57* are exhibited in Hall A of the Museum in Case 1. All the remaining fragments are stored in drawers of this, the single exhibition case in that gallery.

283. *SCA 5*

Fragmentary lower left portion of the acanthus calyx-base. Sheared off at the right; broken at the upper left and top; original lower surface intact. Part of the three tiers of leaves of which the calyx-base was composed is preserved. From it spring a curving, fluted stalk, broken off at the top, and, to the left, a smaller stem emerging from a smaller leafy calyx. Traces of original contact between the smaller stem and the large stalk are preserved on the left side of the latter.

   Lower margin roughly finished. Original rear surface preserved (roughly picked) at left, indicating that the central akroterion was generally triangular in plan. The sloping surface behind the stalks (see the restored section, Pl. CXIII) is picked and contains two roughly cut dowel-like holes for a metal brace or armature.

   Preserved height 0.607 m.; preserved width at bottom 0.482 m.; depth 0.43 m.

SCA 2. 53.330. (Figs. 281, 282.)

Tip of overhanging acanthus leaf falling to the left. Broken at the right. Drill hole between two left lobes not fully pierced. Restored to No. *1* with interval of plaster.

   Preserved width 0.12 m.

SCA 3. (Figs. 281, 282.)

Tip of upright acanthus leaf restored to No. *1* with interval of plaster. Broken below.

   Preserved height 0.045 m.

SCA 4. (Fig. 281.)

Worn tip of overhanging acanthus leaf falling to the left. Broken on top and right side.

   Preserved width 0.103 m.

SCA 5. 53.301. (Figs. 281–283.)

Fragmentary ribbed, fluted stalk emerging from leafy calyx at node of fluted stem of smaller size than the related curving stalk of No. *1*. Tips of two upright acanthus leaves of top tier of main calyx (No. *1*), united with and partially overlapping its calyx. Broken at top (i.e., left) and bottom. Broken spur of original connection with stem to left of curving stalk of No. *1* is visible at the right.

Preserved height 0.18 m.

SCA 6. (Figs. 281, 282.)

Tip of upright acanthus leaf, broken below. Restored to No. *1* with slight interval of plaster, since connecting surface is not preserved.

Preserved height 0.03 m.

SCA 7. 53.331. (Figs. 281, 282.)

Tip of overhanging acanthus leaf falling to the right. Broken below. Restored to No. *1* with interval of plaster, since connecting surface is not preserved.

Preserved height 0.09 m.

SCA 8. 53.313. (Figs. 281, 284.)

Fragmentary, badly worn calyx from which three members emerge: a ribbed, fluted stalk, framed on the left by a leaf curling outward (i.e., to the left), on the right by a tendril dropping inward (toward the right). All three members are broken off close to the acanthus calyx, of which only the upper part is preserved. On the left side of this calyx, a hole ca. 0.025 m. in diameter and 0.036 m. in depth evidently received a member of the metal brace.

Preserved height 0.215 m.

284. *SCA 8*

285. SCA 11

SCA 9. (Fig. 281.)

Worn fragment of a tendril, broken at both ends.

Preserved width 0.034 m.

SCA 10. (Fig. 281.)

Worn fragment of a tendril, broken at both ends. Broken spur on inner side for connection with inner curl.

Preserved width 0.054 m.

SCA 11. 53.303. (Figs. 281, 285.)

Eight-petaled flower with upright pistil. Uppermost petal broken off, along with all but the top of a fragile stem emerging beneath the lowest petal. On the lower left and right sides, traces of original abutment against lateral objects, from which it has broken off.

Preserved height 0.113 m.

SCA 12. (Fig. 281.)

Badly worn tip of overhanging acanthus leaf falling to the right. Broken at both ends. Traces of former contact with another member on upper surface.

Preserved width 0.063 m.

SCA 13. (Fig. 281.)

Badly worn ribbed, fluted stalk curving from broken acanthus calyx. Broken above; at base, trace of leaf growing to the right. Restored from two connecting pieces.

Preserved height 0.272 m.

SCA 14. (Fig. 281.)

Badly worn fragment of ribbed, fluted stalk, broken above and below.

Preserved height 0.082 m.

286. *SCA 19*

SCA 15. (Fig. 281.)

Tip of overhanging acanthus leaf falling to the left. Broken at the right.

Preserved width 0.06 m.

SCA 16. (Fig. 281.)

Badly worn base of a half-palmette, broken above and below. Traces of contiguous palmette petals at top.

Greatest preserved width 0.06 m.

SCA 17. (Fig. 281.)

Fragment of a tendril, broken above and below.

Preserved width 0.033 m.

SCA 18. (Fig. 281.)

Badly worn fragment of a tendril, broken above and below. Back split off.

Preserved width 0.031 m.

SCA 19. 53.305. (Figs. 281, 286.)

Tip of acanthus leaf falling to the left and supporting upper tendril. Broken at the right and below. Section of tendril broken at each end and restored from two connecting pieces. Broken spur on interior of tendril for inner curl.

Preserved width of leaf 0.07 m.; preserved width of tendril 0.088 m.

SCA 20. (Fig. 281.)

Badly worn fragment of a tendril, broken at each end. Trace of spur originally abutting outer coil on exterior.

Preserved width 0.035 m.

287. *SCA 21*

288. *SCA 22*

SCA 21. 53.312. (Figs. 281, 287.)

Fragment of ribbed, fluted stalk, broken above and below. Trace of original abutment of another member on right side.

Preserved height 0.123 m.

SCA 22. 53.302 and 53.310, restored from two connecting pieces. *Pedimental Sculptures,* pp. 24 ff., fig. 57. (Figs. 281, 288, 301, 428.)

Ribbed, fluted stalk, broken at top, springing from acanthus leaf calyx at node of a fluted stalk emerging from a lower calyx, of which traces of the leaf are preserved at the lower right. One fragmentary tendril drops to the left from the upper calyx, while a portion of a second adheres to the left side of the uppermost part of the ribbed and fluted stalk. A fragmentary acanthus leaf curves up from the left and abuts both that stalk and the lower tendril. Calyx leaf chipped above and broken below. Toward the rear of this calyx, a hole ca. 0.023 m. in diameter and 0.026 m. deep for a brace.

Preserved height 0.48 m.

SCA 23. (Fig. 281.)

Badly worn fragment of a tendril, broken at both ends.

Preserved width 0.065 m.

SCA 24. (Fig. 281.)

Badly worn fragmentary rear petal of double palmette, restored from two connecting pieces. Broken at each end. Broken spur on lower surface near tip from another, abutting, member.

Preserved length 0.21 m.

SCA 25. (Fig. 281.)

Badly worn fragmentary rear petal of double palmette. Broken at each end; lower part of petal (i.e., left side) missing.

Preserved length 0.004 m.

SCA 26. (Fig. 281.)

Worn fragment of rear petal of double palmette, broken at each end.

Preserved length 0.105 m.

SCA 27. 53.308. (Figs. 281, 289.)

Fragmentary rear petal of double palmette. Chipped at tip, broken below. Trace of adjacent petal on left side.

Preserved length 0.205 m.

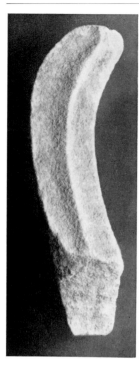

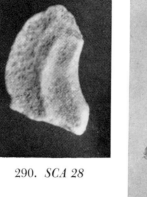

290. *SCA 28*

291. *SCA 33*

292. *SCA 36*

289. *SCA 27*

SCA 28. 49.83. (Figs. 281, 290.)
Tip of front petal of double palmette. Chipped at top, broken at bottom.
Preserved length 0.055 m.

SCA 29. (Fig. 281.)
Fragment of rear petal of double palmette, broken at each end.
Preserved length 0.093 m.

SCA 30. (Fig. 281.)
Badly worn fragment of rear petal of double palmette, broken at each end.
Preserved length 0.10 m.

SCA 31. 51.750. (Fig. 281.)
Badly worn fragment of front petal of double palmette. Chipped at tip, broken below.
Preserved length 0.054 m.

SCA 32. 49.623 A. (Fig. 281.)
Tip of front petal of double palmette, broken below.
Preserved length 0.056 m.

SCA 33. 49.623 C. (Figs. 281, 291.)

Fragment of rear petal of double palmette, broken at each end. Trace of contact with adjacent petal on right side.

Preserved length 0.103 m.

SCA 34. (Fig. 281.)

Tip of a tendril, broken below. Retains trace of spur connecting it with outer coil.

Preserved length 0.029 m.

SCA 35. (Fig. 281.)

Fragment of a tendril, broken at each end.

Preserved length 0.03 m.

SCA 36. (Figs. 281, 292.)

Fragmentary half-palmette restored from five connecting pieces. Three petals partially preserved. Traces of contact with a fourth on bottom of lowest petal, and with adjacent member on exterior of intermediate petal near tip.

Greatest preserved height 0.105 m.

SCA 37. (Fig. 281.)

Worn fragment of base of a half-palmette, retaining traces of four contiguous petals. Broken above and below.

Preserved height 0.087 m.

SCA 38. (Fig. 281.)

Badly worn acanthus calyx with stump of ribbed, fluted stalk emerging below it. Lump in interior where another, now missing, member grew from it toward the left.

Preserved height 0.143 m.

SCA 39. (Fig. 281.)

Badly worn fragment of a tendril, broken at each end.

Preserved length 0.119 m.

SCA 40. 49.821. (Fig. 281.)

Badly worn fragment of a tendril, broken at each end.

Preserved length 0.058 m.

SCA 41. (Fig. 281.)

Worn fragment of a ribbed, fluted stalk. Abutted at lower right by section of a tendril; traces of another member springing from upper right side.

Preserved length 0.155 m.

SCA 42. (Fig. 281.)

Badly worn fragment of a tendril, broken at each end. Trace of spur on exterior for connection with adjacent member.

Preserved length 0.06 m.

SCA 43. (Fig. 281.)

Fragmentary acanthus leaf growing toward the left. Broken at top, bottom, and right side.

Preserved width 0.056 m.

SCA 44. 49.30 A. (Fig. 281.)

Tip of overhanging leaf falling toward the right. Broken at the left.

Preserved width 0.077 m.

SCA 45. 53.304. (Figs. 281, 293.)

Fragmentary ribbed, fluted stalk growing from acanthus calyx from which tendril also springs to the right. Leaf abuts stalk at the right. Stalk and tendril broken above, leaf at each end, and calyx at bottom and sides.

Preserved height 0.23 m.

293. *SCA 45*

SCA 46. (Fig. 281.)

Badly worn fragmentary tendril, broken at each end. Traces of abutting member on each end.
Preserved length 0.093 m.

SCA 47. (Fig. 281.)

Badly worn fragment of a tendril, broken at each end.
Preserved length 0.053 m.

SCA 48. (Fig. 281.)

Badly worn fragment of a tendril, broken at each end. Traces of abutting member on exterior.
Preserved length 0.043 m.

SCA 49. (Fig. 281.)

Worn fragment of a tendril, broken at each end. Trace of spur on interior for connection with inner curl.
Preserved length 0.078 m.

SCA 50. (Fig. 281.)

Worn fragment of a tendril, broken at each end.
Preserved length 0.057 m.

SCA 51. (Fig. 281.)

Badly worn tip of acanthus leaf falling to the left and abutting section of tendril on that side. Sheared off at the right.
Preserved length 0.048 m.

SCA 52. (Fig. 281.)

Badly worn fragment of acanthus calyx, broken on all sides.
Preserved height 0.092 m.

SCA 53. (Fig. 281.)

Fragment of ribbed, fluted stalk, broken at each end. Visible surface patched in antiquity. Lower part of patch has split off, seemingly because an incorrectly placed hole had been drilled into it to attach it to the stalk, then abandoned, leaving the patch weak at that point. Correctly placed hole running through both patch and stalk partially preserved at right end of fragment. Patch left unribbed and unfluted.
Preserved length 0.15 m.

340

SCA 54. (Fig. 281.)

Fragment of acanthus calyx, broken at bottom. Overhanging tips of leaf broken on both sides. Retains stump of stem of round section that once grew from it.

Preserved height 0.085 m.

SCA 55. 53.311. (Fig. 281.)

Fragment of curving, fluted stalk, broken at each end. Trace of abutting member on upper right side.

Preserved height 0.23 m.

SCA 56. 52.777. (Fig. 281.)

Worn fragmentary tip of upright acanthus leaf, broken on all sides.

Preserved width 0.091 m.

SCA 57. 53.306. (Fig. 281.)

Tip of overhanging acanthus leaf falling to the right. Broken at the left.

Preserved width 0.087 m.

SCA 58. (Fig. 281.)

Worn fragmentary tip of overhanging acanthus leaf falling to the left. Broken on left side and below.

Preserved width 0.078 m.

SCA 59. (Fig. 281.)

Fragment of tip of overhanging acanthus leaf falling obliquely toward the front. Broken on top and at sides.

Preserved width 0.123 m.

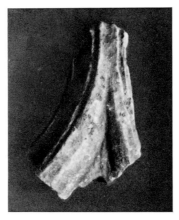

294. *SCA 60*

341

SCA 60. (Figs. 281, 294.)

Worn fragment of fork uniting two fluted, ribbed stalks. Broken at top and bottom. Traces of contact with adjacent member on right side.

Preserved height 0.17 m.

SCA 61. (Fig. 281.)

Worn fragmentary leaf, broken at each end. Trace of contact with another member on left (upper) side.

Preserved length 0.155 m.

Only seven fragments of the central akroterion of the façade were recovered in our excavations to the north and northeast of the building.[175] However few, they indicate that it was identical in scheme with the better preserved floral akroterion from the rear pediment and that, unlike this southern counterpart, it was never replaced, but remained in position until the final destruction of the building. For these fragments from the north side of the Hieron are identical in execution with the analogous pieces of the original Hellenistic central akroterion from the south. They include:

NCA (S)1. 50.564. (Fig. 281.)

Tip of rear petal of double palmette, broken at each end. Trace of contact with adjacent petal on left side.

Preserved length 0.075 m.

NCA (S)2. 55.97. (Fig. 281.)

Tip of rear petal of double palmette, broken at each end. Trace of contact with adjacent petal on right side.

Preserved length 0.105 m.

NCA (S)3. 50.600 B. (Fig. 281.)

Badly worn tip of front petal of double palmette, broken at bottom.

Preserved length 0.045 m.

NCA (S)4. 50.529 F. (Fig. 281.)

Fragment of a tendril, broken at each end.

Preserved length 0.07 m.

175. Only No. *6* is on exhibition in Hall A, the remaining pieces being kept in the previously mentioned case or (No. 7) in storage.

295. *NCA(S)6*

NCA (S) 5. 50.462 D. (Fig. 281.)
Worn fragment of an acanthus leaf, broken on all sides.
Preserved width 0.056 m.

NCA (S) 6. 50.512. (Figs. 281, 295.)
Tip of overhanging acanthus leaf falling obliquely toward the front. Snapped off at back and chipped at sides.
Preserved width 0.145 m.

NCA (S) 7. 50.528–51.218. (Fig. 281.)
Fragmentary fluted, ribbed stalk attached, at the right, to vertical section of large-scale, wind-blown leaf. Present broken edge of leaf, 51.218, restored to 50.528, fitting it break on break. Combined piece broken at top and bottom. Obliquely presented, hence summarily executed. Roughly picked on back.
Preserved height 0.26 m.

In addition to these seven fragments of certain provenance, there are five fragments in Vienna, *NCA (V) 2–6,* which must be attributed to the northern central akroterion, in spite of the fact that their specific provenance is unknown, because they wholly or partially duplicate extant pieces of both the southern Hellenistic akroterion and its Roman replacement or repeat a motif of the southern Hellenistic akroterion that was not retained in identical form on its successor. A sixth fragment, *NCA (V) 1,* which partly duplicates an element preserved on the Roman akroterion but lacking on its predecessor, might theoretically be attributed to either the northern or southern Hellenistic akroterion. Since the other Hellenistic fragments

343

in Vienna can only have come from the northern akroterion, it is reasonable to assume that this fragment was found with them. All six pieces are stored, without individual numbers, with the other akroterial fragments from Samothrace in the Antikensammlung.[176]

NCA (V)1. (Figs. 281, 296.)

Tip of a symmetrical, upright acanthus leaf drooping slightly forward. Broken below; projecting lobe chipped.

Preserved height 0.085 m.; preserved width 0.175 m.; thickness at bottom 0.045 m.

NCA (V)2.

Severely worn fragment of a ribbed stalk, node, and an elongated acanthus leaf flaring toward the tip. Broken at both ends.

Preserved width 0.16 m.

This fragment, the counterpart of *SCA 61*, confirms the restoration of the latter in Pl. CXI. It is a motif that does not occur on the Roman akroterion.

NCA (V)3. S,I, pl. 46, fig. II. (Fig. 297.)

Fragment of the upper part of a small ribbed, fluted stalk from the node of which the lower part of an acanthus calyx grows. Rear half split off.

Preserved height 0.067 m.

This fragment, the counterpart of one of the two small stalks from which the stems of a pair of flowers spring on both the Hellenistic and Roman southern akroteria, duplicates a portion of these stalks that is, or was, once preserved in all four instances, three being attached to the respective calyxes, the fourth being *SCA 54* (cf. Pls. CXI, CXV).[177]

NCA (V)4. S,I, pl. 45, uppermost fragment at the left. (Fig. 298.)

Fragment of a curving ribbed, fluted stalk, broken at both ends. The broken tip of an acanthus leaf adheres to its outer left side.

Preserved height 0.15 m.

This fragment is a partial counterpart to *SCA 22* and differs in shape from its Roman variant *RCA (V)21.*

---

176. There are, in addition, three fragments in Vienna which duplicate extant parts of the Roman akroterion and, therefore, presumably come from the northern Hellenistic akroterion that are too severely worn to allow accurate identification or description. Two were probably tips of lobes from the acanthus leaves of the calyx (one is ca. 0.065 m. high, the other ca. 0.058 m.); the third may conceivably have formed part of the outer left leaf of the upper tier of the calyx.

177. The two comparable fragments on the Roman akroterion in Vienna appear in *S,I*, pls. 44 and 46, fig. x. Careful examination of pl. 44 will reveal that the left stalk was found as a separate fragment before its reattachment to the base in the nineteenth century. It is now missing. The fragment described above, *NCA(V)3*, is not that lost piece—as the differing direction of its fluting attests—but a portion of a fifth such stalk.

296. *NCA(V)1*

298. *NCA(V)4*

297. *NCA(V)3*

299. *NCA(V)6*

NCA (V)5.

Worn fragment of a curving ribbed, fluted stalk that tapers in slightly from bottom to top. Broken at both ends and split longitudinally through the center to be mended. Two circular dowel holes, the upper ca. 0.018 m. in diameter, the lower 0.012 m., have been drilled into the present rear surface for the attachment of a supplementary piece. They are 0.04 m. apart center to center.

Preserved height 0.168 m.

This fragment, which duplicates the lower part of *SCA 38* and the stalk beneath it, is an element that does not recur in identical form on the Roman akroterion.

NCA (V)6. S,I, pl. 45, left side. (Fig. 299.)

Fragment of a fluted stalk from the node of which an acanthus calyx grows. The beginning of a ribbed, fluted stalk emerges from this calyx, which is overlapped on its lower side by portions of two upright acanthus lobes, the left one rising slightly higher than the right and being only half preserved. Traces of an abutting member project from the right side of the

345

acanthus calyx above the node. The upper tip of this calyx is chipped, as is the tip of the right upright lobe. The tip of the calyx, once a separate fragment, has been reattached to it. Rear surface roughly picked.

Preserved height 0.245 m.; preserved width 0.158 m.; thickness from outer face of upright lobes to rear surface ca. 0.135 m.

This element, the counterpart to *SCA 5*, is also preserved on the Roman akroterion, where it recurs at a larger scale.

The reconstruction of the central floral akroterion of the Hieron, illustrated on Pl. CXI, incorporates all sixty-one of the fragments of the original southern akroterion possessing sufficient shape to be identified and drawn, supplemented by four pieces from the northern akroterion: three in Samothrace (*NCA* (*S*) *3, 6, 7*) the fourth in Vienna (*NCA* (*V*) *1*, fig. 296). Although it would be tedious to justify the precise position of each of these sixty-five fragments within the proposed reconstruction, it may be useful to point out certain governing factors or features which determined or revealed their positions within the total composition and allowed this shattered, openwork sculpture to be reconstructed with exceptional precision.[178]

The obvious point of departure in this investigation was offered by the largest of the fragments, the calyx-base *SCA 1* (Pl. CXI; fig. 282). Preserving nearly, but not quite, half the original width of the Hellenistic akroterion at its base,[179] its full width could be calculated, at least approximately, from that of its Roman replacement in Vienna (fig. 300).

178. I should like to emphasize that Philip Oliver-Smith is wholly responsible for the reconstruction drawings reproduced on Pls. CXI–CXIV. The reconstruction of the Hellenistic floral akroterion presented here is the product of joint activity on his and my part in the summer of 1960. The original drawings for Pls. CXI, CXII were made at 1:1 scale, each of the sixty-four fragments in Samothrace being measured and drawn, and introduced into the position assigned it within the composition as a whole as a result of our joint deliberations. It may be of interest to mention that our investigation was facilitated by the possibility of working in Hall A of the Museum in the vicinity of the large fragment No. *1*. Here all the akroterial fragments preserved in Samothrace, shaped and shapeless alike, from the north or the south, were not only examined and discussed but also could be placed in tentative positions—from which they were repeatedly moved or shifted—on paper spread on the concrete floor of Hall A, which served as our game board. This direct approach to our movable material was supplemented by the use of paper cutouts or surrogates both of the actual fragments and of their often missing but provable exact counterparts from the opposite side of the symmetrical composition. The ease with which these movable objects could be adjusted to reflect new observations and the gradual growth and unfolding of this mighty plant, in which the position and characteristics of a given fragment often had far-reaching effects on others, proved a great asset to our procedure. When the reconstruction had been worked out to our mutual satisfaction, it was traced in outline, at 1:1 scale, and the individual fragments were portrayed at the same scale. The many resulting pencil drawings were combined and the full-scale reconstruction drawings executed in ink in a studio of the American Academy in Rome, to which we are greatly indebted for its generous provision of the necessary facilities.

Three of the four reconstruction drawings were first published in *Pedimental Sculptures*, figs. 58–60.

179. Until the present reconstruction of the floral akroterion had been worked out, it was not possible to determine the proportion of the base preserved—hence the slightly inaccurate description in *Guide*, p. 78; *Guide*², p. 81.

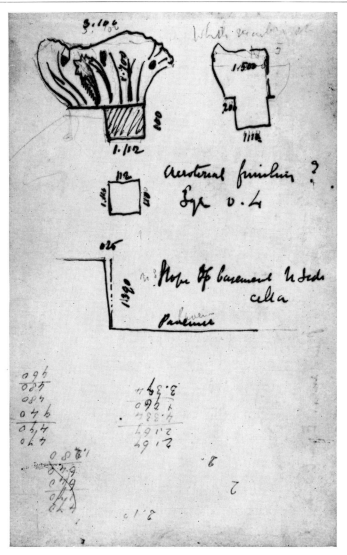

316. Fragmentary floral akroterion from the Temple of
Dionysos at Teos, after Pullan

the Temple of Dionysos at Teos (fig. 316).[202] Although certain of these filigree akroteria may
be precisely dated, notably the fragment from the Temple of Hera Basileia, they are either
too incompletely preserved or too ill published to afford further evidence of the specific date
of the central akroteria of the Hieron. As its technical features may be paralleled within the
century, so the rococo grace and exuberance of its composition accord with one stylistic

202. As reported by W. R. Lethaby, *Antiquities of
Ionia*, Pt. V (London, 1915), pp. 28 f., on the basis of
R. P. Pullan's Notebook II, in the Department of Greek
and Roman Antiquities of the British Museum. The
entire page is reproduced above, fig. 316, with the kind
permission of the Keeper, Mr. D. E. L. Haynes, to
whom I am also indebted for the opportunity of examining all five of Pullan's notebooks and of reproduc-

ing this page in *Pedimental Sculptures*, fig. 55. It is not
surprising that Pullan did not draw on this piece
of evidence and include akroteria, however hypothetical their form, in his reconstruction of the temple.
Comparison of the sketches in his field notebook with
his published plates makes it clear that he tampered
with the evidence he had recorded for a building in
which he was disappointed, as Lethaby has very properly indicated in this volume.

current of that complex age. But the most telling evidence of the date of this best preserved of Greek openwork floral akroteria is provided by the lateral figural akroteria, which logic demands were added to the building at the same time.

The Lateral Figural Akroteria
(Pls. CV, CVII–CIX; Figs. 317–344)

The majority of the fragments of the original lateral akroteria of the Hieron come from its rear, southern corners. Like the remnants of the central floral akroterion from this side of the building, they were found close to it, below the latest antique ground level. There they were buried when the severely damaged figures to which they had belonged were replaced by Roman counterparts. All but the restored statue, *SLA 1,* exhibited in Hall C, are stored in the Museum in Samothrace.

> *SLA 1.* 49.1042. *Hesperia,* 20 (1951), 25 f., pls. 15, 16; *Guide,* pp. 63 f., 66, 89, fig. 43; *Guide²,* pp. 65, 67, 92 f., fig. 46;[203] *Pedimental Sculptures,* pp. 24 f., figs. 44, 51. (Figs. 317–324, 334–337, 344.)

Statue of a winged female figure, standing with her weight on her left leg, the right being bent, lightly poised, and drawn to the rear. The right foot is missing. The left arm is bent, rests against the left hip, and extends forward, its missing wrist and hand having been separately carved and doweled to it. (The dowel hole is 0.0265 m. wide, 0.015 m. high, and 0.044 m. deep.) The right upper arm, preserved to and including the elbow, extends outward from the body, the arm having been raised and bent. The ponderation of the figure, the position of the arms, the presence of a circular strut (preserved length 0.10 m.; diameter 0.028 m.) above the right breast that evidently once braced the right forearm, and the broken dowel set in lead below the left hip, in line with but to the right of the extended left hand, indicate that the figure held an object in each hand, the left one being doweled to the left thigh. These characteristics and the existence of *NLA* 7 (pp. 374 ff.), a fragmentary hand holding a jug, attributed to the northwestern akroterion, suggest that the figure held an oinochoe in her right hand, a patera in her left, and was occupied in pouring a libation. The position of the leaded dowel on the left thigh and of the strut attached to the bent right arm confirm this supposition. The head and the greater part of the neck are missing, but sufficient of the latter is preserved to indicate that the head was turned toward the statue's left. Although virtually the entire right wing is lost, its original contour where it joined the figure is visible and, together with the preserved parts of the left wing, shows that the wings were full length, their tips resting on the base of the statue—an implication confirmed by

---

203. The date of discovery is mistakenly reported as 1950 in both *Guide¹* and *Guide².*

317. *SLA 1*

318. *SLA 1*

the fragmentary wing tips *SLA 4* and *NLA 5*. Only on the lower parts of the wings were the feathers carved in shallow planes receding from the inner to the outer edge; higher up such details, if present, must have been added in paint.

The figure wears a sleeveless, girdled chiton and, over it, a himation. This outer garment has slipped down behind the back and the left shoulder, lies wrapped around the left forearm and looped about the waist (the upper edge having dropped down over the right thigh), and falls in broad zig-zag folds on her left side. Her left foot, shod in a soft shoe [204] with notched sole, emerges beneath the vertical folds of the mantle.

The statue has been restored [205] from three primary fragments: the largest, one intact piece including the entire lower part of the figure from the hips down, as well as the forepart of the left arm from above the elbow downward; and the two joining left and right sides of the torso, including the upper part of the left arm. The irregular line of the split running

204. For similar shoes on the Telephos frieze, see *Pergamon,* III, pt. 2, pl. 32, fig. 3, and the more elaborate but related variety worn by the figure of Tragoidia, ibid., VII, no. 47, pls. 14, 15.

205. By Giorgios Kontogeorgis, former chief restorer of the National Archaeological Museum in Athens and, from 1949–61, responsible for all restoration in Samothrace.

319. *SLA 1*, right side

320. *SLA 1*, seen from the rear

down from the right side of the neck, passing between the breasts and on toward the navel, is visible in figs. 317, 318. These three primary pieces fitted together break on break even before the smaller fragments fitted into the interstices of the abdomen were added to them (see fig. 321). They were supplemented by the right upper arm, itself repaired from four contiguous fragments; the upper portion of the left wing (put together from three pieces); a section of the lower part of that wing adjacent to the himation, below the mass of folds dropping from the left arm (figs. 317, 318, 323); the outermost section of the circular strut below the right shoulder; and a strip of the outermost edge of the second vertical fold of drapery to the right of the right leg.

The area between the wings on the back of the figure is only roughly picked (fig. 320). Within it, below the line of the girdle, is an irregular hollow 0.08 m. deep retaining traces of iron. In line with it, immediately above the base, there is a square cutting. Presumably these holes, like the smaller cuttings on the central akroterion, were used for the attachment of a metal rod or brace.

The rear surfaces of the wings, too, are roughly picked, the entire back of the figure having been essentially invisible. The left wing was evidently damaged and repaired, whether at the time the figure was made or as a result of some injury sustained by it prior to its replacement. The three clamp holes indicative of this repair are visible in figs. 317, 320: two on the rear, one on the front; traces of lead from a fourth appear in fig. 322, above the elbow.

The statue was carved in one piece with its base and doweled to the southwestern corner sima block (figs. 317, 318, 319, 320, 323).[206] Although the base is broken and the greater part of the triangular area defined by the inner surface of the right wing and the rear and left edges of the plinth is missing, part of that large dowel hole is preserved (depth 0.095 m.; preserved right side in fig. 320, 0.07 m. long.) The figure is slightly weathered, especially on the oblique surface of the right thigh, in the depths of the folds of drapery, and on the upper part of the left wing.

Preserved height (without base) 1.43 m.; height of base 0.063 m.; preserved depth of base 0.475 m.; preserved width 0.235 m.; restored height (without base) ca. 1.53 m.; with base ca. 1.593 m.

Found 9 m. north of the southwest corner of the Hieron in the narrow interval between it and the Altar Court. The three major pieces and the smaller fragments belonging to them were found together, neatly buried beside and below the surface of the euthynteria of the Hieron.

SLA 2. 51.546 and 49.1046 A. (Cf. Figs. 317, 320.)

Two joining fragments from the upper outer edge of the left wing of No. *1*, retaining three clamp holes: one on the front, two on the back. Although obviously part of the repair to this wing, visible in figs. 317 and 320, this mended piece could not be reattached to the statue without marring its appearance. Weathered on the front; traces of fire on the back of 51.546.

Preserved height of combined fragments 0.185 m.

49.1046 A was found with the fragments belonging to No. *1*; 51.546 was recovered from an Austrian excavation dump to the west of the Hieron.

SLA 3. 49.1046 B.

Weathered fragment of the upper curving edge of a wing.

Preserved length 0.068 m.

Same provenance as No. *1* and 49.1046 A.[207]

---

206. See above, pp. 76 f.

207. The numerous tiny splinters, crumbs, and shapeless fragments of marble found in the immediate vicinity of No. *1* and taken to the Museum at the time of its discovery to be examined in connection with its reconstruction, but which proved to have no discernible place in the statue, were later stored there. Their size and condition precluded individual accessioning.

321. *SLA 1,* detail

322. *SLA 1,* left side, detail

323. *SLA 1,* detail

324. *SLA 1,* left side, detail

SLA 4. 49.490, 50.117, and three unnumbered fragments. (Figs. 325, 326.) Fragmentary right wing restored from five joining pieces. The restored fragment, irregularly broken on all sides, preserves the lower portion of the wing, including two carved feathers, part of its junction with the adjacent folds of the himation, and a section of the broken base. It provides additional proof that the wings of the lateral akroteria were full length, their tips touching the base. This fragmentary wing, the lower right margin and base of which partially duplicate preserved areas of No. *1*—hence, cannot be fitted onto it or attributed to it—must come from its counterpart. The back of this wing, too, is only roughly picked.

Like No. *1*, this statue was damaged and repaired before its replacement. The rear edge of the restored fragment retains four circular dowel holes indicative of the attachment of a supplementary piece of marble. Below and adjacent to the lowest dowel hole, the fragment has been roughly dressed to receive that repair piece.

Height of restored fragment 0.551 m.; height of base ca. 0.55 m.

50.117 was recovered on the surface in the interval between the Hieron and the Altar Court, 4.50 m. north of the southwest corner of the former; 49.490 and the three unnumbered fragments were found somewhat to the east in the western aisle of the cella. These varied provenances reflect the activity of our Austrian predecessors in this area of the building and the fact that over its surface we excavated earth previously excavated and moved by them, thus no longer in its original undisturbed context.[208]

SLA 5. 52.520.

Fragment of drapery from the portion of the himation wrapped about the extended forearm of the akroterial figures. Identical in style of execution and weathering with the comparable area of No. *1*, which it duplicates. Since this motif does not occur on the Roman replacements of the original akroteria, this fragment must come from the Hellenistic counterpart to No. *1*.

Preserved width 0.054 m.

Found between the Hieron and the Altar Court, 2 m. north of the southwestern corner of the former—again, in earth previously excavated by our predecessors.

SLA 6. 49.1047 A.

Fragment of the outer edge of a right wing, preserving traces of a feather.

Preserved height 0.101 m.

Found at the southeast corner of the Hieron.

208. This repaired wing was mistakenly attributed to one of the Roman replacements of the original akroteria in *Hesperia*, 21 (1952), 40, n. 84, before all the akroterial pieces in Vienna had been examined. For reference to the technical differences between the wings and bases of the two sets of akroteria, see below, pp. 373 f.; text II, pp. 119 ff.

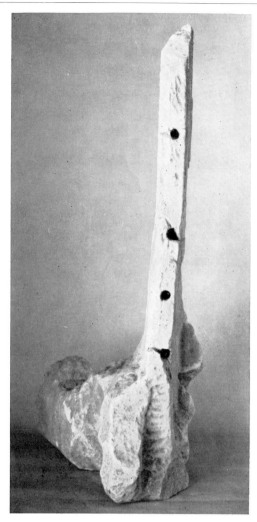

325. *SLA 4*

326. *SLA 4*, seen from the rear

SLA 7. 52.851.

Fragment of a vertical fold of drapery identical in scheme with the vertical folds of the himation of No. *1.*

    Preserved height 0.083 m.

    Found at the southeast corner of the Hieron.

SLA 8. 52.393.

Fragment of a vertical fold of drapery analogous to No. 7.

    Preserved height 0.061 m.

    Found south of the Altar Court.

Fourteen additional fragments of drapery, too worn and calcinated to warrant itemizing, were found in the Roman fill at the southeast corner of the building and apparently come from one of the rear lateral akroteria, presumably the eastern. They are catalogued under

371

Acc. Nos. 49.990 and 54.15. A last small fragment, 49.1045, conceivably a section of a right forearm, may have belonged to one of the figural akroteria.

Given the provenance of *SLA 1–3*, it is reasonable to assume that when this life-size statue was irreparably damaged and replaced it was buried near the corner over which it had once stood. To have transported it from any distance to its place of discovery in the narrow lane between the Hieron and the Altar Court would have been pointless. Under the circumstances, it must be ascribed to the southwestern corner of the cella. Nos. *4–5*, from its rear counterpart, must therefore be attributed to the original southeastern akroterion, an attribution confirmed by the provenance of Nos. *6–7*, fragments that unmistakably come from an akroterial figure. The provenance of No. *8*, on the contrary, is too equivocal to allow it to be attributed with certainty to one rather than the other rear corner.

Although only small fragments of the lateral akroteria that once adorned the façade of the Hieron were recovered to the north of the building, they are sufficient to prove that such figures existed and were identical in type and execution with the well-preserved south-western akroterion. They consist of the following items:

NLA 1. 51.122. (Fig. 327.)
Fragment of a right waist below the girdle. The vertical folds of the forward edge of the himation are visible clinging close to the underlying chiton. Identical with the comparable area of *SLA 1* and, like it, marked by slight horizontal *Liegefalten.*

Preserved circumference ca. 0.23 m.; greatest preserved height 0.09 m.

Found 18 m. northwest of the northwest corner of the Hieron in the debris of its final destruction.

NLA 2. 51.206. (Fig. 328.)
Fragment of a right waist below the girdle. Very possibly from the area immediately below *NLA 1.*

Greatest preserved height 0.092 m.

Same provenance as *NLA 1.*

NLA 3. 51.843. (Fig. 329.)
Fragment of a right leg, preserving the knee and contiguous areas of the lower thigh and upper shin. The curving edge of the fallen upper part of the himation lying over the knee exactly parallels the same area of the *Spielbein* of *SLA 1* and, together with its identity of style and scale, indicates that this fragment belonged to an exact duplicate of that figure—i.e., to the northeastern akroterion. Strongly weathered.

327. *NLA 1*

328. *NLA 2*

330. *NLA 5*

329. *NLA 3*

Preserved height 0.175 m.

Found west of the southwest corner of the Hall of Votive Gifts.

NLA 4. 50.590.

Splinter of the outer edge of a vertical fold of the himation of the type well preserved on *SLA 1*.

Preserved height 0.06 m.

Found northeast of the northeast corner of the Hieron.

NLA 5. 52.164. (Fig. 330.)

Fragment of the tip of a right wing. The terminations of two feathers are preserved, as well as a small broken portion of the projecting mass of the mantle to their right. The invisible back of the wing is hollowed and roughly picked like *SLA 1* and *4*. Unlike them, however, it shows no trace of the base below the feathers, which end at the same distance above the

373

bottom surface of the statue as their counterparts on *SLA 4* (0.005 m.). This technical difference between the northern and southern akroteria is doubtless one feature of the previously noted change in the system whereby the northern akroteria were moored to the blocks beneath them.[209] The bottom surface of the fragment is roughly picked. Severely weathered.

Greatest preserved height 0.12 m.

Found at some distance northwest of the façade.

NLA 6. 52.75.

Tip of one feather and broken background behind it. Similar in scale, style, and weathering to *SLA 5*.

Preserved length of feather 0.06 m.

Found west of the southwest corner of the Hall of Votive Gifts.

The character and provenance of *NLA 1–6* make their attribution to the northern akroteria certain. The following fragments may be ascribed to these figures with a high degree of probability but not with absolute certainty.

NLA 7. 38.36. Samothrace Museum, exhibited in Hall B, Case 4. (Figs. 331, 332.) Fragmentary left hand of a female figure grasping the handle of a vessel. The index finger and last joint of the thumb are missing. The globular body of the broken vessel (of which only the rear outer surface is partially preserved) and its handle allow it to be interpreted as a jug or oinochoe. The fragment is severely weathered; the fingers, the deep intervals between them, and the top and palm of the hand are all deeply pocked and indicative of long exposure.

Inasmuch as it is reasonable to predicate precisely such a hand and vessel to complete the statuary type of the akroterial figures, and this fragment is not only appropriate in scale but also similar in style to the sculptures of the Hieron,[210] it is plausible to ascribe it to one of the four lateral akroteria. The fact that, like the pedimental sculptures and the certain fragments of the northern akroteria, it bears traces of long exposure to the elements suggests that it comes from one of the northern figures. The southern akroteria, which were in place a far shorter time, are less weathered. Hence, since it is a left hand, it may be ascribed to the northwestern akroterion.

---

209. Above, p. 106.

210. Theoretically, such a fragment could be attributed to one of the pedimental figures; but since it supplies an element hypothetically required by the lateral akroteria for which there is no evidence in the pediment, this alternative is less likely. On the whole, the stylistic differences between the pedimental figures and the akroteria, especially in regard to their drapery, are so marked that it is easy to separate the smallest fragments of the two groups of figures into one or the other category. For further reference to this point, see below, pp. 384 f.

331. *NLA 7*

332. *NLA 7,* seen from the side

333. *NLA 8,* seen from above

Preserved length of hand from wrist to knuckle of third finger 0.085 m.; width across knuckles 0.068 m.

Provenance unknown; purchased from a Samothracian in Palaiopolis on June 29, 1938.

NLA 8. 51.422. (Fig. 333.)

Fragmentary right hand. Broken at the wrist and shattered on all surfaces; the four fingers, broken at the tips, are discernible, as are the deep, weathered intervals between them.

Despite its severely damaged condition, this fragment is sufficiently similar to No. 7 to suggest that it may have been the raised right hand of the northeastern akroterion.

Preserved length 0.115 m.; width across knuckles 0.07 m.

Found in the Austrian dump west of the Hieron and over the Hall of Votive Gifts.

Three additional fragments found northwest or west of the northwest corner of the building conceivably come from the figural akroteria of the façade: 51.631, three broken outstretched fingers from a hand holding a patera (?); 50.30 and 51.130, presumably fragments of upper arms, theoretically attributable to either the pedimental or akroterial figures.[211] Five others recovered from the Austrian excavation dump west of the northern part of the Hieron can have come from either the northern or the southern akroteria: 51.221, fragment of himation over a thigh; 51.304, fragment of chest retaining trace of round strut (?); 51.667, fragment of an upper arm; 51.359, splinter from an upper arm (?); and 51.429, fragment of drapery. None of these fragments warrants description or illustration.

These fragments, however sparse and small, are sufficient to prove that the lateral akroteria of the porch were identical in type and style with the original lateral akroteria at the rear of the cella.[212] NLA 1–3, fragments that duplicate areas of SLA 1, must therefore be ascribed to the northeastern akroterion; very likely NLA 4–6 and 8 come from the same figure. The fact that all but one were found to the northwest or west of the Hieron, curious as it may at first sight seem, simply reflects the prevailing direction of the mighty earthquake in which the Hieron and its neighbors collapsed, a tremor that threw the upper parts of their superstructures in a northwesterly direction.[213] Like the pedimental sculptures beneath them, the northern akroteria remained in place throughout later antiquity. Hence, they became more

---

211. 50.30 was identified in *Hesperia*, 21 (1952), 40, n. 84, as a fragment of one of the northern akroteria.

The fragment of drapery illustrated by Schober, p. 20, fig. 19, and interpreted as having belonged to a counterpart to the Vienna Victory seems, on the contrary, to be Hellenistic. Like *SLA 1* and *4*, it has been repaired. The area around the drill hole has been picked, and the rear surface, which is slightly concave, has also been picked: that is, it has itself been used to

repair a statue—quite possibly, given the motif, one of the Hellenistic akroteria.

212. Schober's attribution of a different statuary type to the northern akroteria was made before any of the akroterial fragments discussed here had been found. For discussion of this figure, which comes from the pediment, see above, pp. 268 f., *NP(V) 14*.

213. For amplification of this point, see above, pp. 18 f., and Vol. 4, pt. II, p. 119.

weathered than their Hellenistic counterparts at the south and, as their exceedingly fragmentary condition attests, were subjected to the dual hazards of destruction by earthquake and through the activity of lime-burners.

From the Archaic age onward, such winged female figures were popular akroterial types.[214] Their continuing use as late as the second century is documented outside Samothrace in Pergamon.[215] Whether they alight on the apex or the corners of a pediment, they are normally represented as moving figures whose garments billow about them. The lateral akroteria of the Hieron, figures poised lightly but quietly on the corners of the building, are seemingly unique among akroterial Nikai in their posture and action.[216] Less orthodox bearers of Victory than winged acolytes of the Great Gods, they pour libations in honor of the divine power whose life-giving force is so eloquently, if abstractly, expressed in the great floral akroteria that crown the building.[217]

As freestanding architectural sculptures placed high above the spectator's eye level, these figures were certainly designed to be seen foreshortened, from below. The impossibility of photographing the southwestern akroterion at the proper height results in exaggeration of its intrinsic elongation. Even the slight correction of what was clearly a degree of intentional distortion of the figure obtained by raising it two-thirds of a meter above ground is apparent (fig. 334).[218] But the fact remains that the statue is characterized by

214. For archaic examples, see Karl Volkert, *Das Akroter in der antiken besonders der griechischen Baukunst*, I, *Archaische Zeit* (Düren-Rheinland, 1932), pp. 19 ff., 32 ff. For classical examples, see, among others, the lateral akroteria of the Athenian Temple in Delos (Fernand Courby, *Les temples d'Apollon* [*Délos*, XII], pp. 237 ff.) and of the Stoa of Zeus Eleutherios (T. Leslie Shear, "The Sculpture Found in 1933" [Excavations in the Athenian Agora], *Hesperia*, 4 [1935], 374 ff.). At Epidauros, winged female figures fluttered over both gables of the Temple of Artemis, as the recent identification of a fourth figure in the National Museum in Athens has established. (For the three figures ascribed to the façade, see P. Kavvadias, Γλυπτὰ τοῦ Ἐθνικοῦ Μουσείου. Κατάλογος περιγραφικός [Athens, 1892], nos. 159–61; idem, *Fouilles d'Épidaure*, I [Athens, 1893], pls. 9, 10; A. Defrasse and H. Lechat, *Épidaure* [Paris, 1895], pp. 167 ff.)

215. On the Upper Market Temple: *Pergamon*, III, pt. 1, p. 110.

216. But precisely their attributes, the patera and the jug, are characteristic of the goddess in her capacity as handmaid of other divinities: see the article by Bernert in *RE*, XVII, cols. 293 f., s.v. *Nike*. Similar attributes have been proposed for a wingless female

figure (Hebe?) identified as the central akroterion of the Temple of Ares in the Agora (P. N. Boulter, "An Akroterion from the Temple of Ares in the Athenian Agora," *Hesperia*, 22 [1953], 141–47, pls. 47, 48).

217. Winged female figures normally interpreted as Nikai occur elsewhere as akroteria on temples dedicated to none other than Demeter and Persephone: cf. the fragmentary figures from the third-century Temple of Demeter at Pergamon (Hugo Hepding, "Die Arbeiten zu Pergamon 1908–1909, III. Die Einzelfunde," *AM*, 35 [1910], 495 ff., pl. 23, figs. 3, 4), and the reference to such figures, specifically called Nikai, on a temple to Persephone in Paros in an inscription from the Imperial period (*IG*, XII [5], 229). I owe the latter reference to my husband. Cicero's reference (*In Verrem* 2.4.49, sec. 110) to a colossal statue in the Sanctuary of Ceres at Enna which showed the goddess bearing a figure of Victory in her right hand offers another example of this association.

I cannot attempt here to resolve the question whether such figures are invariably to be interpreted as Nikai or, at times, as personifications of another sort explicable only within the context of a specific cult. For convenience, I shall retain the term "Nikai" for the lateral akroteria of the Hieron.

218. The most obvious example of intentional

334. Southwestern Hellenistic akroterion of the Hieron. Samothrace Museum

335. Southwestern Hellenistic akroterion of the
Hieron, seen from the left side. Samothrace
Museum

slenderness of proportion. The narrow-shouldered, high-waisted girlish torso curves
pliantly above the long legs. The unyielding verticality of the left leg, intensified by the reiterated, straight folds of the mantle, provides a firm base for its resilience, imparting stability
to the figure. Juxtaposed to its rigidity are the long, broken curves of the relaxed right leg,
indeed, of the entire right side—those curves echoed and elaborated by the line of the
mantle clinging close to the torso, moving across the abdomen in sweeping, staccato diago-
nals, and falling, on the opposite side, in powerful zig-zag masses that combine the sharp
angularity of the vertical folds with the pliant fullness of the fallen upper mantle. Seen from
the left side (figs. 322, 335), the drapery wrapped around the left arm and hanging from
it unites the plastic irregularity of the fallen mass of mantle across the abdomen with the

distortion, the extreme elongation of the left arm from
shoulder to elbow when the statue is viewed frontally,
is perceptibly altered when it is seen from the side,
even at near ground level (cf. fig. 335).

336. Southwestern Hellenistic akroterion of the Hieron. Samothrace Museum

337. Southwestern Hellenistic akroterion of the Hieron. Samothrace Museum

vertical direction of its adjacent outer edge, repeating it in varied form. The singular combination of movement and quiet, of dynamic, plastic curves and rectilinear precision—a contrast consciously exploited by such details as the emergence of the right knee and left forefoot from the severe vertical folds of the himation—is especially marked from this viewpoint. From the right side (figs. 319, 336), the contrasts are less sharp, the long loops of the mantle, whether over the back and thigh or over the bent leg, being set off against the primary contour of the figure. This emphasis on contour recurs in more formal fashion when the statue is viewed from the front (figs. 317, 337). Then the spontaneous grace of the natural profile is replaced by a conscious use of outline to reiterate the contour of the torso on its outer side, to curve boldly across the body, defining major areas of it before

380

338. Detail of the frieze of the Hekateion at Lagina. Archaeological Museums of Istanbul

339. Detail of the frieze of the Hekateion at Lagina. Archaeological Museums of Istanbul

dropping down in the reiterated vertical folds of the mantle, those sharp, thin folds set off from each other by wide, deep intervals of strong shadow that play so primary a role in the effect of this statue. The differentiation in the angles of the wings—the right one barely visible from the front, hence leaving the animated contour of the outer side exposed; the left one emerging diagonally from the figure and doubtless contributing further to its stability—can no longer be fully grasped.[219]

Figures analogous to this statue in ponderation and proportion, if not in quality, occur repeatedly on the frieze of the Hekateion at Lagina. Closest of all are those illustrated in figs. 338, 339.[220] Tall, slender, narrow shouldered, and high waisted, they are similar in their elongation of form, in their long-drawn, quiet curves, and in their expression of similar formal contrasts. The relaxed leg is repeatedly sharply differentiated from the *Standbein*, set off from it by emphatic, defining folds, kept simple in surface in contrast with its multiplicity of reiterated, vertical folds. Here, too, these vertical folds conceal the supporting leg and are massed between it and the *Spielbein*. Far inferior to the akroterial sculptures of the Hieron in vigor, lacking both their richness of invention and precision of execution, these figures from Lagina are, nonetheless, strikingly similar in style.

Schober proposed a date shortly after 130 B.C.[221] for the Hekateion. Certain other

219. It can, however, be deduced. The reconstructed figures shown in Pls. CVII–CIX are based on drawings prepared under my direction by Miss Patricia Tobacco of the class of 1962 at Smith College, to whom we are indebted for this contribution to Vol. 3.

220. *Lagina*, p. 30, fig. 18, and pl. 5. Cf. also pls. 3, 6.

221. Ibid., p. 26. This date is mistakenly quoted by Zschietzschmann (op. cit. [n. 125, above], as ca. 160 B.C.

341. Reverse of silver tetradrachm of Alexander I Balas. The British Museum, London

340. Bronze statuette of Athena from Caesarea in Cappadocia. Staatliche Museen, Berlin

342. Detail of the frieze of the Hekateion at Lagina. Archaeological Museums of Istanbul

343. Bronze statuette of Athena from Caesarea in Cappadocia, seen from the rear. Staatliche Museen, Berlin

344. Southwestern Hellenistic akroterion of the Hieron. Samothrace Museum

critics have inclined to date it toward the close of the century,[222] if not still later.[223] The earlier date is probably correct. It is bolstered by the stylistic implications of another late Hellenistic monument—a bronze statuette of Athena from Caesarea in Cappadocia (figs. 340, 343).[224] Slender, narrow shouldered, high waisted, and long flanked, once again, girlish in figure like the Nike, the youthful goddess is even more closely related to a torch-bearing divinity on the frieze (fig. 342),[225] owing to the almost identical forms of their costume, the belted peplos, and their stance. They have in common the sharp differentiation of their legs—the right rigid, its organic function emphasized by revelation of the sandaled forefoot, the left drawn obliquely backward. On both figures, the vertical folds over the

222. For example, Valentin Müller, "A Chronology of Greek Sculpture 400 B.C. to 40 B.C.," *The Art Bulletin,* 20 (1938), 407; Hahland, op. cit. (n. 23, above), p. 108; Bieber, *The Sculpture of the Hellenistic Age,* p. 165; Karl Schefold, *Klassische Kunst in Basel* (Basel, 1959), p. 81. Cf. also Dinsmoor, p. 282, and Lawrence, op. cit. (above, n. 19), p. 219.

223. Horn, op. cit. (n. 125, above), p. 73; Louis Robert, *Études anatoliennes (Études orientales,* V [Paris,

1937]), p. 427, n. 2.

224. K. A. Neugebauer, *Die griechischen Bronzen der klassischen Zeit und des Hellenismus (Staatliche Museen zu Berlin, Katalog der statuarischen Bronzen im Antiquarium,* II [Berlin, 1951]), no. 64, pp. 72 ff., pl. 32. Height 0.265 m.

225. *Lagina,* pl. 21. Neugebauer (loc. cit.) has pointed out the general relationship between this statuette and the frieze at Lagina.

right leg and those massed between the legs give way to long loops that frame the relaxed left leg. Seen from the side, the insistent, almost symmetrical pattern of the two edges of Athena's peplos recalls the motif of the Victory's himation (cf. figs. 335, 343, 344). But these zig-zags are flat and schematic, a classicistic echo of a traditional motif still rendered on the Nike with richly varied contrasts of texture, movement, and detail.[226] This feature, coupled with its languid grace, could be construed to imply that the bronze statuette reflects a later phase in the development of Hellenistic style than the akroterial sculptures. And, in fact, it has been ascribed to the first century B.C.[227]

But there is evidence that precisely the qualities most characteristic of this statuette, in particular, its elongated proportions, occurred as early as the mid-second century. The silver tetradrachm struck under the Seleucid king Alexander Balas in the year 148 B.C. illustrated in fig. 341 [228] bears an image of Athena strikingly similar to the statuette from Caesarea. In stance, in the now familiar attenuation of form, in the sharp contrast between the tiny torsoes and the remainder of the long-flanked figures, even in the manipulation of the lower edge of the peplos into fluent curves to reveal the similarly placed feet, the two figures are virtually identical. In view of this correspondence of style, it is scarcely possible to avoid antedating the statuette by decades and drawing the conclusion that a mannered form of neoclassicism, stamped by extreme elongation of the figure, existed as early as the third quarter of the second century and constituted one current of contemporary style.[229]

These interrelationships imply that on stylistic grounds alone the figural akroteria of the Hieron must be dated in the second half of the second century B.C., in all probability, in the third quarter of the century.[230]

The origin of this style is more difficult to define. Its sphere includes both Asia Minor and Samothrace. Theoretically, the unknown designer of the lateral akroteria can have been a Carian. Yet the fact that the figures from Lagina are in a sense blurred images of a figural style seen in sharp focus in Samothrace—that they are pallid versions of its creative vitality—makes this alternative unlikely and raises the question whether the akroteria are not the products of a Samothracian master and his shop.[231] If so, it is clear that that master

226. A prototype of this classicistic scheme is to be found on the Telephos frieze: *Pergamon*, III, pt. 2, pl. 31, fig. 5.

227. Ibid.; Horn, op. cit., pp. 82 f., placed it earlier, toward the end of the second century.

228. Percy Gardner, *A Catalogue of the Greek Coins in the British Museum*, IV (*The Seleucid Kings of Syria*) (London, 1876), pl. 15, no. 5. Minted in Antioch in the year 164 of the Seleucid era, i.e., 148 B.C.

229. As Herbig has observed, the metopes of the so-called Corinthian-Doric temple in Paestum are related in style to the frieze at Lagina: Friedrich Krauss

and Reinhard Herbig, *Der korinthisch-dorische Tempel am Forum von Paestum* (*Denkmäler antiker Architektur*, 7 [Berlin, 1939]), pp. 65 ff. He accepted Schober's date for Lagina (p. 66, n. 1), and saw in these Sullan metopes a slightly later, more mannered phase of the figural style of the Hekateion.

230. I have proposed this date on the basis of the same comparisons in *Pedimental Sculptures*, pp. 24 f.

231. Schober (*Lagina*, pp. 85 ff.) has emphasized the coexistence of diverse stylistic currents on the frieze at Lagina and assumed that they reflected the collaboration of sculptors of varied artistic schooling.

was not the sculptor who designed the pedimental sculptures.[232] The linear component of his style, which found expression both in his emphasis on contour and in the clear articulation of his drapery, is wholly lacking in the pedimental sculptures. Those sharply-defined vertical folds (figs. 317, 323), so many thin membranes of stone widely set and deeply carved to attract and hold shadow, that make small fragments of this drapery immediately recognizable are not to be found in the pediment beneath them—nor can their execution be exactly duplicated elsewhere.[233]

But it is quite possible that this master was responsible for the central akroterion. Seen from the side, in particular (Pl. CXIV; fig. 335), the figural and floral akroteria have in common their swaying, sinuous profiles. Pliant and plant-like,[234] the figures are defined by a contour that moves forward and backward, as the stalks of the floral akroterion bend in similar rhythm. The sculptor who conceived the exuberant movement of the central akroterion, when it is seen from the front, could well have created the complex, sweeping forms of the mantles worn by the lateral figures. From the front, too, the dynamic frame of the openwork central akroterion shimmering against the sky and dominating the façade was contained by the quiet figures poised lightly over its corners, those figures neither static

He has also assumed that the masters called to work at such a site were for the most part outsiders (see especially p. 104).

232. As, again, different sculptors executed the pedimental and akroterial figures on the Temple of Asklepios at Epidauros: see Crome, op. cit. (n. 131, above), passim.

233. If Schober's view (*Lagina,* pp. 103 f.) that the linear style of the later second century stems from Athens is correct, we should expect to find tangible connections between our Nikai and Athenian sculpture. Yet I am aware of only two worth mentioning. The seated figure of Aphrodite (fig. 265), which I have suggested above (p. 317, n. 151) may come from a small pediment, has a certain litheness, a similarity in the proportions of the slender, willowy torso and small, flat breasts and in the rendering of the sheer crinkled chiton and its rounded belt, that recall the analogous areas of our statue. A similar contrast between the rendering of the chiton and the heavy, loose mass of the doubled-over mantle is also evident, together with a taste for widely spaced folds set off by deep, shaded hollows in the lower parts of the drapery.

A second statuette in the National Museum (No. 2585), a standing female figure wearing chiton and himation, bears a certain relationship to our statue in its still more exaggerated contrast between the verticality of the left side of the figure and the long, bold curve of the right; in the manner in which the himation is clasped to the crinkly chiton by the high girdle and forced to cling close to the torso on the right side;

and in the springy resilience of the figure. It is coarsely executed, the folds of the mantle often being incised rather than modeled, and doubtless, as has been suggested, reflects a later, mannered development of the type of figure exemplified by our Nikai. See Gerhard Krahmer, "Stilphasen der hellenistischen Plastik," *RM,* 38/39 (1923/24), 182 and figs. a, b; Horn, op. cit., p. 89, pl. 37, fig. 3; Bieber, *The Sculpture of the Hellenistic Age,* p. 166 and figs. 710, 711.

One prominent motif in the drapery of our akroterion, the little wad of material belonging to the mantle that has been pulled up vertically above the diagonal mass of folds over the right thigh, occurs early in the Hellenistic age on an Attic statue, the Themis of Rhamnus (for an illustration, see ibid., fig. 516), as well as on a second-century figure of Aphrodite, again in the National Museum in Athens (No. 3248). But whatever the origin of this motif, its subsequent use was not restricted to Attic work. See, for example, a marble statuette from Camirus: Luciano Laurenzi, "Monumenti di scultura del Museo Archeologico di Rodi-IV e dell'Antiquarium di Coo-II," *Clara Rhodos,* IX, 40 ff., pls. 2 ff.

234. It is worth recalling that long before the discovery and reconstruction of the Hellenistic floral akroterion, Karl Lehmann stressed the "flowery grace" and "plant-like elasticity" of the newly-found figural akroterion (*Hesperia,* 20 [1951], 26), so marked is this aspect of the statue, an emphasis that can now be seen to spring from a conscious correlation of the figural and floral akroteria.

nor moving but filled with inner life and potential movement. The very scale of the central akroterion, rising high above both the summit of the tympanum and the lateral akroteria equated with it in Vitruvian fashion,[235] must have intensified the evident emphasis on the flourishing of life implicit in the sculptures of the Hieron: whether in the front pediment, with its theme of the nurturing of the infant hero-founder of the mysteries by beneficent forces; in the rear pediment, with its image of divinity, the very source of life, including the new life entered into through the rites; or in the profuse floral forms of the simas and central akroteria symbolic of eternal life.[236]

However varied the personal styles of the masters who produced the sculptures of the Hieron, their artistic affinities have in each case proved to lie with Pergamon or Lagina.[237] The high reliefs of the pronaos ceiling, ultimately dependent upon, yet later than, the Gigantomachy of the Great Altar, may well have been executed close to the mid-century. So, too, may the sculptures of the front pediment, in view of their one tangible connection with the Telephos frieze. Given their structural position and the resulting fact that they cannot be earlier than the completed porch or later than the akroteria, they were certainly carved at some point in the third quarter of the second century. The akroteria, floral and especially figural, have been shown to be closely related to the Hekateion at Lagina, a temple surely built no later than the late second century and possibly dating from somewhat earlier in the second half of that century than has hitherto been proposed. Simply on the basis of their stylistic connections, the sculptures of the Hieron must be dated, broadly speaking, in the second half of the second century B.C. The specific character of their relationship to the Great Altar and the definite possibility that the other monuments with which the akroteria are linked should be antedated make it conceivable that coffers, pediments, and akroteria

235. 3.5.12, where it is prescribed that lateral akroteria be equal to the height of the tympanum and that they be exceeded in height by the central akroterion (see above, pp. 351 ff., n. 183, for comment on the latter point). When restored to their theoretical height of ca. 1.53 m., the Nikai of the Hieron are approximately equal to the 1.47 m. high tympanum wall and three-quarters the height of the central akroterion (2.03 m.); that is, the latter is one-third larger than the lateral akroteria and the tympanum wall beneath it. Precisely the same proportion recurs on the late-fifth-century Temple of the Athenians at Delos, where the western tympanum and the lateral akroteria are 1.20 m. high, the central group 1.80 m. (see F. Courby and H. Lechat in *Délos*, XII, 138, 237 ff.), and, in the following century, governs the relative sizes of the akroteria on the Temple of Asklepios at Epidauros.

Using Crome's figures for the extant statues, op. cit. (above, n. 131), pp. 20 ff., and allowing an appropriate amount for the missing head of the central akroterion, one finds that the latter is, again, one-third larger than the lateral sculptures. (The height of the tympanum is disputed.) Hence Thompson's statement, loc. cit. (above, n. 183), that the scale of the Delian akroteria is extraordinary is incorrect. On the contrary, it would seem that in the Classical period and later, this proportion was normal. See above, pp. 351 ff., n. 183, for further discussion of this topic, and text II, pp. 83 ff., for the Roman southern akroteria of the Hieron, which repeat the size and scale of their predecessors almost to a millimeter.

236. The leaves and tendrils decorating the seats on which the *epoptai* sat and the outlet draining the lustral area in the cella, like the rinceaux on the sima,

alike were made soon after the mid-century. They are, in any case, products of the third quarter of the second century B.C.[238]

With the completion of the porch, the Hieron became one of the two most richly adorned buildings in the Sanctuary of the Great Gods, vying in splendor with its small neighbor, the Propylon of the Temenos. Meaningful alike to initiate and uninitiate, its sculptures glorified the Samothracian Gods and the legendary heroes who installed their cult and carried it to other shores. Local though their content and regional their style, they reflect the widespread revival of architectural sculpture in the second century B.C. In its final late Hellenistic form, the Hieron exemplifies the renascence of classical forms characteristic of that age. The solitary Doric survivor of that classicistic movement, it occupies a unique position in the history of Greek sculpture.

---

reflect the same emphasis (see above, p. 204, n. 147).

In his interesting discussion of the decoration of the Tholos at Epidauros, Roux, pp. 195 ff., has interpreted its ornamental forms in meaningful fashion and seen in the acanthus tendrils of its ceiling and its crowning floral akroterion symbols of immortality. The occurrence of such crowning floral akroteria on a variety of funerary monuments, as well as on cult buildings, and the meaning of this motif within such contexts deserve thorough investigation.

237. As both the architect who completed the porch and his fourth-century predecessor who de-signed the building have proved to be most closely affiliated with architectural practice in Asia Minor. See above, pp. 215 ff., 235.

238. It was suggested in *AJA*, 61 (1957), 123, that work on the porch extended over several decades from ca. 170 to 140 B.C. The relationship between the Hieron, Lykosoura, and Temple A at Kos (for which see above, pp. 221 ff.), on the one hand, and, on the other, the probability that the pedimental and akroterial sculptures were executed in a short time and in closer sequence to each other than was once apparent make this alternative unlikely.

[Volume 3 is concluded in Text II,
which contains the indexes to
both Text I and Text II.]